Management of Sustainable Development in India

Management of Sustainable Development in India

Editors:

J.R. ARORA

ARATI BASU

NEW DELHI INSTITUTE OF MANAGEMENT
Approved by AICTE since 1996 & Accredited by NBA GOI
60, 50 (B&C), Tughlakabad Institutional Area, New Delhi 110062

GRP

GLOBAL RESEARCH PUBLICATIONS
NEW DELHI (INDIA)

First Published – 2011

ISBN: 978-81-89630-41-6

Published by

GLOBAL RESEARCH PUBLICATIONS
4800/24, 1st Floor, Ansari Road
Darya Ganj, New Delhi-110002 (India)
Phone : 23245225. Fax : 91-11-23272135
E-mail: globalresearchpublications@gmail.com, grpindia@vsnl.net

CONTENTS

Acknowledgement *ix*
Executive Summary *xi*
List of Contributors *xvii*

PART ONE

Challenges of Sustainability: Infrastructure, Entrepreneurship Development, Technology & General Economics

1 Infrastructural Development for Sustained Growth in India 3
Kawal Gill

2 Woman Entrepreneurship: A New Breed to Achieve Sustainable Development 22
Sanjay Manocha & Sanjoy Roy

3 Rural Entrepreneurship through Microfinance for Sustainable Development 34
Dimple Tresa Abraham & S.S. Kalamkar

4 Measuring Entrepreneurship Development: A Study Conducted on Women Entrepreneurs of Micro Credit Centered Enterprises in India 42
Vasanthkumari. P.

5 Emerging Issues in Entrepreneurship Development 51
Rudra Chakrapani & P. Kannaih

6 Management Education in India - A Critical Assessment 56
Arunava Narayan Mukherjee

7 Triple Bottom Line Reporting-In Search of True Corporate Transparency 64
Sumanta Dutta

8 EQA Modelling on Indian IT Majors: Cases of Infosys and TCS 70
Ashish Varma & Ishika Varma

9 Mobile Technology 76
Sadhna Jha

10 A Comparative Study of Personality and Depression in Internet Addicts and Non Addicts 81
Saba Shamim, Bharathi Kumari & Aanchal Ahuja

11 E-Governance 87
Parveen Kaur, Kamaldeep Kaur & Abha Grover

12 Sustainability Management- Need to Focus 103
Rekha Gulia

PART TWO
Dynamics of Finance & Sustainable Development

13 State of Commodity and Derivative Market Performance in India 113
Khyser Mohd.
14 FII and Its Impact on Indian Stock Market 120
Pritpal Singh Bhullar & Nipun Aggarwal
15 Changing Trends of Asset Preference of the Public: Key to the Sustainability of Economic Growth 129
Arati Basu & Anita Agarwal
16 Micro Finance: Yesterday, Today & Tomorrow 141
Rekha Sachdeva
17 Role of MFI in Sustainable Development of Indian Rural Sector 147
Piali Haldar & Anshu Kumar

PART THREE
Human Resource Management in Sustainability of Development

18 Managing Change in HR 165
Nimmi Agarwal, Agnibesh Samanta & Rohit Parashar
19 Managing Change in Organizations 170
G. Vani
20 Cross Cultural Issues and Managing Diversity 178
K. Sanjeeva Rao
21 Leadership Development in the Context of Sustainable Growth 187
Dhananjay Singh
22 Mental Health Promotion at Workplace: A Key for Organization Growth and Development 193
Dolly Lavania
23 Women Success in Public Relations through Emotional Intelligence 207
Anshu Bhati & Jyoti Sharma
24 Occupational Stress and Mid-career Crisis for Indian Corporate Women in the Service Sector 213
Manidipa Chatterjee
25 Quality of Work Life as HR Practice: The Mediating Link of Commitment 224
Jyoti Sharma
26 A Study on Talent Management System as an Effective Tool for Organization Effectiveness 231
Vijit Chaturvedi & Poonam Batra
27 Principles for Selection of Teaching and Training Methods 240
K. Palani
28 Attaining Global Sustainable Competitive Advantage in the 21st Century through HR Functions Using Web 2.0 Technologies 247
Tanushree Gulati

PART FOUR
Dynamics of Marketing & Sustainable Development

29 Distribution Strategies Adopted by Small Scale Industries of Uttarakhand 259
Gajendra Singh & Pratima Negi

30 Sustainability Measures for Efficient Markets and Good Governance: An Impact Study on the Extension of Trading Hours in India 277
Deepak. R

31 Designing an International Advertising Strategy 287
Amit Thukral

32 Changing Global Marketing Environment 292
K.G. Chaubey, Shanti Ranjan Upadhyay & Jyoti Bajpai

33 Global Branding Strategy 301
S.K. Tannan

Index 306

ACKNOWLEDGEMENT

Bringing out a publication on a topic which is diverse in nature involves all round efforts and commitments of the Management, Faculty, Administration and above all the participation of delegates, speakers and distinguish experts in providing us deep insight and understanding of this important subject. We are indeed indebted to them for their cooperation and inputs. We sincerely thank the management of NDIM, its Chairman, Shri V.M. Bansal for his inspiration, encouragement and providing the financial Support.

We are particularly thankful to our resource persons from SREI Infrastructure Finance Ltd, Engineering Project India LTD, PowerCon Knowledge Services Pvt. Ltd., Haier Appliances India Pvt. Ltd, RBI, RKJ Group, SMC Global Securities Ltd. for their invaluable contribution for the development of ideas on the issue of Management of Sustainable Development in India. Special thanks to Mr. Ved Jain, CA, Ex–President, ICAI, Dr. D.N. Paliwal, Member Secretary, National Board of Accreditation (NBA) and Mr. S.K. Goel, Member and Special Secretary, CBEC, GOI for their contributions and encouragement.

We received unfettered support from our colleagues and our students. Without them this work could not have been successful.

New Delhi Institute Of Management
New Delhi
August 2011

Prof.(Dr.) J.R. Arora
Prof.(Dr.) Arati Basu

EXECUTIVE SUMMARY

Two days' national conference on "Management of Sustainable Development in India" organized by New Delhi Institute of management was timely and appropriate at a time when this has been a topic of discussion and deliberation worldwide. Earlier centuries only pursued faster economic growth and were insensible to environmental destruction which brought the globe to an impasse . Now the very existence of the globe is at challenge unless we change every aspect of our living and life style. The recession of 2008-09 taught the world the value of financial discipline - one vital aspect of sustainable Development. The sustainability of Development has multiple dimensions. In the last century, the sustainability of development was perceived as triple bottom line- Social, economic and environmental: the "people, planet, profit". Now Scholars, Educationists and experts from the corporate of the public and private sectors are engaging themselves to evolve strategies of growth with environmental preservation, redressing inequities, achieving a more dynamic and stable world economy. This definitely calls for changes in the management styles of all the functional areas. NDIM has been able to contribute to this decisive issue of global as well as national importance through discussions, deliberation and interactions that were carried out in two day long National conference on 1st and 2nd April, 2011.

In the first section , we have attempted to summarize the highlights of the deliberations of Resource Persons from, the public, private and the Govt. Sector. Then in the Second section, key points from the delegates presentations have been provided for our readers to be benefitted from the conference of National importance.

Chief Guest Mr. Ved Jain, CA Ex-President, ICAI, emphasized that the sustainability of development is a necessity and all round efforts and reorientation of resource use, new direction of innovation, accounting standard as well as programme for inclusive growth were to be pursued vigorously to achieve the sustainability.

Dr. R. Mandal, Former Adviser of Planning Commission, Chief Executive Officer, SREI Infrastructure Finance Ltd, in his keynote address emphasized the need for sustaining the high rate of growth of GDP in India having the highest number of working class population with middle class aspirations. The Govt. has been evolving the models of Private and public Partnership as a solution for huge funds for infrastructure development and inclusive growth through the involvement of the corporate in the welfare of all sections of stakeholders.

Mr. S.P.S. Bakshi, CMD, Engineering Project India LTD. in the technical session on " **Challenges of Sustainability: Infrastructure, Entrepreneurship"** rightly pointed out that the challenges of sustainable Development is not one but many interconnected issues such as continuous innovation, organizational reorientation, creating environment for entrepreneurship development, the proactive Govt.'s policies and human resource training.

Management schools could contribute by creating new brand of managers to lead India towards these directions. In this session, **Mr. Vijay Rai, President & CEO, PowerCon Knowledge Services Pvt. Ltd.,** talked about the need for skills formation for Sustainable Development and Global Capacity building through knowledge management. According to him, another aspect of sustainability i.e. inclusive growth can only be achieved through development of communication channels.

In the technical session on '**Dynamics of Finance & Market in Sustainable Development**", the chairperson , **Dr. D.N. Paliwal, Member Secretary, National Board of Accreditation (NBA)** and an eminent educationist , pointed out that the economic growth is the basis for sustainable development and that could only be achieved through scientific approach through use of money- the lesson learnt from the housing bubble in the USA. The deliberation by **Mr. Sandeep Tyagi, Director, HR Haier Appliances India PVt. Ltd.** a Chinese subsidiary in India, mentioned that Human Resource is fundamental to the sustainability of any organization. He then described how his organization had been practicing human resource development through employee engagement. **Mr. R. Giridhar DGM, RBI,** mentioned how the Govt. of India is attempting to link financial management with the Environmental Sustainability through the promise of 50 percent discount on the share price of the green technology. Financial aspects of sustainability cannot be ignored and hence there should be trade off between sustainability and profitability.

In the dedicated technical session on the Second day, discussions and deliberations of on the theme **"Human Resource Management in Sustainability for Development"** were carried on. The Chairperson, **Mr. V.P. Singh, Director-HR, RKJ Group** and the key speaker, **Mr. Rajan Sinha, CEO, Mantrana Consulting**, brought forth points that that the Sustainable Development can only come through social involvement and long term practices in the society, political and economic arenas. The concept of inclusion needs to be embedded in all the above spheres. The team playing attitude should be inculcated in the childhood itself. The organization needs to develop competency model through inclusion of not only skills and knowledge but also attitudes and habits so that inclusive culture can be developed in the organization. The corporate needs to invest on the well thought schemes to develop quality of its employees specially those who are at the forefront of the organization a la Japanese philosophy.

In the session on "**Derivative Market and Micro Finance for Sustainable Development**", **Mr. Jagannadham Thunuguntla, Chief Strategist & Head of Research, SMC Global Securities Ltd**. through tracing the cyclical path of a few successful companies e.g. Airtel, Naukri.com Educom and Sizcom, showed that the company depends on venture capital to start with, then goes for private equity and lastly company opts for IPO when it is ready to be listed. One needs to have rare intelligence rather than common sense, to be successful in the financial market. Dr. **Dinesh Tyagi, Adviser, Infrastructure Advisory Division, SREI Infrastructure Ltd.,** the key speaker of the session pointed out that more than 60 per cent of India comprises of district and rural economy and hence the Sustainability of Development cannot be possible without a definite plan of actions and availability of technology to these areas. Inclusive growth will be possible through development of infrastructure and ICT. Programmes such as Bharat Nirman and PURA are modeled to provide connectivity, electricity, information technology (internet and ICT), irrigation, sanitation and water supply which would ensure health, education and business growth in the rural area. These are basic accelerators for sustainable Development.

Valedictory speech was delivered by **Mr. S.K. Goel, Member & Special Secretary, CBEC, GOI**. In his speech he mentioned that sustainable Development is not a choice any more but a compulsion. Poverty in India has been increasing in spite of high GDP growth. There is high demand for energy especially clean energy. India is planning to introduce solar power by 2022 and National biogas energy by 2017.

Section II
Key Points from the Presentations of Delegates

On the basis of subthemes, papers are arranged in four parts and accordingly a brief summary of each is provided.

In **Part one**, papers on Challenges of sustainability of Development are explored through the presentation of delegates. **Gill's** paper analyses the role of private sector in infrastructural development and then discusses the specific bottlenecks to infrastructural development and suggests the way forward. The study of **Manocha** and **Roy** analyses how the positive changes in socio-economic attitudes towards women and the advantage of innovative technology are creating opportunities for women to be the successful entrepreneurs. The empirical study by **Abraham** and **Kalamkar** on micro finance helping micro enterprises suggests that microfinance, micro credit and micro entrepreneurship should be interlinked and only then microfinance would promote sustainable income generation among the poor. Another empirical study on microfinance by **Vasanthakumari** views the micro enterprise development based on micro credit as an opportunity for providing gainful employment to the poor, for improving their incomes and standard of living. The paper by **Chakrapani** and **Kannaiah** explains that though to-day's entrepreneurs in the emerging market start the new type of business with little capital investment, they are able to become successful global players. They are providing opportunities to Multinationasl to capture new ideas, customers, suppliers, and talent and creating employment in the Indian economy. **Mukherjee** finds that structural maladies and dysfunctional outcomes of present Indian management education system are the result of random imposition of American model and consumerisation of education in the current era of liberalization; some suggestions have been made in this paper for restructuring the system. **Dutta's** analysis explains the relation between CSR and sustainability based on triple bottom line reporting; this could enhance economic value addition for the stake holders though it still remains challenging. **Varma** and **Varma** applied Earnings Quality Assessment (EQA) on two prominent Indian Information technology companies viz Infosys and TCS and find that the technique is useful for monitoring the performance of a company.

Jha in her paper explores the usage and contribution of mobile technology in the growth of commerce and Business. **Shamim, Bharathi Kumari** and **Ahuja** in their paper provides results of their research conducted on 100 college and school going students' of both internet addict and non addicts in assessing their depression levels. The paper by Ms. **Parveen**, Ms **Kamaldeep** and Ms **A. Grover** analyze the role and scope of ICT in the process of E-Governance for govts at all levels for providing basic services and support to the stakeholders. **Gulia** finds that to-day's companies are facing great challenges to fulfill the twin objectives of the environmental sustainability as well as the pursuit of the sustainability of their own companies

In **part two**, papers focus on discussion of the dynamics of finance in sustainable Development. The paper by **Khyser Mohd.** finds that the risk averse investors in the commodity market at present are gaining in a big way by choosing derivative products to minimize the impacts of fluctuations in asset prices on profitability and cash flows. **Bhullar** and **Agarwal** in their paper discussed the impact of FII's on the Indian Stock market in the recession year 2008 while FII is observed to be the most critical factor for the depression in the Indian stock market. **Agrawal** and **Vashishtha** shows that investments by venture capitalists on serial entrepreneurs would be successful to generate higher returns though the success could only come through skills and efficiency of both entrepreneurs and venture capitalists The paper by **Basu** and **Agarwal**, analyzing the changing trends of asset preference of Indian public through trend analysis for the period of 1970-71 to 2008-09 shows that there is a definite shift of asset holdings from physical to financial assets. Time deposits of banks amongst financial assets still are the most preferred asset holdings by Indian public, though they are also now investing more on insurance products. Stockholdings are still not popular and the paper finds that constraints of Indian stock market to a great extent are responsible for this. **Rekha Sachdeva's** paper discusses the state of SHG-based microfinance in India and concluded that microfinance movement in India is presently too small to create a massive impact in poverty alleviation, but if pursued with skills it holds the promise to alter the socioeconomic face of the poor. **Shikha Makkar's** analysis shows that banks have not been able to include vast segment of the population, especially the underprivileged sections of the society into the fold of basic banking services. The paper by **Haldar** and **Kumar** seeks to answer how to reach out to over 700 million citizens across six lakh villages, and meet the financial needs of the rural poor to improve their self confidence and status in the society- a key to the sustainable development of India.

In the **third part**, papers on Human Resource Management in Sustainability of Development are presented. **Agarwal, Samanta** and **Parashar** emphasizes that human resource management has a vital role in organization success and hence this needs to evolve itself to meet the challenges of sustainable development. The research project by **G Vani** finds that only those organizations which are able to undertake suitable programs in the changing and demanding economic order of the world, can remain ahead of others and sustain in the race. **Rao** suggests that well designed cross-cultural training programs would help employees in coping up with the stress and cultural shocks in the multicultural organization. He also finds that working effectively in cross-cultural context is becoming vital competence for aspiring managers in the modern corporate world. According to **Singh** in his paper critically examines the strategic intervention policies by Aditya Birla Group (ABG) for leadership development and talent Management Process in their diverse businesses in the pursuit of sustainable growth. **Dolly Lavania,** an organization needs to address the stigma and discrimination on mental health problems and make positive changes for overall development of the organization. The paper by **Bhati**, and **Sharma** attempts to understand the role and importance of Emotional Intelligence of Public Relations profession with various facets . These may assist Public Relations professionals to recognize these emotions in various situations. The article by **Chatterjee** highlights the causes and consequences of occupational stress for women executives and suggests the strategies to cope with such trends. **Sharma**'s study attempts to prove that when organization's quality of work life is encouraging and flexible enough to facilitate employees' growth, commitment and these in turn would reflect the employees' concern for and identification with the organization. **Srivastav** and **Pandey** in their paper raise the issues of violence in the society to explain how these are destroying peace and harmony among people, causing environmental destructions thus creating barrier for sustainable Development. The study by **Chaturvedi** and **Batra** focuses on the role of Talent management system in building organization effectiveness and building the knowledge capital for creating competitive advantage for the organization. **Palani** finds that the relevance of teaching and training technologies is continuously changing in real life through changes in the concepts and innovation processes. **Gulati** in her paper tries to establish how online societies formed through the social network services has made a positive impact on fast, transparent, convenient and cost-effective flows of HR business practices which definitely is promising the advent of a new era in HR practices.

In the **fourth** and **last part** on Dynamics of Marketing in the context of sustainable development, **Singh** and **Negi**, in their empirical study on marketing strategies of small scale industries of Khadi, woolen and handicraft in Uttarakhand, show how these sectors choose the locations of distribution, maintain healthy relations with the dealers and take care of other functions related to sales as the distributional strategy. The paper by **Deepak. R**. using the volatility measures, examines the effect of extension of trading hours and confirms that better informational flows leads to efficient market. **Thukral** in his analysis deals with the dilemma of the firm entering into international market on choosing between standardized or differentiated strategy of advertising in different international markets. The paper by **Chaubey**, **Shanti Ranjan** and **Bajpai**, points out that the marketers have now been adopting to aggressive marketing strategies for survival and growth due to the fierce competition in the emerging markets arising out of the change in lifestyles, and consumption patterns. **Tannan** deals with the debate on the supremacy of global brands and the inadequacy of the local brands and then answers whether the brands should adapt to the local needs and cultural preferences.

Conclusion: In conclusion, following points that emerged from the deliberations of the resource persons and papers of the delegates:

1. Challenges of management of sustainability are many and can be pursued only in the environment of proactive Govt.'s policies
2. Innovation and knowledge management through continuous training and development at the organizational level are essential part of sustainable development.
3. Discipline in the financial system are essential to ensure the sustained growth of the corporate.
4. Inclusive culture is created through empathy rather than sympathy. The team playing attitude could help to inculcate the culture of inclusion. Changes of these kind need to come at all level - social, political and economic.
5. Rural Development for sustainable and inclusive growth can be achieved through adaptation of technology and micro financing.
6. The Govt., Society and the Corporate are the stakeholders of the sustainable growth and its management.

This book definitely is a valuable document of the conference and views expressed. We sincerely hope this is going to be a useful reading for the researchers and the policy makers.

We express our sincere thanks to our Chairman, Prof. V.M. Bansal, and Ms Bhumika Bansal, Director Technical for intensive guidance, support and encouragement in organizing the conference and later on for the publication of the proceedings .Their ideas were valuable inputs for us to prepare this book. We thank our faculty members and admistrative staff for all cooperation they provided for the success of the conference.

Prof.(Dr.) J.R. Arora
Dean NDIM

Prof. (Dr.) Arati Basu
NDIM

LIST OF CONTRIBUTORS

Kawal Gill, Fellow- Commerce, Institute of Life Long Learning, University of Delhi and Associate Professor, Sri Guru Gobind Singh College of Commerce, University of Delhi.

Sanjay Manocha & **Sanjoy Roy**, Lecturer, Bharati Vidyapeeth University Institute of Management & Research.

Dimple Tresa Abraham, Asst. Professor, New Delhi Institute of Management, Tughlakabad, New Delhi, and Ph.D. scholar at the Gokhale Institute of Politics and Economics, Pune & **S.S. Kalamkar,** Reader and Research guide at the Gokhale Institute of Politics and Economics, Pune.

Vasanthakumari. P., Associate Professor. Dept. of Commerce, N.S.S. College, Ottappalam,Palakkad, Kerala, India.

Rudra Chakrapani, SV University, Tirupati, AP, India. & **P. Kannaiah**, Vani Nikethan Institute of Management Studies, Karimnagar.

Arunava Narayan Mukherjee, Faculty of Human Resource Management, International School of Business & Media, Kolkata & Ph.D. Research Scholar, The University of Burdwan, West Bengal, India.

Sumanta Dutta, Department of Business Administration, Dinabandhu Andrews Institute of Technology & Management, Kolkata.

Ashish Varma, Assistant Professor, IMT Ghaziabad & **Ishika Varma,** Visiting Faculty: Economics and International Business.

Sadhna Jha, Lecturer, Lingaya's Lalita Devi Institute of Management and Sciences.

Saba Shamim, Bharathi Kumari & **Aanchal Ahuja,** Dept. of Psychology, JMI, New Delhi-110025.

Parveen Kaur, Assistant Professor (HRM), **Kamaldeep Kaur**, Assistant Professor (IT), & **Abha Grover**, Assistant Professor (Marketing), New Delhi Institution of Management, Delhi.

Rekha Gulia, Lecturer, Lingaya's Lalita Devi Institute of Management and Sciences.

Khyser Mohd., Associate Professor & Head, Dept. of Business Management, Telangana University, Dichpally, Nizamabad (A.P.).

Pritpal Singh Bhullar & **Nipun Aggarwal,** Research Scholar, School of Management Studies, Punjabi University, Patiala.

Arati Basu, Professor & **Anita Agarwal,** 2nd Year PGDM (2009-11), New Delhi Institute of Management, New Delhi.

Rekha Sachdeva, Lecturer–MBA, Manav Rachna College of Engineering, Faridabad.

Piali Haldar, Asstt. Professor, Asia Pacific Institute of Management, New Delhi & **Anshu Kumar,** PGDM (Student 2nd Year), Asia Pacific Institute of Management, New Delhi.

Nimmi Agarwal, Assistant Professor, SBS, **Agnibesh Samanta,** MBA (1st year) & **Rohit Parashar,** MBA student, [Sharda University].

G Vani, Assistant Professor in Business Management, Telangana University.

K. Sanjeeva Rao, Assistant Professor in Business Management, Danavanthri Institute of Management Science.

Dhananjay Singh, All India Management Association, New Delhi.

Dolly Lavania, Assistant Professor, G.L.A. University, Mathura.

Anshu Bhati & **Jyoti Sharma**, Associate Professor, International Institute of Professional Studies, Devi Ahilya Vishwavidyalaya, Indore.

Manidipa Chatterjee, Asst.Professor, Meghnad Saha Institute of Technology (Techno India Group), West Bengal University of Technology.

Jyoti Sharma, Associate Professor, International Institute of Professional Studies, Devi Ahiliya Viswavidiyaliya, Indore-M.P.

Vijit Chaturvedi, Assistant Professor & **Poonam Batra**, Lingaya's University, Faridabad (Haryana).

K. Palani, Principal, Dr.Ambedkar Memorial Institute of IT & Management Science.

Tanushree Gulati, Assistant Professor, Department of Business Administration, Manav Rachna College of Engineering, MRIU Campus, Faridabad.

Gajendra Singh, Associate Professor & **Pratima Negi,** Research Fellow, Department of Business Management, H.N.B. Garhwal University.

Deepak. R, Faculty, Bhavan-Marshall Institute of Management, Bangalore-560001.

Amit Thukral, Assistant Professor, Dept. of Management Studies, Amrapali Institute, Shiksha Nagar, Haldwani, Nainital-263139, Uttarakhand.

K.G. Chaubey, Shanti Ranjan Upadhyay & Jyoti Bajpai, Associate Prof., Naraina Vidhya Peeth, Kanpur (U.P.).

S.K. Tannan, International Institute of Business Studies, Noida.

PART ONE

Challenges of Sustainability: Infrastructure, Entrepreneurship Development, Technology & General Economics

1

INFRASTRUCTURAL DEVELOPMENT FOR SUSTAINED GROWTH IN INDIA

Kawal Gill

Introduction

High growth and sustainable development are the principal objectives of developing countries in the present world. In the globalised framework, this requires efficiency in production and availability of resources- both materials and services- so that the output can be augmented up to the fullest potential and prices are competitive. A major precondition for attaining those goals is availability of a host of infrastructural facilities in adequate quantity and reliable quality. Interlinkages between infrastructure and economic growth are well documented. A large body of research has found that infrastructure investment has high social rates of return, especially in low income countries and is a key determinant of economic growth (Aschauer, 1989; Munnell, 1990; World Bank, 1994; Calderon and Serven, 2003; Estache, 2006; Sahoo and Dash; 2008; 2009).

Infrastructure spending accounts for a significant proportion of national income and consumption in many countries; as such, any reform affecting the sector is likely to have wider repercussions on the economy. Empirical evidence indicates that infrastructure spending has a positive and statistically significant effect on long-run economic growth (World Bank 2002). Ghosh and De (2005), for instance, have noted that infrastructure in least developed countries contributed towards a hinterland's output, income, employment growth and quality of life. Meanwhile, Esfahani and Ramirez (2003) have found that if Africa had East Asia's growth rate in telephones per capita (10% vs 5%) and in electricity generation (6% vs 2%), its per capita growth rate would have been at least 0.9% higher. Richards (2008) has shown that due to the lack of adequate investment in infrastructure during the 1990s, Latin America's long-term growth was lower by 1 to 3%. Because infrastructure service provides valuable inputs to other commercial activities, the removal of infrastructure bottlenecks contributes to overall growth. In East Asia, recent studies have indicated that greater stocks of infrastructure were indeed associated with higher growth (Seethepalli et al. 2008).

Other empirical studies have highlighted the importance of infrastructure in promoting growth and reducing poverty. A UNESCAP (2006) study on infrastructure in developing

Asian countries has shown that road transport and electricity, in particular, play a key role in poverty reduction. Similarly, a study on road infrastructure in the Philippines has found that rural roads generate the largest impact in terms of income growth. The same study revealed that rural household's production and income-generation potential is optimized with access to networks that alleviate their isolation (Barrios 2008).

Infrastructure development, both economic and social, is one of the major determinants of economic growth, particularly in developing countries. Direct Investment on infrastructure creates (i) production facilities and stimulates economic activities; (ii) reduces transaction costs and trade costs improving competitiveness and (iii) provides employment opportunities to the poor. In contrast, lack of infrastructure creates bottlenecks for sustainable growth and poverty reduction (Sahoo and Dash.2009)

Bhattacharyay (2008) has identified a number of major roles for infrastructure in regional socio-economic development and integration.

First, basic infrastructure promotes economic exchange among various sectors of an economy, both locally and internationally. It provides greater access to key inputs for economic growth, such as resources, technology, and knowledge.

Second, infrastructure improves socio-economic and environmental conditions by providing basic needs and utilities such as roads, water, sanitation, hospitals, clinics, schools, environment-friendly power, and telephone lines—all of which are part of the United Nation's Millennium Development Goals (MDGs). It can reduce: (i) non-income poverty by facilitating the poor's access to basic services; and (ii) income poverty by increasing economic opportunities and income generating capacity, particularly for poorer groups and communities in remote areas.

Third, it enhances physical connectivity both within and among countries, facilitating the improved customs procedures and trade rules and regulations— improves logistics, resulting in reduced trade costs and the speedier movement of goods and services.

Fourth, greater regional integration through enhanced physical connectivity supports trade and investment (including FDI) expansion, and financial market development.

In case of India, the importance of infrastructure for overall economic development and enhancement of trade and business activities need hardly be emphasized. India on attaining Independence, accorded highest importance to the development of infrastructural facilities. The successive plans were formulated on such line that the infrastructureal sectors claimed the lion's share of the plan outlays and actual expenditures. If all the ten plans along with annual plans are taken together, it is observed that the total allocated spending of Rs 33954 billion, the infrastructural sectors claimed Rs 22452 billion i.e more than 66 percent of the total allocation (Majumdar,R, 2008). It has been because of such paramount importance being attached to the development of the infrastructure in our economic planning that long strides have been made in the physical availability of such facilities in India. There has been a remarkable growth in the absplute level of such facilities, as well as in the level relative to the size of the nation and population i.e in standardized forms. However, the progress is not that commendable if we compare it to the global standards. In fact India lags behind not only the developed nations, but also the middle – income group countries, to which group it belongs.

According to the World Economic Forum's 2010-11 Global Competitiveness Index, India is ranked 86th out of 139 countries in quality of overall infrastructure—well below the rankihg of China (50th) and Brazil (62nd). Rankings in quality of roads, port infrastructure, and electricity supply are 90th, 83rd, and 110th respectively. Only 1.7 per cent of road network is covered under National Highways catering to about 40 per cent of traffic and barely 14 per cent of the roads are four-laned; major ports have inadequate berths, suffer from draft constraints, and lack efficient rail/road connectivity; airports, especially in Tier II and III cities, have inadequate infrastructure; railways lack modern freight terminals, have slow average freight and passengers speeds, very low payload to tare ratio, and the growth of rail network is lagging far behind the increase in traffic; the power sector has a 14 per cent peaking deficit, 11 per cent energy shortage, and 27 per cent transmission and distribution losses. The progress of rural infrastructure has also not been at the desired pace.

Investment climate surveys repeatedly show that the limited and poor quality of infrastructure facilities acts as a major impediment to business growth in India. Indian policymakers realize that any credible efforts toward sustainable economic growth in India must involve a substantial upgrade of infrastructure investment and provision of good quality infrastructure facilities. India has many advantages to offer to potential investors, including high and steady economic growth, single-digit inûation, vast domestic markets, a growing number of skilled personnel, an increasing entrepreneurial class and constantly improving ûnancial systems, including expanding capital markets. However, only provision of good quality infrastructure would enable India to reap these beneûts.

Infrastructure demands strong planning, coordination, decentralization, private participation and commercialization of service providers rather than a top-down approach. Since private participation in infrastructure is limited in developing countries, particularly in India, cost recovery and measures to improve policy and institutional frameworks are important for creating a virtuous circle of investment and growth (Sahoo and Dash, 2009).

Against this background the present paper is structured as follows: section I presents an overview of Infrastructural development in India since independence to post reform period, section II analyses the role of private sector in infrastructural development and section III discusses the specific bottlenecks to infrastructural development and the way forward.

Section I

Overview of Infrastructural Development in India Since Independence to Post reform Period

Government Strategy on Infrastructural Development

Till 1990's the public sector was assigned a prominent role for building infrastructure in the country, rather investments in infrastructure development was considered to be a monopoly of the public sector due to the large financial outlays, long gestation periods, uncertain returns and associated externalities involved in the infrastructural projects.

But, the change in policy regime that occurred in the early 1990s, essentially moving to more market oriented solutions and to a more open trade regime, led to a change in the strategies for infrastructure development also. With the objective of stimulating and mobilizing increased private-sector investments, either from domestic sources or foreign avenues, the Government has offered various incentives for the infrastructure sector for sustained economic growth. These include: allowing 100 per cent FDI(under the automatic route) in all infrastructure sectors including the roads, power, ports, and airport sectors; 74 per cent in telecom services and 100 per cent in telephone equipment; 49 per cent to100 per cent for various services in the aviation sector; extended tax holiday periods up to ten-year tax holidays (under section 80-IA of the Income Tax Act 1961) to enterprises engaged in the business of development, operation, and maintenance of infrastructure facilities; and emphasis on PPP as one of the preferred modes for project implementation.

The ongoing eleventh five year plan (EFYP) that spans the period 2007-08 to 2011-12 has laid great stress on both infrastructure and inclusive growth. The EFYP plans to double the investment in seven core infrastructure sub sectors like roads, ports airports, electricity, irrigation, telecommunication and railways. The relevant quantitative targets are for these sectors in the Eleventh Plan are presented in Table 1.

With the projected average rate of 9 percent growth in GDP during the EFYP the total investment requirement amount to US $ 492 billion. The financing of the projected investment during the 11th Plan indicates that while budgetary support could be to the tune of Rs2,00,000 crore, private sector investment in infrastructure could be Rs6,01,959 crore or US $ 147 billion. This combined with the Internal and Extra Budgetary Resources (IEBR) of both the centre and states will amount to Rs14,06,388 crore or US $ 343 billion. Assuming that 30% of this will be in the form of equity, internal resources and other non-debt sources, the total debt component is envisaged at Rs 9,84,472 crore or US $ 240 billion. The sources of the debt would be domestic credit from banks, non-banking finance companies, pension/insurance companies and external commercial borrowings (IIFCL 2008).

The resource requirements as projected above poses a challenge in mobilization. The large debt requirements suggest that debt service obligations will also be huge which can be met only if public sector improves its efficiency, economise on costs and rational user charges are levied to improve revenue streams of the infrastructure projects. At the same time, private sector investments will also have to increase substantially and its share in total investment should be around 30%. In sectors like ports and airports, private sector investment will have to be higher and Public-Private Partnership (PPP) could offer a viable solution, by providing infrastructure services on commercial principles.

Overview of Major Sectors Covered Under Infrastructure

Roads Infrastructure

The Indian road network has emerged as the second largest road network in the world aggregating at around 3.7 million km and consisting of national highways, state highways and other road comprising major district roads, other district roads and village roads. The US tops the list with a road network of 6.4 million km. Currently, China has a road network of over 1.8 million km only. Roads occupy a crucial position in the transportation matrix of India as they carry nearly 65 per cent of freight and 85 per cent of passenger traffic. Over the past decade several major projects for development of highways linking the major cities have been planned – and work started on most of them. What is of significance is that private sector involvement (BOT projects) has finally been found to be feasible in the Indian context. This has led to an accelerated growth in this sector – which had long been faced with financial constraints. This has also facilitated improvement in the quality of the new highways and introduction of the latest concepts for toll collection, signages etc. The process of development of the new highways is expected to continue for many years to come.

Railways

The Indian Railways enterprise was nationalised in 1953. It is now one of the world's largest rail network under one management. It plays an important role in not only meeting the

Table 1
Infrastructure—Deficit and Eleventh Plan Physical Targets

Sector	*Deficit*	*Eleventh Plan Targets*
Roads/Highways	65590 km of NH comprise only 2% of network; carry 40% of traffic; 12% 4-laned; 4-lane 20000 km; 2-lane 50% 2-laned; and 38% single-laned	6-lane 6500 km in GQ; 4-lane 6736 km NS-EW; 20000 km; 1000 km
Ports	Inadequate berths and rail/road connectivity	New capacity: 485 m MT in major ports; 345 m MT in minor ports
Airports	Inadequate runways, aircraft handling capacity, parking space and terminal	Modernize 4 metro and 35 non-metro airports; buildings 3 greenfield in NER; 7 other greenfield airports
Railways	Old technology; saturated routes; slow speeds (freight: 22 kmph; passengers: 50 kmph); low payload to tare ratio (2.5)	8132 km new rail; 7148 km gauge conversion; modernize 22 stations; dedicated freight corridors
Power	13.8% peaking deficit; 9.6% energy shortage; 40% transmission and distribution losses; absence of competition	Add 78577 MW; access to all rural households
Irrigation	1123 BCM utilizable water resources; yet near crisis in per capita availability and storage; only 43% of net sown area irrigated	Develop 16 mha major and minor works; 10.25 mha CAD; 2.18 mha flood control
Telecom/IT	Only 18% of market accessed; obsolete hardware; acute human resources' shortages	Reach 600 m subscribers—200 m in rural areas; 20 m broadband; 40 m Internet

Source: Planning Commission, Eleventh Five Year Plan, chapter 12, page 255

needs of the country, but also in bringing together dispersed areas and integration. From a very modest beginning in 1853, when the first train Thane (a distance of 34 km), Indian Railways has grown into a over a route length of 63,327km (Table 3).

Power Infrastructure

Installed power generation capacity in the country has increased significantly over the years from about 2,301MW in 1950-51 to 1,54,664 MW by 2006-07. Correspondingly, the overall generation increased from 2,519GWh during 1950-51 to 7,25,454 GWh during 2006-07. Consequently, the annual per capita Power generation increased from 17.28 kWh in 1950-51 to 671.89 kWh in 2006-07(Table 4).

Ports and Shipping Infrastructure

India is the 20th largest maritime country in the world. The maritime sector in India comprises ports, shipping, shipbuilding and ship repair, as well as inland water transport systems. Ports have played an important role in facilitating India's international trade and also in generating economic activity in their surroundings. The12 major and 200 minor ports scattered across its 7,517 km coastline handle both domestic and international trade (Table 5).

India has a long coastline of 7,517 km. The existing 12 major ports control around 76% of the traffic. Due to globalization, India's ports need to gear up to handle growing volumes. A number of the existing ports have plans for expansion of capacities, including addition of container terminals. The government has launched the National Maritime Development Programme, to cover 276 port projects (including related infrastructure) at an investment of about INR 600 billion by the year 2012. Also, States are increasingly seeking private participation for the development of minor ports, especially on the west ports.

Telecommunications Infrastructure

In the initial plans, telephones were not considered a necessity or for mass use. As a result, telephone penetration levels were very low and the quality of service was poor. However, long waiting lists, technological advancements and pressure from various domestic and international stakeholders pushed the government to initiate reforms in this sector in the mid-1980s. Further, after liberalisation the results in this sector have been impressive. Teledensity increased from less than 1 per cent in 1991 to around 18.23 per cent by 2006-07 and the number of phone lines from 5.07 million to 205.89 million over the same period. Wireless has been the principal engine for telecom growth in the country. The wireless subscriber base grew from less than 1 million in 1997-98 to 165 million in 2006-07; this figure has leaped to 543 million by November 2009 (Table 6).

Development of the telecom industry in India illustrates the huge potential benefits from the growth of infrastructure sectors. India's telecommunication network is now the third largest in the world and the second largest among the emerging economies of Asia. India is also among the fastest growing telecom markets in the world. The Indian telecom industry manufactures a complete range of telecom equipment using state-of-the-art technologies designed specifically to match the diverse terrain and climate conditions in the country.

Civil Aviation Infrastructure

With air travel becoming popular and cheaper, the civil aviation sector is experiencing high growth in domestic passenger carriage, cargo movement and international air traffic. The

Table 2
Development of Roads and Road Transport

Sector	*Units*	*1950-51*	*1960-61*	*1970-71*	*1980-81*	*1990-91*	*2000-01*	*2006-07*
Total length	000kms	400	525	918	1,491	2,331	3,374	3,709
National Highways	000kms	20	24	29	34	34	58	67
State Highways	000kms	43	62	89	127	127	132	137
Other Roads	000kms	338	439	800	2,170	2,170	3,184	3,506
				Road Transport				
Total	000Nos	306	665	1,865	19,173	19,173	48,857	89,618
Goods Vehicles	000Nos	82	168	343	1,173	1,289	2,715	4,436
Buses	000Nos	34	51	94	312	312	562	992
Cars, Jeeps, Taxis	000Nos	159	310	682	2,733	2,733	6,143	11,526
Two-Wheelers	000Nos	27	88	576	12,525	12,525	34,118	64,743
Other Vehicles	000Nos	4	42	170	2,314	2,314	5,319	7,921

Source: NCAER, 2010, Infrastructure Development in India, an Assessment of Status and Strategies.

Table 3
Development of Railways

Sector	*Units*	*1950-51*	*1960-61*	*1970-71*	*1980-81*	*1990-91*	*2000-01*	*2006-07*	*2007-08*
Route Length	km	53596	56247	59760	61240	62367	63,028	63,327	63,273
ElectrifiedRoute length	km	388	748	3706	5345	10083	14,856	17,786	18.274
Locomotives	Number(in thousands)	8209	10624	11158	10908	8417	7566	8153	8330
NumberOf Wagons	Number	100	152	226	269	278	246	243	247
Wagon Capacity	Million tonnes	4.14	6.3	9.35	11.14	11.5	10.9	10.06	10.24
OriginatingFreight traffic	Million tonnes	93	156.2	196.5	220	341.4	473.5	727.75	793.89
Net tones Km	Million tonnes km	44.12	87.68	127.36	158.47	242.2	312.4	481	521.4
PassengersOriginating	Millions	1284	1594	2431	3613	3880	4,833	6,219	6524
Passenger km	Million km	66,517	77,665	118,120	208,558	295,644	457,022	694,764	769,956

Source: NCAER, 2010, Infrastructure Development in India, an Assessment of Status and Strategies.

airlines passenger kilometers flown on international and domestic routes recorded more then 20 per cent growth per year between 2005-06 and 2007-08; India jumped to the 9th position in the world aviation market in 2007 from the 12th place that it occupied in 2006. Though the rate of growth dropped in 2008-09 due to the global economic crisis, India's new status as an international IT and manufacturing hub has led to a growth in international air traffic considering the increase in air traffic and the entry of new airlines, the government has taken steps to re-structure and modernize existing airports and set up new Greenfield airports. .Mumbai and Delhi airports have already been handed over to private players. Kolkata and Chennai airports will also be developed through JV route.

Irrigation

The net irrigated area (NIA) in the country has increased from 20.85 Mha in 1950-51 to 60.20 Mha by 2005-06 and the gross irrigated area (GIA) had increased from 22.56 Mha to 82.63 Mha during the same period. The country accounts for 31.4 per cent of Asia's total irrigated land and 17.9 per cent of the world's total irrigated land. The country's total agricultural land is 16.8 per cent of Asia's total agricultural land and 11.9 per cent of the world's total agricultural land. India now has the largest irrigated area in the world (Table 7).

There has been a striking change in the sources of irrigation over the plan periods. The importance of groundwater has increased considerably. In 1951, tube wells were little known and the entire area under groundwater irrigation was served mainly by shallow dug wells. Tube well irrigation initially started under state patronage in the 1950s. However, its coverage was insignificant till the early 1960s. Thereafter, the growth of tube wells picked up significantly due to government support. Further, the private profitability of tube wells increased with the introduction of new technologies and subsidies in electricity as a result of which the number of tube wells had increased from barely 200,000 in 1961 to 5 million in the late 1990s and then to 8.8 million by 200-01. Tube wells are now a major source of irrigation correspondingly; the share of canals in the NIA has decreased.

Section II

Role of Private Sector in Infrastructure Development

At present, the private sector is the engine of growth for many countries and the expansion of the private sector has became a central theme in the development agenda of many of these countries. Sustained economic growth is critical for job creation and poverty reduction. In addition, a thriving, private sector-led economy is probably the best defense against corruption, as economics and clear rules have less scope for corruption. In most countries of south Asia, the largest investment by the private sector has been in the telecommunications sector – nearly US $ 29,926.2 million during 2000-2005 – followed by energy, transport and water and sanitation. India has received the maximum investment in the region, followed by Bangladesh and Pakistan. (Table 8).

Private sector participation in infrastructure development was actively pursued first in electricity and telecommunication sectors. New institutions were created to regulate the industry to ensure competition and at the same time ensure commercial substantially of the operations. Entry of private sector operators in ports, civil aviation and telecom has led to very rapid growth of these sectors. In the case of electricity, the non-conventional and renewable energy sources such as wind energy and small hydro projects have been largely

Table 4
Development of the Power Sector

Sector	*Units*	*1950-51*	*1960-61*	*1970-71*	*1980-81*	*1990-91*	*2000-01*	*2006-07*
Power generationcapacity	MW	2,301	5,377	16,270	33,316	74,699	113,221	154,664
-hydro	MW	560	1,917	6,382	11,794	18,757	23,904	34,714
-thermal	MW	1,741	3,460	9,468	20,662	54,346	85,422	108,112
-Nuclear	MW	0	0	420	860	1,565	2,680	3,900
-Renewable	MW	0	0	0	0	30	1,215	7,938
Gross electricityGeneration	6574	20,123	61,212	119,260	289,439	536,452	752,454	
-Hydro	GWh	2,519	7,837	25,248	46,557	71,656	80,854	113,719
-Thermal	GWh	4,055	12,287	33,546	69,702	211,610	440, 840	609,856
-Nuclear	GWh	0	0	2,417	3,001	6,141	13,249	18,802
-Renewable	GWh	0	0	0	0	32	1,509	10,076
Annual per capitaConsumption of power	KWh	17.28	38.12	89.76	119.36	237.95	364.45	467.68

Source: NCAER, 2010, Infrastructure Development in India, an Assessment of Status and Strategies.

Table 5
Development of Ports

Sector	*Units*	*1950-51*	*1960-61*	*1970-71*	*1980-81*	*1990-91*	*2000-01*	*2006-07*
Total traffic handled	M.Tonnes			62.46	87.14	163.82	368	635.76
Major ports	M.Tonnes	19.2	39.9	55.7	80.41	152.55	281.1	463.84
Minor ports	M.Tonnes	NA	NA	6.76	6.73	11.27	86.9	171.92
No. Of major ports	M.Tonnes	5	9	10	10	11	12	12

Source: NCAER, 2010, Infrastructure Development in India, an Assessment of Status and Strategies.

Table 6
Development of Telecommunications

Sector	*Units*	*1950-51*	*1960-61*	*1970-71*	*1980-81*	*1990-91*	*2000-01*	*2006-07*
Number of telephones Per 100 population	Millions	0.03	0.08	0.18	0.31	0.60	2.86	18.23
Total no. Of telephones	Millions	0.10	0.33	0.98	2.15	5.07	30.36	205.86
Fixed lines (DELs)	Millions	0.10	0.33	0.98	2.15	5.07	26.51	40.75
Cellular mobile telephones	Millions	0	0	0	0	0	3.85	165.11
Number of telephonesPer 100 rural population	Number	NA	NA	NA	0.03	0.08	0.90	5.8

Source: NCAER, 2010, Infrastructure Development in India, an Assessment of Status and Strategies.

in the private sector. There has been limited success in attracting private operators in thermal electricity generation although the stage seems to have been set for progress here as well. Private sector has begun operations under 'build, operate and transfer' contract or its variants in the development of roads, airports and ports. Major and medium irrigation projects remain in the public sector. Nevertheless, public private partnerships (PPP) and the increasing role of the private sector are becoming established as a critical element of the energy of the strategy for infrastructure development.

PPP projects that are economically essential but commercially unviable are provided financial assistance in the form of Viability Gap Funding (VGF) and long tenor loans through the India Infrastructure Finance Company (IIFC) Limited. IIFC (UK) Ltd., a subsidiary of the IIFCL at London, has been established with the objective of borrowing funds from the RBI and lending to Indian companies implementing infrastructure projects in India solely for meeting capital expenditure outside India. In order to ensure quality project development activities by the States and Central Ministries, the India Infrastructure Project Development Fund (IIPDF) supports up to 75 per cent of the project development expenses in the form of interest-free loans. The projects, sponsored by State Governments and municipalities represent various sectors where PPPs are increasingly being adopted, namely urban sector, health and education, civil aviation, and roads.

Development and use of PPPs for delivering infrastructure services has now at least 11 years of precedence in India, with the majority of projects coming in line in the last 5 years. Policies in favor of attracting private participation as well as innovation with different structures have met with varying degrees of success. Some sectors like telecommunications, power, and ports and roads, have done very good progress compared to limited success in other sectors.

Some states have undertaken far more PPPs than others, and a much heavier use of PPPs in some sectors than others. As far as current status of projects in place as per our database, there have been at least 450 PPP projects in our main sectors of focus where a contract has been awarded and projects are underway in the sense that they are either operational, have reached construction stage, or at least construction/implementation is imminent. The total project cost is estimated to be about Rs. 2, 24,175.75 Crore.

The above table highlights that road projects account for 60% of the total number of projects and 45% by total value because of the small average size of projects. Ports though account for 10% of the total number of projects have a larger average size of project and contribute 30% in terms of total value.

It is noteworthy that if ports and central road projects are excluded from the total, there is in fact a relatively small value of deal flow, at only Rs 55757.02crs in basic infrastructure PPPs to-date, suggesting a significant potential upside for PPP projects across sectors.

In terms of main types of PPP contracts, almost all contracts have been of the BOT/ BOOT type (either toll or annuity payment models) or close variants. In terms of approach to provider selection, almost all the 450 projects are competitively bid (either national or international competitive bidding).

Section III

Specific Bottlenecks and Challenges of Infrastructure

1. Table no 1 highlight prevailing infrastructural gaps in quantity and quality at the beginning of Eleventh plan. The plan has proposed a comprehensive plan to bridge these however

Table 7
Development of Irrigation

Sector	Units	1950-51	1960-61	1970-71	1980-81	1990-91	2000-01	2006-07
Gross Irrigated Area	Mn.ha.	22.56	27.98	38.20	49.78	63.20	76.57	83.56
Net Irrigated Area (NIA)	Mn.ha.	20.85	24.04	31.10	38.72	48.02	51.63	60.64
Net irrigated area by type								
Canals	000 ha.	8,295	10,370	12,838	15,292	17,453	14,578	14,156
Tanks	000 ha.	3,613	4,631	4,112	3,182	2,944	2,258	2,083
Tube wells	000 ha.	0	0	4,461	9,531	14,257	20,711	28,031
Wells	000 ha.	5,978	7,083	7,426	8,164	10,437	9,231	9,277
Other	000 ha.	2,967	2,209	2,266	2,551	2,932	4,849	7,094

Source: NCAER, 2010, Infrastructure Development in India, an Assessment of Status and Strategies.

the mid term appraisal during the first three years of the Eleventh Plan indicates an optimistic outlook for infrastructure sector as a whole. Yet, to accelerate the pace of infrastructure development further, certain challenges need to be overcome. The foremost is to make huge capacity addition in a time-bound manner while ensuring that projects embody value for money and investment results in world class infrastructure. Infrastructure should at the same time be affordable and sustainable.

2. According to the recent Economic Survey 2010-11, 'the country needs $1 trillion worth of infrastructure investments by 2017 to upgrade roads, bridges, ports, metros and power plants. Half of the projected investment is to come from private sector. Some innovative ideas and new models of financing would be required. Channeling domestic and foreign financial savings of this scale into infrastructure requires a judicious mix of policy interventions which balances the growth and stability objective'. Thus financing infrastructure would be a big challenge in the years to come.

3. Apart from the need for substantial financial outlays for infrastructure, there are several non- financing constraints that need to be addressed to avoid time and cost overruns. Urgent action is called for in addressing the problems of (i) tendering of unviable projects; (ii) bad quality of engineering and planning at DPR stage; (iii) lack of standardized and sub-optimal contracts; (iii) land acquisition delays and slow approval processes, especially environmental and forest clearances; (iv) insufficient optimization of procurement costs (of PSUs); (v) weak performance management in nodal agencies and PSUs and; (vi) inadequate availability of skilled and semi-skilled manpower.

4. To speed up roads and bridges construction, the Ministry of Road Transport and Highways has made several policy and procedural changes. As a result, total works in progress, at any point, are at present about 9000 km as compared to 6000 km about ten months ago. Yet the gap between physical targets and achievement is huge. There have been inordinate delays in acquisition of land in some States, mostly due to procedural formalities, court cases, low levels of cooperation from other stakeholders, and delays in disbursement of compensation by the competent authority to affected landowners.

   Some of these problems can be overcome if projects are awarded on the basis of a transparent and hands-off auction system. In order to raise the efficiency bar and make the tendering process in road projects more effective, there is need to put into effect a transparent well-designed system of auction whereby private developers are made to properly compete with one another with no involvement of the Government.

5. Creative capacity augmentation in the railways sector is needed as in the past five years goods traffic has increased by above 8 per cent per annum whereas the rail network has been augmented by barely 0.08 per cent. The Ministry of Railways has proposals for capacity augmentation, rolling stock, and dedicated corridors and accordingly projects for construction of a dedicated freight corridor, high-speed rail corridors, world class railways stations, etc. are at different stages of planning and implementation. There is need to streamline the institutional framework for public- private partnership (PPP) projects in the railways sector so as to attract significant private-sector investment.

6. The biggest challenge in the civil aviation sector is to build and modernize infrastructure in pace with the manifold increase in demand. By 2020 the sector would need about 100 airports of international standard and a commercial fleet of 1,000 aircraft as passenger traffic is expected to reach 150-170 million (from about 55 million) and Air freight to

Table 8

Investment in Infrastructure Projects with Private Participation, South Asia (US$ million)

Country/Region	Telecommunications		Energy		Transport		Water and Sanitation	
	1995-99	2000-05	1995-99	2000-05	1995-99	2000-05	1995-99	2000-05
Bangladesh	438	1294	555	502	-	-	-	-
India	7457	20642	7166	8286	1273	4281	-	113
Nepal	-	109	98	39	-	-	-	-
Pakistan	76	6595	4298	525	421	71	-	-
Sri Lanka	602	766	176	271	240	-	-	-
South Asia	8605	29926	12293	9623	1934	4352	-	113
East Asia and Pacific	29305	29854	43590	30742	24636	20562	8988	10486
China	5970	8548	16916	10493	10803	13797	720	3477

Source: NCAER, 2010, Infrastructure Development in India, an Assessment of Status and Strategies.

Table 9
Sector wise Break up, PPP Projects in India, 2009

Sector	*Total Number of Projects*	*Based on 100 Crore*	*Between 100 to 250 Crore*	*Between 251 to 500 Crore*	*More than 500 Crore*	*Value of Contacts*
Airports	5	0	0	303	18808	19111
Education	1	93.32	0	0	0	93.32
Energy	24	175.59	558	2669	13708	17110.59
Ports	43	96	970	2440	62992.95	66498.95
Railways	4	0	102.22	905	594.34	1601.56
Roads	271	3162.5	5526.49	32861.87	60453.92	102004.7
Tourism		742.56	674.52	0	1050	2467.08
Urban Development	29	1283.86	1468.7	2403.91	10132	15288.47
Total	450	5638.83	9299.93	41582.78	167739.21	224175.8

Source: www.pppindiadatabase.com

increase to 9 million MT (from about 1.5 million MT). The sector has seen some success in attracting private-sector investment in recent years. The sector needs to upgrade existing non- metro airports, construct greenfield airports, and upgrade communication systems, air traffic management and equipment.

7. In the port sector, the Government has already put in place a comprehensive National Maritime Development Programme focusing on building inclusive maritime infrastructure. However, the challenge is to ensure time-bound implementation of projects as the delay in execution of several projects has resulted in congestion and inadequate infrastructure. Also the focus of public-funded investment need be on commercially non-viable but essential common infrastructure facilities so as to attract private-sector investment into commercially viable projects.
8. The challenge for the power sector is to make capacity addition and decongest inter-regional and regional transmission corridors. This capacity addition is expected to be three times more than the achievement of the 10th Plan but, keeping in view the persistent energy deficit of about 14 to 15 per cent, more efforts are needed. The long-term challenge is to increase the share of non-fossil fuel-based hydro and nuclear power generation.
9. The telecommunications sector has been successful in achieving tele-density targets ahead of time. With an overall tele-density achievement of 61 per cent (137 per cent urban and 28 per cent rural), the sector has been a success story so far. It has also been highly successful in attracting private investment and generating additional revenues for the Government. The challenge for the sector lies in fulfilling the government's vision of on-demand availability of telephone and broadband facilities across the country. Penetration and quality of rural broadband services are key to removing the digital divide and for provisioning of quality and cost-effective health and education facilities for rural masses. A transparent and consistent policy framework would ensure further growth of the sector.
10. Finally, there are several cross-cutting, regional- and local-level challenges. Protection of the environment, cutting of greenhouse gas emissions, and promotion of green technology are challenges on the path to rapid infrastructure development. The policy framework in each sector needs to strike a balance between rapid and sustainable development.

References

Aschauer, D.A. (1989), Is Public Expenditure Productive? Journal of Monetary Economics 23: 177-200.

Barrios, E. (2008), Infrastructure and Rural Development: Household Perceptions on Rural Development. Progress in Planning 70: 1–44.

Bhattacharyay, B.N. (2009), Infrastructure Development for ASEAN Economic Integration. ADBI Working Paper 138. Tokyo: Asian Development Bank Institute. Available: *http://www.adbi.org/workingpaper/2009/05/27/3011.infrastructure.dev. asean.economic/*

Esfahani, H.S., and M.T. Ramirez (2003), Institutions, Infrastructure and Economic Growth. Journal of Development Economics 70: 443-477.

Estache, A., and A. Goicoechea (2005), A "Research" Database on Infrastructure Economic Performance. Policy Research Working Paper 3642. World Bank: Washington, DC.

Ghosh, B., and P. De. (2005), Investigating the Linkage between Infrastructure and Regional Development in India:Era of Planning to Globalization. Journal of Asian Economies 15 (16): 1023–1050.

Government of India (2010), Planning Commission, Mid-Year Analysis.

Government of India (2007-12), Planning Commission, Eleventh Five Year Plan.

Majumdar, R. (2008), Infrastructure for Sustainable Growth: A Demand Projection Exercise for India, Journal of Quantitative Economics, Vol 5, No 2 Online at *http://mpra.ub.uni-muenchen.de/12812/ MPRA* Paper No. 12812, posted 17. January 2009/08:05

Munnell, A.H. (1990), Why has Productivity Growth Declined? Productivity and Public Investment. New England Economic Review, Federal Reserve Bank of Boston.

Richards, D. (2008), Global Infrastructure-a Growth Story. In Infrastructure Finance: Trends and Techniques, edited by H.A. Davis. London: Euromoney Books.

Sahoo, P and Dash, R.K. (2009), Infrastructure Development and Economic Growth in India, Journal of the Asia Pacific Economy, Rutledge, 14, 4, pp. 351-365.

Seethepalli, K., M. Bramait, and D. Veredas (2008)M, How Relevant is Infrastructure to Growth in East Asia? Policy Research Working Paper 4597. Washington, DC: World Bank.

United an and the Pacific (UNESCAP). Nations Economic and Social Commission for Asiia, 2006. Enhancing Regional Cooperation in Infrastructure Development including that related to Disaster Management. New York: UN.

World Bank (1994), World Development Report 1994: Infrastructure for Development. New York: Oxford University Press.

World Bank (2002), Empowerment and Poverty Reduction: The World Bank's Agenda Bank: Washington, DC.

Websites

www.coolavenues.com

www.pppinindia.com

www.ibef.org

2

WOMAN ENTREPRENEURSHIP: A NEW BREED TO ACHIEVE SUSTAINABLE DEVELOPMENT

Sanjay Manocha & Sanjoy Roy

Introduction

Entrepreneurs are normally considered as agents of change in the socio-economic development of a country. They are also seen as innovators, risk-takers, decision-makers and people with a definite vision. They have different characteristics as compared to the people accepting jobs or wage employment and also managerial functions. Earlier, it was believed that entrepreneurs are born and entrepreneurship is hereditary. But in the last couple of decades, it was confirmed that people could be indentified, trained and developed as entrepreneurs. The misconception that entrepreneurship is a monopoly of some communities and restricted to certain regions prevailed for a long time. But now it is evident that entrepreneurship does not belong to a particular region, community, sex, education, age, income level or a specific stratum of community.

In India, even today, certain regions and states are industrially and economically backward and among the regions certain communities are economically backward. It does not mean that they do not posses entrepreneurial traits. But socio-economic surveys of these regions and communities have proved that their entrepreneurial skills are dormant. If the proper conductive atmosphere is provided, even these regions and communities would respond favorably.

Motivational input and the infrastructure of the support system occupied a significant position in equipping "the first generation entrepreneurs". In this context, various "target groups" are identified for concentrating the efforts of entrepreneurial development. One such important target group is "woman". To bring them into the mainstream of entrepreneurship, the government formulates special schemes and policies.

Now, target group is widened due to the ever-increasing backlog of unemployment in India. Particularly, the increasing rate of unemployment among the educated youth with technical qualifications poses as a serious threat. As the employment market is saturated in India new employment opportunities are not generated. As a result, people have become frustrated hunting for jobs. Unable to seek a job, they turn towards self-employment and entrepreneurship. But this is a negative attitude. Entrepreneurship Development Training Programme (EDP) focuses on motivating the people to deveop a positive attitude towards adopting entrepreneurship as a better career option.

Liberalization, globalization and open economy concepts have posed a challenge for the small-scale industry. Is this true? The small-scale industry in India is set to play a distnict role in the country's economic development. Even though, industrial climate has turned to be fiercely competitive, the strength of being small is wonderful. The advocacy in favour of the small-scale sector which is still strong and valid is based on the grounds of:

- Promotion of economic well-being of masses
- Decentralization of economic power
- Diffusion of regional disparities
- Creation of large-scale employment
- Quick production
- Capital saving
- Import substitution and export promotion
- Saving foreign exchange
- Promoting the sense of participation in the economic development efforts

In the days of multinationals, small-scale industry and first generation entrepreneurs have to contribute significantly in the country's economic development. The main thrust of all the policies is on the development of new entrepreneurs.

The concept of **entrepreneurship** has a wide range of meanings. On the one extreme an **entrepreneur** is a person of very high aptitude who pioneers change, possessing characteristics found in only a very small fraction of the population. On the other extreme of definitions, anyone who wants to work for himself or herself is considered to be an entrepreneur.

The word *entrepreneur* originates from the French word, *entreprendre*, which means "to undertake." In a business context, it means to start a business. The Merriam-Webster Dictionary presents the definition of an entrepreneur as one who organizes, manages, and assumes the risks of a business or enterprise.

Schumpeter's View of Entrepreneurship

Austrian economist Joseph Schumpeter's definition of entrepreneurship placed an emphasis on innovation, such as:

- new products
- new production methods
- new markets
- new forms of organization

Wealth is created when such innovation results in new demand. From this viewpoint, one can define the function of the entrepreneur as one of combining various input factors in an innovative manner to generate value to the customer with the hope that this value will exceed the cost of the input factors, thus generating superior returns that result in the creation of wealth.

Entrepreneurship vs. Small Business

Many people use the terms "entrepreneur" and "small business owner" synonymously. While they may have much in common, there are significant differences between the entrepreneurial venture and the small business. Entrepreneurial ventures differ from small businesses in these ways:

Amount of Wealth Creation - rather than simply generating an income stream that replaces traditional employment, a successful entrepreneurial venture creates substantial wealth, typically in excess of several million dollars of profit.

Speed of Wealth Creation - while a successful small business can generate several million dollars of profit over a lifetime, entrepreneurial wealth creation often is rapid; for example, within 5 years.

Risk - the risk of an entrepreneurial venture must be high; otherwise, with the incentive of sure profits many entrepreneurs would be pursuing the idea and the opportunity no longer would exist.

Innovation - entrepreneurship often involves substantial innovation beyond what a small business might exhibit. This innovation gives the venture the competitive advantage that results in wealth creation. The innovation may be in the product or service itself, or in the business processes used to deliver it.

ENTREPRENEURSHIP IN INDEPENDENT INDIA

1. In a mixed economy, as India was defined by architects of this republic, with the public sector having the definite upper hand, the role of the state becomes very crucial. By its very nature such an economic system could not adequately focus entrepreneurs as catalyst of economic development. The state rather assumed the role of the major entrepreneur. Possibly and rightfully so, the overriding concern of the newly independent country related to correcting the anomalies and distortions created by the colonial rule.
2. Issues like employment generation, distributive justice and balanced regional development thus occupied the centre stage of industrial policy making in India. The first Industrial policy resolution of 1948 was a solid statement of the country's philosophy of growth, the vital aspect of which was industrialization under government regulation. Naturally neither this policy nor the subsequent ones made any specific reference to the entrepreneur or entrepreneurship. It is interesting to note that even the small scale sector, which later came to be known as 'the breeding ground of indigenous entrepreneurship', has been promoted and nurtured for its potential for addressing the larger developmental concerns. Such concerns, together with a gradually expanding public sector had set out a framework of industrialization where the cornerstones were controls, regulation and restrictions for the large industries and a wide protective umbrella with special incentives and institutions for the small ones. This was the scenario till late 1980s.

THE GROWTH OF ENTREPRENEURSHIP IN INDIA

1. Through unrecognized by policy statements, entrepreneurial initiative was breaking new grounds in the small industry scene over the past four decades banking mainly upon the ingenuity and determination of individuals. The late sixties and early seventies also witnessed a few sporadic attempts to create entrepreneurs from non traditional

communities with a view to breaking the monopoly of the dominant groups and diversifying the entrepreneurial base in the country. The state of Gujarat was the forefront of this movement.

2. By the late sixties it became quite evident that two resources are the most critical (in spite of favorable policies) for development of entrepreneurship, finance (credit) and managerial capabilities. The industrial policy exercises were woefully oblivion of these two basic factors though there were incentives and special institutions. When industrial development picked up in the sixties the bankers limited credit mainly to established industrialists and merchants for existing projects with assured success and sufficient collaterals. A study of 53 projects financed by banks and the Gujarat State Financial Corporation during the period 1965-68 revealed many interesting things. More than two thirds of institutional loans were for diversifications and expansion of existing enterprises. Of the new loans, 30% were given to merchants and traders with adequate financial resources and hence the required collateral. The entrepreneur's financial stake stood very high in the transactions tat a debt equity ratio 1:1. Such policies evidently were holistic to an aspiring and an otherwise competent young entrepreneurs but without enough financial resources and tangible assets. As an innovative alternative to the conventional banking system an Industrial Investment Corporation was set up as a State company in Gujarat in 1968 with attractive and unconventional credit schemes.
3. The task next was to identify and groom potential new entrepreneurs from a variety of socioeconomic backgrounds. The entrepreneurship development programme with well ell designed inputs for motivating, informing and skilling entrepreneurial individuals was pioneered in 1970. Something started as an experiment soon spread to other parts of the country (and now to many developing countries) and became a deeply entrenched strategy for new enterprise creation over the years. Difficult models and methodologies have been evolved and tasted by different organizations. Several modifications have been carried out to suit the profile and needs of various groups of trainees. For example, potential micro enterprises in the rural sectors by the poor, whose ventures have only limited investment and low levels of technology must be addressed differently from those of enterprising women whose talents and creativity have been suppressed by age-old socio-cultural norms and practices. Both need appropriate approaches so that they become capable of manifesting their entrepreneurial competence.
4. Despite efforts made by a host of institutions, only less than 20% of the new entrepreneurs have access to training every year. This means that a large mass of potential entrepreneurs are still outside the reach of training interventions.

THE TRANSFORMING SENERIO

1. While training can provide the necessary skills and motivation to entrepreneurial individuals, it is the government that should create an encouraging environment so that creative individuals commercialize their innovative ideas. In other words, the spirit of enterprise comes directly in contact with the 'system' at the stage of launching a business venture. Unfortunately, enquiries among entrepreneurs time and again reiterate the negative impact of the system on the morale of the entrepreneur and the growth of enterprise. Unfriendly bankers, procedural delays, bureaucratic indifferences all impede the smooth launching of enterprises. Ironically enough, the policy imperatives with

their trust on protecting the new entrepreneurs in the small sector from the shocks of unequal market relations with the large sector, have turned out to be the hardest stumbling blocks on their path to growth and prosperity. Complex and burdensome regulatory and administrative environment created as a result of excessive state intervention became the major deterrent to the emergence of new entrepreneurship. An uncanny situation has thus been created. On the one hand the numbers look impressive almost 15 million jobs, over two million enterprises; around 7500 products. On the other, a good number of firms are observed to be failing due to financial inadequacy, technological obsolescence and managerial inefficiency. We have to sit back and take stock of the past now to see where and why we have gone wrong in our assessment and planning.

2. The changing economic scenario domestically and globally warrants that this exercise is done in right earnest without losing much time. The goals of economic policy in the nineties and beyond appear now to be two fold: developing a viable, efficient and internationally competitive small industry and creating an innovative, socially responsible and liberated class of entrepreneurs who can take on the challenges that spring up as the process of liberalization and reform progress.
3. With liberalization setting in, it was bound to be sooner, rather than later, that a new business class would emerge. Never could we have predicted that Azim Premji, who inherited a vegetable oil company, could beat traditional industrialists in becoming the richest India. And that a school teacher's son, Narayana Murthy, would own the most valued company in the country, Infosys. Such twists of fate, possible only in today's India, were a far cry a decade ago.

Role of Woman Entrepreneurs

In the traditional Indian society, a distinction was made between 'men's' work and 'women's' work, particularly that of the women with family responsibilities. It curtailed the employment opportunities for woman in conventional and unconventional fields of economic activity. This led to the concept of work suitable for woman. The persisting concept of women's work as auxiliary to that of men has resulted in the continuance of the traditional definition of women's work. This obviously reflects the past rather than the present or the future.

In India, the rights of women to public employment recognized under Constitution, Articles 16(1) and 16(2) of the Constitution, grant the right of equal opportunities in regard to employment to men and women without any distortion.

Often a question is posed, "Are women entrepreneurs a separate category?" or "Do women entrepreneurs need a separate treatment?" briefing this, entrepreneur and entrepreneurship are economic concepts. The entrepreneur represents distinct qualities, skills, attitudes, beliefs, capacities and values. Irrespective of sex, an individual with these distinct qualities can become an entrepreneur.

Therefore, women entrepreneurs should not be considered as a separate category. But in the male-dominated, traditionally orthodox Indian society, economic independence of women did not have a social sanction. The entry of women in the field of industry and business as an owner of the enterprise is a recent development. To facilitate women to take up more challenging entrepreneurial careers, to equip them with essential support system and strengthen them to establish themselves economically, socially and culturally at par with men in the initial stages, additional motivation, guidance, support and opportunity is necessary.

The Indian women have basic characters in themselves in the present sociological and cultural setup as follows.

- Indian women are considered as Sakthi, which means source of power.
- Effectively coordinating the available factors and resources.
- Efficient execution of decisions imposed on them
- Clear vision and ambition on the improvement of family and children.
- Patience and bearing the sufferings on behalf of others and
- Ability to work physically more at any age.

To harness women in the economic restructuring programme and to actuate them as productive human resource, it is necessary to provide special schemes, incentives, benefits and concessions in the form of a special treatment. Not as the weaker sex, but as an economically weaker class, a separate treatment to women entering the gamut of entrepreneurship is justified.

The main reasons behind the entry of women in entrepreneurial careers are:

- Limited job opportunities
- Pressing need to earn income to supplement the family income due to a high cost of living
- Social pressure of increasing standard of living
- Utilization of spare time
- Self-esteem need
- Increasing socio-economic awareness
- Impact of role models in industry and business ('She is doing, why not me?' feeling)
- Constant motivation by government institutions
- Impact of media
- Attractive incentives, subsidies and schemes

Problems/Challenges of Women Entrepreneurs in India

Women in India are faced many problems to get ahead their life in business. A few problems cane be detailed as;

- The greatest deterrent to women entrepreneurs is that they are women. A kind of patriarchal – male dominant social order is the building block to them in their way towards business success. Male members think it a big risk financing the ventures run by women.
- The financial institutions are skeptical about the entrepreneurial abilities of women. The bankers consider women loonies as higher risk than men loonies. The bankers put unrealistic and unreasonable securities to get loan to women entrepreneurs. According to a report by the United Nations Industrial Development Organization (UNIDO), "despite evidence that woman's loan repayment rates are higher than men's, women still face more difficulties in obtaining credit," often due to discriminatory attitudes of banks and informal lending groups (UNIDO, 1995b).
- Entrepreneurs usually require financial assistance of some kind to launch their ventures - be it a formal bank loan or money from a savings account. Women in

developing nations have little access to funds, due to the fact that they are concentrated in poor rural communities with few opportunities to borrow money (Starcher, 1996; UNIDO, 1995a). The women entrepreneurs are suffering from inadequate financial resources and working capital. The women entrepreneurs lack access to external funds due to their inability to provide tangible security. Very few women have the tangible property in hand.

- Women's family obligations also bar them from becoming successful entrepreneurs in both developed and developing nations. "Having primary responsibility for children, home and older dependent family members, few women can devote all their time and energies to their business" (Starcher, 1996, p. 8).The financial institutions discourage women entrepreneurs on the belief that they can at any time leave their business and become housewives again. The result is that they are forced to rely on their own savings, and loan from relatives and family friends.
- Indian women give more emphasis to family ties and relationships. Married women have to make a fine balance between business and home. More over the business success is depends on the support the family members extended to women in the business process and management. The interest of the family members is a determinant factor in the realization of women folk business aspirations.
- Another argument is that women entrepreneurs have low-level management skills. They have to depend on office staffs and intermediaries, to get things done, especially, the marketing and sales side of business. Here there is more probability for business fallacies like the intermediaries take major part of the surplus or profit. Marketing means mobility and confidence in dealing with the external world, both of which women have been discouraged from developing by social conditioning. Even when they are otherwise in control of an enterprise, they often depend on males of the family in this area.
- The male - female competition is another factor, which develop hurdles to women entrepreneurs in the business management process. Despite the fact that women entrepreneurs are good in keeping their service prompt and delivery in time, due to lack of organisational skills compared to male entrepreneurs women have to face constraints from competition. The confidence to travel across day and night and even different regions and states are less found in women compared to male entrepreneurs. This shows the low level freedom of expression and freedom of mobility of the women entrepreneurs.
- Knowledge of alternative source of raw materials availability and high negotiation skills are the basic requirement to run a business. Getting the raw materials from different souse with discount prices is the factor that determines the profit margin. Lack of knowledge of availability of the raw materials and low-level negotiation and bargaining skills are the factors, which affect women entrepreneur's business adventures.
- Knowledge of latest technological changes, know how, and education level of the person are significant factor that affect business. The literacy rate of women in India is found at low level compared to male population. Many women in developing nations lack the education needed to spur successful entre-preneurship. They are ignorant of new technologies or unskilled in their use, and often unable to do research and gain the necessary training (UNIDO, 1995b, p.1). Although great advances are

being made in technology, many women's illiteracy, strucutural difficulties, and lack of access to technical training prevent the technology from being beneficial or even available to females ("Women Entrepreneurs in Poorest Countries," 2001). According to The Economist, this lack of knowledge and the continuing treatment of women as second-class citizens keeps them in a pervasive cycle of poverty ("The Female Poverty Trap," 2001). The studies indicates that uneducated women donot have the knowledge of measurement and basic accounting.

- Low-level risk taking attitude is another factor affecting women folk decision to get into business. Low-level education provides low-level self-confidence and self-reliance to the women folk to engage in business, which is continuous risk taking and strategic cession making profession. Investing money, maintaining the operations and ploughing back money for surplus generation requires high risk taking attitude, courage and confidence.
- Achievement motivation of the women folk found less compared to male members. The low level of education and confidence leads to low level achievement and advancement motivation among women folk to engage in business operations and running a business concern.
- Finally high production cost of some business operations adversely affects the development of women entrepreneurs. The installation of new machineries during expansion of the productive capacity and like similar factors dissuades the women entrepreneurs from venturing into new areas.

How to Develop Women Entrepreneurs?

Right efforts on from all areas are required in the development of women entrepreneurs and their greater participation in the entrepreneurial activities. Following efforts can be taken into account for effective development of women entrepreneurs.

- Consider women as specific target group for all developmental programmes.
- Better educational facilities and schemes should be extended to women folk from government part.
- Adequate training programme on management skills to be provided to women community.
- Encourage women's participation in decision-making.
- Vocational training to be extended to women community that enables them to understand the production process and production management.
- Skill development to be done in women's polytechnics and industrial training institutes. Skills are put to work in training-cum-production workshops.
- Training on professional competence and leadership skill to be extended to women entrepreneurs.
- Training and counseling on a large scale of existing women entrepreneurs to remove psychological causes like lack of self-confidence and fear of success.
- Counseling through the aid of committed NGOs, psychologists, managerial experts and technical personnel should be provided to existing and emerging women entrepreneurs.

- Continuous monitoring and improvement of training programmes.
- Activities in which women are trained should focus on their marketability and profitability.
- Making provision of marketing and sales assistance from government part.
- To encourage more passive women entrepreneurs the Women training programme should be organised that taught to recognize her own psychological needs and express them.
- State finance corporations and financing institutions should permit by statute to extend purely trade related finance to women entrepreneurs.
- Women's development corporations have to gain access to open-ended financing.
- The financial institutions should provide more working capital assistance both for small scale venture and large scale ventures.
- Making provision of micro credit system and enterprise credit system to the women entrepreneurs at local level.
- Repeated gender sensitization programmes should be held to train financiers to treat women with dignity and respect as persons in their own right.
- Infrastructure, in the form of industrial plots and sheds, to set up industries is to be provided by state run agencies.
- Industrial estates could also provide marketing outlets for the display and sale of products made by women.
- A Women Entrepreneur's Guidance Cell set up to handle the various problems of women entrepreneurs all over the state.
- District Industries Centres and Single Window Agencies should make use of assisting women in their trade and business guidance.
- Programmes for encouraging entrepreneurship among women are to be extended at local level.
- Training in entrepreneurial attitudes should start at the high school level through well-designed courses, which build confidence through behavioral games.
- More governmental schemes to motivate women entrepreneurs to engage in small scale and large-scale business ventures.
- Involvement of Non Governmental Organisations in women entrepreneurial training programmes and counselling.

The existing women entrepreneurs in India can be classified into three main categories:

- Forced entrepreneurs who are compelled by circumstances or family business responsibilities to take up a career in business and industry
- Chance entrepreneurs who went into business by luck or accident without any preparation
- Created entrepreneurs, who are specifically identified, motivated, trained, equipped and developed as entrepreneurs. In recent years, there is an overwhelming response from women for the entrepreneurship development training programmes, which is increasing the band of women entrepreneurs in India.

Opportunities for Women Entrepreneurs

Considering the flow of women entrepreneurs in the traditional and conventional industries and product lines, it is often criticized that the women entrepreneurship in India is caught up in "3 Ps," (papads and pickles, food industry, petticoats, readymade garment industry, paintings and handicrafts). The entry of women entrepreneurs in the conventional product is justified on the grounds that they have acquired the skills required for these products traditionally. If they could excel in these product lines let them excel. But many all-India surveys proved that in recent years, women entrepreneurs have entered all fields of business and industry.

In the last decade, there has been a remarkable shift in emphasis from the manufacturing industry to the service industry. Considering this, some important opportunities are identified for the women in urban areas:

- Computer services and information dissemination
- Trading in computer stationery
- Computer training at various levels
- Computer maintenance
- Travel and tourism
- Quality testing, quality control laboratories
- Sub- assemblies of electronic products
- Nutrition clubs in schools and offices
- Poster and indoor plant library
- Recreation centers for old people
- Culture centers
- Screen printing, photography and video shooting
- Stuffed soft toys, wooden toys
- Mini laundry, community eating centers
- Community kitchens
- Distribution and trading of household provision as well as saris, dress materials, etc.
- Job contacts for packaging of goods
- Photocopying, typing centers
- Beauty parlours
- Communication centers like STD booths, cyber cafes, etc.
- Crèches
- Catering services
- Health clubs, etc.

The opportunities enlisted above for urban women are representative and such opportunities can be identified.

Opportunities for Women in Semi-urban Areas

Considering the socio-economic, cultural and educational status and the motivational levels of women in semi-urban areas, particularly projects with low investments, low technical know-how and assured market are suggested for them. Important opportunities identified for semi-urban women are enlisted below:

- Production of liquid soap, soap powder, detergents, deodorants etc.
- Office stationary like cushion pads, gum, ink, ink pads etc.
- Convenience, readymade, instant food products including pickles, spices, papads etc.
- Community kitchens
- Communication services
- Different types of training and coaching classes
- Child care centers and culture centers for children
- Nursery classes
- Manufacturing of leather goods
- Garments

Opportunities for Women in Rural Areas

In the recent industrial policy, the government has given tremendous importance for the agro-based products and allied products. Only one to two percent of the total production of fruits and vegetables is processed every year in India. This reveals a huge scope for the food, fruit and vegetable processing industry. Women have a natural flair and instinct for food preparation and processing. A new market is developed for the processed fruits and vegetables in form of baby foods, ice cream, convenience foods, cold drinks, canned products, traditional medicine preparations etc. thus, there are plenty of opportunities available for women entrepreneurs.

Conclusion

Business is Business! That's what they say! But is there any particular way a business has to be done? Partly yes and partly no. Partly yes because there isn't any particular way we wouldn't have learnt and tried to master it. And partly no because continuous change in technology and vast amount of information is making it much more challenging, and demands something new every time. Add to it the global competition, business is never the same. As somebody said, "You never cross the same river more than once." Always there are new waters in the river, so there are new challenges and new people in business every time.

So evolving is the new concept of knowledge worker, and the problems of attrition have shifted the focus of organizations to the women as future workforce, especially as knowledge workers. Obviously, there are many examples where a woman has reached to the top, like Indira Nooyi, CEO of PepsiCo, and many more. So organizations have started seeing women with a new hope, they are taking-up women of ability, pairing them with men of ability, to make the best organization and a profitable one too.

The truth is that successful business is led by people of experience with specific business skills and the right mind-set. This is why we must develop women managers further through learning experiences, coaching and training that ensures the results a corporation needs to obtain highly skilled women leaders.

Therefore a key consideration by the government should be to critically evaluate the exiting macro economic policies and their impact on grassroots entrepreneurship development.

References

Kaulgud Aruna (2003), *Entrepreneurship Management*, Thomson Learning.

Taneja. Satish and Gupta. S.L. (2001), *Entrepreneur Development*, Galgotia Publishing Company.

Oates David (2007), *A Guide to Entrepreneurship*, Jaico Publishing House.

http://www.quickmba.com/entre/definition/

http://www.indianmba.com

3

RURAL ENTREPRENEURSHIP THROUGH MICROFINANCE FOR SUSTAINABLE DEVELOPMENT

Dimple Tresa Abraham & S.S. Kalamkar

Introduction

India, in recent years has grown to achieve a sustainable gross domestic product (GDP) of 8.1% (Planning Commission revised estimate for the Eleventh Five Year Plan), but the weak and the marginalized sections that constitute farmers, artisans, and women has remained largely sidelined. Equitable growth requires employment generation, which would ensure sustainable livelihoods to the poor and the marginalised in the urban and rural areas of the country. Self employment can be generated through the development of micro enterprises and according to Otero and Rhyne (1994, p.1) "for increasing numbers of poor people around the world, micro enterprises are a source of income and employment where no other alternatives are available". These enterprises which require only a small amount of initial investment enable income generation through self employment and ensure livelihood security for the poor. Rural micro entrepreneurship can lead to generation of higher non-farm employment and incomes leading to sustainable development. A number of micro enterprises has been promoted through micro-credit which is a main component of microfinance, a tool for providing finance to the poor, and in the words of Koveos and Randhawa (2004:p82)

"The heart of the idea of microfinance is the belief that poverty can be reduced and eventually eliminated through provision of credit to those too poor to access the formal financial system".

Literature Review

The objective of microfinance, considered as a grassroots instrument to alleviate poverty by many researchers, Anderson et al (2002); Evans et al (1999); Tietze et al (2007); Woller and Woodworth (2001a, b), is primarily to be achieved through micro enterprises that would ensure livelihoods. Anderson and Locker (2002), McKernan (2002), Hermes et al (2005), in separate studies conducted in some of the developing regions had reported that various social programs providing micro-loans without collateral have helped the poor to earn their livelihoods thereby leading to social and economic development in these areas.

Micro enterprises require small loans, or 'Microcredit' which is the term used for extending of small loans to very poor people, especially women, for generating income through self-employment activities. Kulshrestha (2000) identified the lack of capital as a major constraint to the development of women owned enterprises in rural areas, which was mainly due to lack of identity and assets as collateral security. Dowla (2006) has mentioned that it was the Grameen Bank of Bangladesh that pioneered lending without any collateral to the poor, especially to groups of poor women, who were illiterate and landless. The advent of microfinance and micro-credit and the self help grouping as Shylendra (2008) mentions brought about a change in to this, bringing about greater inclusion of the poor especially the women, into the formal banking sector.

The objective of microcredit according to Anderson et al (2002) is to break the vicious circle of poverty consisting of low capital, productivity, income and savings and is intended to enable the borrowers, primarily the poor women, to buy the goods that are needed to start or improve a small business. Lepenies(2004), wrote that the poor commonly face obstacles in the form of unfavourable market environments, inadequate financial infrastructure, location, market and infrastructure constraints, with poor transport infrastructure being one of the important impediment to rural microenterprise development.

The Asian Development Bank (ADB) has grouped micro enterprises into high return entrepreneurial and low return survival activities with the former being larger, more highly capitalized, employing more number of labour and using better technologies. They also tend to operate continuously, reinvest surpluses, and are usually primary household income sources mostly operated by men across regions, insulated from seasonal fluctuations and exhibiting lesser closure rates in comparison. Survival activities on the other hand are usually secondary sources of income and are mostly operated by women. They are characterized by low barriers to entry, undifferentiated products, saturated markets and inefficiencies which limit their competitiveness. They often rely on inputs which their owners gather themselves from locally available sources which may be seasonal, and the production processes are also prone to climatic fluctuations leading to very few of these enterprises earn income which is very close to the poverty line.

Mead and Leidholm (1998) defined micro enterprises as those requiring very small amount in terms of start-up capital, with initial capital requirements ranging from 49 dollars in Sierra Leone to 2,104 dollars in Jamaica. Dhar (2005), who researched on IRDP, identified microenterprises as those whose loan requirement was ranging from Rs. 6,000 and Rs. 10,000. Many of them may be involved in activities ranging from part-time income-generating activities run by individuals, to larger family-operated enterprises and also smaller enterprises employing hired labour. They may encompass all types of urban and non-farm rural activities, extending from manufacturing to commerce and even include enterprises engaged in transport business. Variations in business type, based on agricultural seasons were common in the rural areas. The researchers also recorded that in the case of women-owned and operated microenterprises, the cash associated with one microenterprise were frequently mingled with that of other household activities, including other enterprises.

In India, initiatives like the IRDP and the SGSY were undertaken to reach the poor in the rural areas aimed at increasing income through self-employment. Many of these programmes, gave thrust to promoting group entre-preneurship as group approach according to many like Bogaert and Das (1989) was considered to be more suitable and therefore to be promoted. These government-sponsored programmes, provided wide range of incentives as well as financial support, namely subsidy, to support small enterprise development. The national level programmes like the Rajiv Gandhi Udyami Mitra Yojana had provided handholding or support to microenterprises. A major support provided is the subsidy which was referred to as 'margin money' in the Prime Minister's Employment Generation Programme (PMEGP), a government initiative that began in 2008, with the objective of generating 37.38 lakh additional employment opportunities by facilitating self-employment and entrepreneurship in the rural and urban areas having a subsidy component of Rs.4485 crores.

Table 1
Estimated Targets Under PMEGP from 2008-09 to 2011-12

Year	*Employment (in Nos)*	*Margin Money (Subsidy) (Rs.crore)*
2008-09	616667	740.00
2009-10	740000	888.00
2010-11	962000	1154.40
2011-12	1418833	1702.6
Total	3737500	4485.00

Note: In addition, Rs.250 crore has been earmarked for backward and forward linkages.
Source: www.kvic.org.in

These measures have been taken to achieve or enable inclusive growth as the focus today, according to Woodworth (2000) has shifted towards enabling the poor to improve their lives by imparting the necessary training to successfully launch their own small businesses ("micro-enterprises"), including the acquisition of small business acumen and entrepreneurial skills.

As sustainable micro enterprises can ensure and provide livelihoods for the poor, it can play a role in alleviating poverty, but the degree of permanence, productivity and profitability varies considerably among these micro enterprises. The study aims to look in to the performance of women run micro enterprises in rural areas, particularly by group of women who had grouped themselves in to self help groups.

Research Methodology

Sixty group run microenterprises from fifteen panchayats in the district of Ernakulam in Kerala were selected for the study. Purposive selection of panchayats was done, and the enterprises that were in operation for at least a period of 18 months were selected randomly. These were owned and operated by women belonging to self help groups promoted with the handholding support of *Kudumbashree*, a government run poverty eradication programme. The panchayats as well as the enterprises were selected randomly from the lists maintained at the district office of the *Kudumbashree* mission.

Data was collected in May- June 2010, by interviewing the women who were running the enterprises using a structured questionnaire which contained both close ended as well as open ended questions. There was over representation of certain kind of enterprise activities (such as tailoring), because of the predominance of choice of such livelihood activities by the rural women. The performance of enterprises for the research is measured based on the average monthly turnover and the average monthly income generated per member. The research worked out correlation between the subsidy amount and the income generation per member and the turnover as these were considered to be important performance measures of the enterprise.

In all, there were seven tailoring units, five of Nutrimix and dairy units, four units each of catering, home made snacks, handicrafts, and readymade garments. The sample also had three units of restaurants, paper bag units, provision store, rice and spice powder and soap powder units. There were also two paper plate & cup units which had some amount of machinery. The rest of the ten units were all single units representing activities like candle and umbrella making, oil processing, direct marketing, data processing centre and others.

Findings and Discussions

Out of the sixty group run rural enterprises that were selected in the sample, 20 per cent of the total was 'inactive' as they had not carried out any enterprise operations in the past twelve months or more. Of these, only one had not received any subsidy support while, five had received subsidy ranging from 10000 to 30000. Six of the enterprises that had become inactive had received subsidy support ranging from 50,000 to 1, 00,000 rupees. The initial investment in capital assets of these inactive enterprises ranged from 2,500 to 50,000 with the total investment ranging between rupees 23,000 and 200,000.

Amount of Subsidy

Ranged from Rs.0 to 1,10,000, with just one group run enterprise with eleven members receiving the highest amount as each member was entitled to a subsidy of Rs.10,000 each. From Table 1 it can be observed that six enterprises received zero subsidy, while eight only received Rs.10,000 as the subsidy component. It can also be observed that 58.33 per cent (or 35 units) received a subsidy of Rs.50,000 or more. Out of the inactive enterprises, 50 per cent had received subsidy support, with three receiving a subsidy of 50,000 each and one with Rs.1 lakh subsidy support.

Table 1
Subsidy Received by Micro-enterprises

No. of Micro enterprises	6	10	2	2	4	1	12	1	1	2	18	1
Subsidy Amount(Rs.000)	0	10	15	20	25	35	50	60	62.5	80	100	110

Source: Field Data collected from rural enterprises

Per Capita Monthly Income Per Member from Enterprise and Inactive Enterprises

In 2010, twenty per cent of the enterprises were inactive, with all enterprises producing the product 'nutrimix' having the highest percentage of members staying with the activity as well as each member receiving a respectable monthly income which averaged about Rs.3000. The enterprise was able to exhibit such returns as the market or the forward linkage of the product was ensured as the buyer, as mentioned in the case was the ICDS. Out of the five dairy units selected only one became inactive and this was because of some intentional effort by the group members.

Table 2
Monthly Income/ Member at Inception and Last Year

Income /Member/Month at Inception(Rs)	*Income/Member/Month in 2010 (Rs)*
100(5)	100 to < 500(4)
200(6)	500 to < 1000(6)
250(7)	1000 to < 1200(3)
300(9)	1200 to < 1500(4)
400(3)	1500 to < 2000(8)

Contd.

Income /Member/Month at Inception(Rs)	*Income/Member/Month in 2010 (Rs)*
500(14)	2000 to < 2500(6)
750(1)	2500 to < 3000(8)
800(3)	3000 to < 3500(3)
1000(7)	4000 to < 5000(1)
1500(4)	6000 to < 7000(1)
6000(1)	7000 to < 8000(2)

Source: Field Data collected from rural enterprises.
The figures in brackets denote the number of enterprises generating the given average monthly income at inception and in 2010.

Relation between Monthly Income Per Member from Enterprise and Subsidy

In order to find whether there was any relation between monthly income per member and the subsidy received by the group, correlation was calculated. The correlation was -0.1488 in the case of relation between subsidy and monthly income per member at inception, while it was -0.2681 in the case of monthly income per capita in 2010. The negative correlation indicates that there is no positive effect of subsidy on income generation by micro enterprises. Rather, even if subsidy is not availed, the enterprise may thrive if other enabling factors like 'forward linkages' are made available.

Relation between Initial Investment and Income Per Member in 2010

It was seen that out of the 20 per cent of the enterprises that were inactive, half had an investment that was greater than 1 lakh rupees or above. A quarter of all the enterprises that were closed had an initial investment of Rs.100, 000 and Rs. 200, 000 respectively. Only four enterprises had generated an average monthly income of Rs.4000 or more per member and it was seen that all the four enterprises had an initial investment ranging from Rs 10,000 to Rs.90, 000. In the case of the rural enterprise that had generated the highest average monthly income (Rs.7500/ month) per member, the initial investment was only Rs.10, 000. The members had invested later and were running under the initiative of one member who had taken a personal loan to make an additional investment which had improved the earning potential of the enterprise. Thus we can conclude from this analysis that there may not be any significant relationship between the initial investment and the income generated per member from the enterprise after a few years of operation.

Selected Cases of Rural Enterprises: The success of micro enterprises and economic activities of the poor depends greatly on the empowering environment that the local and state governments can ensure, and one of the successful strategies for promotion of successful microenterprises has been through the conversion of social needs into business opportunities.

Nutrimix Enterprises: This enterprise is 'innovative' as 'Nutrimix' is a product that was designed as the take home ration or food supplement for the "Anganwadi"[1] children aged below three years. Earlier the ICDS (Integrated Child Development Services) in Kerala was providing this as primarily eggs and milk powder, which was being sourced from the local market and from the neighbouring states, as large scale purchases. The 'Kudumbashree' mission found the opportunity where by a wholesome take home ration would be manufactured by the Neighbourhood group (NHG) entrepreneurs which would be wholly procured by the ICDS in the state. ICDS services are primarily aimed at addressing the needs of children below six years of age, and were launched by the government of India in

1975. The aim of the kudumbashree mission is to scale up to five hundred nutrimix manufacturing enterprises set up in various panchayats to serve the requirement of all the Anganwadi in the state. These enterprises are run by five member activity groups formed from various neighbourhood groups with the project cost of one five member unit being Rs 2.20 lakh, with a subsidy component and an entrepreneur contribution of Rs 50000 and Rs 10000 per enterprise which is supplemented by a bank loan component of Rs 1.60 lakh. All nutrimix units in the district of Ernakulam were run by two or more five member groups, for availing the required loan from the bank, and subsidy benefits from the government, as the capital requirement for these enterprises was higher. Also each unit required at least a minimum of ten people to carry out the various activities in the production as well achieve some amount of economies of scale.

In 2007, when the nutrimix unit at Edathala village began its operations, its monthly production was 9000 kilograms while in 2010, it had increased to 12,000 kg due to the hike in recommended monthly entitlement per child to 3.375kg/child from 2.5kg/child. The group which had 20 women initially became 14 members just one month in to the operation. Since then, all have worked in perfect unison towards the success of the enterprise sacrificing present monthly income (keeping it a bare minimum at first) for enabling monthly repayment of Rs.11,500 regularly. The wages for eight hour was raised to Rs.100 per person from the second year onwards. Every year, the group had shared profits in the month of April-May, regularly buying gold, which was primarily to meet short term capital requirements when ever a need arose. The total profit that was shared amounted to around Rs 60,000 per member in the three years of operation.

Ruchishree: The case deals with Ruchishree, a pickle and savouries enterprise that was originally formed by five women, who were neighbours and belonged to the neighbourhood group (same as SHG) 'Amma'. The enterprise began its operations in 2004, with a bank loan of Rs.100, 000 from the Central Bank of India, and a subsidy of Rs.50, 000. Within four months of operations, four members left, as they did not find the activity worthwhile. The remaining two members Thankamani and Janani struggled on and continued with the enterprise nurturing it, making different varieties of traditional items, until October 2009 when they also parted ways(after completing the bank repayment) dividing the assets that the business had namely, some steel containers and utensils. Today both are in the same business but as single entrepreneurs with the help of their family members and sell their products separately through their regular clients (small retail shops and restaurants) and also in the various monthly markets organised by the kudumbashree mission in the district.

The break-up of the group run enterprise in to individual run enterprises can be divided in to two phases. The first break-up happened with in the first six months when three members left. The main reason was returns or income earned by each of the individual members being too low. The final breakup in to individual enterprises after five years of jointly running the venture was because of issues related to sharing of work and money, with one woman working harder in the marketing activity with the help of her husband who was helping the wife who was not getting much help from her partner as she also had a salaried job and hence had less time to engage in marketing activity. After the break up in to individual enterprises, Thankamani, who had earlier worked as a nursing attendant while the enterprise was run jointly, resigned worked full time for developing the enterprise, actively involved in both production and marketing. The income from the enterprise became the main source of family income for both the women, contributing about 75 per cent of the total family income with both earning an average income of 6000-7500 per month. In the case of both, the individual income was more than double of what each had received earlier when they were working together and running just one jointly owned enterprise. Thus both were happier to run individually owned enterprises than the jointly (group) owned enterprise. Janani said, *"At least one is motivated to work hard as the income generated from one's efforts is substantial enough to support the family needs"*.

Conclusion

Rural Entrepreneurship would help to generate sustainable livelihoods, if the enterprise activity is suitable for the micro as well as the macro environment. It is important to promote entrepreneurship in the rural areas where the choice of the activity itself is critical to survival and growth of the enterprise. Market demand for the product is critical to the success and long term growth, as it is imperative that the enterprise activity should either meet an unmet need of the local or the marketable population. Marketing tie-ups and forward linkages may help the firm more than the subsidy, and therefore support strategies other than subsidy may have to be devised for the long term sustainability. It was observed that if the product or service had lot of local demand as in the case of 'tailoring' and 'dairy', there was a greater possibility of the enterprise generating a decent income to the members, provided there was no discord among the members.

The study has some limitations, one of them being the fact that the sample is chosen from just one district in the state, Ernakulam, which is also one of the better developed districts in terms of number of micro enterprises as well as economic opportunities available. Again the state chosen Kerala, is distinct in the sense that the demarcation between the urban and rural areas are indistinct. Therefore, it is possible for the rural enterprises to tap the urban markets better, which may not be the case in other states. Hence studies should be conducted in various states, region-wise, to understand the enabling factors affecting the sustainability and performance of rural microenterprises. This study could only conclude that in the case of group run enterprises, subsidy or a higher initial investment could alone not ensure better performance or a sustainable income to the entrepreneurs, but their linkage with the market as well as the choice of the product was more important for ensuring sustainability and performance in the long run.

References

Anderson, C.L and Locker, L. (2002), "Microcredit, Social Capital, and Common Pool Resources", *World Development*, Vol. 30 No.1, pp.95-105.

Evans, T.G., Adams, A.M., Mohammed, R. and Norris, A.H (1999), "Demystifying Non-participation in Micro Credit: A Population-based Analysis", *World Development*, Vol.27,No.2, p.419–430.

Hermes, N., Lensink, R. and Mehrteab, H.T. (2005), "Peer Monitoring, Social Ties and Moral Hazard in Group Lending Programs: Evidence from Eritrea", *World Development*, Vol. 33 No.1, pp.149-69.

Koveos, P and Randhawa, D. (2004), "Financial Services for the Poor: Assessing Microfinance Institutions", *Journal of Managerial Finance*, Vol. 30 No. 9, pp.70-95.

Lepenies, P.H. (2004), "Exit, Voice and Vouchers: Using Vouchers to Train Microentrepreneurs-Observations from the Paraguyan Voucher Scheme", *World Development* 32 (4), pp.713-724

Mead, D.C and Leidholm, C. (1998), "The Dynamics of Micro and Small Enterprises in Developing Countries", *World Development*, Vol.26, No.1, pp.61-74.

McKernan, S-M. (2002), "The Impact of Micro-credit Programs on Self-employment Profits: Do Non-credit Program Aspects Matter?" *Review of Economics and Statistics*, Vol. 84 No. 1, pp.93-115.

Morduch, J. (1999), "The Microfinance Promise", *Journal of Economic Literature*, Vol. 37, pp.993-1006.

Shylendra, H.S. (2008), "Role of Self Help Groups", *Yojana*, January 2008, pp.25-28.

Shylendra, H.S. (2004), "The SHG Bank Linkage Programme", *Journal of Rural Development*, Vol.23, No.4, pp.411-450.

Tietze, U., Siar, S., Upare, S. M. & Upare, M.A. (2007), *Livelihood and Micro-enterprise Development Opportunities for Women in Coastal Fishing Communities in India– Case Studies of Orissa and Maharashtra*, FAO Fisheries Circular. No. 1021, Rome, FAO. 69p.

Woller, G. and Woodworth, W. (2001a), "Micro Credit and Third World Development Policy, *Policy Studies Journal*, 29,145–65.

Woller, G. and Woodworth, W. (2001b), "Micro Credit as a Grass-roots Policy for International Development", *Policy Studies Journal*, 29, 202–14.

4

MEASURING ENTREPRENEURSHIP DEVELOPMENT: A STUDY CONDUCTED ON WOMEN ENTREPRENEURS OF MICRO CREDIT CENTRED ENTERPRISES IN INDIA

Vasanthakumari. P.

Of the total 950 million people in India, narly 50 percent are women. Female headed families form a higher percentage of the poorest households in the country. Gender inequalities have resulted in the concentration of women in unorganized sectors and unequal pay for equal work. Women contribute a higher proportion of their income for family survival. Even then they have limited command over resources. Micro credit centered enterprises have significance in this context .Micro credit institutions view micro enterprise development as an opportunity for providing gainful employment to the poor, improving their income and standard of living. But the survival and growth of these enterprises depend on the entrepreneurship among the beneficiaries. It is against this background that the present study has been conducted.

Part - 1

Introduction

The position of women in the society is determined by her contributions to economic and social process. Her contributions to the society are affected by control over resources and bargaining power. There are different modes for the women to reach out to the society. Involvement in economic and social activities provide adequate space for women. Employment is considered to be the main factor contributing to the economic and social status of women.

Though India is the largest democracy in the world, with regard to education, employment and status of women, the country is far behind the developed nations of the world. The census statistics indicate that majority of Indian women are illiterate, ill fed, unemployed and low paid occupying poor status in the society. The concept of self employment and entrepreneurship among women deserves special emphasis in this context.

In India rural women especially those belonging to weaker sections of the society have limited access to resources or employment opportunities that would make them economically independent and socially significant. Micro enterprises have a significant role in India in the prevailing ambience of industrial backwardness, mounting rate of unemployment and scarcity of capital Micro enterprises are more attractive to the rural poor women as they require low capital and low risk. It aims at the identification of innovative and creative activities that go along with the specific environment in which people are living and try to solve the problem faced by them especially in the area of finance by the technology and resources already available.

Though the Government of India launched several programmes to eradicate poverty and provide employment to women, they did not yield desired results. This is because they failed to take into account the local needs, entrepreneurial talents, marketing potential and resource handling capacities of the beneficiaries. These problems can be overcome by the formation of micro enterprises by micro credit institutions. Hence through this paper an attempt is made to examine the role of micro credit centered enterprises in India and to measure its impact on entrepreneurship.

METHODOLOGY

Micro enterprises functioning as group enterprises, operated by women linked with micro credit institutions have been taken for the study As the largest number of such groups are functioning in Kerala . Kerala has been selected.1950 micro group enterprises having at least 4 years have taken. Of these 2% has been selected at random. Of the selected enterprises, 5 entrepreneurs are taken for measuring entrepreneurship. Thus 39 micro enterprises and 195 entrepreneurs constitute the samples for the present study. Scaling technique based on five point Likert scale was the main tool used for analysis.

Part - 2

Women Entrepreneurship

Traditionally women's occupation status has always been identified with family and children. Recent changes in economic, political, social and education scenario in the global context have necessitated changes in the women's status and her role. This has resulted in rapid strides in women's progress.

India also witnessed rapid transformation in women's status in recent years. Though 48% of Indian population consists of women, their participation rate in the economic activities is only 34%. Among many other fields, women of today have moved into the world of entrepreneurship, both in the domestic and global markets. Even then, less than 5% of business units are owned and operated by them. Kerala is no exception to this. Active participation of women in management and leadership is still found to be lacking. Their position can be improved by providing them with gainful employment. Hence the self employment schemes including micro enterprises are highly significant.

In India, the poor are plagued by high levels of unemployment, low incomes and significant debt. The crux of poverty alleviation programmes in India lies in the employment generation potential leading to income generation. The origin and growth of micro enterprises in India can be traced to lack of employment opportunities and inadequate income generation. To address the issues of poverty reduction, creation of employment and income opportunities in rural areas, the government has initiated Micro Enterprise Development Programme. Micro enterprise development is viewed as an opportunity for providing gainful employment to the people below poverty line, thereby improving their income and standard of living

Micro enterprises represent an important means of earning income for women in developing countries. It is not easy for women to find a job that will be suitable to her family responsibilities and household work. Thus many women are attracted by the idea of self employment in micro enterprises adjoining their houses with flexible working hours which allow them to take care of both home and business. It provides employment and income to alleviate poverty. Micro enterprises are small undertakings run by individuals or groups who take up responsibility of managing a business venture and are often involved in the family activities. The micro enterprises suit the life style of women because of their multiple roles and need to re-organise time. Micro enterprises embody an impressive array of initiatives, skills and talents, which, if effective forms of assistance can be developed, have the potential to make an enormous contribution to the economic growth.

Micro enterprises commonly share certain characteristics like low fixed capital, low technology and a few workers. Micro enterprises come into existence out of either market driven or non market driven forces. Market driven ones are managed and controlled by the entrepreneurs themselves. In non-market driven enterprises a government agency or a NGO plays an active role. Non-market driven micro enterprises are fostered by Government or its agencies as a part of poverty alleviation. Non market driven micro enterprises are considered for the purpose of this study.

One of the main objectives of initialing non-market driven micro enterprises is to help the beneficiaries to take up and manage their own business activities which could supplement their household employment and income leading to improved standard of living. At the same time these enterprises are expected to serve as instruments which could bring about economic awareness and empowerment among the women members. The idea of starting micro enterprises has raised lot of hopes and expectations, particularly among women below poverty line. Through the operation of micro enterprises, asset management ability of the poor women will increase along with their profit margin and wages

Micro enterprises development is viewed as an emerging process which starts with low capital, low risk and low profit at the initial stage, gains momentum and later switches from low to medium capital and then from low risk to medium risk. At an advanced stage it can reach medium capital medium risk and medium profit with appropriate technology, emerging technology or even with low technology. To achieve their objectives, entrepreneurs of micro enterprises need to be supported by technological know-how, institutional finance and an effective marketing network system for their products. For this women micro entrepreneurs are assisted in: (a) identification of innovative and creative activities suited to the specific environment in which the poor people are living and help to solve the problem faced by the community by using the technological know-how already available (b) In the absence of entrepreneurial talents continued support by means of 'hand holding' and 'support services', (c) Training in functional areas of management like production finance, marketing and human resources, (d) Utilising the existing potential of resource persons available in and around the state for developing entrepreneurship, and (e) experiencing the marketing network system.

In addition to the above, entrepreneurs of micro enterprises receive various financial assistance and subsidies. They are provided with funds ranging from one lakh to nine lakhs as special assistance to various Grama Panchayats for financing micro enterprises. Challenge fund, matching grant, revolving func etc. are other forms of assistance given to SHGs linked micro enterprises. Innovative funds are provided to innovative projects ranging from Rs.1 lakh to 1.25 lakhs subject to 50% subsidy. Technological funds are provided for launching enterprises using new technology. A series of training programmes were arranged on the functional areas of management. Assistance from banks and other financial institutions including thrift and credit societies were channeled for achieving the objectives of micro enterprises. There are certain common features in the funding of the various enterprise programmes. All micro credit linked enterprises are bank linked and a minimum of 50% of the project cost has to be obtained through bank loans. The subsidy components are limited to 50% of the total project cost and the entrepreneurs share is limited to 5% of the total project cost.

Micro credit linked enterprises in Kerala aim to promote innovative business ideas rather than 'tried and tested' ideas. The method devised for identifying enterprises is (i) generating the idea that could solve a problem existing in the society (problem solving) (ii) fill the gap that existed (gap filling) (iii) converting new and emerging opportunities into an enterprise. Most of the entrepreneurs are first generation entrepreneurs and it is expected that women with the right attitude can be trained and developed to run the business. A systematic step by step process is normally followed for enterprise development. Brain storming sessions for enterprises development in the SHG meetings are held. The idea generated are analysed in the light of market feasibility, technology, existing skills, training needs, competition, funding etc. General awareness training to create an awareness of the potential of the enterprise to alleviate poverty, Entrepreneurship Development Programme training on various aspects of setting up and operating an enterprise, and on developing leadership quality and communication skills, training on skill development and training under Performance Improvement Programme provided to entrepreneurs would help to equip them to operate the business effectively.

Inspired by the encouragement provided under Central and State Government Schemes, the number of micro enterprises has increased from 10,604 individual micro enterprises and 685 group enterprises in 1999-2000 to 21,754 individual and 5054 group enterprises in 2007-2008 (Economic Review 2007).

Part - 3

Socio-Economic Profile of Entrepreneurs

- Majority of the entrepreneurs (59%) in Kerala fall under the age group of below 30 years.
- 82.8% of the respondents are married. As majority of the respondents are from BPL families, married women need more income. They look upon micro enterprises as a source for supplementing the family income.
- The highest percentage (50.8%) has only school education. Lack of employment opportunities for women with low educational back ground forces them to start enterprise
- 100 percentage of the sample respondents are first generation entrepreneurs and poverty forced them to become members of SHGs and thereby entrepreneurs of micro enterprise
- 97.4% of the sample entrepreneurs have no experience in the same line of business.
- Economic motive is the major motivating factor for the entrepreneurs to start the business because majority of them are from economically backward families and their main motive was to earn income to supplement the income of the families.
- Majority of the respondents (43.1%) had no prior occupation as they were the home makers before joining the enterprise.

- Average remuneration per month of the micro entrepreneurs was Rs. 2003. As the average monthly income exceeds Rs. 1,500 it can be concluded that micro enterprises have succeeded in yielding the minimum monthly income specified as per the operational definition, i.e., Rs.1,500 per month.
- After joining the enterprise 100% of entrepreneurs had attended training. Among these 75.9% attended training only once. The training modules designed for micro entrepreneurs consist of more than one area and the highest percentage (65.6%) attended training in the area of accounting: Even then they expressed the need for further training in the areas of accounting, marketing, entrepreneurship etc.
- Majority (53.8%) of the sample entrepreneurs have families with more than 5 members. 53.8% of the sample respondents have 2 children in their house below the age of 5 years. The study also reveals that though the high proportion of respondents has families with more than 5 members, 83.1% have families with only two earning members.

Part - 4

Impact on Entrepreneurship

Here an attempt is made to measure and analyse the extent of entrepreneurship development among micro entrepreneurs of micro credit linked enterprises Scaling technique based on five point Likert Scale was used to measure entrepreneurship development. To measure it, elements or skills affecting it are divided into two, viz., Individual Related Skills and Business Related Skills. Ten sub variables under each variable, viz., individual related skills and business related skills were identified and were placed before the respondents to mark their choice showing their degree of agreement or disagreement to each sub variable. The values for choices were assigned as; 2 for strongly agree, 1 for agree, 0 for undecided, -1 for Disagree and -2 for strongly disagree. Data were collected from 195 respondents in Kerala. Then frequencies for each sub variables were counted for the total micro enterprises and for each category. Then values assigned were multiplied with their corresponding frequencies and Entrepreneurship Development Index was calculated.

To arrive at the degree of entrepreneurship, the following decision criteria were used;

Below Zero and zero = No empowerment

Between Zero and 33⅓ = Low empowerment

Between 33⅓ and 66⅔ = Moderate empowerment

Above 66⅔ = High empowerment

Based on readings on empirical studies on entre-preneurship, focus group discussions with experts in this area and pilot study conducted by the researcher individual related skills and business related skills were identified.

Individual Related Skills

Individual related skills identified include flexibility, farsightedness, dynamism, effective communication, creativity, initiative, confidence and optimism, result oriented, accepting challenges, energetic and hard working. The result of analysis on individual related skills is given in Table 1.

Table 1
Entrepreneurship Development Index for Individual Related Skills

Variables	*Overall Indices*
Flexibility	86.5
Far sightedness	67.0
Dynamism	65.0
Effective communication	70.0
Creativity	75.5
Initiative	66.5
Confidence and optimism	76.5
Result oriented	54.0
Accepting challenges	58.5
Energetic and hard working	82.8
Composite Index	75.0

Source: Survey data
: Average Index

The above table shows that the Composite Index for women entrepreneurship was 75, which was above 66⅔, which indicates entrepreneurship development based on individual related skills was high. The over all indices among sub variables ranged between 86.5 and 54.0. A detailed examination into the sub variables reveals that, of the 10 sub variables, 6 indicate high level of empowerment, ie, the over all average indices for these variables were above 66⅔. The overall average indices for these sub variables were; flexibility (86.5), energetic and hard working (82.8), confidence and optimism (76.5), creativity (75.5), effective communication (70) and fàrsightedness (67). For two variables, viz taking initiative (66.5) and 'dynamism' (65.0), the indices were very close to the high level of Entrepreneurship Development Index. The rest two sub variables viz.., 'accepting challenges' and 'result oriented' scored average indices of 58.5 and 54.0 respectively indicating moderate level of entrepreneurship development.

To conclude, in individual related skills for entrepreneurship development the areas that demand special attention includes 'resulted oriented' 'accepting challenges', 'dynamism' and 'initiative'. While designing the training programmes special attention should be paid to include modules to develop these personal related business skills.

Business Related Skills

For assessing the business related skills, 10 variables which are essential for business were identified. These includes ability to: promote new business, administer the business, generate new ideas, undertake risk and uncertainty, planning, coordination and control; handle cash and bank transactions, accounting, conduct market survey, time management, and 'financial management'. All these skills related to the management aspects of business and are pre-requisites for a successful entrepreneur. For analysis, average Entre-preneurship Index for each variable and Composite Index for each category and an over all Composite Index, were computed. Table 2 gives details of entrepreneurship development index for business related skills.

Data in the table above reveals the average entrepreneurship development indices among variables ranged between 76 and 17.5, with a Composite Index of 43.5. In business related skills, entrepreneurship development index of only one variable, ie, 'handle cash and bank transactions', was above 66⅔ and indicates high entre-preneurship development. For all other variables except one, the entrepreneurship development indices were between 33⅓ and 66⅔ and showed moderate empowerment. For one variable, i.e., 'ability to conduct market survey', the Index was 17.5 representing low empowerment.

Table 2
Entrepreneurship Development Index for Business Related Skills

Variables	*Overall Indices*
Ability to promote new business	47.0
Administer business	56.0
Generate new ideas	48.5
Undertake risk and uncertainty	55.0
Plan, co-ordinate and control	55.0
Handle cash and bank transactions	76.0
Accounting	36.5
Conduct market survey	17.5
Time management	46.5
Financial management	43.0
Composite Index	43.5

Source: Survey data
: Average Index

The above discussion on entrepreneurship development in business related skills throws light on the fact that the development was more in 'handling cash and bank transaction' and the least in 'conducting market survey' for each category as well as for the entire sample of micro enterprises. Discussions reveal that marketing is the most severe problem faced by micro enterprises and none of the units had conducted an in depth market survey. While attempting to identify the areas for further training, the highest percentage of entrepreneurs expressed the need for training in marketing (Table 2). All these emphasises the need for developing marketing skills among the entrepreneurs. For this special care should be given to this aspect while designing training module and to impart training both on theoretical and practical aspect in this regard. Apart from marketing, accounting should also be given importance. From the discussions with the entrepreneurs as well as on scrutiny of the accounts maintained by majority of the enterprises, the researcher was convinced that most of entrepreneurs have no knowledge in maintaining accounts and most of them followed single entry system of accounting. In handling cash and bank transactions the Entrepreneurship Development Index is high. This is because, as SHG members, they have had enough experience and get trained in handling cash and bank transactions.

An effort is also made to analyse the entrepreneurship development in total by combining both individual and business related skills.

Table 3
Combined Composite Entrepreneurship Development Index

Elements	*Over all Composite Index*
Individual related skills	75.0
Business related skills	43.5
Combined Composite Index	59.3

Source: Survey Data

The Combined Composite Index of both individual and business related skills was 59.2. As the total Combined Composite Entrepreneurship Development Index was 59.2 it was inferred that entrepreneurship development in the micro enterprises sector of Kerala is only moderate.

Part - 5

Suggestions

- The proper selection of activity for the 'group' is crucial for its survival and expansion. Efforts should be made to identify the suitable activity based on resources, skills and markets.
- The women micro entrepreneurs should be given training for developing managerial and leadership skill to carry out their responsibilities effectively. The convener and joint convener of the enterprise should be rotated normally once in a year. Such rotation helps in leadership development in all the entrepreneurs.
- The training facilities do not often reach the required level. Though 100 % have attended training, they respondents expressed the need for further training in the areas of accounting, marketing, entrepreneurship etc. Need based training to members on modern techniques of production and on management, organizing a management wing consist of management experts at district level would solve technical and managerial problem to some extent. Regular monitoring of performance of micro enterprises should be done by this team.
- Study on business related skills reveals that accounting is one of the greatest hurdles for the micro entrepreneurs. Simple accounting is essential for conducting business. Opportunities shall be provided to entrepreneurs to interact with the educational institutions and banks. Students of educational institutions shall be encouraged to assist the women entrepreneurs of micro enterprise in the basics of accounting under National Service Scheme or Social Service Scheme or NCC. The assistance of local banks especially the lead bank can be availed in this regard.

Conclusion

Micro credit centered enterprises have a prominent role in the rural India in stimulating the skill among the poor women. These enterprises are accepted as a vibrant tool to achieve economic and social empowerment .Being an effective tool to provide command over resources, it enables women to earn adequate income to ensure a reasonable standard of living. It also helps them to identify their strength sand weaknesses. But care should be taken to upgrade their individual and business related skills to survive the global competition

References

Bandyopadhyay (1986), *A Study on Poverty Alleviation in Rural India through Self Employment Creation Programmes*, ARTEP, ILO.

Chen Marthu (1996), *Beyond Credit: A Subsector Approach to Promoting Women's Enterprises*, Aghakhan Faudation, Canada.

Dawson, Elsa L. (1998), "Assessing the Impact: NGO's and Empowerment", in (Ed.) Afshar, Haleh, *Women and Employment: Illustrations from the Third World*, Macmillan Press Ltd., Great Britain.

Nagayya (2005), "Enhancing Competitiveness Among Rural Non Farm Small Enterprises", (Ed) in Rao, Narasimha, *Rural Development in India*, Serials Publications, New Delhi.

Pandian, Sundara and G. Saravanan (2008), "Observations of SHG in Micro Enterprise Activity", *Empowerment of Women through Entrepreneurship,* (Ed) by L. Radhakrishnan, Gyan Publishing house, New Delhi.

Pradeep Kashap (2008), "Livelihood Promotion among SHGS", in (Ed.), Karmakar, K.G, *Micro Finance in India,* , Sage Publications, Delhi.

Prasad, C.S. et.al (2007), *Sixty Years of Indian Economy 1947 to 2007,* New Century Publications, New Delhi.

Somu Criappa (2004), *Financing Development of Small Scale Enterprises,* Mohit Publications.

Anand, Vinod (2004), "Micro and Small Enterprises in Selected Urban and Semi Urban Locations in Botswana: Basic Characteristics", *Indian Journal of Economics.*

Biradar, R R. (2008), Growth of Rural Non-agricultural Employment and Poverty Alleviation in India: What does Emerging Evidence Indicate", *Journal of Social and Economic Development,* Vol. 10 (2), July–December.

Bliss and Garatt (2001), "Supporting Women Entrepreneurs in Transitioning Economics", *Journal of Small Business Management,* Vol. 39 (4).

Edward, Millard (1996), "Appropriate Strategies to Support Small Community Enterprises in Export Markets", *Small Enterprise Development,* Vol.7 (1), March.

Gary, B. Hansen (1996), "Using Group Entrepreneurship to Create New Enterprises Systematically", *Small Enterprise Development,* Vol. 7(1), March.

Gustave Rayo and Julio Cordoba, "Micro Enterprises Promotion– The Case of FOSIS in Chile", *Small Enterprise Development,* Vol. 7 (3), September.

Hyman, Eric and Kirk, Deardan (1998), "Comprehensive Impact Assessment Systems for Non–Governmental Organization Micro Enterprise Development Programmes", *World Development,* Vol. 26 (2).

Shaw, Judith (2004), "Micro Enterprise Occupation and Poverty Reduction in Micro Finance Programmes: Evidence from SriLanka", *World Development,* Vol. 32 (7).

Vasantha Kumari, P. (2008), "Women Empowerment Through Micro Enterprises Development", *Southern Economist,* Vol. 47 (15), December 1.

Government of India (2009), *Report of the Committee on Credit Related Issues under SGSY,* Ministry of Rural Development.

Government of Kerala, *Economic Review 2000,* 2001, 2002, 2003, 2004, 2005, 2006, 2007, 2008 State Planning Board, Thirvanantha-puram.

Government of Kerala (2003), *Women in Kerala 2001,* Economics and Statistics Department.

Government of Kerala (2007), *Micro Enterprises Survey Report,* Kudumbhasree.

Institute of Small Enterprises and Development, *India Micro, Small and Medium Enterprises Report 2007,* ISED, Cochin, 2008.

5

EMERGING ISSUES IN ENTREPRENEURSHIP DEVELOPMENT

Rudra Chakrapani & P. Kannaiah

INTRODUCTION

The Global Entrepreneurship Monitor 1999 defined entrepreneurship as "any attempt at new business or new venture creation, such as self-employment, a new business organization, or the expansion of an existing business, by an individual, a team of individuals, or an established business.

"I had to make my own living and my own opportunity! But I made it! Don't sit down and wait for the opportunities to come. Get up and make them!"–*Madam C.J. Walker, creator of a popular line of African-American hair care products and America's first black female millionaire*

THE TRADITIONAL APPROACH

The traditional approach to entrepreneurship is a methodical, scientific process. Generally speaking, the approach consists of researching the market, identifying a need, and creating a business to fill it. More specifically, the steps of the process are:

- Select the industry you're interested in working in.
- Research the kinds of businesses and various business models within that industry.
- Perform market research to see where there is an unmet need—geographically, pricewise, complementary products and services, etc.
- Analyze the competition.
- Develop a preliminary business plan for a business to meet that need.
- Do some more market research to assess the realistic market potential for your business. *Will people buy it?*
- Revise the business plan and determine your funding requirements.
- If needed, seek out lenders or investors.
- Start the business.

Needless to say, this is not something you just knock out in a weekend. The most obvious problem to this approach is that it's extremely labor-intensive and potentially expensive to even decide whether or not to go into business. Of course, that time spent on the front end reduces the risk of failure down the road.

It doesn't matter where the idea comes from. What matters is what you do with it. And no matter how brilliant you think the idea is, you need some external input - a "sanity check", if you will. Even if you don't have the time or money for extensive formal market research or business planning, do the informal research yourself to find out if there's a market for your idea and to assess the viability of your business concept.

You can ask your friends and family, but when you do, make sure to let them know exactly what you are looking for– honest, detailed feedback on the idea. True friends will be supportive of your ability to succeed, but they will also be willing to be honest with you.

If you make it past the friends and family round and still think you've got a viable business concept, put together a basic business plan. There are extensive resources to help you with this in our Business Plan section. It doesn't have to be incredibly detailed — you're not going to the bank or investors with it.

Now, think of the three to five most successful entrepreneurs you know. (If you don't know that many, you'd better meet some — it's going to be very difficult to be a successful entrepreneur yourself without several of them in your network.) Contact them and see if they'll take a look at your business plan and meet you over coffee or lunch (your treat!) to discuss it. Now would also be a good time to find a mentor.

If you feel you need some market research, turn to an online community in which you participate regularly, or find an online community of people who match your target market. Ask a few questions in the discussion forums, preferaby open-ended ones that will get you qualitative information, rather than just quantitative data. It may not be as statistically accurate as formal market research, but if you're not talking about risking huge sums of money, it's probably good enough. The higher the risk, the more formal research you need. With this approach, you can pursue your passion, tempered by proven practices, and improve your possibilities of prosperity.

ENTREPRENEURIAL ACTIVITY - AN HISTORICAL PERSPECTIVE

Entrepreneurship is a major contributing factor to the economic well-being of a country both in terms of economic growth and job creation. Traditionally, entrepreneurial ability tended to focus on the following four attributes:

Initiative - the entrepreneur takes the initiative to bring together the economic resources of land, labor and capital to produce a commodity (whether a good or a service) with the hope that such production will create a profitable business venture.

Decision-making - the entrepreneur makes the basic business policy decisions for the business, thereby setting the course of the enterprise.

Innovation - the entrepreneur is an innovator, attempting to introduce new products and new ways of doing things.

Risk-taker - the entrepreneur risks his or her time, effort, business reputation and invested funds in the entrepreneurial venture.

THE MODERN ENTREPRENEUR

Until recently, the above attributes, especially innovation and risk-taking, were the dominant factors that defined the characteristics of those who chose to become entrepreneurs.

Now, however, with corporate downsizing being a fact of life, many entrepreneurs find themselves thrust into the role by default. The question for anyone either finding themselves in this position involuntarily or thinking about leaving corporate life for the heady world of entrepreneurship is whether you have what it takes to be successful ... the "right stuff" in other words. Some people do, in spades. Others simply don't. If you're one of the ones who just doesn't, either resign yourself to working for someone else or cultivate in yourself the qualities that successful entrepreneurs share. Believe it or not, entrepreneurs are not just "born". Well, some, of course, seem to be natural-born entrepreneurs, but for the rest of us, the qualities of entrepreneurship can definitely be acquired by hard work and application.

COMMON ISSUES

The "common denominator" issues facing all entrepreneurs are planning, finance and implementation.

Planning: All entrepreneurs face the challenge of starting a new business, be it through innovation (inventing something new or doing something a different way), finding the right opportunity to get into, or buying a franchise. Whichever road you choose, it will involve serious planning.

Financing: Unless you have ready funds at your disposal, getting finance is the next major challenge and cannot be attempted until your business plan is in place. You will need to prepare funding proposals and applications for loans, venture capital, and funds from angel investors.

Implementation: This is make or break time. Many people think just getting started is the hard part - and it is hard. But where many businesses stumble is not in the planning and financing stages but in implementing their business plan. Why this is so is not certain. There are various hypotheses including the idea that ideas people and implementation people are two very different breeds and it is highly unusual to find one person who can do both: More likely though, is the simple fact that implementation requires such a broad range of skills that no one person can possibly be adept at all of them.

The real challenge and skill of the entrepreneur, then, is to recognize what you do well and then appoint employees or subcontractors to do the rest. Of course, if you're running a business on a shoestring, this simply may not be possible! So be brutally honest and objective in assessing your particular strengths and weaknesses BEFORE you cash in your day job and your 401K.

The areas to think about in terms of implementation are the same as those encompassed by a broad definition of management: promotion (marketing and advertising), public relations, sales, employees, communications, legal issues, plant and equipment, risk management, disaster planning, crisis management, insurance, technology, computer systems, taxes, bookkeeping, finance, and the internet.

PERSONAL QUALITIES

Equally important as the common issues shared by all entrepreneurs are the personal qualities of the entrepreneur him or herself. To start you thinking about whether you have the right stuff to make a success of an entrepreneurial venture, here's a list of character traits and work ethics common to successful entrepreneurs. Although it is not necessary that you possess all of them, you should possess most:

Passion - entrepreneurs have a strong passion for their idea or concept, so much so that their work is their play. If you don't like what you do, you won't stick it out when challenges come along, as they inevitably will.

Curiosity - entrepreneurs need to understand how things work. They ask a lot of questions. Curiosity therefore triggers innovation.

Sponges - entrepreneurs are sponges. They devour information about their industry and are always current on new and emerging trends and technologies, not only in their specific industry but in closely related industries. This habit of scanning their environment is a rich source of discovery of new opportunities. Entrepreneurs are ALWAYS looking for new markets, applications, products or twists on an old concept.

Optimism - entrepreneurs think of problems as opportunities for improvements and new ideas.

Forward looking - entrepreneurs are never satisfied with the status quo and are always proactively carving out their future.

Careful about Money - entrepreneurs are careful with money and have a firm grasp on what things cost and their value to the business. This allows them to recognize a true bargain when they see one.

Started Earning at a Young Age - entrepreneurs commonly displayed entrepreneurial leanings as a teenager seeking out entrepreneurial activities such as babysitting, lawnmowing and lemonade stands.

Competitive - entrepreneurs are naturally competitive and don't let the grass grow under their feet.

Time Conscious - entrepreneurs know the value of time and how to make the best use of it. You won't find entrepreneurs spending much time on nonproductive activities. That said, entrepreneurs typically also recognize the value of downtime and time with family and will factor these activities into their schedule.

Risk Takers - entrepreneurs are not afraid of taking calculated risks. They typically trust their hunches and act on them.

Usually Loners - entrepreneurs generally prefer a solitary work environment as opposed to teamwork.

Professional - entrepreneurs are professional in their approach to work. They operate as they would in a corporate environment and don't allow themselves to be distracted by outside influences.

High Energy - entrepreneurs have a plan and a vision and they work it. Entrepreneurs are often health-conscious too, recognizing that the fitter they are, the better their minds work. So entrepreneurs will take time from their schedule to work out and eat well.

Flexible - entrepreneurs are nothing if not responsive to change. Although they appreciate the importance of having a plan and working that plan, they allow themselves room to react and respond to opportunities that may suddenly reveal themselves.

Nurture Entrepreneurial Spirit - entrepreneurs seek out and nurture the entrepreneurial spirit in their employees and reward them accordingly.

Confident Goal-setters - entrepreneurs are confident and set long-term goals, both for themselves personally and their businesses. They view money and financial security as a measure of accomplishment and a source of peace of mind.

Persistent - entrepreneurs never give up. They persist until they succeed.

Learn from Failure - entrepreneurs learn from their failures and those of others. Failure to an entrepreneur is nothing more than an opportunity waiting to be discovered.

Self Responsibility - entrepreneurs take the initiative and personal responsibility for their success or failure (which is always a merely temporary state).

Resource Utilization - entrepreneurs utilize ALL of their available resources.

Internal Locus of Control - entrepreneurs don't believe in luck. They firmly believe that success and failure lies within their personal control or influence.

THE FUTURE OF ENTREPRENEURSHIP

A recent Purdue University study concluded a number of factors seem to favor continued high rates of new firm formation:

- Continuing high rates of change (change creates opportunities for new firms).
- Continued growth of the service sector (the highest growth area for new firm formation).
- Increasing number of virtual corporations in which firms outsource their functions, creating opportunities for entrepreneurs.
- Positive climate for small business - a general perception that small business is a positive influence on the economic wellbeing of the country giving entrepreneurs legitimacy and respect.
- Growth in international business opportunities.

CONCLUSION

With the traditional corporate-employment track seemingly on the decline, the trend of forming strategic alliances with other businesses that are closely aligned with yours or with someone who can add value to your product is emerging. In fact, futurists envision a return to extended community living with shared resources but individual living and working relationships with entrepreneurial activities being the basis of these communities. Strategic alliances are a first step along this path.

So, if you have determined entrepreneurship is for you, you can be confident that you are part of the wave of the future. But understand what it will demand of you and whether you are prepared to give what it will take. The allure of entrepreneurship is undeniably strong for many but make sure you're going into it for the right reasons. Being miserable in your job does not automatically make starting your own business the best idea in the world. In fact, it could be the worst reason of all to get into business for yourself. The right choice may instead be to find another job that you won't be miserable in. But if, taking into account everything that's been said above, you're adamant that you have what it takes, by all means take the bull by the horns and create something absolutely fabulous.

References

Madhurima Lal & Shikha Sahai (2008), *Entrepreneurship*, Excel Books, Second Edition, pp. 43-52 & 63-169.

H. Nandan (2007), *Fundamentals of Entrepreneurship*, Prentice Hall of India Pvt. Ltd., New Delhi, pp. 1-37.

Bholanath Dutta (2009), *Entrepreneurship Management Text and Cases*, Excel Books, Edition, pp.1-36 & 45-53.

Vasanth Desai (2010), *The Dynamics of Entrepreneurial Development and Management*, Himalaya Publishing House, 6th Edition, pp.28-48 & 244-256.

Dr. CSG Krishnama Charyulu, Dr. R. Lalitha (2009), *Innovation Management*, Himalaya Publishing House, 2nd Edition, pp.175-199 & 276-299.

Robert J. Calvin (2004), *Entrepreneurial Management*, Tata Macgraw Hill Edition, pp. 37-59, 61-91 & 237-263.

6

MANAGEMENT EDUCATION IN INDIA- A CRITICAL ASSESSMENT

Arunava Narayan Mukherjee

Introduction

The time has come when Indian management education must make an ideological shift. Quality management education is still not available to enough number of aspirants. Management education in India functioning in an elitist line, has been generating only the expectation of quick materialistic rewards among the management graduates who are indifferent to ethical and social perspective. There is no overall emphasis on issues concerning inclusive growth, sustainable development and social entrepreneurship etc. Moreover there is not enough indigenous, progressive research in the field of management education. The ideological reorientation calls for an urgent need to move away from the neo-colonial mindset that opts for processes which are in conformity with the US system as well as commoditization of Education. In this article an effort has been made to critically evaluate the management education system in India with a view to provide prescriptions for reorienting it and thereby making it more relevant and effective.

The Current Scenario-An Incongruous System

The State of Management Education in India is Experiencing Quite a Paradoxical Situation. On one hand, there is the emergence of elitist schools which has been creating power distance from the national cultures: on the other hand, *Democratization of MBA Education* due to privatization of Higher Education has resulted into the fall of quality of Management Education leading to mismatch between demand for and supply of required quality of human resources. The concept of quality business education is defined differently in different cultures. Indian culture is characterized by high power distance and consequently high quality may denote elitism, reflecting pre-eminent standing among peers, as ascribed by public beliefs, and reinforced by cultural media, rewards and rankings (Gupta, Hanges & Dorfman, 2002). On the other end, in low power distance cultures, excellence could reflect action orientation, and be more a symbol of accomplishment indicating the core mission and strategic commitment to all-round quality of the business education. ***The concept of quality as defined by low power distance cultures is what is useful to compete in the current global economy where success needs action orientation and team work. This suggests, that Indian business schools might***

need to change their culture and adapt to a new world economy by viewing quality more in terms of achievements than a reputation. Failure to do so will result in the top tier schools becoming increasingly elitist till they lose touch with the actual needs of Indian businesses and national development as a whole. (Gupta, Kamala, Ancheri, 2003). According to the *Arjun Sengupta Committee Report* of 2006, there are over 340 million (92 percent of the country's working population), in the unorganized sector in India. They contribute 60 percent to the national economic output. Yet, they constitute the poorest and most vulnerable segments of our population without any formidable business leadership or guidance from formally trained managerial acumen. This is clearly indicative of the fact that Indian management education system mainly produces managers for 8 percent of the country's working population.

Indian Management Education should come out of this elitist notion. It is the high time the policy makers and the people controlling management education should realize this. Other wise it will be too late to manage. Realization of this criticality in current times particularly in the context of recent global melt down is evident. (Mukherjee, 2011) .It has been reported crore-plus salaries offered on B-school campuses will be tempered through a new system that proposes to segregate guaranteed pay from fringe benefits. The system will make packages appear slimmer; forcing corporate recruiters to become more realistic while enticing MBA graduates with puffed-up-offers. The placement standards prepared by the Indian Institute of Management Ahmedabad (IIM,A) will remove performance-linked compensation like variable pay and annual bonus and fringe benefits like employee stock options and club memberships while reporting final salaries. (Nair & Dave, The Economics Times, Kolkata, 2nd February 2011).

Experts have started exploring the relationship between various aspects of the global economic scenario and leadership crisis and emphasizing on the emerging paradigms of sustainable business organisations. They agree that in a highly "volatile" and "mercurial" global financial set-up, the need of the hour was to nurture a new crop of leaders- "not regimented managers". In this context, the Management gurus are welcoming the launch of new breed of academic programmes on business leadership and human resource leadership which focus on creating entrepreneurships, compassion and sustainability.[1] In order to achieve the goal we need to make a through assessment of the prevalent system of management education in India and suggest appropriate remedial measures. An effort has been made to the aforesaid direction in the following paragraphs under specific rubrics.

Linking National Priority with Universal Wellbeing - Growing Need for Social Entrepreneurship Training in Management Education

India needs to create Indian Managers for serving Indian cause which will ultimately lead to global development; Indian Management Education system should not be producing Managers who become glorified agents of converting Indian needs to foreign lusts. Ideally C.K. Pralhad's bottom of the pyramid theory requires to be implemented in Indian Management Education system. The benefits of quality management education should be made available to the working community of un-organised sector and common man instead of only catering to the requirements of corporate houses. Management education is meant for serving grater socio economic goal. It should aim to create social entrepreneur rather than creating a class of social compradors.

In today's context India needs not mere entrepreneurs, but Social Entrepreneurs who will carry out successful business with a social goal. For whom earning wealth and taking care of well being of fellowmen in the society is equal important A Social Entrepreneur basically play the role of change agents in the social sector, by:

- Adopting a mission to create and sustain social value (not just private value),
- Recognizing and relentlessly pursuing new opportunities to serve that mission,
- Engaging in a process of continuous innovation, adaptation, and learning,
- Acting boldly without being limited by resources currently in hand, and
- Exhibiting heightened accountability to the constituencies served and for the outcomes created. (Dees, 1998)

In other words, a social entrepreneur is someone who recognizes a social problem and uses entrepreneurial principles to organize, create and manage a venture to make social change. Social Entrepreneurship aims at developing a sustainable business model, at the same time, tries to help persons at the Bottom of the Pyramid (BoP). In a nutshell social entrepreneurship can be defined as a mechanism to create human capacity in the social sector. In the current era of globalization social entrepreneurship can play a formidable role by successfully organizing the indigenous social capital for business to avert the threats of multinational aggression.

Although social entrepreneurship is becoming part of higher education and management education all over the globe, there are typical problems that prevent its growth and development as an academic discipline which are summarised below:

- There is a lot of confusion on who will teach the course on social entrepreneurship? At the same time there is no clear natural path to develop faculty to teach social entrepreneurship.
- Business schools still view social entrepreneurship as a practice, not a discipline. There is not enough academic research on social entrepreneurship; more research works are needed in order to advance the credibility of social entrepreneurship as an academic field.
- Most business schools still cover social issues by including a term paper or holding discussions of superficial nature. Social Entrepreneurship coursework and extracurricular activities are rarely connected to the mainstream, for-profit, business training of the rest of the MBA programme.

The specialization offered by most of the B-schools In India mainly confines to Human Resource, Marketing, Finance, Retail and Systems– the typical conventional structure. Hardly a few business schools offer courses on social entrepreneurship, Sustainable Development or Entrepreneurship. Apart from the reasons mentioned above the factors which are responsible for this state of affairs are following–

- The commercial mind set of the management of B-schools in India (most of whom are privately run) who feel conventional areas of specialization will help their students to get a good placement in industry which in turn will be useful for them to promote the brand of their B-school in the education market- an invariable offshoot of commoditization of management education.
- Neither the private B-schools nor University system providing higher education in management is interested in going for experimentation or adopting innovative approach in the study of management. They would like to follow the conventional model which fits into the existing corporate structure.

- The Indian social psyche is also extremely averse towards taking risk. All the stake holders of management education – be it the aspiring MBA, parents of the management students, the institution of higher learning running the management course – all are mainly interested in placement, to be more precise in how the management student bags a safe, secured, high paying job in a good company is the chief concern of all. This might be the colonial hang over of a nation which for two hundred years believed secured employment is the most coveted goal of life. Practice of this philosophy have made working population this nation morally and intellectually crippled, dependent for whom entrepreneurship is a foreign phenomenon.

In India, barring a few Tier I B Schools like, Indian Institute of Management Ahmedabad, Indian School of Business, Hyderabad, N.S. Raghavan Centre for Entre-preneurial Learning at Indian Institute of Management, Bangalore, S.P. Jain Institute of Management & Research, Mumbai, hardly there is any systematic endeavour on the part of institutions imparting higher education in management to promote the study of entrepreneurship as a whole and social entrepreneurship in particular. This is an alarming situation for Indian Management Education system which calls for immediate rectification. (Mukherjee, 2011)

Management Education-Adopting a Holistic Developmental Approach

Apart from being a technical subject the application of Management is universal and developing expertise in management to a great extent depends on the ability and acumen of the individual and a few of his distinct qualities such as how he perceives and interacts with his surroundings, his social awareness, his networking skills, his comprehension of ground realities, his understanding of culture, values and human feeling not merely on attainment of his theoretical and technical knowledge of Management. Of course, the theoretical and technical knowledge of Management helps an individual to become an effective manager provided he is able to make a fine blend of his technical knowledge of Management and mature comprehension of intricacies of life. But, a manager only full of theoretical and technical knowledge devoid of basic understanding of life is neither a manager nor a product of the discipline of Management in true sense of the term. Not a single business tycoon of the world who is the super manager and creator of business empires-from Henry Ford to Dhirubhai Ambani- started their managerial venture as a B School product equipped with theoretical and technical knowledge of management. Unfortunately, the policy makers have failed to take cognizance of this simple fact as they are in a habit of looking at simple things in a complicated manner. In the words of Warren Buffett

"The business schools reward difficult complex behavior more than simple behavior, but simple behavior is more effective." (Warren Buffett as quoted by Maxwell ,page 98)

This phenomenon can be well elucidated in the words of Professor Ishwar Dayal the pioneer of management education in India.

"Management education, over the years, has changed in certain ways, and not changed in other ways. The basic disciplines continue to remain the same. You can't run business without Accounting, you can't run business without Marketing or Finance or Organisation Behaviour. The main change that has come about is in the context of business......Therefore, any management institution will have to be also concerned with developing understanding of how one can go about understanding different cultures in their own context....This is where management education has to develop a framework. The curriculum has to be different.

The courses that you devise have to be more focused on cultural and social aspects than the courses that were taught earlier."

Apart from Prof. Dayal, other scholars since long back also have been emphasizing, the humanities in general and business ethics in particular should be more firmly embedded in business management programmes. (Small, 2006).

Ideally Management Education should be a judicious mix of theory and practice, and ideal convergence of knowledge of various disciplines, with a strong focus on experimentation research and development. The content and delivery of management education must be designed in accordance with the changing requirement of industry, national as well as international business scenario and socio cultural surrounding-which is a continuous process.

Unfortunately, the aforesaid phenomena are alarmingly missing in Indian management education in general particularly in the wake of privatized education system. Management courses are taught mechanically for pure commercial point of view. The current system hardly provides any opportunity for research innovation and experimentation. The entire process of management education is "Placement" oriented. Instead of trying to asses the potential of the management student and requirements of industry and thereby trying to strike a chord between them by way of imparting proper training, most of the business schools try to push the management students for earliest available employment which the student concerned may not retain since there exist a mismatch among his potential, training and employment. This mismatch between potential skill and employment leads to underutilization of skills paving the way for a kind of underemployment. Not only that once for them the job becomes simply a means to earn money, a mechanical delivery where there is no liking for the work they do, they loose the opportunity of becoming successful manager thereby developing problem of stagnation for themselves as well as becoming unproductive for the posterity. Because successful managers who like their jobs either become thought leader, visionaries or successful entrepreneur in future (for example N.R. Narayana Murthy, Nandan Nilekani, Gurucharan Das etc.). At the same time particularly in India escapist, malinger, frustrated managers either become management teachers or management consultants.

The private owned B Schools always insist students to take up those specializations (irrespective of whether the student is competent enough to take up the specialization) which will help them to place the students easily and finally help them to advertise their placement record in education market to attract more and more student admission leading to accumulation of their profit.

The system of management education should undergo a thorough restructuring leading to the emergence of a long term vision of knowledge development with greater social awareness and commitment.

Systematizing Indian Management Education-Developing the System for "Training the Trainer"

Till date there has not been systematic effort to stream line management education. Despite its unique applied orientation no policy framework has been developed so far which answers following glaring questions in connection with the faculty of management education :

1. How to accredit a management teacher?
2. Ideally what should be the eligibility criteria to become a management teacher besides usual academic qualification?
3. What kind of training should a management teacher undergo before joining the profession?

4. What is the nature of upgradation programme that management teachers will under go periodically during their service life? What will be their role in industry-institute interaction?
5. How to develop the research acumen of management teachers?

Here, it is worth mentioning that India has the system and infrastructure for teachers' training from primary school level to university teacher level, but astonishingly no formidable system of training the management teachers exist although management as a discipline and avocation occupies a distinct position in the nation's socioeconomic life. There exists a typical vacuum in this area which has been ignored by the policy makers for reasons beyond comprehension. This fundamental flaw should be addressed immediately.

Besides, the approach to management education needs to be Indian in nature. (Dayal). It is futile to work on the knowledge which was developed in America or Europe because the context of that knowledge is directly related to their culture and tradition and absolutely different from Indian culture and tradition. If the knowledge is acquired within India's own culture and environment, it shall be more applicable and produces faster results. Indian management teachers in general hardly think in this line and not at all original in their approach to study and delivery of the subject. Accordingly the materials that are used are mostly based on the foreign experiences. Indian management education could not produce a body of well researched, original management literature of international standard. Such kind of literature should be developed in India.

Shunning the Existing Classist Character of Indian Management Education

It seems the policy maker have deliberately designed the management education in an elitist line which strictly adhere to the class bias. Following examples will elucidate logic.

In so far as the faculty members are concerned, in a Tier-I B School (either approved by AICTE or not) they are usually the products of Tier-I B School or elite academic institutions. The teachers in Tier-II B School (either approved by AICTE or not) are generally from Tier-II B School or the products conventionally recognized academic process. The rest of the system covers institutes conducting MBA/Management Courses under distance education programme of various universities and regular undergraduate Management colleges affiliated to various universities where different courses on management are conducted. Any person can somehow fit into this segment as the faculty -be a retired frustrated manager, a young unemployed MBA without a single day industry experience, a post graduate who is technically disqualifies to teach the subject in which he/she has done his/her Master Degree in UG or PG level becomes a management teacher. This way, Management Education Institutes have become a shelter for rehabilitating a community of intellectually handicapped !!

As a result Students are separated into a hierarchical system of groups on the basis of instruction received that are openly labeled. The characterization of the labels is carried over into the minds of the corporate and society in general as being a certain type: high ability, low achieving, slow, average, etc. Students of management institution belonging to general category (below Tier-II) are not being given any quality training towards definite career direction while students in elite B schools are prepared to become strategist and future business leaders.

In this connection arguments have already been advanced by well researched sociological studies like *Schooling in Capitalist America* by Bowles and Gintis, *Learning to Labour* by Paul

Willis, *Keeping Track: How Schools Structure Inequality* by Jeannie Oakes and *Social Class and the Hidden Curriculum of Work* by Jean Anyon etc.

This is a kind of reincarnation of colonial paradigm!!! It very much resembles the implementation of "The Filtration Theory of Education" of British Raj - an educational system designed by the British rulers for India, the basic principle of which says, educate the top few, education will filter down (percolate) in due course!

This classist character of the management education system should be changed, at the same time new objectives and new pedagogical methods for management education, particularly for the less privileged students should be developed. The basic ethos of HRD–*Trainer should help disadvantaged trainees* (socially or otherwise) *to realize their potentials,* must be implemented in management education.

Although Government of India through University Grants Commission officially announces the policy decision that private franchising of higher education is not allowed (vide UGC Circular No. 1-52/99(CPP-II) dated 9th August 2001 and recent Circular No. F.8-4/2009(CPP-I/PU dated 14th July 2010). But this prohibition has actually confined to paper work only. The effect of mushroom growth of study centers of various Universities under distance education system who are *technically approved by UGC – AICTE – DEC joint committee* has been disastrous for management education system in India. In the name of imparting management education these study centers are actually dignified "coaching classes" of management subjects under the cloak of University Education. Most of them are having poor infrastructure, no check on the quality of faculty members, no real endeavour to ensure the development of students as grooming managers – in fact they are "Kiosks of Higher education" who simply sell the degree of management.

Unless more stringent and drastic actions are taken at national level to stop this menace, in near future we will find the future of management education at a stake.

Conclusion: Changing the Prevalent Degenerative Societal Outlook towards Management Education

The attitude of MBA wannabe their guardian and society in general towards management education has to be changed. Now, attainment of management education is a shortcut to success. The B Schools in their advertisement declares "100% Placement" if not "100% Placement Assistance". Off course, the cost of such lucrative future proposition is quite heavy an amount, but in the era of consumerism the logic goes straight-in order to get good management education and good placement one has to pay more-the more you pay the better facility and opportunity you get for your career. Worse is that it has a typical perversion-even if you are not good in studies, your Placement is secured because you have paid money. Perhaps, the most pathetic sacrifice of ideals of education reducing the status of "Management Schools" to "Finishing Schools". Accordingly, the management graduates develop a street smart attitude-"why should I study? I am smart enough to have paid the amount of my course fees, I am bound to get a job"

In fact, in a way studying management or for that matter MBA has become a status symbol for the Generation Y. For them management education is merely a magic tool to secure a happy materialistic life. Their management training has got nothing to do with the betterment of society and pubic life. It is an insular selfish journey to materialist success and to ensure it by hook or crook Perhaps, there lies the origin of one of the serious social maladies of modern society-the corrupt corporation and the corruption they spread in public life and civil society for ensuring their own profit (a conspicuous form of Crony Capitalism) which finally leads to a vitiated corrupt society.

Finally it can be said this is the high time for all the stakeholders of Indian Management Education system to realise Management Education is not only aimed at ensuring the earned income, it should engage in innovative, creative ways to tackle business as well as socio-economic issues by imparting quality education with due emphasis on research and development.

References

Deb Nirmalya (2009), Between Morality and Responsibility, *The Statesman*, Kolkata, 3rd March, Report on Proceedings on Seminar organized by School of inspired Leadership.

Dees Gregory J. (1998, 2001), 'The Meaning of Social Entre-preneurship': October 31, 1998, Reformatted and revised: May 30, 2001, Paper funded by The Kauffman Foundation *http://www.fuqua.duke.edu/centers/case/documents/dees_SE.pdf.* Accessed on March 15, 2011.

Gupta, V., Hanges, P.J. & Dorfman, P.W. (2002), 'Cultural Clustering: Methodologies and Findings', *Journal of World Business*, Vol. 37, No. 1, p. 11-15.

Gupta, Vipin, Gollakota Kamala & Sreekumar Ancheri (2003), *Quality in Business Education: A Study of the Indian Context*; Paper Prepared for and Presented at the Business Education and Emerging Market Economies: Trends and Prospects Conference, Technology Square, Atlanta, Georgia, USA, 7th November

Maxwell John C. (2008), *Leadership Gold*, Thomas Nelson, Tennessee.

Macaulay's Minutes. Quoted in Saine S.K. (1980), *Development of Education in India: Socio-economic and Political Perspectives*, Cosmo Publications, New Delhi.

Mukherjee Arunava Narayan (2011), Paper titled "Social Entrepreneurship– An Emerging Value based Alternative Leadership in Business – Lessons for Indian Management Education" presented in National Conference on Management of Sustainable Development in India organised by New Delhi Institute of Management at New Delhi 1st & 2nd April, 2011.

Nair Avinash and Dave Parag (2011), "B-School Pay Packs to be Slimmer", The Economics Times, Kolkata, 2nd February.

Prahalad C.K. (2009), Revised and Updated 5th Anniversary Edition) *The Fortune at the Bottom of the Pyramid: Eradicating Poverty through Profits* Pearson Prentice Hall.

Report of National Commission for Enterprises in the Unorganized Sector (NCEUS), Govt. of India, 2009.

Small M.W. (2006), 'A Case for Including Business Ethics and the Humanities in Management Programs', *Journal of Business Ethics*, Vol. 64, No. 2 (Mar), p. 195-211.

Websites Visited

http://www.ecell-iitkgp.org/competitions/eclairez/faq

www.beyondgreypinstripes.org,

www.caseplace.org

http://iwsbfaculty.wordpress.com/2009/02/27/professor-ishwar-dayal-on-management-education-today/

7

TRIPLE BOTTOM LINE REPORTING-IN SEARCH OF TRUE CORPORATE TRANSPARENCY

Sumanta Dutta

Introduction

The wind of transformation of the global economy has transcended geographical boundaries and has converted the world into a global village. The rapid growth of international trade and internationalization of business firms, the development of communication and information technologies, emergences of global financial reporting convergence practices are perturbing the financial environment to a great extent. Because of these pressures and the current attention to corporate integrity, many companies find that being recognized for responsible business practices are considered to be new business imperative. Ethical business practices are no longer a matter of private domain, rather an extended financial performance aspects involves sustainability measures that take reporting beyond the traditional measures of performance and quality **(Gary Cokins, 2009).**Sustainable development espouses new priorities that widen the agenda for business enterprise performance beyond the myopic "short –termism" of earning profits.**(K.Chatterjee,2005).**Today stakeholders becomes more and more aware of the ecological and social footprints adopted by multinational companies (MNCs) worldwide, accountability, transparency and governance issues are considered to be main stream agenda in the corporate boardroom discussion. Sustainability reporting evaluates the performance of company's based on three distinct parameters such as economic, environmental and societal. Corporate world is looking for a holistic solution to the planet's economic, environmental and social problems. Since, then, ecologically conscious leaders have had to encounter the challenge of holistic management **(Harman, 1982, 1994; Capra, 1996)** in seeking to balance ecological security, resource security as well as socio-economic security for creating a sustainable enterprise that can make resource-efficient product offerings with minimal social environmental impact and maximum value to customers' quality of life. **(Fussler and James, 1996, P-120).**

TBLR is Complementary to Financial Reporting

Sustainability reporting is complementary to traditional financial reporting in that it transcends the limits of financial reporting by providing material non financial information to help assess the quality and quantity of a firm's intangible assets, such as integrity, reputation, capacity to innovate, quality of management, and human capital, for an undefined constellation of stakeholders. It provides information beyond financial results that investors, employees, customers, and other corporate stakeholders may use to make decisions. Triple Bottom Line Reporting is step forward in this regard.

There is no universally accepted definition of TBLR. The Group of 100 Incorporated (2003), in Australia, defines TBLR as a "corporate communication with stakeholders that described the company's approach to managing one or more of the economic, environmental and/or social dimensions of its activities, and through providing information on these dimensions. "TBLR, thus, involves cerebrating comprehensively about what constitutes 'performance' and success' for business. Its symbolizes an attempt to integrate the traditional financial bottom line of financial prosperity in accounting with a bottom line of environmental quality and that of social equity. While most businesses are familiar with the traditional 'Bottom line' of profit, the must also consider their social and environmental performance today much the same way as they consider economic performance.

This has been rightly conceptualized by Kenichi Ohmae regarding the role of corporations as follows: "A business is no longer just an economic instrument. The principal purpose of a business is not to make profit; it is to make profit in order to continue to do things and to do so even better and more abundantly."**(Kenichi Ohmae, 2003)** The view oppose the concept what Milton Friedman said in 1970 "the social responsibility of a business is to increase profits". Hence, CSR has moved from being a public relations tool or a feel good factor to a key parameter to keep companies open & transparent. It now no longer stands in isolation but has become a part of good corporate governance practices.

The Global Reporting Initiative (GRI) (2002) makes it clear that the corporations do not operate in isolation and that their continuing existence, i.e. sustainability, depends on an acknowledgement of their embeddedness in a broader social context. **(Painter & Moorland, 2006)**

The GRI provide the following threefold mission to the Corporate:

- To elevate and make routine, sustainability reporting at a global level so that it may be at par with financial reporting in terms of comparability, audit-ability, and generally accepted practices;
- To design, and continually improve standardized reporting, core measurements applicable to all enterprises, and customized, sector-specific measurements for reflecting the TBL dimensions of sustainability.
- To ensure a permanent and effective institutional host to support such reporting practices and to build a global, independent institution to become steward of the Guidelines.

With the introductions of **GRI (Global Reporting Initiative)** in 2000, the era of sustainability reports were introduced which has set certain guidelines to incorporate social, environmental & financial reporting of many companies. Presently, nineteen companies in India following GRI based sustainable reporting practices.

Table-3 shows that there is a growing acceptance of Triple Bottom Line based sustainability reporting by the corporate houses in India. The evaluation and auditing are carried out by a third party following GRI standards. Over the decades, through sustainability reporting an organization discloses the nonfinancial performance of an organization & its impact on the economy at large. Public disclosure of sustainability information also indicates

Table 1
Building Blocks of TBLR

Attribute	Economic/Financial	Environmental	Social
		← *Bottom Line* →	
Capital	Financial capital + Physical capital + Human Capital	Critical Natural Capital + Renewable/Substitutable Natural capital	Organization + Culture + Trust+ Integrity + Teamwork
Accountability	Obligation to account for financial performance via Annual Report	Obligation to account for environmental performance via Corporate Environmental Reports	Obligation to account for CSR to stakeholders via Values Reports.
Accounting	Annual / monthly / quarterly accounts prepared according to GAAP, with full results of income and financial position produced annually.	Separate identification of environment-related costs and revenues within the conventional accounting system, new forms of valuation and increased investment in environmental protection; tracking environmental performance indicators; incorporating sustainability considerations into mainstream accounting.	Assessment of the impact of a company in terms of community relations, product safety, training and education initiatives, charitable donations, sponsorships, and employment of disadvantaged groups.
Indicators	Profit & Loss Account, Balance Sheet, Statement of Retained Earnings, Cash Flow Statement, Accounting and Financial Ratios.	The Eco-balance sheet, the Eco-compass, integrated, organizational and site-specific performance indicators.	Human Development Indicator (HDI), Index of Sustainable Development Welfare (ISDW).
Auditing	Internal audits to ensure the effectiveness of management controls, and external audits for an independent examination and attestation of the credibility of the financial statements of the company.	Environmental audit for assessing use of eco-efficient technologies, energy intensity of products and production processes, waste reduction and recycling possibilities, overall environmental impacts of the organization, and compliance against regulations and standards.	Social audit covers the non-financial impact of a company be aiming to assess its performance in relation to society's requirements and expectations.

Source: K Chatterjee, 2004

INDICATOR TYPE	CATEGORY	ASPECT
Economic Performance Indicators	Direct Economic Impacts	Customers
		Suppliers
		Employees
		Providers of Capital
		Public Sector
Environmental Performance Indicators	Environmental Impacts	Materials
		Energy
		Water
		Biodiversity
		Emissions, effluents & waste
		Suppliers
		Products and services
		Compliance
		Transport
		Overall
Social Performance Indicators	Labour practices and decent work	Employment
		Labour management/ relations
		Health and safety
		Training and education
		Diversity and opportunity
	Human rights	Strategy and management
		Non-discrimination
		Labour / management relations
		Freedom of association & collective bargaining
		Child labour
		Forced and compulsory labour
		Disciplinary practices
		Security practices
		Indigenous rights
	Society	Community
		Bribery and corruption
		Political contributions
		Competition and pricing
	Product responsibility	Customer health and safety
		Products and services

Source: http://www.group100.com.au.2003

Table 2: GRI Indicator Matrix

a company's ability to monitor & manage the risks & fruitful utilization of the opportunity associated with GRI or G3 sustainability parameters.

Table 3
Global Reporting Initiative (GRI) Status of Indian Companies

Name of Organization	*Guideline*	*Application Level*	*Status*
BPCL	G3	A+	Third Party checked
Chemplast Senmar	G3	A+	GRI checked
Dr.Reddy's	G3	Undeclared	
Free scale	G3	Undeclared	
Grasim Industries	G3	A+	GRI checked
Infosys Technologies	G3	A+	GRI checked
ITC	G3	A+	Third Party checked
Jubilant Organosys	G3	A+	GRI checked
Larsen & Toubro	G3	A+	GRI checked
Mahindra	G3	A+	GRI checked
Moser Baer India	G3	A	Self declared
MSPL	G3	Undeclared	
Reliance Industries	G3	A+	GRI checked
Shree cement	G3	A+	GRI checked
Sterlite Industries	G3	Undeclared	
Tata Motors	G3	A	Self declared
Tata Tea	G3	A+	Third Party checked
VS Dempo & Co	G3	B+	Third Party checked
WIPRO	G3	A+	Third Party checked

Source: http://www.globalreporting.org

The concept of sustainability reporting which emanated from the TBL accounting, originated during the 1980's through an awareness campaign that urged nations to find alternative means of economic expansion without destroying the environmental resources or sacrificing the well being of future generations. Sustainability, since then become a buzzword in corporate mainstream agenda, the credit goes to John Elkington, who first coined the term & propagated it a cross the world in order to educated the people about the three way reporting framework for **People, Planet and Profit**, that goes beyond the boundaries of traditional reporting practices.

The concept of TBL, however, does not imply that companies are required to maximize-returns across all the three dimensions of corporate performance. The TBL paradigm aims at encouraging managers to think beyond the old-fashioned financial bottom line, in terms of two additional 'bottom lines', namely the 'social bottom line' and environmental bottom line'. It focuses on the corporate entities not only on the economic value they add, but also on the environmental and social value they add and/or often destroy (Elkington, 1997; Sustainability, 1998).

Conclusions

As more & more companies are reporting on their efforts to meet social & environmental goals as well profit targets. European commission to propose a legislative framework for mandatory reporting, requiring multinational companies to publish an independently verified annual report that would take "Triple Bottom-Line" Reporting approach to integrate social, environmental & economic criteria.

Mr. Larsson argues that "there is a brand issue connected to this". Hans Leeuwerik, a business representative at **EFRAQ (European financial reporting advisory Group)** believes "that sustainability data is not a hard & clear as normal financial data, so it is not as easy to draw up definitions or to gather information". He also argued that such sustainable reporting should not be made mandatory "As we are still at the development stage, making it mandatory would block a lot of the good work now in progress". **(The Economist Intelligence Unit Ltd, 2003).**

In last words, it can be said that CSR has moved from being a public relations tool or a feel good factor to a key parameter to keep companies open and transparent. It now no longer stands in isolation but has become a part of good corporate governance practices. Hence, such sustainable reporting mechanism which focus on people, planet and profit are based on the principle that goodwill earned from the stakeholders leads to benefits the corporation. This in turn enables the corporation to further enhance stakeholder value.

References

Aguilera, R., Rupp, D. and Ganapathi, J. (2007), Putting the S back in Corporate Social Responsibility: A Multilevel Theory of Social Change in Organizations, Academy of Management Review, 32:836-63.

Aras, G. & Crowther, D. (2009), " The Durable Corporation: Strategies for Sustainable Development" (Grower Publishing Ltd.).

Bowen, H.R (1953), Social Responsibilities of the Businessman(Harper & Row, New York).

Campbell J.L. (2007), "Why would Corporations Behave in Socially Responsible Ways?"Academy of Management Review, Vol. 32, No. 3.

Capra, F. (1996), "The Challenge" in Steering Business Towards Sustainability edited by F Capra and G Pauli, New Delhi: Response.

Carroll.A.B. (1979), "A Three –Dimensional Conceptual Model of Corporate Performance", Academy of Management Review 4(4), 497-505.

Carroll.A.B. (1999), "Corporate Social Responsibility", Business and Society 38(3), 268-295.

Chatterjee, K. (2004), "Towards a Generally Acceptable Sustainability Reporting Framework: Is the Global Reporting Initiative a Panacea, Precept or Parameter?" in Trade, Technology and Environment edited by M Mallikarjun and PW Chugan, NICOM 2004, Ahmedabad:Institute of Management, Nirma University of Science and Technology.

Chatterjee, K. (2005), "Triple Bottom Line Reporting: Is the Global Reporting Initiative Heading for Standardized Credibility in Corporate Communication?" The ICFAI Journal of Accounting Research, July, 2005.

Cokins, Gary (2009), "Measuring the New 'Triple' Bottom line-People, Planet and the Profit" Financial Executives, November, 2009.

Elkington, J. (1998), Cannibals with Forks: The Triple Bottom Line of 21st Century Business (New Society Publishers).

Friedman M. (1970), "The Social Responsibility of Business is to Increase Its Profits" The New York Times, 1970, 13 September.

Fussler, C. and James, P. (1996), Driving Eco-Innovation: A Breakthrough Discipline for Innovation and Sustainability,London:Pitman

Goodpaster, K.E. (1983), "The Concept of Corporate Social Responsibility", Journal of Business Ethics 2, 1-22.

Harman,W. (1982), Changing Belief Systems, Calif: SRI International VALS Report#33.

Laud, R.L. and D.H. Schepers (2009), " Beyond Transparency: Information Overload and a Model for Intelligibility", Business and Society Review, 114:3, 365-391.

Painter, Mollie & Moorland (2006), "Triple Bottom Line Reporting as Social Grammer: Integrating Corporate Social Responsibility & Corporate Codes of Conduct, Business Ethics: A European Review,Vol.15, No.4, Oct-2006, pp. 352-364.

Prahalad. C.K. and A.Hammond (2002), "Serving the World's Poor, Profitably", Harvard Business Review 80(9), 48-57.

Schepers, H. Donald and Laud, Robert L. (2009), "Beyond Transparency: Information Overload and a Model for Intelligibility. Business and Society Review, 114:3 (365-391).

Valor, C. (2005), "Corporate Social Responsibility and Corporate Citizenship: Towards Corporate Accountability", Business and Society Review 110(2), 191-213.

Waddock, S.A. C. Bodwell and S.B. Graves (2002), "Responsibility: The New Business Imperative" Academy of Management Review, 16(2), 132-148.

Waddock, S.A. (2000), "The Multiple Bottom Lines of Corporate Citizenship: Social Investing, Reputation and Responsibility Audits", Business and Society Review 105(3), 323-346.

Zadek, S. (2001), "The Civil Corporation: The New Economy of Corporate Citizenship. (Eartscan, London).

Websites

http://www.accountability.org.uk

http://www.globalreporting.org

http://www.sustainability.org

http://www.group100.com.au.2003

The Economic Intelligence Unit Ltd, 2003

8

EQA MODELLING ON INDIAN IT MAJORS: CASES OF INFOSYS AND TCS

Ashish Varma & Ishika Varma

Introduction

As per Healey, P.M., Wahlen, J.M., (1999), earnings can include Revenues, Operating Income, Net Income and the Forecasted earnings. There are various differences in calculating these earnings measures and often one cannot rely only on the Income statement for the data needs. This makes earnings quality assessment challenging.

Of the eight models only the Lev Thiagarajan and Empirical Research Partners models have been empirically tested for evidence of usefulness related to quality of earnings. Lev and Thiagarajan's findings confirm that their fundamental (earnings) quality score correlates to earnings persistence and growth, and that subsequent growth is higher in high quality-scoring groups. Empirical Research Partners model is based in part on methodology developed and tested by Piotroski, whose findings indicate a positive relationship between scores based on the model and future profitability.

In this paper Earnings Quality Assessment (EQA) is applied on two prominent Indian Information technology companies viz Infosys and TCS. This gains special significance especially after the SATYAM scam and the resultant apprehension on the stated figures of the earnings quality of IT majors in India.

Objectives

Main objectives of the study are :

- To critically examine the Earning quality assessment model (EQA Model)
- To study application of EQA to two IT companies Infosys and TCS and find the results thereto.

Earning Quality Assessment Model

The Bellovary J.L, Giacommino D.E, Arkers M D (2005) EQA consists of a model that uses 20 criteria that impact earnings quaiity applied as a "rolling evaluation" of all periods presented in the financial statements. The EQA is more comprehensive than the similar models available in the literature. The EQA evaluator assigns a point value ranging from 1 to 5 for each of the 20 criteria, with a possible total of 100 points. A score of 1 indicates a negative effect on earnings quality and a score of 5 indicates a very positive effect on earnings quality. EQA scores, then, can range from 20 to 100.

While the EQA evaluator needs to use professional judgment in assigning scores to each of the criteria, the guidelines written below can be used.

Criteria	*Score*	
1. Revenue recognition issues	1-5	
(Shifts of revenues to other periods: low EQA score of 1.)		2.
Gross margin/sales ratio	1-5	
(High and improving relative to industry: high EQA score of 5.)		3.
Operating earnings/sales	1-5	
(High and improving relative to industry: high score.)		4.
Earnings variability (Great variability: low score.)	1-5	
5. Cash flow from operations exceeds net income	1-5	
(Greater difference: high score.)		
6. Expense recognition issues	1-5	
(Shifts of expenses to other periods: low score.)		
7. Operating leases (Greater occurrence and amount: low score.)	1-5	
8. R&D (Decreasing R&D: low scare.)	1-5	
9. Pension expenses and gains	1-5	
(Consider trend and industry. Greater occurrence and amount: low score.)		
9. Employee stock option expense	1-5	
(Pro forma and large impact on EPS: low score.)		
10. Gain (loss) from asset sales/sales	1-5	
(Incidence is negative. Look at trend and industry.)		
11. Acquisitions/dispositions (Evaluate soundness relative to goals.)	1-5	
12. Discontinued operations	1-5	
(Consider trend and industry. Greater occurrence and amount: low score.)		
13. Ongoing restructuring charges	1-5	
(Consider trend and industry. Greater occurrence and amount low score.)		
14. One-time items	1-5	
(Consider trend and industry. Greater occurrence and amount: low score.)		
15. Extraordinary items	1-5	
(Consider trend and industry. Greater occurrence and amount: low score.)		
16. Accounting changes	1-5	
(Consider trend and industry. Greater occurrence and amount: low score.)		
17. Reverses prior charges/provisions	1-5	
(Consider trend and industry. Greater occurrence and amount: low score.)		
18. Tax-rate percentage	1-5	
(High variance from statutory rate and high variance: low score.)		
19. Share buyback/issuance	1-5	
(Examine degree and trend. High incidence: low score.)		
20. Total possible rating	1-5	

Application of EQA on IT Companies and the Resultant Scores

EQA Performance of Infosys

Infosys has performed well on the criteria of revenue recognition which is good for an IT company. It has also performed well on earnings variability parameter, expense recognition parameter, pension expenses parameter, gain from asset sale criteria, discontinued operations criteria, on going restructuring charges criteria, accounting changes and extraordinary items criteria. However Infosys can do better on its Cash flows and one time items. Overall **Infosys** gets a score of **74 (See Exhibit).**

EQA Performance of TCS

TCS, just like Infosys has also performed well on the revenue recognition criteria. It had done well on the earnings variability parameter and expense recognition parameter. Certain items are not applicable to TCS and thus the resultant score is high such as discontinued operations, on going restructuring, one time items, exceptional items, and accounting changes.

Overall **TCS** gets a score of **66 (See Exhibit).**

Insight regarding the challenges for these two companies:

- Focus on Research and Development should be more
- Cash flow is less than the Net Income in both the companies
- Slow pace of acquisitions and large amount bonus share issuance from capitalization of the reserves.

Conclusion

Infosys has performed better in the EQA model score. However the score for both the companies is respectable. This is reassuring since both happen to be the iconic Indian IT companies. Both companies display a reasonably conservative accounting policy that results in prudent assessment of a companies financial status and income measurement. Both companies have a pre tax income stream which is from recurring main line of business. For both Infosys and TCS, the sales are converted to cash within a time frame which is at par with the industry average and there is a lack of dependence on tax rates. All this points towards sound earnings quality in these firms. Also the earnings are not at the mercy of currency gains. Further the earnings are stable and consistent.

For best results the EQA model should be applied by an unbiased professionals on a multi period data pertaining to the relevant companies. In the present study the application of the EQA Model was on 5 years data (2004-08). Further improvement can be done in the form of applying the model in a rolling fashion. Overall score from each year can be compared to find out any significant changes.

Overall both the firms have good earnings quality. They are conservative, they follow reasonable and justifiable assumptions, and are not volatile in their earnings. Both Infosys and TCS, in the given time period, have reasonable earnings quality.

References

Healey, P.M., Wahlen, J.M. (1999), A Review of the Earnings Management Literature and Its Implications for Standard Setting Accounting Horizons 365-383.

Bellovary J.L, Giacommino D.E, Arkers M.D. (2005), "Earnings Quality: Its Time to Measure and Report" The CPA Journal ; Nov 2005 pp. 32-37.

Lo, K. (2007), Earnings Management and Earnings Quality, Journal of Accounting and Economics (2007).

Beneish, M. (1999), The Detection of Earnings Manipulation, Financial Analysts Journal, pp. 24-36.

Piotroski, J. (2000), Value Investing: The Use of Historical Financial Statement Information to Separate Winners and Losers, Journal of Accounting Research, Supplement, 2000, pp. 1-41.

Jones, J. (1991), Earnings Management during Import Relief Investigations, Journal of Accounting Research, pp. 193-223.

Ball, R., Shivakumar, L. (2005), Earnings Quality in UK Private Firms: Comparative Loss Recognition Timeliness, Journal of Accounting and Economics, 83-128.

DeChow, P.M, Sloan, R.G., Sweeney, A.P. (1995), Detecting Earnings Management. The Accounting Review 193-225.

Graham, J.R. Harvey, C.R., Rajgopal , S. (2005), The Economic Implication of Corporate Financial Reporting, Journal of Accounting and Horizons 365-383.

Schipper, K. (1989), Commentary on Earnings Management, Accounting Horizons, 91-102.

Narayanaswamy, R, Financial Accounting: A Managerial Emphasis, 3e, PHI.

Penman S, Financial Statement Analysis and Security Valuation, 2e, TMH.

Exhibit 1

Criteria in INFOSYS EQA	*2008*	*2007*	*2006*	*2005*	*2004*	*Overall Score*
Revenue recognition issues(Rs. Cr)	15648	13149	9028	6860	4760.89	5
Gross margin/sales ratio (%)	43.28	44.65	45.87	46.72	47.59	3
Operating earnings/sales (%)	31.72	32.13	33.11	33.89	33.26	3
Earnings variability (Net Income) (Rs. Cr)	4470	3777	2421	1859	1243.47	5
Cash flow from operations exceeds net income(Rs. Cr)	-654	-510	-184	-500	390.5	1
Expense recognition issues (Rs. Cr)	10685	8924	6039	4535	3177.24	5
Operating leases (Rs. Cr.)	50	47	34	34	38.88	3
R&D/ Revenue (%)	1.3	1.3	1.13	1.03	0.94	4
Pension expenses and gains (Provident Fund Contibtion) (Rs. Cr.)	184	156	95	87	4.64	5
Employee stock option expenses (Pro forma)	13	12	40	115	12.9	3
Gain from asset sales	0	0	0	1.00	0.04	5
Acquisitions/dispositions(Rs. Cr)	127	635	31	63	83	2
Discontinued operations	0	0	0	0	0	5
Ongoing restructuring charges	0	0	0	0	0	5
One-time items (Special Dividend)	1144	0	830	0	666.41	2
Extraordinary items (Rs Cr)	0	0	0	0	0	5
Accounting changes	N/A	N/A	N/A	N/A	N/A	5
Reverses prior charges/provisions	N/A	N/A	N/A	N/A	N/A	5
Tax-rate percentage(%)	15.46	9.98	5.58	6.17	9.42	4
Share buyback/issuance (Bonus shares by capitalization of General Reserves)	0	148	3	101.97	0.74	2
(Includes shares issued on conversion of options)						74

Exhibit 2

Criteria in TCS EQA	*2008*	*2007*	*2006*	*2005*	*Overall Score*
Revenue recognition issues(Rs. Cr)	18533.72	14939.97	11214.86	8027.59	5
Gross margin/sales ratio (%)					
Operating earnings/sales (%)	29.49	30.24	29.75	31.82	3
Earnings variability (Net Income) (Rs. Cr)	4508.76	3757.29	2716.87	1831.42	5
Cash flow from operations exceeds net income(Rs. Cr)	-680.85	-206.03	-372.45	147.57	1
Expense recognition issues (Rs. Cr)	13513.61	10639	7946.59	5568.54	5
Operating leases (Rs. Cr.)	176.46	204.64	47.96	25.23	1
R&D/ Revenue (%)	0.2	0.22	0.28	0.26	1
Pension expenses and gains (Provident Fund Contibtion) (Rs. Cr.)	192.41	94.81	102.77	82.55	3
Employee stock option expenses (Pro forma)	0	0	0	186.65	2
Loss from asset sales	0.36	0.51	4.49	10.4	2
Acquisitions/dispositions(Rs. Cr)	156.84	180.41	658.06	45.1	2
Discontinued operations	N/A	N/A	N/A	N/A	5
Ongoing restructuring charges	N/A	N/A	N/A	N/A	5
One-time items (Special Dividend)	N/A	N/A	N/A	N/A	5
Exceptional items (Rs Cr)	N/A	N/A	N/A	N/A	5
Accounting changes	N/A	N/A	N/A	N/A	5
Reverses prior charges/provisions	N/A	N/A	N/A	N/A	5
Tax-rate percentage(%)	15.83	9.75	10.49	10.44	3
Share buyback/issuance (Bonus shares by capitalization of General Reserves)	0	48.93	0	9.11	3
(Includes shares issued on conversion of options)					66

9

MOBILE TECHNOLOGY

Sadhna Jha

Introduction

Mobile technology is the technology that is portable. Some examples of mobile technology devices are:

1. Laptop and netbook computers.
2. Palmtop computers or personal digital assistants.
3. Mobile phones and smart phones.
4. Global positioning system (GPS) devices.
5. Wireless debit/credit card payment terminals.

Mobile devices can use a variety of communications technologies such as:

1. Wireless fidelity (WiFi) – a type of wireless local area network technology.
2. Bluetooth – connects mobile devices wirelessly.
3. Dial-up services – data networking services using modems and telephone lines.
4. Virtual private networks – secure access to a private network.

Laptop and Netbook Computers: A laptop computer, usually called a notebook computer by manufacturers, is a battery- or AC-powered personal computer generally smaller than a briefcase that can easily be transported and conveniently used in temporary spaces such as on airplanes, in libraries, temporary offices, and at meetings. A laptop typically weighs less than 5 pounds and is 3 inches or less in thickness. Among the best-known makers of laptop computers are IBM, Apple, Compaq, Dell, and Toshiba.

Laptop computers generally cost more than desktop computers with the same capabilities because they are more difficult to design and manufacture. A laptop can effectively be turned into a desktop computer with a docking station, a hardware frame that supplies connections for peripheral input/output devices such as a printer or larger monitor. The less capable port replicator allows you to connect a laptop to a number of peripherals through a single plug.

Laptops usually come with displays that use thin-screen technology. The thin film transistor or active matrix screen is brighter and views better at different angles than the STN or dual-scan screen. Laptops use several different approaches for integrating a mouse into the keyboard, including the touch pad, the trackball, and the pointing stick. A serial port also allows a regular mouse to be attached. The PC Card is insertable hardware for adding a modem or network interface card to a laptop. CD-ROM and digital versatile disc drives may be built-in or attachable.

A **Netbook** is a new type of laptop computer, defined by size, price, horsepower, and operating system. They are small, cheap, under-powered, and run either an old or unfamiliar operating system.

Netbooks run either Windows XP Home edition or Linux. They do not run XP Professional, Vista, or OS X. Microsoft arbitrarily restricts Netbooks from running the Professional Edition of Windows XP. Likewise, Apple arbitrarily restricts OS X to Apple hardware and it has never played in the low-end realm that Netbooks occupy. Vista requires too much horsepower to run well on a Netbook. HP has been the only company to offer Vista on a Netbook.

Palmtop Computers or Personal Digital Assistants **:** A **palmtop computer** is a very small computer which can be hold in one hand and manipulate with the other. These kinds of computers have specialized keyboards or keypads to enter data, or small QWERTY keyboards. Other names for palmtops are *handheld* computers, pocket computers and *PDA*.

The main features of these computers are that they are small, light, draw power from a battery and are intended for general usage. Their input includes a typewriter keyboard and the output consists of a small, full-color LCD *display* The palmtop has a word processor, a spreadsheet *program*, a calendar and a phone book. An important characteristic is that its *operating system* is compatible with that of a PC. Various programs can be installed and run and the data may be transferred to and from a desktop computer. In contrast to personal digital assistant, it has more memory, a keyboard and many available programs. Handheld computers usually do not have disk drives due to their small size. They have PCMCIA slots where disk drives, modems, memory or other devices could be put into. Palmtops that do not use a keyboard but a pen are called PDAs or hand-held computers.

(Personal Digital Assistant) A handheld computer for managing contacts, appointments and tasks. PDAs typically include a name and address database, calendar, to-do list and note taker, which are the functions in a personal information manager application. Wireless PDAs may also offer e-mail and Web browsing, and data are synchronized between the PDA and desktop computer via USB or wireless.

Mobile Phones and Smart Phones: An electronic telecommunications device, often referred to as a cellular phone or cellphone. Mobile phones connect to a wireless communications network through radio wave or satellite transmissions. Most mobile phones provide voice communications, Short Message Service (SMS), Multimedia Message Service (MMS), and newer phones may also provide Internet services such as Web browsing and e-mail.

A **smartphone** is a mobile phone that offers more advanced computing ability and connectivity than a contemporary feature phone. Smartphones and feature phones may be thought of as handheld computers integrated with a mobile telephone, but while most feature phones are able to run applications based on platforms such as Java ME, a smartphone usually allows the user to install and run more advanced applications. Smartphones run complete operating system software providing a platform for application developers. Thus, they combine the functions of a camera phone and a Personal digital assistant (PDA). A cellular telephone with built-in applications and Internet access. It provides digital voice service as well as any combination of e-mail, text messaging, pager, Web browsing, voice recognition, still and/or video camera, MP3, TV or video player and organizer. In addition, **smartphones** have become application delivery platforms, turning the once single-minded cellphone into a tiny mobile computer.

Global Positioning System (GPS) Devices: The Global Positioning System (GPS) is a satellite-based navigation system made up of a network of 24 satellites placed into orbit by the U.S. Department of Defense. GPS was originally intended for military applications, but in the 1980s, the government made the system available for civilian use. GPS works in any weather conditions, anywhere in the world, 24 hours a day. There are no subscription fees or setup charges to use GPS.

How it Works: GPS satellites circle the earth twice a day in a very precise orbit and transmit signal information to earth. GPS receivers take this information and use triangulation to calculate the user's exact location. Essentially, the GPS receiver compares the time a signal was transmitted by a satellite with the time it was received. The time difference tells the GPS receiver how far away the satellite is. Now, with distance measurements from a few more satellites, the receiver can determine the user's position and display it on the unit's electronic map.

A GPS receiver must be locked on to the signal of at least three satellites to calculate a 2D position (latitude and longitude) and track movement. With four or more satellites in view, the receiver can determine the user's 3D position (latitude, longitude and altitude). Once the user's position has been determined, the GPS unit can calculate other information, such as speed, bearing, track, trip distance, distance to destination, sunrise and sunset time and more.

Wireless Debit/Credit Card Payment Terminals: A **Credit card terminal** is a device that can do transactions with a debit card or a credit card. Several types of credit card terminals are available to merchants. Most have the same basic purpose and functions. They allow a merchant to swipe or key in required credit card information and transmit such data to the merchant service provider. Most newer models processes credit cards, gift cards, and are expandable to perform check verification. The majority of credit card terminals transmit data over a standard telephone line or the internet. Wireless terminals can transmit card data using either cellular networks or satellite networks. Some also have the ability to store data and transmit over a standard telephone line when one becomes available.

Using a smartphone and the appropriate software, a merchant can replace the functionality of a dedicated hardware credit card terminal using a credit card terminal app running on their smartphone. These credit card terminal apps support manual entry of the credit card

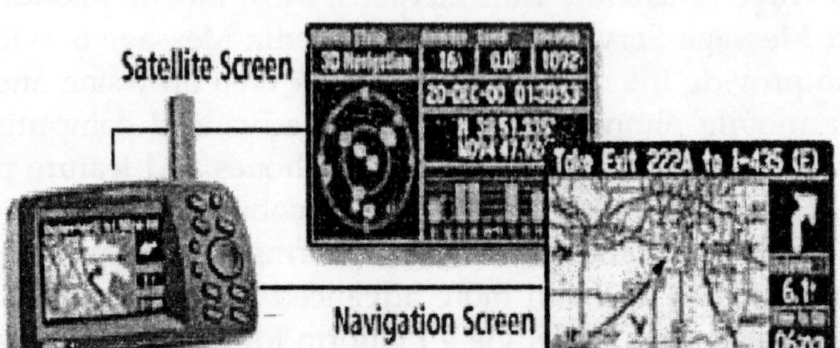

number. The apps may work with hardware devices known as swipers or credit card readers to transfer the credit card track data to the app. An app which is capable of reading the credit card track data will help the merchant receive a better discount rate on their credit card processing costs.

Mobile Devices - Communications Technologies

Wireless Fidelity (WiFi)

A type of wireless local area network technology. A communication technology that uses the 'Direct-sequence spread spectrum radio technology' and the 'Orthogonal Frequency Division Multiplexing radio technology', Wi-Fi is the trademark used by a trade group known as Wi-fi Alliance. The essence of the Wi-Fi technology is that, it acts as a bridge between wireless devices that operate on different technologies. The term Wi-Fi is used for wireless fidelity.

How Does Wi-Fi Work: Radio waves are used for the working of Wi-Fi technology. The wireless adapter of the computer and the wireless router play an important role in its working. The adapter receives data from the computer in digital form. This data, after its conversion in radio waves is sent to the router by means of an antenna. The router decodes the signal and sends it to the Internet. The process is reversed when information is sent from the Internet to a computer.

Bluetooth – Connects Mobile Devices Wirelessly

Bluetooth is a wireless technology for connecting various devices. Bluetooth is even capable of communicating through walls. However, in practice this largely depends on the properties of the walls and the device class. There are three device classes with maximum transmission ranges between ten and a hundred meters.

In Bluetooth, services are defined by means of profiles, such as the file transfer profile, the basic printing profile, and the personal area network profile. To enable a device to use the services of another device, both must understand the same profile — a piece of information that is often missing on the device package and in the manual.

To be able to use Bluetooth, you need a Bluetooth adapter (built-in or external), drivers, and a Bluetooth protocol stack.

Dial-up Services – Data Networking Services Using Modems and Telephone Lines

Dial-up Internet access is a form of Internet access that uses the facilities of the public switched telephone network (PSTN) to establish a dialed connection to an Internet service provider (ISP) via telephone lines. The user's computer or router uses an attached modem to encode and decode Internet Protocol packets and control information into and from analogue audio frequency signals, respectively.

Virtual Private Networks – Secure Access to a Private Network

A **virtual private network** (**VPN**) is a computer network that uses a public telecommunication infrastructure such as the Internet to provide remote offices or individual users secure access to their organization's network. It encapsulates data transfers using a secure cryptographic method between two or more networked devices which are not on the same private network so as to keep the transferred data private from other devices on one or more intervening local or wide area networks.

Benefits: The growth and development of mobile technology has positive effects on society. Through Mobile technology you can access all of the market data you require using your mobile phone. With the introduction of 3G technology, mobile technology and smart phones with capabilities of handling video calls, browsing the internet and sharing large files, mobile technology has made it more efficient to conduct business.

Mobile technology enables you to get breaking news as and when it happens. Mobile technology enables you to make speedy and informed decisions.

Mobile technology has played a great role in the education sector by enabling people to access the Internet, even in remote locations using mobile broadband. This enables students and researchers in these far flung areas to carry out research using this feature of mobile technology.

Number of people use mobile technology, businesses are adopting the use of M-commerce. By doing so, businesses are able to increase their revenues and client base. Banks are also adopting mobile technology to conduct mobile banking. This not only brings convenience in terms of transferring money but also saves a lot of time.

Drawbacks: The cost involved in setting up the equipment and training required to make use of mobile devices. Mobile devices can expose valuable data to unauthorized people if the proper precautions are not taken. Ensure that the devices, and the data accessed, are kept safe.

References

http://www.businesslink.gov.uk

http://searchmobilecomputing.techtarget.com/definition/laptop-computer

http://news.cnet.com/what-is-a-netbook-computer/#ixzz1HmJp9Dfs

http://www.answers.com/topic/pda#ixzz1HmM0GzOu

http://www.tech-faq.com/what-is-a-pda.html

http://www.cheap-computers-reference.com/palmtop-computer.html

http://www.webopedia.com/TERM/M/mobile_phone.html

http://encyclopedia2.thefreedictionary.com/Smartphones

http://en.wikipedia.org/wiki/Smartphone

http://www8.garmin.com/aboutGPS/

http://en.wikipedia.org/wiki/Credit_card_terminal

http://www.buzzle.com/articles/what-is-wi-fi-wireless-fidelity.html

http://www.novell.com/documentation/suse91/suselinux-adminguide/html/ch08s04.htm

http://en.wikipedia.org/wiki/Dial-up_Internet_access

http://en.wikipedia.org/wiki/Virtual_private_network

http://www.wapalize.co.uk/advantages-of-mobile-technology/

10

A COMPARATIVE STUDY OF PERSONALITY AND DEPRESSION IN INTERNET ADDICTS AND NON ADDICTS

Saba Shamim, Bharathi Kumari & Aanchal Ahuja

Introduction

It was originally proposed by Goldberg in1995 for Pathological, Compulsive internet usage

- it is defined as the habitual compulsion to engage in a certain activity or utilize a substance
- It manifest both physical and psychological dependence
- Conceptually the diagnosis is a compulsive – impulsive spectrum that involves online/offline computer usage

Types of Addictions

- *Cyber-sexual Addiction:* individuals who suffer from this type of addiction are typically engaged in viewing, downloading online pornography and involved in fantasy.
- *Cyber-relational Addiction:* this is a addiction to chat rooms, instant messaging or social networking sites become over involved in online relationship. Online friends quickly become more important at the expense of real life relationship with family and friends.
- *Net Compulsions:* addiction to online gambling and ebay are fast becoming new mental problems in the post internet era with the instant access to virtual casinos, interactive games, and ebay addicts loose excessive amounts of money and even disrupt their jobs and significant relationships.
- *Information Overload:* the wealth of data available on the world wide web has created a new type of compulsive behavior regarding excessive web surfing and database searches and will spend greater amount of time searching and collecting data from web and organizing information.

- *Computer Addiction*: in the 80's , first computer games started (solitaire and minesweeper) and research found that computer game playing become problematic in organizational settings as employees spend most of their time playing rather than working.

Prevelance

- 2.1 % (age 6 –13) of the children of South korea suffers from internet addiction
- 13 % of the Chinese children meet the criteria for internet addiction
- 4.7 % of the Indian population is suffering and many are on the risk of developing the disorder.
- Male are reported to have high rate of Internet usage(ASSOCHAM 2010)
- 71 % of the office workers abuse internet during working hours by visiting social networking sites, shopping online, gaming
- Individual who suffers from depression, anxiety, social phobia and other compulsive disorders are more likely to develop internet addiction
- Level of depression and suicidal ideations were highest in internet addicts group
- Children with single parent family, homesickness and the age of the person were significantly associated with addiction
- Hostility and aggressive behavior is associated with internet addicts

Ye Ying et al (2011) tried to explore the psychological and behavioral characteristics of severe internet addicts. 30 severe internet game addicts (aged from 16~25 years) and 43 non-addicts participated in the investigation. Measures included Internet Addiction Scale, Eysenck Personality Questionnaire (EPQ), Social Support Questionnaire, Life Purpose Scale and Sensation Seeking Scale. Internet addicts got significantly lower scores than non-addicts on Social Support Questionnaire, Life Purpose Scale and Thrill and Adventure Seeking (TAS) . Scores of Objective Support, Utilization of Support and Sensation Seeking could predict the Internet Addiction score of the addict group. Internet addicts have significantly lower score on factor Lie of EPQ than nonaddicts. Severe internet game addicts have the characteristics of low social support, less purposes in life and less adventure tendency.

Sensation Seeking and Social Support have predictive function for internet addiction degree.

Ko, C et al (2006) aimed to examine the differences in personality characteristics between adolescents with and without Internet addiction and substance use experience as defined by the Tridimensional Personality Questionnaire (TPQ), In the cross-sectional investigation 3662 students (2328 boys and1334 girls) from high schools in southern Taiwan. Our investigation was conducted using the TPQ, the Chen Internet Addiction Scale, and Questionnaires for Experience in Substance Use. Adolescents with Internet addiction were more likely to have substance use experience. High novelty seeking (NS), high harm avoidance (HA), and low reward dependence (RD) predicted a higher proportion of adolescents with Internet addiction. High NS, low HA, and low RD predicted a higher proportion of adolescents with substance user experience. Of the 4 groups, the Internet addiction group had the highest HA scores and the comorbid group had the lowest HA scores. Adolescents with high NS and low RD should be provided with effective strategies for preventing Internet addiction and substance use. In addition, the Internet addiction group and the comorbid group should be provided with different preventative strategies focused on HA.

Objectives

- To assess the depression of internet addicts and non addicts in school and college students.
- To assess the neuroticism of internet addicts and non addicts in school and college students.
- To assess the introversion/ extroversion dimension of internet addicts and non addicts in school and college students.

Hypotheses

- There will be significant difference in depression of internet addicts and non addicts in school and college students
- There will be significant difference in neuroticism of internet addicts and non addicts in school and college students.

3. There will be significant difference in introversion and extraversion dimension of internet addicts and non addicts in school and college students.
4. There will be positive correlation between depression and neuroticism in school and college students.

Variables

Independent Variable

- School v/s college
- Addicts v/s non addicts

Dependent Variables

- Depression
- Personality

Sample

A total of 100 students were taken, out of which 50 were school students and 50 of college students. Each group (school and college) are further divided into 25 addicts and 25 non addicts.

Procedure

The data was collected from school and college of Delhi. Permission was granted by school and college authority to collect the data from the students. A good rapport was established with the students and they were provided proper instructions regarding the scales. They took all three tools and after filling the questionnaires the students were thanked for their contribution.

Tools Used

- Internet addiction test
- Maudsley personality inventory
- Beck depression inventory

Statistical techniques used : 2X2 ANOVA was calculated , coorelational analysis was used.

Results

Table 1
Two Way Analysis of Variance for Depression

Source	*SS*	*df*	*MS*	*F calc*
Rows	163.84	1	163.84	15.96
Columns	1102.24	1	1102.24	107.4
Rows*columns	129.96	1	129.96	12.66
Error	984.96	96	10.26	
Total	2381.00	99		

Table 2
Two Way Analysis of Variance for Neuroticism

Source	*SS*	*df*	*MS*	*F calc*
Rows	67.24	1	67.24	9.33
Columns	57.76	1	57.76	8.02
Rows*columns	.360	1	.360	.050
Error	691.20	96	7.2	
Total	816.56	99		

Table 3
Two Way Analysis of Variance for Extraversion

Source	*SS*	*df*	*MS*	*F calc*
Rows	187.69	1	187.69	22.71
Columns	32.49	1	32.49	3.93
Rows* columns	59.29	1	59.29	7.17
Error	793.28	96	8.26	
Total	1072.75	99		

Table 4
Depression Level of Addicts and Non-addicts in School

	Minimal	*Mild*	*Moderate*	*Severe*	*Total*
	(0-3)	*(4-8)*	*(9-12)*	*(13-21)*	
Addicts	1(4%)	2(8%)	14(56%)	8(32%)	25
Non-Addicts	18(72%)	6(24%)	1(4%)	0%	25

Table 5
Variables

	Mean	*SD*	*Mean*	*SD*	*t-value*
Depression	6.8	4.8	2.47	2.10	4.16**
Neuroticism	6.64	2.62	5.24	2.77	1.8
Extroversion	8.12	4.21	7.72	2.18	0.42

Discussion

Table 1 shows the two way analysis of variance for depression the f values are highly significant for both the variables and their interaction effect (12.66**). The f value for the type of institution is 15.96** which is highly significant at 0.01 level. The f value for internet addicted and non addicted is 107.4**. School students have obtained higher mean (11.64) in comparison to college students (6.8).

Table 2 represents the 2 way ANOVA for the neuroticism dimension here also the type of institution and the addicted and non – addicted differs significantly. The f value for the type of institution is 9.33** . the f value for addicted and non addicted group is 8.02**. And their interaction effect is not significant at 0.050. college students(6.64) have obtained the higher mean neuroticism dimension in comparison to the school students (5.12).

Table 3 represents the 2 way annova for the extraversion dimension. The f value (22.71) is significant for the type of institution. The interaction effect of type of institution and the addicted and non addicted group is significant (7.17**). The data was further ananlysed on the basis of level of depression (BDI). Higher percentage of the children from college(86%) had minimal depression in the non addicted group than the school students (72%). In the addicted school sample 56% were having moderate depression and 32% severe depression. In the college sample 24% has moderate depression and 16% has severe depression.

Correlation was calculated between depression, neuroticism, extraversion in college students . Most of the correlations are low ie. Less than .4 there is positive and significant correlation between depression and neuroticism (.388**).

In school students most of the correlations are very low. The correlation between depression and extraversion in the addicted group is .235 which is very low. Whereas there is negative correlation between extraversion and depression is (-.23) in the non addicted college students also there is negative correlation between depression and extraversion (- .23).

Hypotheses 1 is related to the significant difference of internet addicts and non addicts in school and college. The hypotheses is accepted here as there is significant difference. Studies conducted by the following people have found the more or less similar type of result for example Helen Petrie and David Gunn (1998) showed that there is a significant relationship between high internet use and positive attitudes towards the internet with both self-reported depression and introversion, supporting the view that internet "addicts' are indeed introverted, and more likely to be suffering from depression.

Young and Rodgers (1998) An on-line survey administered on a World Wide Web site utilized the BDI as part of a larger study. A total of 312 surveys was collected with 259 valid profiles from addicted users, which again supported significant levels of depression to be associated with pathological Internet use.

Hypothesis 2 related to the neuroticism dimension of the internet addicts and non addicts of school and college. Here also hypothesis 2 is accepted. Elizabeth Hardie and Ming Yi Tee (2007) analysis revealed that only neuroticism and perceived support from online social networks were significant predictors of excessive internet use.

Hypotheses 3 is related to the introversion and extraversion dimensions of personality. Significant difference was found. Here the hypotheses was partially accepted as there is significant difference in the type of institution. Katherine chak et al. (2004).

studies have indicated that some patterns of Internet use are associated with loneliness, shyness, anxiety, depression, and self-consciousness, attempted to examine the potential influences of personality variables, such as shyness and locus of control, online experiences, and demographics on Internet addiction. Results indicated that the higher the tendency of one being addicted to the Internet, the shyer the person is, the less faith the person has, the firmer belief the person holds in the irresistible power of others, and the higher trust the person places on chance in determining his or her own course of life.

Hypothese 4 is related to relationship between depression and neuroticism. The hypothese is true in college students but not in school students. Partial support is there for this hypotheses 4. Cheung LM and Wong WS (2010) there is high comorbidity between internet addiction and insomnia. Both insomnia and internet addiction emerged as significant explanatory factors, but they exerted differential effects on depression. Future research should be directed at determining the causal relationship between internet addiction and insomnia, and its underlying mechanism with depression.

References

Beck AT. Steer. R.A. (2000), Beck Depression Inventory- Fast Screen for Medical Patients USA. Psychological Corporation.

Cheung LM, Wong WS, Journal of Sleep Research (2010), The Effects of Insomnia and Internet Addiction on Depression in Hong Kong Chinese Adolescents: An Exploratory Cross-sectional Analysis.

Elizabeth Hardie and Ming Yi Tee (2007), Excessive Internet Use: The Role of Personality, Loneliness and Social Support Networks in Internet Addiction. *Australian Journal of Emerging Technologies and Society*. 5, 34-47.

Helen Petrie and David Gunn(1998), The Effects of Sex, Age, Depression and Introversion, Paper presented at the British Psychological Society, London Conference, Psychology Department, University of Hertfordshire, College Lane Hatfield, Herts. AL10 9AB United Kingdom.

Jalota.S & Kapoor.S. (2000), Eysenck's Maudsley Personality Inventory. Agra (Psychological Research Cell).

Katherine. C, and Louis. L. (2004), Cyberpsychology & Behavior, Shyness and Locus of Control as Predictors of Internet Addiction and Internet Use Volume 7, 5 Mary Ann Liebert, Inc.

Kimberly S.Y and Robert C.R. (1998), The Relationship Between Depression and Internet Addiction. Paper published in *CyberPsychology & Behavior*, 1(1), 25-28.

Kimberly. S.J. (1998), Caught in the Net. Canada. John Wiley and Sons.

Ko, C., Yen, J., Chen, C., Chen, S., Wu, K., & Yen, C. (2006), Tridimensional Personality of Adolescents with Internet Addiction and Substance Use Experience. *Canadian Journal of Psychiatry, 51*(14), 887-894.

Ying. Y. & Wenbin. G. (2011), Institute of Psychology, Chinese Academy of Sciences, No.4 Datun Road, Chaoyang District, Beijing.

11

E-GOVERNANCE

Parveen Kaur, Kamaldeep Kaur & Abha Grover

E-Government

The forces of globalization are achieving impetus with the innovative technological advancements smoothening the progress of the processes .The growth of ICT (information and communication technology has revolutionized the entire world scenario. The worldwide growth of e-Commerce has transitioned into electronic delivery of services at all levels of government activities. This has created urgency for restructuring the traditional way of carrying out the processes, that affect the way in which public and business communities deal with the government. It is also imperative to amalgamate Government services with inter-operable Standards with convergence across departments thus avoiding redundancy of meta-data and processes. This also requires a transformation in entire architecture and structure of the organization. Apart from restructuring of business processes there is a need of networking of organizations and information systems, with public administration operation on a networked base, making an exodus from hierarchical structures which were error prone and victim of mal practices..The quick acceptance of e-governance is aided by forceful technological and telecommunication modernization. In many countries, Information and Communication Technologies (ICTs) are seen as a catalyzing tool for e-Governance.

E-Governance

E-Governance is a method used by government to employ the new-fangled technologies for providing expedient access of government information and services to citizens. It aims to improve internal efficiency, speedier delivery of public services, reformation of administrative processes and participation in government processes. E-government or electronic government refers to the use of Information and Communication Technologies (ICTs) by government agencies. E-Government proffers numerous remarkable opportunities to move ahead in the era of conversant citizens, with improved quality, cost-effective, government services and an enhanced association between citizens and government .Today technology is ever growing and ever powering, it affects the organization and its employees. The benefits of Governance are quicker decision making, decrease in redundancy of work, exposure of corruption and illegitimate transactions, deterrence of knowledge depletion and crisis handling. Information and communication technology (ICT) provides an opportunity for advancement in civic service delivery and administrative practices. ICT leads to a makeover of administrative service. Delivery, lower cost and better allocation of responsibility and its accountability.ICT facilitates a complete technical revolutionization of government processes by amalgamation of Government processes and communication with access enabled on an on-line real time basis, with status tracking and status information.

The term E-Governance leads to many other diffused neologisms as mentioned below.

E-administration- e-Administration is subset of e-Governance for productivity improvement, transparency and accountability of Governments. The prime objective of e-administration is to create paperless offices which would improve the efficiency and reduce the burden of staff. It is usage and execution of the ICT in the administrative departments held with the government.

E-services- E-services, is entering a new phase where many services can be provided for citizens using the Web. Online services can be utilized by users, thus providing a convenient and easy access. such services are fast and more reliable e.g. Online Registration of E-Return Intermediary, Online Status Enquiry of Passport Application, e-filing of Service Tax Returns etc

E-democracy- U.S. president Abraham Lincoln defined democracy as "Government of the people, by the people, for the people". It is an era of immense technological progress which has impact over democracy and transforming democracy into e-democracy .Today there exist various online e-democracy systems like e-complaint system, online disclosure policies, online grievance redress forums etc via which people can communicate their mind to government authorities. Tools on internet like online blogs, forums, communities and interactive surveys assist people to communicate with various government agencies.

Delivery Models of E-Government

Every government has two vital components in its functioning the Administration and Citizen of the nation. The administration component can be inter-department and intra department. Inter-department activities include knowledge and resource sharing, monitoring etc. while the intra-department functions exist within specific department of the government, they are usually hierarchy based. Similarly Citizen & Government has two foremost elements such as citizen to government and government to citizen. The monetary facets of Citizen-to-Government include taxes, bills, penalties etc. The nonmonetary aspects of Citizen-to-Government are voice of the people's opinions, complaints, requests, and elections etc. The monetary facets of Government-to-Citizen comprise loans, relief funds, and B2C transactions, B2B transactions while the non-monetary aspects of Government-to-Citizen are education, polls, survey, intelligence and reports.

E-Governance if often considered as a government using internet facilities to provide improved services and better accessibility of public services. But concept of E-Governance is little less understood by limiting it to internet as there are many non-Internet based E-Governance models which can be used in this context.

With relevance to IT e-governance has following important aspects:

- IT helps in automating various functions of government like Online Pension Payment Order, Online Status Enquiry of Passport Application etc

- Direct communication channel with citizens using websites Online Registration of E-Return Intermediary, e-filing of Service Tax Returns, Lodge Investor Complaint Online etc
- Enhancing Government processes

E-Governance Models

The primary delivery models of e-Government can be divided into Five models as Government-to-Citizen or Government-to-Consumer (G2C), Government-to-Business (G2B), Government-to-Government G2G), Government-to-Employees (G2E), Business to Government (B2G)

Government to Citizen: In this model there is open communication channel between government and citizens. The citizens can perform various functions online and do not need to go to government offices and stand in a long queue to deposit bills, taxes etc. Information Technology and Information Highway together eliminate the precincts between diverse sub-functions of government. In addition it eradicates the precincts between governments worldwide because service delivery is federal around the requirements of citizens and not on political arrangement. These models include monetary and non-monetary aspects. Monetary aspects like E-Filing of Income Tax Returns, e-filing of Central Excise Returns, e-filing of Service Tax Returns. While non-monetary aspects include Lodge Investor Complaint Online, online complaint lodging etc.

Government to Business: It is the online interaction between Government organizations and commercial business firms. Over years it has been seen that government has tried the business model for selected activities when the target is to cope or make profits in supervising these activities. In some cases, governments have used the business model for a particular activity using a proprietary fund format. Since funds are traditionally the foremost mode of putting in order governmental accounting and financial reporting, the proprietary mode is still prevalent. Fund activities in government, which use the business model, are referred to as proprietary funds. The governmental fund group manages wide-ranging government activities such as public safety and other governmental activities.

Government-to-Government refers to the non-commercial communication between Government organizations, departments, and authorities and other Government organizations, departments, and authorities. Its use is common in the UK, along with G2C, and G2B the online non-commercial interaction of local and central Government and the commercial business sector. G2G systems can be internal or external systems. Internal systems are the ones that function within the single government departments, agencies, organizations and authorities. While the external G2G system functions across multiple Governments IS systems.

Business-to-government (B2G) is an interaction between commercial business organizations and government by marketing products and services to various government levels - including federal, state and local. it uses integrated marketing communications techniques such as strategic public relations, branding, advertising, and web-based communications.B2G networks provide a platform for businesses to bid on government opportunities. Government agencies typically have pre-negotiated standing contracts vetting the vendors/suppliers and their products and services for set prices.

Government-to-employees G2E) is the online interactions through instantaneous communication tools between government units and their employees. The model is used to maintain a database of employee records and other details. It can also be used by employees to get information about compensation and benefit policies, training and learning opportunities and civil rights law. G2E is adopted in many countries including the United States, Hong Kong and New Zealand.

E-Governance and Information Technology

With regard to software engineering, Governance is amalgamation of two components-the integration component and the interaction component. It entails sound technology and infrastructure to successfully access and utilizes this knowledge database. Governance needs to sustain a dominant incorporated hardware and software network. This is the integration part of Governance. High-quality Governance models offer a platform for citizens of nations can represent themselves and freely communicate with government. It provides an unproblematic way for individuals to find the groups and communities of interest to them. It should bridge the gap among people of different communities. It puts together an environment with focused expertise that can facilitate answer questions, and direct them to come across various alternative solutions.

IT-Action Plan

For developing an IT based solution to various government problems, an IT action plan needs to be developed. There are certain basic pre-requisites that need to be followed for the development of an IT based solution. IT Infrastructure: the foremost requirement for an e-government is the development of basic infrastructure .Wide range of hardware and software need to be installed, it requires Personal Computers (PCs) with necessary software support to all functionaries.

For e-governance following exclusive IT infrastructures is required:

- Latest high-end machines those are able to support all sorts of hardware and software.
- Server
- Router
- Latest software that should be updated from time to time
- Skilled professionals with suitable training aids
- Skilled and dynamic manpower
- Sound network and security policies

Website: For automating various government processes and creating an efficient communication channel government, there is a need of a web based solution. Through websites citizens can have access to various services online. Government should enable anyone visiting a government website to communicate and interact via the Internet with graphical user interfaces any way more sophisticated than a simple email. Further, there is the need to enhance the contents of the website by including forms and guidelines pertinent to various citizen services being provided by the Department. The National Policy Research Council, a nonprofit think tank, examined the Web presence of the 50 states and all 38,987 counties, municipalities and townships in the U.S and found the top state websites. (Source: *Computerworld/National Policy Research Council "E-Government 2006" report)*

Table 1
Top US Cities E-government Sites

Grade	*State*	*URL*
A+	Michigan	www.michigan.gov
A	Idaho	www.accessidaho.org
A	Indiana	www.in.gov
A-	Nebraska	www.nebraska.gov
A-	Utah	www.utah.gov
B+	Arizona	az.gov
B+	Arkansas	www.state.ar.us
B+	Colorado	www.colorado.gov
B+	Georgia	www.georgia.gov
B+	Texas	www.state.tx.us

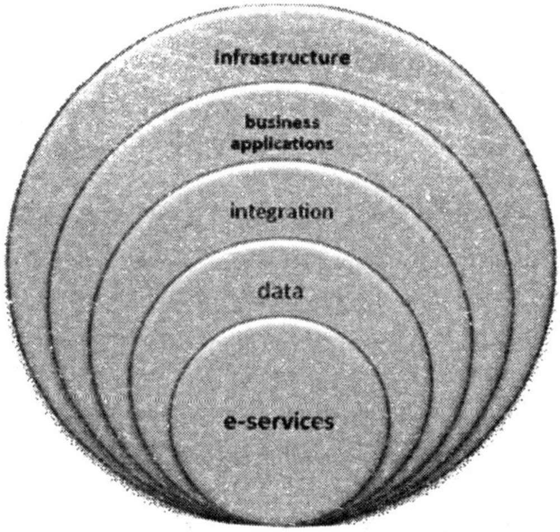

Figure1: IT Infrastructure

Networking: A computer network is a collection of autonomous computer systems for the purpose of information exchange and resource sharing. For an e-governance system there is a requirement to establish Local Area Network (LAN) and develop an Intranet to facilitate file and information sharing between various functional units.

Office Automation: Next important requisite for e-governance is implementing an office automation system to keep up records of receipt, issue of letters and movement of files.

IT Training: Once an e-government system is developed it is very important to provide pertinent dedicated training courses to the staff and Officers, to enable them working on computers.

E-Reports: E-reports are used for Converting the Acts, Rules, Circulars and other published material of interest or importance to the public in electronic form.

E-Governance and Information Systems

Information Systems (IS) Planning is accepted as an essential step in ensuring that IS/IT in organizations planned and implemented in an optimum manner, remembering that IS/IT is becoming a dominant part of an organization. The activity is also a conscious effort to ensure that there is alignment between IS/IT activities with the organization's objectives. In terms of characteristics government organization are naturally different to those of a private sector, even when compared to the largest multinational corporation. Governments do not aim at making profits. For governments the measure of bottom line success is not an objective. Governments are driven by constraints such as rules and regulations, which translates into bureaucracy. The characteristic is further complicated by different government models of different countries another factor which drives uniqueness.It has following objectives:

- To develop a good service system with reasonable cost. The focus is to extend and improve the quality of information, communication network, and information security system.
- To develop management system of central and local government. The focus is to improve the quality of services needed by the community, to manage the changes, to enforce the leadership and to improve the product of the regulation.
- To optimize the use of information technology.
- To improve the participation of private sector and information technology industry.
- To develop manpower capacity in the central and local government. The objectives are to develop ICT culture in government institutions, to optimize the use of ICT.

Steps to Develop an IS

The development of an information system for e-governance requires following steps:

Set up Priorities, Drivers, Critical Success Factors and Project Structure: The purpose of this phase is to identify the government priorities, Drivers, Critical Success Factors and Project Structure.

Verify Established Processes: The prime objective of this step is to determine responsibilities for the IT components based on processes used in government.

Determine Application and Database Portfolio: The objective is to determine the application and database portfolio.

Identify Infrastructure Requirement: This phase is concerned with identifying various infrastructure requirements like hardware ,software ,networking, training etc.

Establish Human Resource Requirement: Next step is to determine the Human Resources requirement to support the application and infrastructure requirements.

Project Phasing and Budget: This step identifies overall project phasing and budget requirements. It also determines budget allocation to individual phases and requirements.

Discuss Plan: The aim of this stage is to let all stakeholders and others know about the program.

Execution of Plan: Once the planning is complete final step is to execute the plan. This phase is also concerned with overall coordination and control

There are immense varieties of e-governance examples all over the world, both at the local and national level. The use of ICT tools in governance can be illustrated through the following examples:

Categories of E-Governance Applications

1. Informing the citizen category tries to make information extensively available to citizens with the aim of increased transparency and answerability, providing data about the political process, services and choices available.
2. Improved service delivery is giving the citizens wider range of options, faster delivery and improved efficiency of services.

3. Increasing citizen participation helps in improving accessibility of citizens to their elected members, creating a vision for partnership in the decision making process.

Fighting Corruption Using the Internet in Kenya

The Information Technology Standards Association (ITSA) of Kenya has initiated a pilot project that aims to increase public responsiveness and promote public participation in fighting corrupt practices. The project will offer an online reporting facility in six towns, two remote locations. The media will form the source points of information which will be routed to the Electronic Graft Management (EGM) Centre. The centre will filter this information electronically and forward it to the relevant authorities for action.

Government Procurement System in Mexico

Mexico's federal government established "Compranet" for government procurement to fight corruption by automating procurement procedures. The process of bidding and reverse bidding has been made online. It helps to make government purchasing more efficient and transparent. The system allows public accessibility to the products and services the government is spending its resources on and gives them information on the vendors or companies which are providing them with these services. There are more than 6000 public sector tenders logged daily, and more than 20 000 service-providing firms are regular users.

E-seva Center in Andhra Pradesh State of India

The goal of e-seva is to make the delivery of city services much simpler. It provides a wide spectrum of citizen friendly services that will save peoples time and effort of running around to various departments.

Services provided include

- Payment of utility bills
- Reservations of train tickets
- Getting birth and death certificates,
- Vehicle permits, driving licenses;
- Transport department services etc.

The use of e-seva services has made the task of a common man easier, wherein an umbrella of services is available at the same place.

Increasing Citizen Participation

Iperbole Internet Civic Network in Bologna, Italy

This represents a hub of collective knowledge focusing on "two-way" communication and citizen participation in the information exchange process. Local citizens benefit from a network of internet public places, free internet access points, e-mail and newsgroups. It provides people with online healthcare support; online services for senior, disabled people and young people.

Democracy Project in North Jutland, Denmark

The task of the Democracy Project was to create an electronic forum for e-democratic dialogue among citizens and politicians, with a particular aim towards November 20, 2001: County

Council Election Day. In 1997, North Jutland experienced the lowest voter turnout in the Danish election. The object of the Democracy Project was to make visible the decisions made on a regional political level, and to involve the citizens in the process of democracy. Specifically, the County Council also wanted to reach first-time voters, who were known to show a low turnout. Citizens, politicians and first-time voters were invited to take part in the project.

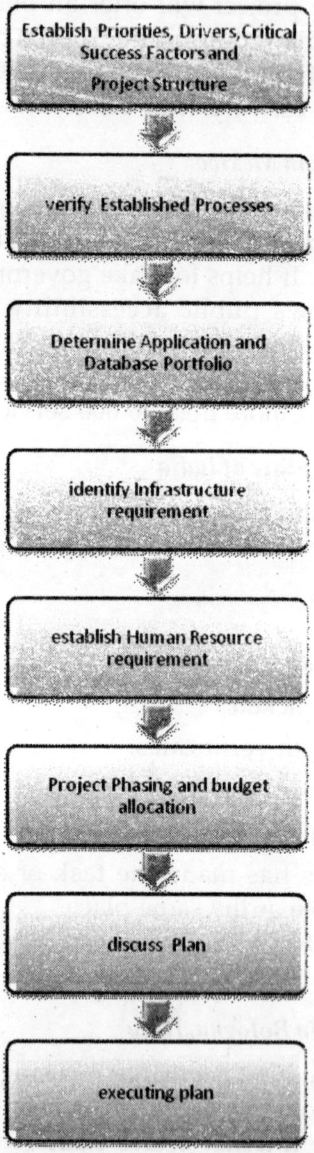

Figure 2: Stages of Development of E-Government Applications

UN e-Government Readiness Index ** Source Wikipedia*

The United Nations Public Administration Network conducts a bi-annual e-Government survey which includes a section titled *e-Government Readiness.* It is a comparative ranking of the countries of the world according to two primary indicators: i) the state of e-government readiness; and ii) the extent of e-participation. Constructing a model for the measurement of digitized services, the Survey assesses the 191 member states of the UN according to a quantitative composite index of e-government readiness based on website assessment; telecommunication infrastructure and human resource endowment.

The following is the list of the top 50 countries according to the UN's 2010 e-Government Readiness Index.

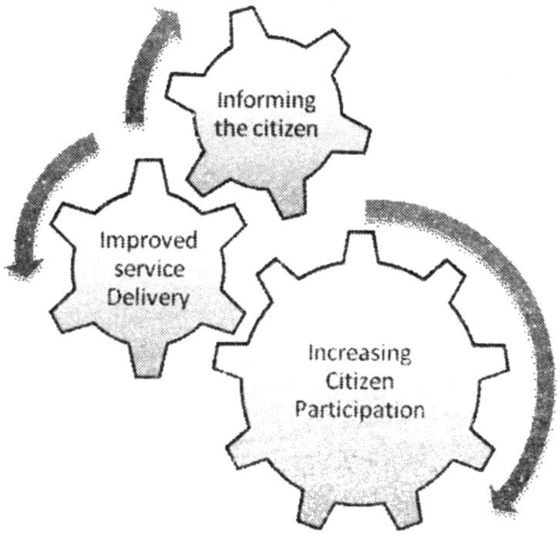

Figure 3: Basic Objectives of E-governance

E-governance Initiatives in India

In India almost all the states have made a creative use of e-governance and Information systems to bring about a paradigm shift in their service delivery methods. The manual work has been overtaken by the inline mode of service delivery. The service delivery kiosks or hubs at centrally located for the easy accessibility to the common people. These counters are usually manned by public or private agencies and they offer a wide spectrum of services under one roof.

Some of the initiatives taken by different states are discussed as follows:

Karnataka

Project Bhoomi

Being an agrarian state it was a cumbersome process to maintain the land records manually. The patwari was the main person who was responsible for the maintainenece, updation and upkeep of the records regarding land ownership, cropping pattern and village maps as per the government procedures. This used to be a tiring process till project Bhoomi was launched. This project helped in the automation of around 20 million records that included 6.7 million farmers. The online record kiosks are popularly known as "Bhoomi Center".

Project 'Bhoomi' very quickly became a huge success as it made the task simpler and the easy accessibility reduced the hardships of the poor farmers in terms of delays, and ensured an accountable and a transparent system.

Madhya Pradesh

Project Gyandoot

Gyandoot is a Government to Citizen Delivery initiative, which has been initiated at Dhar district of Madhya Pradesh in January 2000 with an objective of providing information to the rural population and acting as an interface between the district administration and general public. The basic objective behind this project was to set up and foster a technologically innovative project which is owned and operated by the community itself.

The computers and intranet was installed in twenty village panchayats and these centers were known as *Soochanalayas* which were operated by local rural youth selected for this purpose (called *Soochaks*). The basic services offered by these soochanalayas are

- Daily agricultural commodity rates (*mandi bhav*)
- Income certificate
- Domicile certificate
- Caste certificate
- Public grievance redressal
- Rural Hindi email

Uttar Pradesh

Project Lokvani

Lokvani is a project at Sitapur District in Uttar Pradesh which was initiated in November, 2004. Its objective is to provide a single window to e-Governance solution with regard to handling of grievances, land record maintenance and providing a mixture of essential services. As most of the population in the villages are not educated enough, the programme had to be planned in a way which was user-friendly and within the reach of the people. To achieve this, the programme format uses the local language, Hindi, and is spread throughout the district to a chain of 109 Lokvani Kiosk Centres. These Kiosks have been established by licensing the already existing cyber cafes. The services offered by Lokvani are.

- Availability of land records on the internet
- Online registration, disposal and monitoring of public grievances
- Information of various Government schemes
- Online availability of prescribed Government forms etc

Kerela

Project FRIENDS (Fast, Reliable, Instant, Efficient Network for the Disbursement of Services)

A FRIEND (Fast, Reliable, Instant, and Efficient Network for the Disbursement of Services) provides wide variety of facilities under one roof for citizens to pay taxes and other financial dues to the State Government. It was launched in Thiruvananthapuram in June 2000 and replicated in other district headquarters during 2001-02. The services are provided through FRIENDS *Janasevana Kendrams* located in the district headquarters.

This project is a classic case of attaining front end computerized service delivery to citizens without waiting for completion of back end computerization in various government departments. This project tries to evade the multifaceted issues involved in business process re-engineering in the participating departments.

Rajasthan e-Mitra

This e-Governance initiative obtained its origin from the experiences gained through the LokMitra and *JanMitra* pilot projects launched in 2002. While LokMitra was centered in the city of Jaipur, *JanMitra* was piloted in Jhalawar district to provide information and services under one roof to urban and rural populations.

e-*Mitra* is an amalgamation of these two projects in all the 32 districts using PPP model. There are two major components – 'back office processing' and 'service counters'. Back office processing comprises computerization of participating departments and establishing an IT enabled hub in form of a mini data centre at the district level (e-*Mitra* data centre). All participating departments and the service centres connect to this data centre. It is managed by the Facility Management Service Provider on behalf of the district e-Governance Society Private partners (Local Service Providers) run the kiosks/centres.

Rank	Country	Index
1	South Korea	0.8785
2	United States	0.8510
3	Canada	0.8448
4	United Kingdom	0.8147
5	Netherlands	0.8097
6	Norway	0.8020
7	Denmark	0.7872
8	Australia	0.7863
9	Spain	0.7516
10	France	0.7510
11	Singapore	0.7476
12	Sweden	0.7474
13	Bahrain	0.7363
14	New Zealand	0.7311
15	Germany	0.7309
16	Belgium	0.7225
17	Japan	0.7152
18	Switzerland	0.7136
19	Finland	0.6967
20	Estonia	0.6965
21	Ireland	0.6866
22	Iceland	0.6697
23	Liechtenstein	0.6694
24	Austria	0.6679
25	Luxembourg	0.6672
26	Israel	0.6552
27	Hungary	0.6315
28	Lithuania	0.6295
29	Slovenia	0.6243
30	Malta	0.6129
31	Colombia	0.6125
32	Malaysia	0.6101
33	Czech Republic	0.6060
34	Chile	0.6014
35	Croatia	0.5858
36	Uruguay	0.5848
37	Latvia	0.5826
38	Italy	0.5800
39	Portugal	0.5787
40	Barbados	0.5714
41	Greece	0.5708
42	Cyprus	0.5705
43	Slovakia	0.5639
44	Bulgaria	0.5590
45	Poland	0.5582
46	Kazakhstan	0.5578
47	Romania	0.5479
48	Argentina	0.5467
49	United Arab Emirates	0.5349
50	Kuwait	0.5290

Table 2: UN's 2010 e-Government Readiness Index (*source: www.wikipedia.com*)

Andhra Pradesh

eSeva

This project was designed to provide 'Government to Citizen' and 'e-Business to Citizen' services. Initially, it was implemented in the form of the TWINS (Twin Cities Integrated Network Services) project in 1999 in the twin cities of Hyderabad and Secunderabad. The focus of the e*Seva* project was that all the services are delivered online to consumers / citizens by connecting them to the respective government departments and providing online information at the point of service delivery. The network architecture was designed as an Intranet on a Wide Area Network (WAN). The network is designed in three tiers, 38 each tier being physically located in different places. The first tier for the client-end is located at the e*Seva* centres. The second tier consists of the data servers and the application servers. The third tier comprises Departmental servers as the backend in the concerned departments (Electricity, Municipality, Passport Office, Transport Department, Registration, Commercial Tax, etc). These. Presently, e*Seva* is providing 'One-stop-shop' for over 66 G2Cand B2Cservices in 46 e*Seva* centres in the twin cities and Ranga Reddy district. Centres have also been opened in 20 other districts. The services include online payment of utility bills, issuing certificates, issuing licenses & permits, e-forms etc. Payments can be made by cash/ cheque /DD/credit card/Internet.

Online Services Under National E-Governance Plan

The National e-Governance Plan of Indian Government seeks out to lay the groundwork and provide the momentum for long-term growth of e-Governance within the country. The plan seeks to create the right governance and institutional mechanisms, set up the core infrastructure and policies and implements a number of Mission Mode Projects at the center, state and integrated service levels to create a citizen-centric and business-centric environment for governance.

The Government of India has launched the National e-Governance Plan (NeGP) with the intent to support the expansion of e-governance within the country. The Plan foresees creation of right environments to implement G2G, G2B, G2E and G2C services.

To ensure Interoperability among e-Governance applications, Government of India has setup an Institutional mechanism for formulation of Standards through joint efforts of stakeholders like Department of Information Technology(DIT), National Informatics Centre (NIC), Standardization Testing and Quality Certification(STQC), other Government departments, Academia, Technology Experts, Domain Experts, Industry, BIS, NGOs etc. In this process there is a provision of formal Public review also.

Some of the online services provided under the E-governance plan are:

Income Tax

- E-Filing of Income Tax Returns Online Registration of E-Return Intermediary
- Online Application for Permanent Account Number (PAN)
- Check Status of PAN Application Online
- Online Application for Tax Deduction Account Number (TAN)

Passport/Visa

- Online Status Enquiry of Passport Application

Company Affairs

- Online Company Directory
- Lodge Investor Complaint Online

Central Excise

- Registration for Service Tax Payers
- Registration for Central Excise Assesses
- Know your Service Tax Tariff
- Know your Service Tax Location Code
- e-filing of Central Excise Returns
- e-filing of Service Tax Returns

Pensions

- Online Pension Payment Order (PPO) Status Enquiry

Land Records

- Check your Land Registration Records

Road Transport

- Obtain Driving Licence
- Vehicle Regsitration

Property Registration

- Land/Property Registration

Agriculture

- Check Agricultural Market Prices Online

Municipalities

- Obtain Birth Certificate
- Obtain Death Certificate

Gram Panchayats (Rural)

- Online Collection and Sale of Handicrafts by Rural Artisans

Police

- Online Status of Stolen Vehicles

Employment Exchange

- Register with State Employment Exchanges as a candidate
- Register with State Employment Exchanges as an Employer

E-Courts

- Caselist of Indian Courts

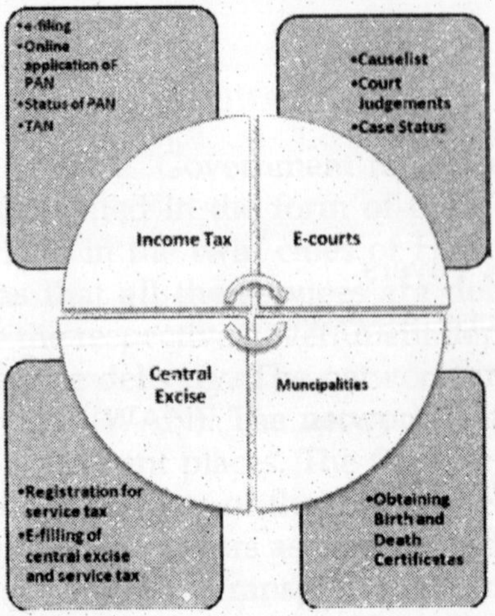

Figure 4: Applications of E-governance

- Court Judgements (JUDIS)
- Daily Court Orders/Case Status

Potential Benefits and Risks of E-Governance

Benefits of E-governance

It is convenient and cost-effective for businesses, and the public benefits by getting easy access to the most current information available without having to spend time, energy and money to get it.

Table 3
E-governance Projects in Different States of India (Source: Dataquest)

Some E-governance Initiatives	
State/Union Territory	*Initiatives covering departmental automation, user charge collection, delivery of policy/programme information and delivery of entitlements*
Andhra Pradesh	e-Seva, CARD, VOICE, MPHS, FAST, e-Cops, AP online-One-stop-shop on the Internet, Saukaryam, Online Transaction processing
Bihar	Sales Tax Administration Management Information
Chattisgarh	Chhattisgarh Infotech Promotion Society, Treasury office, e-linking project
Delhi	Automatic Vehicle Tracking System, Computerization of website of RCS office, Electronic Clearance System, Management Information System for Education etc
Goa	Dharani Project
Gujarat	Mahiti Shakti, request for Government documents online, Form book online, G R book online, census online, tender notice.
Haryana	Nai Disha
Himachal Pradesh	Lok Mitra
Karnataka	Bhoomi, Khajane, Kaveri
Kerala	e-Srinkhala, RDNet, Fast, Reliable, Instant, Efficient Network for the Disbursement of Services (FRIENDS)
Madhya Pradesh	Gyandoot, Gram Sampark, Smart Card in Transport Department, Computerization MP State Agricultural Marketing Board (Mandi Board) etc.
Maharashtra	SETU, Online Complaint Management System-Mumbai
Rajasthan	Jan Mitra, RajSWIFT, Lokmitra, RajNIDHI
Tamil Nadu	Rasi Maiyams–Kanchipuram; Application forms related to public utility, tender notices and display

Contd.

North-Eastern States	
Arunachal Pradesh,	Community Information Center. Forms available on Manipur, Meghalaya, the Meghalaya website under schemes related to Mizoram & Nagaland social welfare, food civil supplies and consumer affairs, housing transport etc.

E-government helps simplify processes and makes access to government information more easily accessible for public sector agencies and citizens. The government benefits from reduced duplication of work. In addition, the processes of data collection, analysis and audit are simplified, and become less tedious. E-governance holds advantages for the business community too, playing the role of a catalyst and a channel for e-business, a fact evidenced

Increased participation: Through the implementation of e governance the government aims at seeking greater citizen participation .Internet acts as a source of communication between civilians all over the country and politicians or public servants. They can voice their opinion and also give their views. A transparent government enables citizens to a larger perspective and this would lead to democratization. The community could turn into a unswerving and major power in government administration to some extent.

Going green: Online government services would lessen the need for hard copy forms and reduce this paper use. Going paperless can save money, boost productivity, save space, make electronic documentation and information sharing easier and minimize environmental damage.

Increased efficiency and convenience: The availability of information on line reduces the time and effort as it is not required to be physically present at the government offices, waiting for the turn.

On the other hand the information requires lesser time to be accessed and processed as compared to hard copies.

Risks of E-governance

There are many considerations and budding implications of introducing e-government, including disintermediation of the government and its citizens, impacts on economic, social, and political factors.

Monitoring: Increased contact between government and its citizens goes both ways. Once e-government begins to build up and become more refined, citizens will be strained to intermingle electronically with the government on a bigger scale. This could potentially lead to a lack of privacy for civilians as the government obtains more and more information on them. This results into loss of privacy of citizens.

Cost: A phenomenal sum of money has been spent on the expansion and implementation of e-government but the outcomes and effects of are often tricky to weigh or are inadequate.

Limited access: This is a major hindrance as the level of literacy is low as well as poverty is the root cause of non accessibility. Citizens are not able to reach the site as a result.

Ambiguity: There is strong questioning whether the information obtained on line is only restricted for the records of the government or for their consumption. The information can be added or deleted as per the desire of the government.

Security concerns and cyber crime

Design of the Study

The present research is Descriptive in nature. **Descriptive research** elucidates data and characteristics about the **population** or phenomenon being studied. Descriptive research answers the questions who, what, where, when and how. Descriptive research is concerned with the present and attempts to determine the status of the phenomena under investigation. Descriptive researchers are oriented towards the description of the present status of a given phenomena. Descriptive research aims to examine the relationships of traits and characteristics.

The present research is the study e-governance. The study has included role of e-governance, its applications, models, use of IT and IS. Apart from this the paper also highlights various benefits and drawbacks of e-governance.

Methodology

The present study shall employ the in-depth analysis of the secondary data available on ethics in academics. The secondary data that has been used is articles, books, journals and previous research work done on the above topic. (The references are given below)

Tools for Data Collection

The data gathering devices were constructed by the researcher herself. The following data gathering devices were used.

- Review of literature
- Visit and review of government portals and websites

Conclusion

The last couple of years have seen emergence of e-governance in India. Though at its infancy but is creating an impact and its presence can be felt via enhanced existing efficiencies, drive down communication costs, and augmented transparency in the execution of various departments. But the growth and extensive development requires computer literacy and infrastructural enlargement across the nation.

References

http://en.wikipedia.org/wiki/E-Government

http://www.it.iitb.ac.in/~prathabk/egovernance/egov.html

http://india.gov.in/govt/studies/annex/6.3.1.pdf

http://www.joaag.com/uploads/5_Monga2EGov3_2_.pdf

http://www.broadllyne.com/Whitepaper%20on%20e-Governance.pdf

http://arc.gov.in/11threp/ARC_11thReport_Ch4.pdf

http://www.dsir.gov.in/a_report/english/2005-06E/Chapter-II-H.pdf

http://www.ijpis.net/issues/no2_2006/IJPIS_no2_2006_p4.pdf

12

SUSTAINABILITY MANAGEMENT- NEED TO FOCUS

Rekha Gulia

Introduction

The world today is facing many problems...Overpopulation, Pollution, Global Warming, War, Stupidity, Obesity/Disease, Habitat Destruction, Species Extinction and the list seems to be endless. The corporate world cannot be isolated from these problems. Rapid economic growth and industrialization have led to the exploitation of natural resources which are limited. The growth of all countries of the world in future is likely to be endangered, if these limited natural resources are completely exhausted. This means that the development should be sustainable and the development in the present should not compromise on the needs of the future generations. Sustainability means living a life of dignity in harmony with nature, creating an economic system that provides for quality of life while renewing the environment and its resources. Sustainability does not (and should not) have a rigid definition. If an environment is not sustained then the ecosystem will overtime fall apart. Overusing one part of an ecosystem can cause the ecosystem to eventually fail. When you overuse one part of an ecosystem then it has dramatic results on the whole ecosystem.

Sustainable management takes the concepts from sustainability and synthesizes them with the concepts of management. Sustainability has three branches: the environment, the needs of present and future generations, and the economy. Using these branches, it creates the ability to keep a system running indefinitely without depleting resources, maintaining economic viability, and also nourishing the needs of the present and future generations. From this sustainable management can be defined as the application of sustainable practices in the categories of businesses, agriculture, society, environment, and personal life by managing them in a way that will benefit current generations and future generations. Sustainable management can be applied to all aspects of our lives. For example, the practices of a business should be sustainable if they wish to stay in businesses, because if the business is unsustainable, then by the definition of sustainability they will cease to be able to be in competition. Communities are in a need of sustainable management, because if the community is to prosper, then the management must be sustainable. Forest and natural resources need to have sustainable management if they are to be able to be continually used by our generation and future generations. Our personal lives also need to be managed sustainably. This can be by making decisions that will help sustain our immediate surroundings and environment, or it can be by managing our emotional and physical well-being.

Objectives

The present paper aims to study the management's role in promoting sustainable practices, benefits such practices accrue; and to identify the practices the firms follow to build their image rather than actually focusing on implementing what they are trying to project to the public.

Methodology

This research is an exploratory research. Secondary data has been used to gather the information. This study highlights that a business that makes the decision to be environmentally-conscious will often promote goodwill among potential customers, while making the world a better place for future generations. Many businesses hesitate to adopt green practices because they fear it will hurt their bottom line and negatively impact profits. They need to focus on the future and follow such practices in true spirit.

Management's Role in Sustainable Management

Management's strategies reflect the mindset of the times. In order to practice sustainable management, one has to be forward thinking, not only in the short term, but also in the long term. Management behavior is a reflection of how accepted conceptions of behavior are defined.. The manager can take some credit for the cultural changes in his or her program, but overall the organization's culture reflects dominant conceptions of the public at that time. This is exemplified through the managerial actions taken during the time periods that lead up to the present day. The sustainability management covers the following areas:

- Top level commitment, culture and decision making
- Future thinking
- What resources are going into business
- Staff
- Operational systems and processes
- What resources are being generated by business
- Relationships and influence
- Communication

To be a manger of sustainability, one needs to be a manger that can control issues and plan solutions that will be sustainable, so that what they put into place will be able to continue for future generations.. Some practical skills that are needed to be able perform the job include:

- Seeing problems/issues
- Being able to set goals/agendas
- Planning Skills
- Creating new ways of doing things (thinking outside the box)
- Taking action when it is needed

- Organizational skills
- Being able to teach, make aware, and train people
- Ability to make tough decisions
- Keeping track of progress
- Taking responsibility
- Ability to project current issues/ideas/plans into the Future
- Possessing whole systems thinking

Benefits of Sustainability

Organizations need to face the fact that the boundaries of accountability are moving fast. The trend towards sustainable management means that organizations are beginning to implement a systems wide approach that links in the various parts of the business with the greater environment at large.

Business leaders from around the world are consistently facing problems. While the perspective on these threats is consistent, the views on the role and responsibility of business differed greatly. These views can be categorized as:

- *Business as bystander.* Leaders in this group feel that problems associated with market capitalism, like income inequality, are most appropriately addressed by government. Business should get out of the way.
- *Business as activist.* In contrast to the first group, leaders in this category don't trust government. They feel that international institutions are inadequate and that business should mobilize and be active in bringing people and organizations together to effect change.
- *Business as entrepreneur.* Members of this group feel that there needs to be a shift in how businesses think and relate to other parts of society. These leaders believe that business can play an important role in addressing social problems. This means transforming how companies do business and measure success.
- *Business as usual.* These leaders feel that the current system of market capitalism is adaptable. They see the current financial crisis as just another bump in the road and believe the system will adapt. As a result, no changes are needed in how business organizations think and relate to the world.

Although some feel that market capitalism solves problems by self-correcting, there is still a belief that business leaders must act ethically. To sustain market capitalism, businesses must earn legitimacy in the eyes of society.

- *Doing the best possible job in operating the company's core business.* This means producing great products, serving customers effectively, treating employees well, and dealing properly with all other constituencies.
- *Committing to good corporate governance practices.* To be legitimate, a company must have good governance.
- Engaging in corporate social responsibility activities.
- *Communicating with the government to try to influence public policy, but not in a self-serving way.*

Economic Benefits of Sustainability

- Direct Cost Savings (energy, water, fuel, procurement)
- Better resale value because of enhanced market image
- Enhanced value - increased value of real estate vis-à-vis a lower cap rate
- Improves retail sales
- Obsolescence reduction - reduced risk of obsolescence = extended asset life
- Demonstration of due diligence
- Easier compliance with environmental regulations
- Risk adverse - reduces risk of litigation, liability, and illness
- Lower health and safety costs
- Lower Absenteeism
- Lower cost of dealing with complaints
- Indicator of management capacity and effectiveness
- Improved Public Relations - free press, product distinction and political support
- Increased Customer Loyalty and Attraction
- Innovation and Development of New Technologies
- Improved image, brand and goodwill
- Increased Profit and Shareholder Value
- Improved Productivity - comfortable environments = happy workers
- Improved Attention and concentration
- Better worker retention and recruitment

Environmental Benefits of Sustainability

- Extended viability term of land
- Conservation of natural resources
- Improvement of air and water quality
- Reduction of Greenhouse Gas Emissions
- Value to Society of Environmental Preservation and Pollution Reduction

Social Equity Benefits of Sustainability

- Greater health and well being
- Increased Employee Retention and Attraction
- Support of environmental/sustainability strategy and vision;
- Enhanced relations with customers, employees and surrounding communities
- Improved employee and community health through cleaner land, air and water

Extended Producer Responsibility

Product Stewardship is often used interchangeably with extended producer responsibility, a similar concept. While both concepts bring the onus of waste management for end-of-life products from the government to the manufacturers, Product Stewardship further extends this responsibility to everyone involved in the life-cycle of the product. This includes not only the manufacturers, but also the retailers, consumers and recyclers as well.

Product stewardship is a concept whereby environmental protection centers around the product itself, and everyone involved in the lifespan of the product is called upon to take up responsibility to reduce its environmental impact. For manufacturers, this includes planning for, and if necessary, paying for the recycling or disposal of the product at the end of its useful life. This may be achieved, in part, by redesigning products to use fewer harmful substances, to be more durable, reusable and recyclable, and to make products from recycled materials. For retailers and consumers, this means taking an active role in ensuring the proper disposal or recycling of an end-of-life product.

Those who advocate it are concerned with the later phases of product lifecycle and the comprehensive outcome of the whole production process. It is considered a pre-requisite to a strict service economy interpretation of (fictional, national, legal) "commodity" and "product" relationships.

The most familiar example is the container-deposit legislation. A fee is paid to buy the bottle, separately from the fee to buy what it contains. If the bottle is returned, the fee is returned, and the supplier must return the bottle for re-use or recycling. If not, the collected fee can be used to pay for landfill or litter control measures. Also, since the same fee can be collected by anyone finding and returning the bottle, it is common for people to collect these and return them as a means of surviving. In general Sustainability principles are

- Reduce dependence upon fossil fuels, underground metals, and minerals
- Reduce dependence upon synthetic chemicals and other unnatural substances
- Reduce encroachment upon nature
- Meet human needs fairly and efficiently

Sustainable Management- A Double Edged Sword

As sustainable management institutions adapt, it becomes imperative that they include an image of sustainable responsibility that is projected for the public to see. This is because firms are socially based organizations. But this can be a double edged sword, because sometimes they end up focusing too much on their image rather than actually focusing on implementing what they are trying to project to the public; this is called green washing. It is important that the execution of sustainable management practices is not put aside while the firm tries to appeal to the public with their sustainable management "practices."

Companies green wash in order to attract consumers and make a profit. As they know that consumers want products that are friendlier to the environment. Yet, for some reason, whether it is lack of funds or willingness, they prefer to give out an eco friendly company image instead of taking actual actions. Visibly, this kind of practice creates many inconveniences for the consumers and the businesses. First of all, when consumers realize that a corporation practices green washing, they lose trust in them. Dishonesty does not attract many clients. From the companies' point of view, if they are willing to take the risk of practicing green washing, they need to know what that implicates. Altogether, greenwashing brings a general doubt to consumers' minds. This lowers their willingness to buy green products and their trust in any green messages. People are no longer as motivated to invest in environmentally friendly products and this is very unfortunate for the business that are actually producing in an eco-friendly way

Examples of green wash

Greenwashers Consulting is a website exemplifying some of the main tactics and strategies of green washing. Some of the examples are.

- Bush Administration's Clear Skies Initiative, which some environmentalists have argued actually weakens air pollution laws.
- Many food products have packaging that evokes an environmentally friendly imagery even though there has been no attempt made at lowering the environmental impact of its production.
- In 2009, European McDonald's changed the colour of their logos from yellow and red to yellow and green.
- An article in *Wired* magazine alleges that slogans are used to suggest environmentally benign business activity: the Comcast eco bill has the slogan of "Paper LESS is MORE" but Comcast uses large amounts of paper for direct marketing.
- The Poland Spring eco shape bottle is touted as "A little natural does a lot of good", although 80% of beverage containers go to the landfill.
- The Airbus A380 airliner is described as "A better environment inside and out" even though air travel has a high negative environment cost. .
- The Advertising Standards Authority in the UK upheld several complaints against major car manufacturers including Suzuki, SEAT, Toyota and Lexus who made erroneous claims about their vehicles
- Kimberly Clark's claim of "Pure and Natural" diapers in green packaging. The product uses organic cotton on the outside, and adds some aloe and vitamin E, but keeps the same petrochemical gel on the inside. Pampers also claims that "Dry Max" diapers reduce landfill waste by reducing the amount of paper fluff in the diaper, which really is a way for Pampers to save money.
- EBay recently created a green hub promoting preowned and sustainable products.
- Ubisoft recently announced that it would no longer include paper manuals with their Playstation 3 or XBox 360 games, claiming that this cost-cutting measure was for the purposes of being environmentally friendly.

Micro-sustainability

Micro-sustainability focuses on the small environmental actions that when calculated collectively result in a large environmental impact. Micro-sustainability centers on individual efforts, behavior modification and creating attitudinal changes, which result in an environmentally conscious individual or community. Micro-sustainability encourages sustainable changes through change agents, which are individuals that are encouraged; and therefore, foster positive environmental action inside their own sphere of influence. Examples of micro-sustainability include recycling, turning off lights when not in use, programming thermostats for efficient use of energy, reducing water usage through conservation, changing driving habits or patterns in order to use less gasoline or modifying buying habits or behaviors in order to reduce waste and consumption.

Economic Opportunity

The economic importance of nature is indicated by the use of the ecosystem services to highlight the market relevance of an increasingly scarce natural world that can no longer be regarded as both unlimited and free. In general, as a commodity or service becomes scarcer the price increases and this acts as a restraint that encourages frugality, technical innovation and alternative products. However, this only applies when the product or service falls within the market system. As ecosystem services are generally treated as economic externalities they are unpriced and therefore overused and degraded. Treating the environment as an externality may generate short-term profit at the expense of sustainability. Sustainable business practices, on the other hand, integrate ecological concerns with social and economic ones. Growth that depletes ecosystem services is sometimes termed "uneconomic growth" as it leads to a decline in quality of life. Minimizing such growth can provide opportunities for local businesses. For example, industrial waste can be treated as an "economic resource in the wrong place". The benefits of waste reduction include savings from disposal costs, fewer environmental penalties, and reduced liability insurance. This may lead to increased market share due to an improved public image. Energy efficiency can also increase profits by reducing costs.

As global population and affluence has increased, so has the use of various materials (Included here are raw materials, minerals, synthetic chemicals (including hazardous substances), manufactured products, food, living organisms and waste), increased in volume, diversity and distance transported. Sustainable use of materials has targeted the idea of dematerialization, converting the linear path of materials (extraction, use, disposal in landfill) to a circular material flow that reuses materials as much as possible, much like the cycling and reuse of waste in nature. This approach is supported by product stewardship and the increasing use of material flow analysis at all levels, especially individual countries and the global economy.

Every economic activity produces material that can be classified as waste. To reduce waste industry, business and government are now mimicking nature by turning the waste produced by industrial metabolism into resource. Dematerialization is being encouraged through the ideas of industrial ecology, ecodesign and ecolabelling. In addition to the well-established "reduce, reuse and recycle" shoppers are using their purchasing power for ethical consumerism.

Sustainable use of materials has targeted the idea of dematerialization, converting the linear path of materials (extraction, use, disposal in landfill) to a circular material flow that reuses materials as much as possible, much like the cycling and reuse of waste in nature. This approach is supported by product stewardship and the increasing use of material flow analysis at all levels, especially individual countries and the global economy.

Conclusion

Companies must make the connection between sustainability as a vision and sustainability as a practice. Managers need to think systematically and realistically about the application of traditional business principles to environmental problems. By melding the two concepts together, new ideas of business principles emerge and can enable some companies-those with the right industry structure, competitive position, and managerial skills- to deliver increased value to shareholders while making improvements in their environmental performance.

References

http://en.wikipedia.org/wiki/Sustainable_development

http://en.wikipedia.org/wiki/Product_stewardship

Ottman JA, Stafford ER, Hartman CL. (2006), "Avoiding Green Marketing Myopia", The Environment, Vol-48, No.-5, June, pp.22-26.

Frankel, C. (1992), "Blueprint for Green Marketing", Marketing Executive Review, 2(5).

http://www.grist.org/article/2010-02-01-how-personal-actions-can-kick-start-a-sustaina bility-revolution

http://www.thejakartapost.com/news/2008/08/28/commentary-when-csr-neither-profit-nor-public-good.html.

PART TWO

Dynamics of Finance & Sustainable Development

13

STATE OF COMMODITY AND DERIVATIVE MARKET PERFORMANCE IN INDIA

Khyser Mohd.

Introduction

Commodity Market: India commodity market consists of both the retail and the wholesale market in the country. The commodity market in India facilitates multi commodity exchange within and outside the country based on requirements. Commodity trading is one facility that investors can explore for investing their money. The India Commodity market has undergone lots of changes due to the changing global economic scenario; thus throwing up many opportunities in the process. Demand for commodities both in the domestic and global market is estimated to grow by four times than the demand currently is by the next five years.

A commodity may be defined as an article, a product or material that is bought and sold. It can be classified as every kind of movable property, except Actionable Claims, Money & Securities.

Commodities actually offer immense potential to become a separate asset class for market-savvy investors, arbitrageurs and speculators. Commodity markets are markets where raw or primary products are exchanged. These raw commodities are traded on regulated commodities exchanges, in which they are bought and sold in standardized contracts.

Derivative Market

Despite of encouraging growth and developments, derivatives market has not yet, realized its full potential in terms of growth & trading. Analysts points out that the equity derivative markets on the BSE and NSE has been limited to only four products- index futures, index options and individual stock futures and options, which in turn, are limited to certain selected stocks only. The growth percentage of Indian infant derivatives market shows the potential opportunities for its development in near future. And it catches the attention of traders, even in the global level as the economy is flourishing even after the financial crisis.

The term 'derivatives', refers to a broad class of financial instruments which mainly include options and futures. These instruments derive their value from the price and other related variables of the underlying asset. Increased financial risk causes losses to normal profitable organizations. There is need to have a strategy of risk management to hedge against uncertainty. Derivatives provide an effective solution to the problem of risk caused by uncertainty and volatility in underlying asset.

Significance

The Indian economy is witnessing a mini revolution in commodity and derivatives and risk management. Commodity trading in India is still at its early days and thus requires an aggressive growth plan with innovative ideas. Liberal policies in commodity trading will definitely boost the commodity trading. The commodities and future market in the country is regulated by Forward Markets commission (FMC).

With the globalization of trade and relatively free movement of financial assets, risk management through derivatives products has become a necessity in India also, like in other developed and developing countries.

India, a commodity based economy where two-third of the one billion population depends on agricultural commodities, surprisingly has an under developed commodity market. Unlike the physical market, futures markets trades in commodity are largely used as risk management (hedging) mechanism on either physical commodity itself or open positions in commodity stock. As Indian businesses become more global in their approach, evolution of a broad based, active and liquid forex derivatives markets is required to provide them with a spectrum of hedging products for effectively managing their foreign exchange exposures.

Need

Despite having a robust economy, India's share in the global commodity market is not as big as estimated. Except gold the share in other sectors of the commodity market is not very significant. India accounts for 3% of the global oil demands and 2% of global copper demands. In agriculture India's contribution to international trade volume is rather less compared to the huge production base available. Various infrastructure development projects that are being undertaken in India are being seen as a key growth driver in the coming days.

Increased financial risk causes losses to even a profitable organization. This needs strategy of risk management to hedge against uncertainty. Derivatives provide an effective solution to the problem of risk caused by uncertainty and volatility in underlying asset. Derivatives are risk management tools that help the organization to effectively transfer risk.

Objectives

The main objectives of the study are;

- T study the Commodity Group-wise Value of Trade
- To study the percentage performance trend of index futures
- To study the percentage performance trend of stock futures
- To study the percentage performance trend index options
- To study the percentage performance trend of stock futures

Scope

The study period is limited to past decade, that is from 2001 to 2010 for Indian derivatives market and it is limited 2000-2008 in case of global derivative market.

Methodology

The data has been collected from websites of BSE, NSE , SEBI Bulletin and other secondary sources. Simple statistical tool Trend Percentages are calculated and descriptive research methodology is used.

Limitations

The data compiled is subject to the limitation in the data collection method used by the concerned authorities.

Current Scenario

This decade is termed as Decade of Commodities. Prices of all commodities are heading northwards due to rapid increase in demand for commodities. Developing countries like China are voraciously consuming the commodities. That's why globally commodity market is bigger than the stock market India is one of the top producers of large number of commodities and also has a long history of trading in commodities and related derivatives. The Commodities Derivatives market has seen ups and downs, but seems to have finally arrived now. The market has made enormous progress in terms of Technology, transparency and trading activity.

As majority of Indian investors are not aware of organized commodity market; their perception about is of risky to very risky investment. Many of them have wrong impression about commodity market in their minds. It makes them specious towards commodity market. Concerned authorities have to take initiative to make commodity trading process easy and simple. Along with Government efforts NGO's should come forward to educate the people about commodity markets and to encourage them to invest in to it. There is no doubt that in near future commodity market will become Hot spot for Indian farmers rather than spot market. And producers, traders as well as consumers will be benefited from it. But for this to happen one has to take initiative to standardize and popularize the Commodity Market.

Though introduced in 2000, financial derivatives market in India has shown a remarkable growth both in terms of volumes and numbers of traded contracts. NSE alone accounts for 99 percent of the derivatives trading in Indian markets. The entry of new instrument 'derivatives' has been well received by stock market players. Trading in derivatives gained popularity soon after its introduction. In due course, the turnover of the NSE derivatives market exceeded the turnover of the NSE cash market (refer table).

Analysis and Findings

Analysis of Commodity Market

The year 2003 is a watershed in the history of commodity futures market. The last group of 54 prohibited commodities was opened up for forward trading, along with establishment and recognition of three new national exchanges with on-line trading and professional management. Not only was prohibition on forward trading completely withdrawn, including in sensitive commodities such as wheat, rice, sugar and pulses which earlier committees had reservations about, the new exchanges brought capital, technology and innovation to the market. These markets notched up phenomenal growth in terms of number of products on offer, participants, spatial distribution and volume of trade. Starting with trade in 7 commodities till 1999, futures trading is now available in 95 commodities. There are more then 3000 members registered with the exchanges. More than 20,000 terminals spread over more than 800 towns/cities of the country provide access to trading platforms. The volume of trade has increased exponentially since 2003-04 to reach Rs. 36.77 lakh crore in 2006-07. Almost all of this (97.2%) of this is now accounted for by the three national exchanges. The other 21 Exchanges have a miniscule share in the total volume.

The growth in commodity futures trade has spawned an upsurge of interest in a number of associated fields, viz. research, education and training activities in commodity markets, commodity reporting for print and visual media, collateral management, commodity finance, ware-housing, assaying and certification, software development, electronic spot exchanges etc. Markets and fields almost non-existent four years ago now attract significant mind-share nationally and internationally.

Table 1
Commodity Group-wise Value of Trade

(Rs. Lakh Crores)

Commodity Groups	*2004-05*	*2005-06*	*2006-07*	*2007-08*
Bullion and other metals	1.80(31.47)	7.79(36.15)	21.29(57.90)	26.24(64.55)
Agriculture	3.90(68.18)	11.92(55.31)	13.17(35.82)	9.41(23.15)
Energy	0.02(0.35)	1.82(8.45)	2.31(6.28)	5.00(12.30)
Others	0.00(0.00)	0.02(0.09)	0.001(0.00)	(0.00)(0.00)
Total	5.72(100.00)	21.55(100.00)	36.77(100.00)	40.65(100.00)

Note: Figures in parenthesis indicate percentage to total value

Futures contracts are available for major agricultural commodities, metals and energy. Commodity group-wise value of trading since 2004-05 is given in **Table–1.** Although agricultural commodities led the initial spurt, and constituted the largest proportion of the total value of trade till 2005-06 (55.32%), this place was taken over by bullion and metals in 2006-07. The growth in 2006-07 was almost wholly (88.7%) accounted for by bullion and metals, with agricultural commodities contributing a small fraction (10.7%). This was partly due to the stringent regulations, like margins and open interest limits, imposed on agriculture commodities and the dampening of sentiments due to suspension of trade in few commodities. Futures market growth in 2006-07 appears to have bypassed agriculture commodities.

Table 2
Index Futures

			Percentage Growth Over Previous Year	
Year	*No. of Contracts*	*Turnover (Rs. in Crores)*	*No. of Contracts*	*Turnover*
2000-01	90,580	2,365	-	-
2001-02	1,025,588	21,483	1032	808
2002-03	2,126,763	43,952	107	105
2003-04	17,191,668	554,446	708	1161
2004-05	21,635,449	772,147	26	39
2005-06	58,537,886	1,513,755	171	96
2006-07	81,487,424	2,539,574	39	68
2007-08	156,598,579	3,820,667	92	50
2008-09	210,428,103	3,570,111	35	-7
2009-10	178,306,889	3,934,389	-15	10

Moreover, there has been a very significant decline in volume of futures trade in agriculture commodities during the year 2007-08, by 28.5%. The overwhelming bulk of this decline is accounted for by Chana, Maize, Mentha Oil, Guar seed, Potato, Guar Gum, Chillies and Cardamom. Trade in these eight commodities, which accounted for 57.9% of total futures trade in agricultural commodities in 2006-07, declined by over 66.4% during 2007-08 compared to previous year. The decline in these eight commodities exceeded the decline of futures trading volumes in all agricultural commodities taken together.

The decade study of index futures trading clearly indicates that in the initial years(200-2002) of introduction of derivatives in India, the growth in number of contracts and turn over was considerably high, but the very next year(2002-03) it is comparatively decreased. In the year 2003-04, there is a significant growth again in the number of contracts and turn over. There is apparent decrease in the business in the year 2004-05, and the following the trend considerable growth in alternative years. In the year 2007-09, the number of contracts increased but the turn over for the years was low touching even the negative figure in comparison to the past year. In the last year that is 2009-10, there is a decrease in the number of contracts, and turn over is also considerably low.

Table 3
Stock Futures

			Percentage Growth Over Previous Year	
Year	*No. of Contracts*	*Turnover (Rs. in Crores)*	*No. of Contracts*	*Turnover*
2000-01	-	-	-	-
2001-02	1,957,856	51,515	-	-
2002-03	10,676,843	286,533	445	456
2003-04	32,368,842	1,305,939	203	356
2004-05	47,043,066	1,484,056	45	14
2005-06	80,905,493	2,791,697	72	88
2006-07	104,955,401	3,830,967	122	37
2007-08	203,587,952	7,548,563	1	97
2008-09	221,577,980	3,479,642	-37	-54
2009-10	145,591,240	5,195,247	-41	49

The table clearly presents the growth trend of stock futures, that the initial years 2002-04 the growth was good, but the next couple of years 2004-06 there is an overall decrease in the growth. In the year 2006-07 there is considerable growth in the derivative market in terms of number of contracts, not in terms of turn over. The trend study of stock futures clearly presents the down ward movement of the market in terms of number of contracts and turn over the year 2007-08. Consecutive years further, 2008 to 2010, the business was decreased making the turnover very low.

The study of index option market for the last decade shows that in the initial years that is 2001-03, there was a encouraging growth of the market, but in the following year 2003-04, it decreased, In the year 2005-06, the number contracts and the turn over increased significantly. But in the year 2006-08, there is a decline in the business, the subsequent year 2008-09 saw considerable growth in terms of number of contracts is similar to that percent growth of 2003-04 but the business is considerably low. The following year that is 2009-10 also the growth rate decreased a maximum extent.

Table 4
Index Options

Year	No. of Contracts	Turnover (Rs. in Crores)	Percentage Growth Over Previous Year: No. of Contracts	Turnover
2000-01	-	-	-	-
2001-02	175,900	3,765	-	-
2002-03	442,241	9,246	151	146
2003-04	1,732,414	52,816	292	471
2004-05	3,293,558	121,943	90	131
2005-06	12,935,116	338,469	293	178
2006-07	25,157,438	791,906	95	134
2007-08	55,366,038	1,362,111	120	72
2008-09	212,088,444	3,731,502	283	174
2009-10	341,379,523	8,027,964	61	115

Table 5
Stock Options

Year	No. of Contracts	Turnover (Rs. in Crores)	Percentage Growth Over Previous Year: No. of Contracts	Turnover
2000-01	-	-	-	-
2001-02	1,037,529	25,163	-	-
2002-03	3,523,062	100,131	240	298
2003-04	5,583,071	217,207	58	117
2004-05	5,045,112	168,836	-10	-22
2005-06	5,240,776	180,253	4	7
2006-07	5,283,310	193,795	1	8
2007-08	9,460,631	359,137	79	85
2008-09	13,295,970	229,227	41	-36
2009-10	14,016,270	506,065	5	121

From the study of percentage growth of stock option for the past ten years, it is observed there is a tremendous growth in the year 2001-02 in terms of number of contracts and turnover but in the consecutive years the growth is there but comparatively low. In the year 2007-08, it is appreciable to some extent and again there is a considerable decrease in the growth of derivative market in India.

Table 6
India-trend in Turnover of Derivatives Trading

Year	No. of Contracts	Turnover (Rs. in Crores)	Percentage Growth Turnover Over Previous Year
2000-01	90580	2365	-
2001-02	4196873	101926	4210
2002-03	16768909	439862	332
2003-04	56886776	2130610	384
2004-05	77017185	2546982	20
2005-06	157619271	4824174	89
2006-07	216883573	7356242	52
2007-08	425013200	13090477.75	78

The table presents the fact that India being in the infant stage of derivative market has experienced a remarkable growth though decreasing growth or trend for the decade.

Findings

The Indian stock market has seen many ups and downs during the last year. It was a series of scams such as 2G scam, housing loan bribery, weak global markets, etc. that led to the sensex and nifty plunging down badly creating a panicky situation during the last phase. And the last week saw the nifty and sensex crossing the 6,000 and 20,000 marks respectively. As per market analysts the share market of India will exhibit positive trends this year with negligible falls. So, there are rays of hope for the investors, especially ambitious investors who are all geared up to make that extra money with their dedicated efforts. For novice investors, the Indian stock market can no doubt turn out to be a lucrative platform only with proper knowledge.

Conclusion

The Indian forex derivatives market is still in a nascent stage of development but offers tremendous growth potential. The development of a vibrant forex derivatives market in India would critically depend on the growth in the underlying spot/forward markets, growth in the rupee derivative markets along with the evolution of a supporting regulatory structure. Factors such as market liquidity, investor behavior, regulatory structure and tax laws will have a heavy bearing on the behavior of market variables in this market. India is one of the top producers of a large number of commodities, and also has a long history of trading in commodities and related derivatives. The commodities derivatives market has seen ups and downs, but seem to have finally arrived now. The market has made enormous progress in terms of technology, transparency and the trading activity. Interestingly, this has happened only after the Government protection was removed from a number of commodities, and market forces were allowed to play their role. This should act as a major lesson for the policy makers in developing countries, that pricing and price risk management should be left to the market forces rather than trying to achieve these through administered price mechanisms. The management of price risk is going to assume even greater importance in future with the promotion of free trade and removal of trade barriers in the world. All this augurs well for the commodity derivatives markets.

References

Trading Statistics of Derivative Segment at BSE, *(www.bseindia.com)*

Bodla, B.S. and Jinda K. (2008), "Equity Derivatives in India", The ICFAI Journal of Derivatives market, Vol-V No.1, pp. 62-82.

Growth of Derivatives Market in India *www.Valuenotes.com/njain/nj-derivatives*

Haush A.S.(2001), 'Potential Derivatives Market in India', The ICFAI Journal of Applied Finance Vol-7, No.5, pp. 1-24.

www.nseindia.com

www.world-exchanges.org

www.businessmapofindia.com

www.icwai.org

www.newyorkfed.org

www.taxmann.net

14

FII AND ITS IMPACT ON INDIAN STOCK MARKET

Pritpal Singh Bhullar & Nipun Aggarwal

Introduction

With the globalization and change in technology, the world has become like a village. All countries seem to be houses of this village. If our ancestors come on earth now, then they would not be able to recognize that they have spent their whole life on this place. 60-70 years ago, due to the lack of technology, people were likely to stay on one place. For them that place was the whole world. They were immunized from what happen on other regions of world. But with the globalization the whole world went shrinked. People from different countries started dealing with each other. Now countries were not immunized as before. Every country's economy somehow depends upon other country because of their interdependence of business. Due to this interdependency, there are some factors which have accumulated affect on the economy of whole world. Due to this reason we can see the effect of the recession due to subprime crisis in US economy over the whole world. All big economies of world come under the threat fire of this recession. The economy of India was also not immunized from this virus of recession. The performance of Sensex and Nifty fall down by 51 % within one year that is year 2008. This makes us curious about knowing the various factors which affect Indian economy during year 2008. So for doing this project, we took stocks of 10 industries which include 46 companies and check the performance of their stocks throughout the year. Then we noticed various other events which happened during the year and affect the economy of India as well as economy of world. This helps us to enrich our knowledge about various factors that have huge impact on economy of any country.

FII

FII stands for foreign institutional investors. These are the one who are from one country and invested in some other country. These are known as short term investors. These may be NRIs or any corporate bodies. They have to register themselves to SEBI (Securities and Exchange Board Of India). In India 1484 FIIs have registered to SEBI for participating in Indian market. They are free to pull out their money any time from the market whenever they want. They have huge impact on economy on the country in which they invested. When they invested in some countries it has positive impact. It provides strong financial base to the companies. It boosts the economy of that country. But when they pull out their money they put companies in deep water. The same thing happened in year 2008 in India.

During the year 2008, the economy of world face the recession after 1921. The sub – prime crisis of us affected the major economies of the world. Indian stock market touched its peak on 10th January 2008. It reached at 21000. All this happened because of FIIs inflow of money. But due to US recession, many investment banks got bankrupted. This all sucked the liquidity in US market. To provide liquidity in their home market, FIIs withdrew their investment from Indian market. This outflow of money from Indian market causes the crash of Indian market in financial year 2008. In year 2008 FIIs invested approximately $ 17 billion but during the same year FIIs pull out $13 billion from Indian market. FIIs showed their keenly interest in investing in debt market. Due to the interest rate in Japan was near to zero, FIIs from Japan showed their interest in investment in India.

The following tables show the monthly analysis of investment done by FIIs in year 2008 in India. It shows how much money they have put in equities and debts and how much money they pull out from equities and debt.

FIIs Investment in Equity in Year 2008

Month	*Purchase*	*Sale*	*Net Investment*
January	103678.20	116713.90	-13035.70
February	73776.60	72043.20	1733.30
March	71159.40	71289.90	-130.40
April	62516.00	61441.00	1074.80
May	58813.70	63825.20	-5011.50
June	62840.80	72936.70	-10095.80
July	63563.30	65400.40	-1836.80
August	47560.20	48771.90	-1211.70
September	66496.20	74774.80	-8278.10
October	49431.30	64778.60	-15347.30
November	30416.10	33013.80	-2598.30
December	31355.20	29604.90	1750.10

FIIs investment in Debt in Year 2008

Month	*Purchase (Rs. Crores)*	*Sell (Rs. Crores)*	*Net Investment (Rs. Crores)*
January	5656.40	3702.70	1953.80
February	5521.80	3025.00	2496.80
March	0.00	879.70	-879.70
April	-186.90	1514.80	-1701.70
May	152.40	315.30	-162.90
June	312.70	1311.30	-998.70
July	6082.30	2463.50	3618.90
August	2579.30	1321.60	1257.80
September	7018.70	3204.20	3204.20
October	2855.30	4713.60	-1858.10
November	9072.60	4857.50	4215.00
December	8955.50	8328.60	626.50

Analysis of Share Price of Differnet Companies in Year 2008

Sector	*Highest*	*Date*	*Lowest*	*Date*	*Highest Closing*	*Date*	*Lowest Closing*	*Date*
Infrastruct								
GMR INFRA	260.4	4/1/08	45.5	27/10/08	252.6	4/1/08	49.5	27/10/08
DLF	1225	14/1/08	154.1	27/10/08	1207.5	14/01/08	178.7	1/12/08
RELINFRA	1478.45	16/5/08	352.75	27/10/08	1462.95	16/5/08	382.6	24/10/08
MAYTASINFRA	932	1/1/08	155.55	31/12/08	912.9	1/1/08	162.15	31/12/08
UNITECH	546.8	2/1/08	21.95	28/11/08	538.25	2/1/08	23.15	28/11/08
IVRCL	627	9/1/08	57	27/10/08	571.2	4/1/08	63.75	27/10/08
Pharma								
CIPLA	244.95	23/07/08	146.7	28/01/08	240.7	20/08/08	160.1	24/10/08
RANBAXY	637.7	19/06/08	163.5	29/10/08	597.5	18/06/08	168.75	29/10/08
SUNPHARMA	1556.9	10/9/08	870	24/01/08	1539.85	8/9/08	925.5	24/01/08
Telecom								
AIRTEL	1010.9	23/1/08	483	27/10/08	975.9	8/1/08	537.1	24/10/08
RCOM	844.7	10/1/08	147.3	27/10/08	821.55	9/1/08	182	20/11/08
TATA TELE	580	27/3/08	323.05	27/10/08	562.8	26/3/08	352.45	3/7/08
IDEA	149.5	15/1/08	34	27/10/08	147.4	15/1/08	36.85	24/10/08
Cement								
ACC	1038.7	1/1/08	365	27/10/08	1028.35	1/1/08	397.1	25/11/08
AMBUJA	149	1/1/08	43	24/10/08	148.55	1/1/08	44.9	24/10/08
Banks								
ICICI	1455.5	14/01/08	283.1	27/10/2008	1435.5	11/1/08	308.5	24/10/2008
HDFC	1825	14/01/08	809	20/11/2008	1788.95	15/01/2008	821.2	20/11/2008
SBIN	2574	4/1/08	965.65	2/7/2008	2464.55	8/1/2008	1025.3	1/7/2008
PNB	720	3/1/08	330.1	2/7/2008	711.35	2/1/2008	350.9	1/7/2008
BANK OF INDIA	465	17/1/08	189.5	1/7/2008	448	17/01/2008	197.9	1/7/2008
BANK OF BARODA	501	3/1/08	188.2	2/7/2008	492.4	3/1/2008	194.75	1/7/2008
IT								
TCS	1077	1/1/2008	415.35	27/10/2008	1054.55	1/1/2008	453.85	17/10/2008
INFOSYS	2046.5	6/6/2008	1040	10/10/2008	1993.55	6/6/2008	1102.3	15/12/2008
WIPRO	535	6/6/2008	180.4	27/10/2008	516	1/1/2008	218.7	20/11/2008
SATYAM	542	2/6/2008	114.55	26/12/2008	524.9	29/5/2008	134.65	26/12/2008
HCL	334.45	1/1/2008	102	15/12/2008	322.05	1/1/2008	103.85	15/12/2008
Energy								
SUZLON	2299	9/1/2008	36.2	2/12/2008	2273.05	8/1/2008	36.9	2/12/2008
NTPC	290.75	15/01/2008	113	27/10/2008	284.65	14/01/2008	125.75	27/10/2008
TATA POWER	1649.8	4/1/2008	530.1	27/10/2008	1629.15	4/1/2008	567.25	27/10/2008
RPOWER	530	11/2/2008	81	27/10/2008	450	25/2/2008	89.65	27/10/2008
POWER GRID	156	4/1/2008	52	27/10/2008	3/1/2008	151.8	58	27/10/2008
Automobile								
MARUTI	1009.95	2/1/2008	433	2/12/2008	997.05	2/1/2008	460	2/12/2008
TATA MOTORS	824.1	4/1/2008	126.45	20/11/2008	793.55	2/1/2008	126.2	20/11/2008
M&M	873.9	1/1/2008	235	3/12/2008	865.1	1/1/2008	243.2	3/12/2008
BAJAJ AUTO	898	26/05/2008	262	2/12/2008	632.4	12/9/2008	301.9	2/12/2008
HERO HONDA	898	3/10/2008	550	22/1/2008	888.4	3/10/2008	592.8	22/1/2008
SWARAJ MAZDA	398	15/1/2008	171.3	27/10/2008	352.7	15/1/2008	175.3	24/12/2008
Steel & Aluminium								
SAIL	290.4	1/1/2008	55.25	20/11/2008	281.1	1/1/2008	58.6	20/11/08
TATA STEEL	957	1/1/2008	137.5	24/11/2008	933.5	9/1/2008	148.8	2/12/2008
HINDALCO	221.4	3/1/2008	38	27/10/2008	219.9	4/1/2008	40.4	27/10/2008
NATINALALUM	566.45	29/5/2008	105.25	27/10/2008	552.05	28/05/2008	139.3	27/10/2008
BHEL	2610	1/1/2008	981	27/10/2008	2583.6	1/1/2008	1079.85	27/10/2008

Contd.

Sector	*Highest*	*Date*	*Lowest*	*Date*	*Highest Closing*	*Date*	*Lowest Closing*	*Date*
Petroleum & Gas								
ONGC	1356	4/1/2008	538.15	27/10/2008	1343.1	4/1/2008	611.8	27/10/2008
RPL	259.8	8/1/2008	68.2	21/11/2008	250.75	7/1/2008	69.95	20/11/2008
IOCL	803.9	1/1/2008	300	27/10/2008	785.1	3/1/2008	314.25	27/10/2008
GAIL	555.5	1/1/2008	164.5	27/10/2008	543	1/1/2008	183.2	20/11/2008

In the above analysis we took 10 major sectors and 46companies belongs to that sectors. For this analysis we took data of the share price of all that companies throughout the year. Then we took the highest intraday price and lowest intraday price of every company in the year 2008. We also check the highest closing price and lowest closing price of the company. From this analysis we came to know when all these companies gave their best and worst performance and at what date? From this analysis we got on what particular date most of the companies touched their highest price and lowest price. We can see that on 27th October most of the companies got their lowest price. Thus we got a clue that on 27th October 2008 most of the companies touched the lowest intra-day price and lowest closing price of their stocks of the year 2008. The month of January 2008 was the bullish month for most of the sectors. Most of the companies touched their highest intra-day price and highest closing price in the month of January.

Analysis of Companies's Volatility in Year 2008

Sector	*Closing Price on 1st Jan.*	*Closing Price on 31st Dec.*	*Fall in 2008*	*% Fall in 2008*	*Volatility*
Infrastructure					
GMR INFRA	250.25	76.9	-173.35	-69.2707292	4.966495254
DLF	1071.25	282.15	-789.1	-73.6616102	5.354283767
RELINFRA	1462.95	579.5	-883.45	-60.3882566	6.060490585
MAYTAS INFRA	932	162.15	-769.85	-82.6019313	4.299367121
UNITECH	507.3	40.65	-466.65	-91.9869899	7.495322768
IVRCL	543.4	143.75	-399.65	-73.5461906	5.793223811
Pharma					
CIPLA	211.1	186.6	-24.5	-11.6058739	2.577558179
RANBAXY	423.35	252.35	-171	-40.3921105	3.986026051
SUNPHARMA	1197.9	1064.15	-133.75	-11.1653727	2.808637221
Cement					
ACC	1028.35	480.15	-548.2	-53.3086984	3.174390155
AMBUJA	148.55	70.05	-78.5	-52.8441602	3.504684654
Banks					
ICICI	1028.35	448.1	-780.65	-63.5320447	4.976384686
HDFC	148.55	998.35	-731.15	-42.2752240	3.626502067
SBIN	1028.35	1288.8	-1094.7	-45.9282567	3.667503547
PNB	148.55	526.7	-144.6	21.54029495	3.549984083
BANK OF INDIA	1028.35	287.05	-86.85	-23.2281358	4.263684077
BANK OF BARODA	148.55	280	-195.15	-41.0712406	3.809687541
IT					
TCS	1054.55	498.3	-556.25	-52.7476174	3.624817602
INFOSYS	1746.85	1132.1	-614.75	-35.1919168	3.072565511
WIPRO	516	243.7	-272.3	-52.7713178	3.703507902

Contd.

Sector	Closing Price on 1st Jan.	Closing Price on 31st Dec.	Fall in 2008	% Fall in 2008	Volatility
SATYAM	443.65	177.2	-266.45	-60.0586047	4.44673838
HCL	322.05	122.3	-199.75	-62.0245303	4.334455237
Energy					
SUZLON	1950.45	62.3	-1888.15	-96.80586531	12.1384569
NTPC	257.45	180.6	-76.85	-29.8504564	3.374075339
TATA POWER	1543.75	749.15	-794.6	-51.47206478	4.212429754
RPOWER	372.3	119.95	-252.35	-67.78135912	5.496038644
POWER GRID	146.6	83.15	-63.45	-43.28103683	3.685912927
Automobile					
MARUTI	991.55	520.2	-471.35	-47.53668499	3.135062283
TATA MOTORS	762.35	159.85	-602.5	-79.03194071	4.031350132
M&M	865.1	274.5	-590.6	-68.26956421	3.948722838
BAJAJ AUTO	604.75	391.1	-213.65	-35.3286482	3.96877523
HERO HONDA	698.45	803.65	105.2	15.06192283	2.621696438
SWARAJ MAZDA	330.2	216.5	-113.7	-34.43367656	4.764800705
Steel & Alumimium					
SAIL	281.1	77.5	-203.6	-72.42974031	4.638143324
TATA STEEL	932.25	217.2	-715.05	-76.70152856	4.671030203
HINDALCO	215.5	51.4	-164.1	-76.14849188	4.63563861
NATIONAL ALUM	509.1	189.45	-319.65	-62.78727166	4.907240318
BHEL	2583.6	1362.6	-1221	-47.25963771	3.791761002
Petroleum & Gas					
ONGC	1249.9	667.1	-582.8	-46.62773022	3.304074718
RPL	226.3	87.2	-139.1	-61.4670791	4.103174191
IOCL	777.3	426	-351.3	-45.19490544	3.470970357
GAIL	543	206.25	-336.75	-62.01657459	0.044714618
Telecomm					
AIRTEL	967.6	715.5	-252.1	-26.054154	3.295607654
RCOM	739.45	227.2	-512.25	-69.274460	4.990305656
TATA TELE	489.55	501.75	12.2	2.49208456	4.274446911
IDEA	136.5	52.65	-83.85	-61.428571	4.165006179

Analysis of Volatility of Stock Exchange

	Closing Price on 1st Jan.	Closing Price on 31st Dec.	Fall in 2008	% Fall in 2008	Volatility
SENSEX	20,300.71	9,647.31	-10653.40	-52.47	2.858702509
NIFTY	6144.35	2959.15	-3185.2	-51.83	2.813917549

The above analysis gave a clear picture of % fall of share price of every company. We took closing price of 1st January 2008 and closing price of 31st December 2008 and see which companies were badly affected in year 2008. From the analysis we got that Infrastructure sector, Automobile sector and IT sector. We can see that Suzlon's (energy sector) share price fall down by 96% and Unitech's (infrastructure sector) stock price fall down by 91% in year 2008. These two were the top worst performance of any companies in year 2008. ICICI bank gave the worst performance in the banking sector. Its stock price fall down by 63.53% in year 2008.its main reason may be the contribution of foreign investors in these sectors. When FII's withdraw their money from these sectors, the performance of these sectors affected. Pharmaceutical sector was least affected sector. The percentage fall in stock price of companies of pharmaceutical sector was least as compared to other sectors companies.

From the above analysis we got that the performance of Sensex and Nifty fall down by 52.47% and 51.83% respectively from 1st January 2008 to 31st December 2008.The stock price of Sensex fall down by 10,653.40 points and nifty fall down by 3,185.2 points. In case of Steel and Aluminium sector Tata steel and Hindalco were equally affected. The stock price of both companies was fall down by app. 76%. This was the highest in this sector.

The Biggest % fall in Sensex in Year 2008

Date	*Day*	*% Fall*
24th October	Friday	10.95%
21st January	Monday	7.4%
10th October	Friday	7.06%
11th November	Tuesday	6.61%
17th March	Monday	6.03%
15th October	Wednesday	5.871%
6th October	Monday	5.784%
17th October	Friday	5.72%

The Biggest Fall in Share Price as Compared to Previous Day Closing Price

Date	*Day*	*Fall*
21st January	Monday	1408.35
24th October	Friday	1070.63
17th March	Monday	951.03
3rd March	Monday	904.84
22nd January	Tuesday	875.41
11th February	Monday	833.98
10th October	Friday	800.51
13th Marc h	Thursday	770.63
31st March	Monday	726.85
6th October	Monday	724.62
11th November	Tuesday	696.28
15th October	Wednesday	674.28

Important Dates and Closing Price

Date	*Closing Price*
18th January	19013.70
21st January	17605.35
8th February	17464.89
11th February	16630.91
12th March	16127.98
13th March	15357.35
14th March	15760.52
17th March	14809.49
28th March	16371.29
31st March	15644.44
3rd October	12526.32
6th October	11801.70
8th October	11328.36
10th October	10527.85
14th October	11483.40
15th October	10809.12
16th October	10581.49
17th October	9975.35
23rd October	9771.70
24th October	8701.07

The above analysis shows the clear pictures of different dates with days when the companies stock price were badly affected. From the above analysis we can conclude that most of the companies gave their worst performance either on Monday or Friday. Monday is the opening day of stock market and Friday is closing day of stock market. Both days show bearish pattern of stock market. We can see that 21st January (Monday) and 24th October (Friday) were the dominating dates of year 2008 when all sectors show bearish patterns. On 21st January Sensex fall down by 1408.35 points and on 24th October Sensex fall down by 1070.63 points. These two were the greatest crash of Indian stock market in 2008. On 24th October Sensex fall down by 10.95% which was the highest in year 2008.

Reasons of Falling Stock Prices

From the above analysis we notice there are some particular days when the performance of Indian market was affected badly. There are some domestic and global reasons behind affecting performance of Indian market. These reasons are following according to date wise.

21ST January

On 21st January BSE Sensex fell down by 1408.35 points or 7.04% than previous day. NSE Nifty fell down by 496.50 points or 8.70% than previous day. BSE was shut down by two times for five minutes before and after 3 pm. On this day 1,323 stocks hit the lower circuit filter means for them there was no buyer only seller were there for these stocks. Only 51 stocks hit upper circuit filter means for these stocks there was no seller only buyer were there.

The main reasons behind falling the share price on this day was

- Huge selling of FIIs
- Weaker global economic prospects
- Huge amount of money sucked by IPOs of Reliance Power and Future Capital
- Margin selling.

24th October

On 24th October Indian stock market saw biggest fall of the year. BSE Sensex fell down by 10.69% than previous day. It closed down by 1070.63 points lower than previous day. Sensex close on 8701.07 on 24th October. NSE Nifty closed down at 2584.

The main reason was selling of FIIs. On this day, FIIs sold shares of worth Rs.1431 Crore where as domestic institutions bought only Rs. 500 Crore equities.

17th March

On this day Sensex fell down by 6.03% than previous day. It close down 951.03 points lower than previous closing point. Nifty fell by 5.11% than previous day.

The main reason behind this was bear sterns fall down. In the previous week (10th March to 15th March) bear stern took off its shares from 25 Indian companies. These companies include Dabur Pharma, Oriental Hotel, Sonata Software, Taj GVK Hotels, Karur Vysya Bank.

Due to bear stern crisis market in us fell down on 14th March (Friday). This crisis had impact on Indian market on 17th March (Monday) FIIs sold stocks of Rs.658 Crore on this day.

Because of this crisis, ICICI share price fell down by 13.76% than previous day.

11th November

On 11th November BSE Sensex fell down by 6.61% as compared to previous day. It was 696.28 points lower than 10th November.

Due to this bad market performance many companies announced their buyback of shares. Some companies were Eicher Motors, Zen Technologies, Godawari Power and Ispat, Maestro Madiline Systems

10th October

10th October was the 3rd biggest looser day for Indian stock market. On this day Indian stock market fell down by 7.06% as compared to previous day. On this day market closed on 10,527.85 that was 800.51 points lower than previous day.

FIIs sold equities worth Rs. 2514 Crore on 10th October. Because many of those FIIs were subsidiaries of Europe and US based financial companies. These were facing liquidity problems at home. Morgan Stanley has offloaded its shares from maximum number of Indian companies.

15th October

On 15th October Sensex fell down by 5.871%. It closed down by 674.28 points lower than previous day. Sensex closed at 10,809 and Nifty closed at 3338. It, Realty and Banking sector companies were biggest loser on this day. FIIs were net seller of equities worth Rs1,030 Crore. TCS fell down by 8.23% than previous day. DLF decreased by 3.5% on this day.

Conclusion

"It is used to be said that when the US sneezes, the whole world caught a cold".

The above saying seems to be practically true in year 2008. When due to subprime crisis US economy saw the recession stage, it affected the whole world economy. Due to globalization and liberalization of economy many foreign investors invested their money in India. But when subprime crisis shackles the firm roots of US economy, FIIs withdraw their money from Indian market to provide stability to US economy. In year 2008 FIIs withdraw $13 billion from Indian stock market which causes to shackles investors confidence in stock market. That's why Indian stock market saw a dominant bearish pattern throughout the year 2008. FIIs invested their money in infrastructure sector and energy sector. when they pull out their money, performance of infrastructure sector and energy sector got worst. The performance of Suzlon (Energy sector) and Unitech (Infrastructure sector) fall down by 96% and 91% respectively in year 2008. Due to bad economy of US, service sector of India also affected. IT sector which was based more on export o US firms also badly affected.

In nutshell we can say due to globalization, interdependency of one economy over other economy is increasing. When one economy does better, it has positive effect on other economy and vice versa. Dependency of Indian economy over FII is true witness of this. It directly or indirectly affects the stoke market.

References

Newspapers

Economics Times, Financial Express, Business Standars

Websites

http://www.businessmonitor.com/bmo/financialmarkets/

http://www.nseindia.com

http://www.bseindia.com

http://www.sharetipsinfo.com/Fii-Newsstockmarket.html/

http://www.economicstimes.com/

http://www.businessline.com/

15

CHANGING TRENDS OF ASSET PREFERENCE OF THE PUBLIC: KEY TO THE SUSTAINABILITY OF ECONOMIC GROWTH

Arati Basu & Anita Agarwal

Introduction

Financial Sector of Indian economy has been changing first as an impact of Globalization and privatization as well as change in national economic philosophy. In the earlier regime, Indian economic policy was based on the concept of public welfare in which the state played the crucial role in economic growth through industrialization. Financial Sector was highly regulated and was used for achieving national economic goals through long term planning. The system was dormant and under developed. Saving rate was low and did not have scope to be institutionalized due to lack of development of financial system. Since welfare sate provided social security to people, incentive for the household to save and invest for future were not there. Govt.'s employees provident funds, pension and health schemes provided cushion for future security for the public. Credit market in this period was underdeveloped; most of credit was directed towards the public sector enterprise and to those sectors which was placed in the national priority list. Financial Institutions were not market driven rather was under direct regulations of the Govt.

Under license Raj, banks were nationalized to deepen and widen the banking service across the country. During this period, the sector experienced more than satisfactory growth. The number of commercial banks increased sevenfold in two decades of nationalization. The asset holding pattern of the households changed from holding physical assets to financial assets in the form of bank deposits and bank deposits increased from 13 per cent in pre nationalization period to 38 per cent. As a result, financial saving as a percentage of total saving increased and bank deposits constituted two fifth of the total financial holding of the households. But Bank deposits were mostly invested in the govt. securities and were kept in the SLR with RBI was diverted to priority sector lending. Consequently, only a small percentage of the banks' funds were available for the private sector and these funds were considerably costly. After liberalization and privatization since 1991, Indian economy witnessed a substantial growth in private sector industrial activities and from 1991-1992 to

1997-1998, the number of private companies doubled from 223,285 to 449,730 while the growth in the number of government companies had slowed down. Number of listed companies increased from 4413 in 1994 t0 5644 in 2003 (Reports of IFC,2011).The growth of private entrepreneurships created a number of positive impacts in India, introducing competition in the market which resulted into cost cutting, efficiency of operation and increase in productivity of labour. Entry of MNCs created competitive environment that enabled Indian corporate to grow and develop world class competency and some of them growing into MNCs taking Indian corporate investment in the developed and developing economies. Indian management system in steel, Parma and IT sector have developed capabilities to go out to acquire companies in the developed economies. Sustainability of development of private enterprises needs funds from the financial market with competitive terms and conditions.

Saving Behavior of the Households

The Figure 1 shows that saving rate in Indian economy has been experiencing the phenomenal increase ever since Reforms in India economy was introduced. From barely 7 per cent of GDP in 1990-91, saving rate jumped up to nearly 33 per cent in 2007-08 and then this has slightly decrease to 30 percent in 2008-9. Indian households are the significant savers in the total savings. From Figure 2, it is apparent that households contributed more than 60 per cent of the total savings. In spite of the fact that Indian households are choosing to be consumption oriented, yet they are the major contributors of the savings of the nation. It can also be noticed from the Fig. 2 that households contribution increased up to 90 per cent in 2002.Thus it is evident that Indian households are the main agents of supplying saving funds to the financial market.

Thus, it is important to analyze how the household savings are used in the financial market for buying different assets. Fig 3 gives an interesting information as to how asset(saving) holding pattern of the households has been changing over the period of 1970-71 to 2008-09. Clearly households are now shifting from holding of physical assets to financial assets as the per cent age of household savings. Households had little more than 30 per cent their savings in the form of financial assets in 190-71 This became more than 60 per cent to more than 50 per cent in just after reforms introduced in the economy in 1991-2 to 1998-99 followed by financial sector reforms. On the other hand Physical form of household savings was 70 per cent of the household savings in 1970-71, which has been reducing as economy's financial sector is deregulated and is maturing. Figure shows the complementarities between financial and physical savings in the ups and downs of their percentage of total household savings.

The paper now will present a conceptual construct to explain the households' decisions to save. The analysis will reflect the expectations and motives of the household from their savings. This enable to point out factors that could influence their choice of assets.

Saving and Investment behavior of the household: Keynesian theory of household savings is based on three motives. Saving for future addition of consumption, for future security, and for trading in the stock market to earn through market capitalization of the stocks. Age, family size, and length of the planning horizon are important factors influencing the household decision to save. After analyzing the theoretical construct, the paper also review some recent empirical studies to find additional factors that influence the household motives for savings. This part of the analysis is important to see how motive for savings influence the asset preference structure of the households..

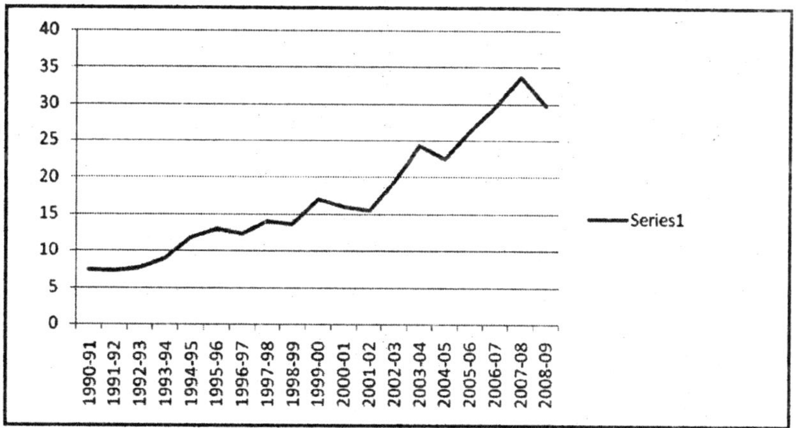

Source: Handbook of Statistics on Indian Economy(2009-10), Reserve Bank of India, Govt. of India

Figure1: Gross Domestic Savings as Percentage of GDP

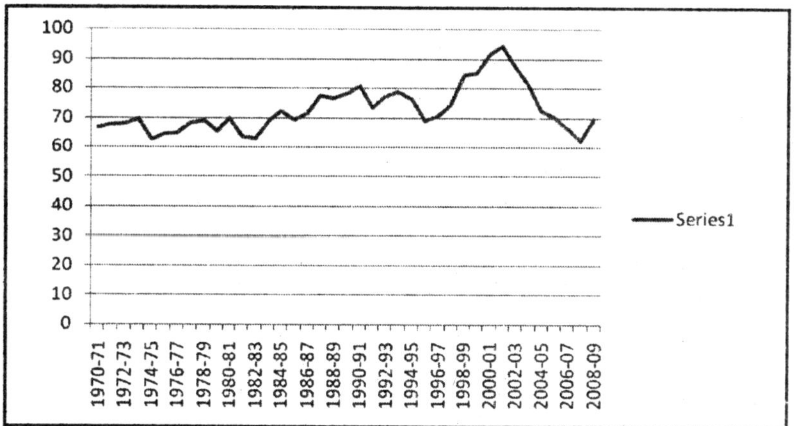

Source: Handbook of Statistics RBI

Figure 2: Household Savings as Percentage of Total Gross Savings

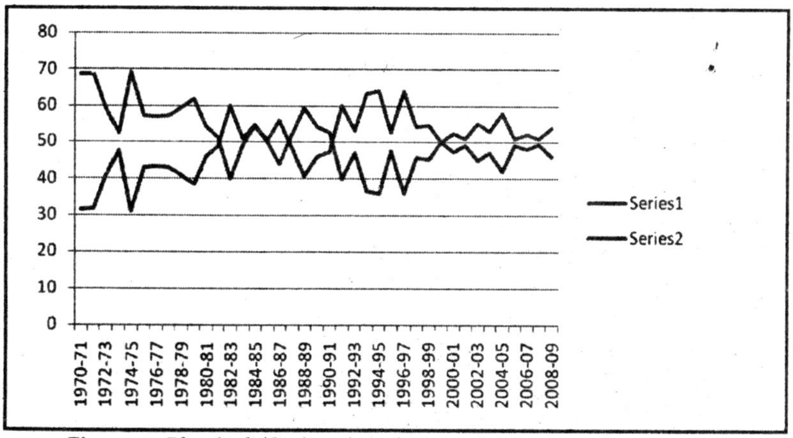

Figure 3: Physical (Series 1) and Financial Savings (Series 2) as Percentage of Household Savings

Theoretical Construct: Time Preference Theory of Saving

This theory is based on the fundamental assumption that the household prefers present consumption to future and hence they will be willing to sacrifice present level of consumption only if they are amply rewarded for the sacrifice. In other words, the household will expect some increase in future consumption over and above amount saved for the sacrifice of the present level of consumption while actual proportion of saving/disserving depends on the ratio of present and future income, rate of time preference as well as prevailing real rate of returns on savings.

Let us take two individuals of the society: Individual "A" and Individual "B" having different endowments of incomes of the present and the Future. " A" has greater scope for future income while B's present income is relatively higher. Future to present income ratio of" A" is greater than "B". The symbolic expression of above statements:

WA = Future income of "A"/ Present income of "A" > **WB** = future income of "B"/ Present income of "B"

Now the time preferences of two are presented in terns of two intertemporal time preference curve by individual "A" & "B". Market rate of interest is the same for both individuals.

Figures 4 & 5 below show that individual "A" decides to borrow from the market while individual "B" decides to save and lend. Factors that the theoretical constructs emerge are that saving decision is influenced by the rational of future to present income, time pretence and the rate of interest while preset to future income could be influenced by age composition of the household. The interest rate is the out come of general economic environment.

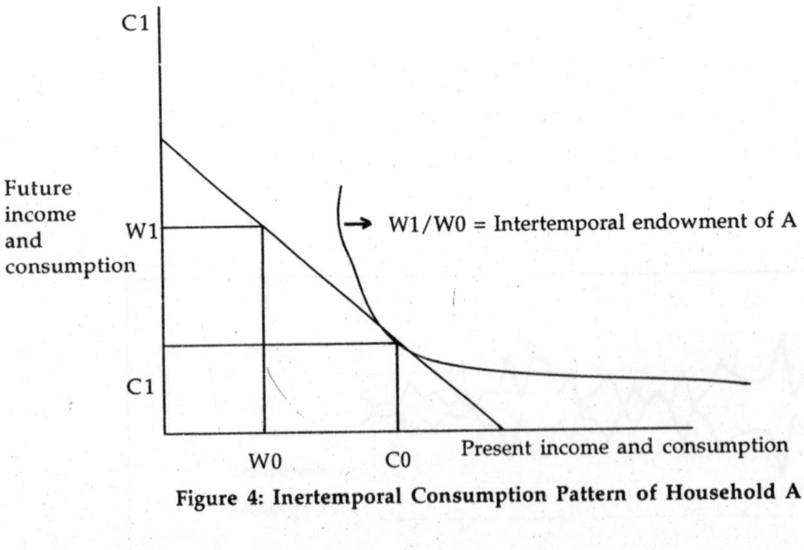

Figure 4: Inertemporal Consumption Pattern of Household A

Empirical literature adds up some more reasons for savings by the households. They find the following major motives for households to save as follows.

(1) "Precaution", which implies building up a reserve against unforeseen contingencies; (2) "Foresight", which includes providing for anticipated future differences between income and expenditure (the life-cycle motive); (3) "Calculation", which refers to the wish to earn

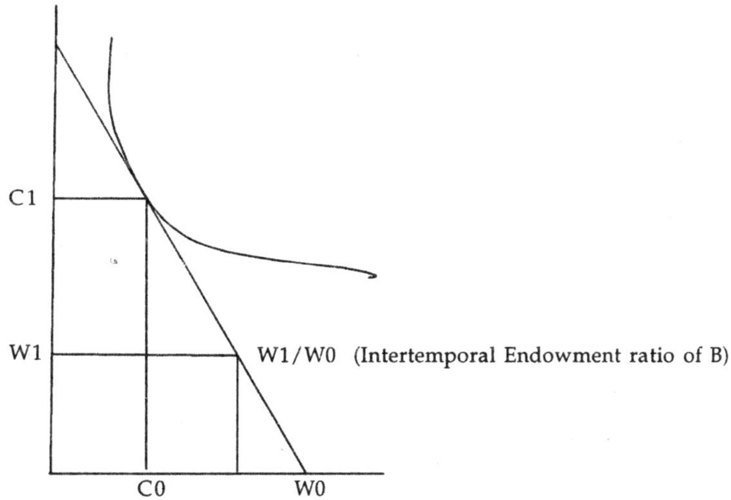

Figure5: Intertemporal Consumption Pattern of Household B

interest; (4) "Improvement", which means to enjoy a gradually improving standard of living over time; (5) "Independence", which refers to the need to feel independent and to have the power to do things; (6) "Enterprise", which means having the freedom to invest money if and when it is favourable; (7) "Pride", which concerns leaving money to heirs (the bequest motive)

As saving decision is taken by the households, they are to find best options to put their saving after weighing three factor e.g. return, risks, liquidity of the assets. Usually individual pretences of risks, reward and liquidity of assets differ as influenced by factors analyzed earlier. One of the objectives of the development of the financial sector is to provide opportunities to the households to select assets according to their choices of these three factors.

Asset Characteristics and Household Asset Preference

Samuelson and Nodhaus in the 19th edition of their illustrious book " Economic" explained that both asset characteristics and individual risk preference at any point of time influence the asset choice of the individual.

In Fig. 5 the. assets are arranged in the scale of returns and risks. The short-term govt. bonds are least risky assets while stocks provide high return though they are most risky assets.

At present Indian households have following options of financial assets:

- *Bank deposits*: These include savings bank accounts, savings and time deposits and certificates of deposit (CDs). These investments pay a low rate of interest apparently this is low risk and high liquid financial assets but risky options in periods of inflation.
- *Debt securities*: This form of investment provides returns in the form of fixed periodic payments and possible capital appreciation at maturity. It is a safer and more 'risk-free' investment tool than equities. However, this option is not at all liquid the returns are also generally lower.

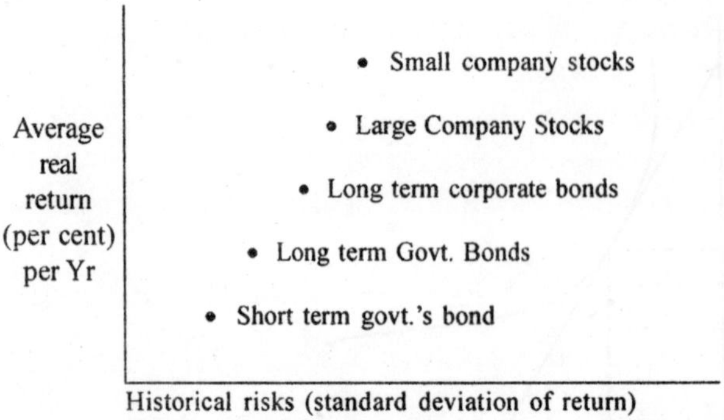

Source: "Economics" by Samuelson and Nordhaus (Indian adaptation,2011)

Figure 6: Characteristics of Assets in the Financial Market

- *Stocks*: Buying stocks (also called equities) makes you a part-owner of the business and entitles you to a share of the profits generated by the company. Stocks are more volatile and riskier than bonds

  Mutual funds: This is a collection of stocks and bonds and involves paying a professional manager to select specific securities for you. The prime advantage of this investment is that you do not have to bother with tracking the investment. There may be bond, stock- or index-based mutual funds.
- *Derivatives*: These are financial contracts the values of which are derived from the value of the underlying assets, such as equities, commodities and bonds, on which they are based. Derivatives can be in the form of futures, options and swaps. Derivatives are used to minimize the risk of loss resulting from fluctuations in the value of the underlying assets (hedging).
- *Commodities*: The items that are traded on the commodities market are agricultural and industrial commodities. These items need to be standardized and must be in a basic, raw and unprocessed state. The trading of commodities is associated with

Table 1
Matrix of Asset Attributes in Terms of Return, Risk and Liquidity

Asset Attribute → *Asset Category* ↓	*Risk*	*Return*	*Liquidity*
Bank Deposits	Less risky	Low return	High liquidity
Insurances	Less risky	Low return	Low liquidity
Mutual Funds	Medium risky	Medium rectum	Medium Liquidity
Derivatives			
Debt securities Bonds/debenture a) Govt.	Medium	Low	Low liquidity
b) Private			
Shares(primary market)	High risk	Un certain return	Low liquidity
Share Secondary Market	High risk	Uncertain return	Medium liquidity
Commodities:	High risk	High return	Low liquidity
Real estate:	High risk	High return	V. Low liquidity

high risk and high reward. Trading in commodity futures requires specialized knowledge and in-depth analysis.

- Real estate: This investment involves a long-term commitment of funds and gains that are generated through rental or lease income as well as capital appreciation. This includes investments into residential or commercial properties.

Table 2
Percentage Distribution of Household Savings in the Total Household Savings
(period 1970-71 to 2008-9)

	Shares+deb	*Prov+pen*	*Insurance*	*Physav/hhsav*	*finsav/hhsav*
1970-71	3.2	23.2	9.8	68.6	31.4
1971-72	0.8	20.4	10.2	68.4	31.6
1972-73	0.9	17.5	10.2	59.5	40.4
1973-74	-0.44	16.85	9.9	52.4	47.5
1974-75	1.8	23.34	10.2	69	30.9
1975-76	0.8	24.16	8.3	57.2	42.8
1976-77	-0.07	17.6	7.8	56.8	43.2
1977-78	2.8	18.4	8.3	57.02	42.9
1978-79	2.2	16.92	7.2	59.1	40.8
1979-80	2.5	17	7.5	61.58	38.4
1980-81	3.4	17.5	7.6	54.01	46
1981-82	3.7	18.2	7.6	51.1	48.9
1982-83	4	17.8	7.7	39.9	60
1983-84	2.9	16.2	7.3	49.1	50.9
1984-85	3.2	15.9	6.6	54.3	54.7
1985-86	5.4	16.38	6.9	49.8	50.2
1986-87	5.6	15.9	6.8	43.9	56
1987-88	2.25	18	7.2	52	48
1988-89	2.8	18.9	8.6	59.4	40.6
1989-90	5.5	19.7	9.2	54	45.9
1990-91	8.4	18.9	9.5	52.6	47.3
1991-92	10	18.4	10.3	40	60
1992-93	10.2	18.4	8.8	47	53
1993-94	9.2	16.7	8.7	36.6	63.4
1994-95	9.25	14.7	7.8	36	64
1995-96	7.1	18	11.1	47.4	52.6
1996-97	4.2	19.17	10.2	35.9	64.1
1997-98	2.6	18.8	11.3	45.7	54.2
1998-99	2.5	22.4	11.3	45.3	54.7
1999-00	6.9	22.8	12.12	49.9	50
2000-01	4.5	19.27	13.6	52.2	47.3
2001-02	3.3	15.71	13.9	50.9	49
2002-03	2.2	15	16.1	55	45
2003-04	2.4	13	13.8	52.8	47.1
2004-05	1.9	13	15.7	57.9	42
2005-06	5.2	10.5	14	50.9	49
2006-07	9.1	11.1	17.7	52.1	47.9
2007-08	12.4	9.9	16	50.7	49.3
2008-09	2.95	9.5	20.1	53.9	46

Source: Hand Book of Statistics on Indian Economy (2009-10) RBI, Govt. of India

Table 2 and Figures 5, 6, 7, 8, 9 exhibit trends of asset preference of Indian household. Clearly data on this table show that in the post reform period households(1990-1993 put their savings in the stock market and this percentage went up to 10 of their total financial savings. Otherwise the stock market only attracted only 2 percent with the exception of 2006-07 & 2007-08 having 9.1 and 12.4 percent of household financial saving being into the stock market. The long term trend shows that percentage of household saving in the earlier years were high and gradually households are preferring to choose insurance for long term assets. Safest form of savings for future security in the earlier periods was provident fund. As insurance market has been liberalized and privatized, fierce competition among market players both in the private, public and foreign have brought in various diversification in the insurance market. Insurance instruments have been tailored to suit the households' preference. Through innovation and application of technology, the costs of insurance products have been reduced thus benefiting both the households and the insurance companies. Also govt.'s incentive through tax exemptions helped the insurance.

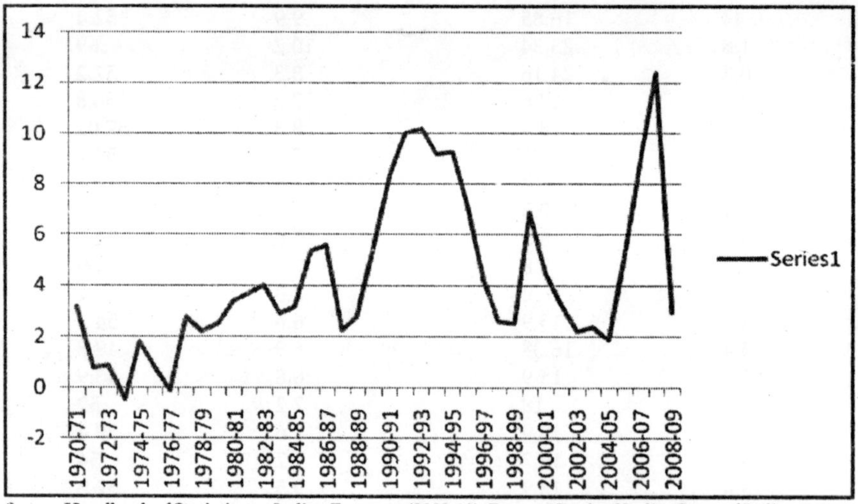

Source :Handbook of Statistics on Indian Economy(2009-10), Reserve Bank of India, Govt. of India

Figure 7: Percentage of Share and Debenture in Total Financial Assets

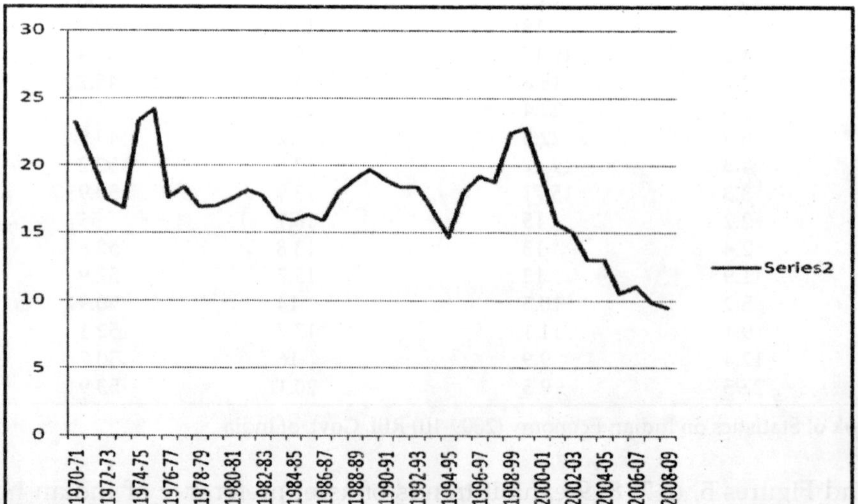

Source :Handbook of Statistics on Indian Economy(2009-10), Reserve Bank of India, Govt. of India

Figure 8: Provident Fund and Pension as Percentage of Finanacial Savings

We have analyzed household's holding of mutual fund over the period of 2000-01 to2008-9 in Fig. 9 and Table 3. Though mutual fund market has been liberalized and it receives govt.'s tax incentive, the households' preference for this asset looks to be volatile. Volatility could be due to its connection with the stock market and Indian stock market has been volatile as discussed in the later part.

Table 3
Resource Mobilization as Percentage of Total Financial Assets

	Mutual Fund as Percentage of tfinassets
2000-01	4.5
2001-02	3.4
2002-03	1.4
2003-04	12.7
2004-05	0.6
2005-06	8.8
2006-07	14.1
2007-08	20.7
2008-09	-3.2

Source: Hand Book of Statistics on Indian Economy (2009-10) RBI, Govt. of India

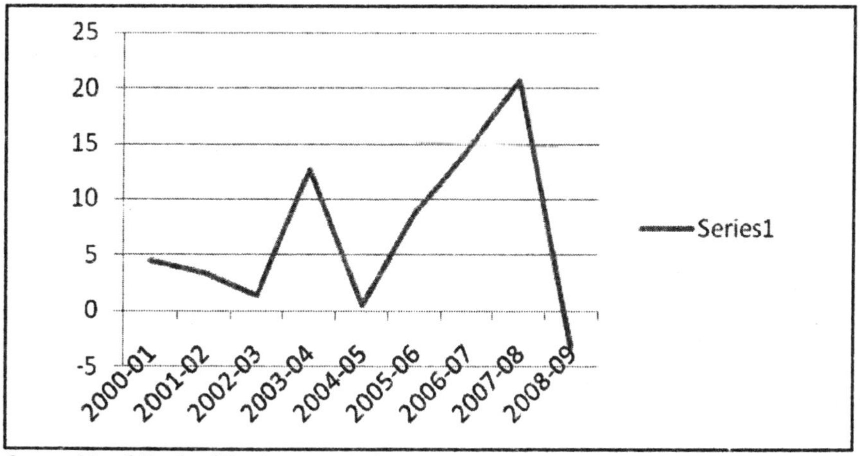

Source: Hand Book of Statistics on Indian Economy (2009-10) RBI, Govt. of India

Figure 9: Mutual Fund as Percentage of Total Financial Assets

Figure 10 exhibits the growth of time deposits as a percentage of GDP. In the absence of availability of data on households holdings of time deposits, we have attempted to get idea about holding of assets through this aggregate data on both households and other stake holders. This asset holding has exhibited phenomenal increase and now is above 70 per cent of GDP. This clearly emerged as the most preferred instrument of savings for the Indian economy. Yet this has been pointed out that time deposits in the commercial banks is not a good finanacial asset form the point of view future income generation. First of all though this is a secure asset, its value erodes with inflation and return on invvestment may turn to be negative in the long run.

Fig. 10 is showing the trend in total fixed deposits as per cent age of GDP over the period of 1970-71 to 2008-09. There has been steady rise in this ratio over time, showing that this is the most favoured form of asset holding in India.

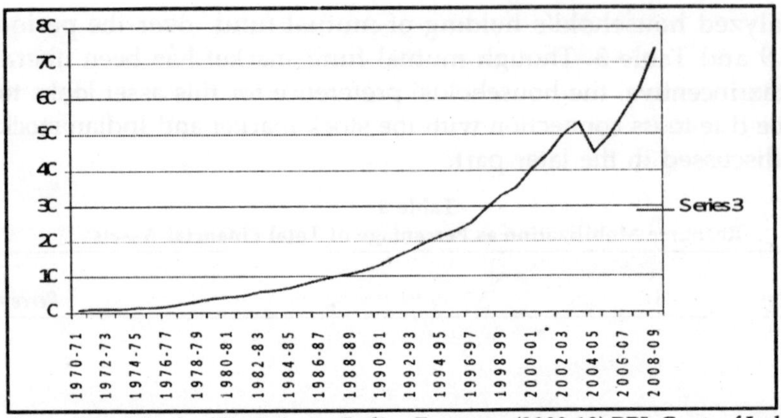

Source: Hand Book of Statistics on Indian Economy (2009-10) RBI, Govt. of India

Figure 10: Total Fixed Deposits as a Percentage of GDP for year 1970-71–2008-09

Next section will analyze the development of Indian financial market to find its possible impacts on the asset holding pattern of the Indian public.

Development of Financial Sector and Channelization of Household Savings to Financial Market

The growth of private companies in a market economy generates demand for funds at a competitive rate through financial market. Recent theoretical literature on development of financial market and growth identifies three fundamental channels through which savings of the economy are channelized to the corporate sector. First, capital market development increases the proportion of savings that is funneled to investments; Second, capital market development may change the savings rate and hence investments; Third, Capital market development increases the efficiency of capital allocation. In compliance to these channels, introducing an efficient capital market to link between the households and net investors (entrepreneurs) results in reduction of transactions costs associated with funneling savings, making the household savings liquid, enabling selection of efficient assets by gathering information on returns efficiently, and providing markets for diversification of risks by the households.

Studies point out that India firms are depend less on capital market for financing their investment. According to IFC reports India's market capitalization is 56 per cent of GDP in 2003 while it came down to 34 per cent in 2011. This is low compared to figure of other emerging market such as Thailand ,Malaysia and Korea **(Table 4).** Economic reforms could encourage development of the stock markets opening up options for the savers of the economy to utilize their savings in a more productive uses. Development of the stock market is also needed as the source of the corporate funds I the situation when that govt. to govt. and external loans to the corporate are fading away. Singh(2008) have pointed out that well developed and regulated stock market could encourage external pension funds which be useful for the industry. Agarwal (2001) suggests that in India the well developed stock market may be able to offer financial services other than those of the banking system and therefore provide an extra impetus to the corporate. Moreover as pointed out by Singh emerging economies find it difficult to regulate stock markets, as is indicated by frequent scams on stock markets. In these markets share prices are volatile and this greatly increases the vulnerability of the economy not only to international shocks, but also to domestic shocks. The main reason for this is that capital inflows lead to an interaction between two inherently unstable markets – the stock market and the currency market expectation which is confirmed by the data. As pointed out in the literature, stock market risks involve two types of information. General market conditions which now a days is much more quick to disseminate through technological advancement. Yet, information pertaining to companies are still not transparent and major risks are occurring from the this factor.

Moreover, the studies show that in India the primary market securities is exhibiting certain features that limit their secondary market liquidity. Firstly, a) Small size of issue b) equity ownership is highly concerted with in founders or controlling shareholders. This limiting feature are small size issue and also as find out by Franklin Allen and Rajesh Chakraborti (2006) equity ownership is highly concentrated with founders or controlling share holders. Indian companies are continually relying in heavily on external sources of finance averaging 60 percent during the period 1985-2006. On the other hand the amount of equity finance has been reducing continually in recent years, it will rise share of the debt in the total finance of corporate firms. Dennis Raja Kumar (2001) suggests that it was not relative cost which induce more of equity financing but was the results of information asymmetry as seen through moral hazards, adverse selection signaling. The dependence on debt finance make India's corporate sector vulnerable to domestic financial shocks.

Table 4
Stock Markets Relative to GDP

	Proportion of GDP 1994	*Proportion of GDP 2003*	*Proportion of GDP 2009*
India	0.44	0.56	0.34
Thailand	0.92	0.96	0.26
Malaysia	2.75	1.95	0.69
Korea	0.50	0.69	0.61
Brazil	0.34	0.47	
Mexico	0.35	0.2	

Source: IFC Factbooks (various issues)

Conclusion

Indian financial system has been developing and asset preference pattern of household has been changing over time from holding of physical to financial assets. Privatization in the finanacial sector and the growth of private corporate sector has definitely attracted asset holdings in the form of insurance products and reduce holding money in the provident funds. Our analysis shows that insurance products are held mostly to cope up with future uncertainty. Stock holdings by the Indian is still very low and highly volatile. Even asset holding in the mutual funds which is believed to be gaining popularity appears to be volatile. The paper has looked into the development of stock market to explain this phenomenon. Under this economic environment, Indian households still preference banks time deposits to other financial assets. It can be mentioned time deposits, though provide a way of saving, this is not considered to be income earning assets due to low inflation adjusted return. Our financial system can provide attractive financial instruments to the household with modernization of the market. This will provide opportunities to the corporate to get funds at the competitive rate from the market.

References

Agarwal R.N. (2004), Capital Market Corporate Financing Pattern and Economic Growth in India, Institute of Economic Growth, University Enclave, Delhi.

Canova Luigina a, Maria Anna, Manganelli Rattazzi a, Webley Paul (2003), *The Hierarchical Structure of Saving Motives*, Journal of Economic Psychology www. Sciencedirect.com Department of General Psychology, University of Padua, Via Venezia 8, Padova 35131, Italy,School of Psychology, University of Exeter, Exeter, UK.

Dennis Raja Kumar J. (2001), Financing Patterns and Investment, A Case Study of Private Corporate Sector in India, Center for Development Studies, Thiruvanathapuram.

Glen Jack (IFC), Lee Kevin (University of Leicester)and Singh Ajit (Cambridge University) (2011) *Competition, Corporate Governance and Financing of Corporate Growth in Emerging Markets.*

Empirical Investigations in the Light of the Asian Crisis, Directorate General for Internal Policies, Policy Department: Economic and Scientific Policies, Economic and Monetary *Aff/Ip/a?Econ?FWC?2009_040/C78March.*

Helge Berger and Pär Österholm (2008), *Does Money Growth Granger-Cause Inflation in the Euro Area? Evidence from Out-of-Sample Forecasts,Using Bayesian VARs,* International Monetary Fund, IMF Working paper, WP/08/53.

Krishnan K.P. (2009), *The Future of Financial Sector Reforms,* Department of EconomicAffairsMinistry of Finance Capital Markets Division, Department of Economic Affairs Ministry of Finance (Paper for the Conference on South Asian Financial Systems).

Samuelson and Nordhaus (2011), "Economics" Tata McGraw Hill Education Private LTD. New Delhi, Indian Adaptation by Sudip Chaudhuri and Anindya Sen.

Singh A. (2003), Corporate *Governance, Corporate Finance and Stock Markets in Emerging Countries,* Working Paper 258, ESRC Center for Business Research, University of Cambridge.

Singh A. (1995), *Corporate Financial Structures in Developing Countries, IFC paper,* Washington D.C.

Singh A. (1997), Financial Liberalisation, Stock Markets and Economic Development, The Economic Journal, Vol 107, No 442,May, pp. 771-782.

Subramaian S. Sriram (1999) Survey of Literature on Demand for Money: Theoretical and Empirical Work with special Reference to Error Correction Models, IMF working Paper WP/99/64, International Monetary Fund.

Sunit P.T. (2009), *An Assessment of the Mobilization of the Household Savings and Corporate Investments Via; Indian Stock Markets.*

Handbook of Statistics on Indian Economy(2009-10), Reserve Bank of India, Govt. of India.

Household savings motives. 22-*JUN*-07.

Journal of Consumer Affairs.

Mishra P K Mishra Uma Sankar, Mishra Biswo Ranjan, MishraPallavi, (2010), *Capital Market Efficiency and Economic Growth: The Case of India,* European Journal of Economics, Finance and Administrative Sciences, ISSN- 1450-2275 Issue 27 (2010)© EuroJournals, Inc. *http://www.eurojournals.com.*

16

MICRO FINANCE— YESTERDAY, TODAY & TOMORROW

Rekha Sachdeva

Introduction

The Indian state put stress on providing financial services to the poor and underprivileged since independence. The commercial banks were nationalized in 1969 and were directed to lend 40% of their loan able funds, at a concessional rate, to the priority sector. The priority sector included agriculture and other rural activities and the weaker strata of society in general. The aim was to provide resources to help the poor to attain self sufficiency. They had neither resources nor employment opportunities to be financially independent, let alone meet the minimal consumption needs. All said and done, Microfinance remains a powerful tool for development. It may be a drop in the ocean, but it has made people self sufficient. Our task is to spread Microfinance and bring down the cost of capital and the operating costs and strengthen the bonding between Microfinance and the Formal Financial System. However, for sustainable development of the poor and rural economy, we have to focus on development of rural infrastructure and the rural economy, otherwise there will be few activities requiring finance. Microfinance sector has traversed a long journey from micro savings to micro credit and then to micro enterprises and now entered the field of micro insurance, micro remittance and micro pension. This gradual and evolutionary growth process has given a great opportunity to the rural poor in India to attain reasonable economic, social and cultural empowerment, leading to better living standard and quality of life for participating households. For the developing countries like India it has come as a breakthrough in the philosophy and practices of poverty eradication, economic empowerment and inclusive growth.

Talk of the Past

With directed priority-sector lending an explicit feature of the formal banking sector, India has built up a network of rural banks that is rare if not unparalleled in the world. 196 RRBs had over 14,000 branches in 375 districts nation-wide, covering, on an average, about three villages per branch. The rural banking system, in its entirety, has an even more impressive coverage. Together, the RRBs, the nationalized commercial banks and the credit cooperatives

— comprising of Primary Agricultural Credit Societies (PACS) and Primary/State Land Development Banks (P/SLDS) — have one branch for every 4,000 rural residents In spite of such an impressive coverage, the formal banking sector has had a limited impact on microfinance or lending to the poor. The RRBs were set up in the mid-70's with a clear mandate for lending to the poor as it was felt that the cooperative banks were being dominated by the rural wealthy an that the commercial banks had an urban bias. Different forms of MF was as follows that were prevalent at that time.

The SHG-Bank Linkage Model– The predominant model in the Indian Micro finance context continues to be the SHG-Bank Linkage Model that accounted for nearly 20 million clients. It started as an Action Research Project in 1989. Under this model, Self Help Promoting Institution usually a NGO, helps groups of 15-20 individuals through an incubation period after which time they are linked to banks. The SHG had proved their efficacy over time but they suffer from a meager resource base which handicapped their capacity to expand the economic activities of their members. The factors received by the SHG members were the lack of information, time consuming and expensive procedures for obtaining bank loans, rigid lending policies of banks in respect of unit costs, unit sizes and group guarantee for loans. There were three linking model in the country:

Model I - SHG formed and financed by banks: - In this model, the banks play the dual role of promotion of SHGs and also provider of credit to SHGs, 21% of SHGs financed were from this category.

Model II - SHGs formed by formal agencies other than banks (NGOs and other), but directly financed by banks: - In this model, the NGOs and other agencies have played the role of facilitator. 72% of SHG financed were from this category.

Model III- SHGs financed by banks using NGOs and other agencies as financial intermediaries: - In this model, the NGOs and other agencies play the role of financial intermediation. Only 7% of SHG financed were from this category.

Grameen Model – Potential clients are asked by the MFO to organize themselves into 'groups' of five members which are in turn organized into 'centres' of around five to seven such groups. The loans for productive purposes are provided by the MFO directly to the members of small groups directly on the strength of group assurance. Grameen Model is being followed in India by Association for Sarva Seva Farms (ASSEFA), Activists for Social Alternatives (ASA) and Other Financial and Technical Services Ltd.

Cooperative Model – This has been initiated by Cooperative Development Forum (CDF), Hyderabad which has relied upon a "Credit Union" involving the Saving First Strategy. It has built up a network of Women Thrift Groups (WTGs) and Men Thrift Groups (MTGs). They are registered under Mutually Aided Cooperative Society Act (MACs) and mobilize savings resources from the members and access outside/ supplementary resources from the institutional systems.

Partnership Model – The partnership model pioneered by ICICI Bank attempted to address the following key gaps:

- To separate the risk of the MFI from the risk inherent in the Micro Finance portfolio.
- To provide a mechanism for banks to incentivize partner MFIs continuously, especially in a scenario when the borrower entered into a contact directly with the bank and role of the MFI was closer to that of an agent.
- To deal with the inability of MFIs to provide risk capital in large amounts, this limits the advances from banks, despite a greater ability of the latter to provide

implicit capital. In this model, the MFI collects a 'service charge' from the borrowers to cover its transaction costs and margins. The lower the defaults, the better the earnings of the MFI as it will not incur any penalty charges vis-à-vis the guarantee it provides.

In the absence of any significant economic development, it is pointed out that there was an unmistakable trend of repayments being made out of reduced consumption, increased working time as farm labour and borrowing from relatives, other groups in vicinity or moneylenders in extreme cases. In such a scenario, while loan volume, outreach and repayment may outwardly justify the intervention and make it attractive for bankers, its

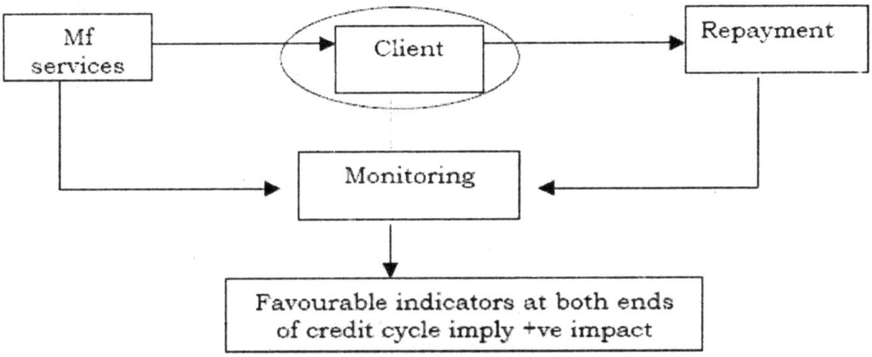

impact on economic gains for clients gets missed out. The common underlying assumption behind reliance on such parameters is belief in the linear cycle of credit, starting from credit off take followed by economic activities, rise in income/assets and repayment out of additional income.

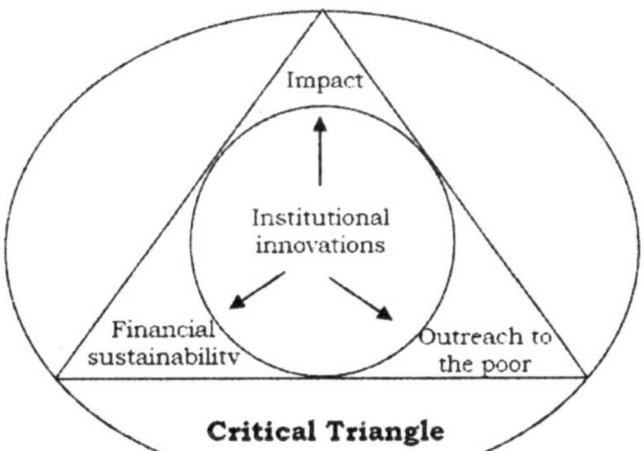

The state accepted the challenge to move from the old paradigm of subsidized credit delivery to sustainable micro banking. By moving towards packaging of credit to meet the needs of the poor, the system had sorted out problems of arbitrage between the cost of credit available from the institutions that were sponsored by the state and the local players. Even the problem of improper identification of the "beneficiary" – leading to a heavy leakage was plugged. The question of continuing access to these services was therefore successfully addressed by embracing the methods of microfinance. Now after a conscious shift towards micro banking – they offer complete financial services of a bank to the poor and to people who transact in small amounts.

The state-wise distribution of SHGs linked with banks shows considerable variation in the share of total SHGs. Andhra Pradesh has a disproportionately large share of over 42% of all linked SHGs. Tamil Nadu and Uttar Pradesh (including Uttaranchal) follow with about 12% and 11% share respectively. Karnataka come next with about 9%. The rest of country thus accounts for about a quarter of the total SHGs combined. From an all-India perspective therefore, the SHG-bank linkage experience has been very strongly biased towards the South and has not provided a balanced access to credit for the poor in India.

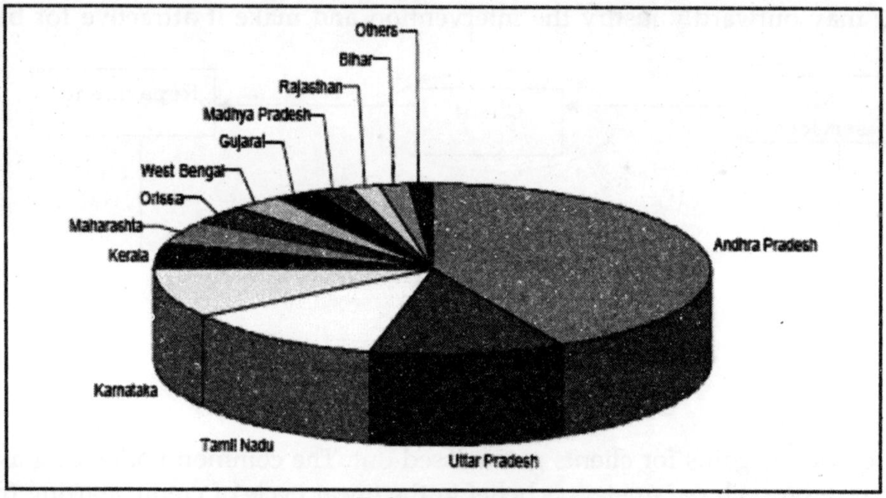

Today's Scenario

The Current Level and Pattern of Access to Formal Finance

India has a deep financial system. Financial assets in India amount to about US$430 billion, in nominal terms, compared to less than US$250 billion in Argentina, US$330 billion in Malaysia, or US$386 billion in Mexico, despite India's significantly lower per capita income. The share of financial assets in GDP in India is about 93%, compared to 81% in Argentina and 68% in Mexico.

Micro Credit by Micro Finance Institutions

Micro Finance Institutions are playing an important role of financial intermediaries in microfinance sector. The MFIs operate under various legal forms,

- NGO MFIs – Registered under Societies Registration Act, 1860 and/or Indian Trust Act, 1880.
- Cooperative MFIs – Registered under State Cooperative Societies Act or Mutually Aided Cooperative Societies Act (MACS) or Multi- State Coop. Societies Act, 2002
- NBFC MFIs incorporated under Section 25 of Companies Act, 1956 (not for profit)
- NBFC MFIs incorporated under Companies Act, 1956 & registered with RBI.

Future

The Indian economy at present is at a crucial juncture, on one hand, the optimists are talking of India being among the top 5 economies of the world by 2050 and on the other is the presence of 260 million poor forming 26 % of the total population. The enormity of the task

Overall Progress Under Micro-finance during the Last Three Years

(₹ in crore)

Particulars		2007-08		2008-09		% Growth (2008-09)		2009-10		% Growth (2009-10)	
		No. of SHGs	Amount	No. of SHGs	Amount	No. of SHGs	Amount	No. of SHGs	Amount	No. of SHGs	Amount
A. SHG-Bank Linkage Model											
Savings of SHGs with Bank as on 31 March	Total SHGs	5009794	3785.39	6121147	5545.62	22.2	46.5	6953250	6198.71	13.6	11.8
	Out of which SGSY	1203070	809.51	1505581	1563.38	25.1	93.1	1693910	1292.62	12.5	(17.3)
Bank Loans disbursed to SHGs during the year	Total SHGs	1227770	8849.26	1609586	12253.51	31.1	38.5	1586822	14453.30	(1.4)	17.9
	Out of which SGSY	246649	1857.74	264653	2015.22	7.3	8.5	267403	2198.00	1.0	9.1
Bank Loans outstanding with SHGs as on 31 March	Total SHGs	3625941	16999.91	4224338	22679.84	16.5	33.4	4851356	28038.28	14.8	23.6
	Out of which SGSY	916978	4816.87	976887	5861.72	6.5	21.7	1245394	6251.08	27.5	6.6

B.(1) MFI-Bank Linkage Model (₹ in crore)

Particulars	2007-08		2008-09		Growth during 2008-09 (%)		2009-10		Growth during 2009-10 (%)	
	No. of MFIs	Amount	No. of MFIs	Amount	No. of MFIs	Amount	No. of MFIs	Amount	No. of MFIs	Amount
Bank Loans disbursed to MFIs during the year	518	1970.15	581	3732.33	12.2%	89.4%	691	8062.74	18.9%	116.0%
Bank Loans outstanding with MFIs as on 31 March	1109	2748.84	1915	5009.09	72.7%	82.2%	1513	10147.54	(21%)	102.6%

Bank Loan Provided to MFIs

Agency	Years	Amount of loan disbursed to NGOs/ MFIs		Loan Outstanding against NGOs/ MFIs as on 31 March		Percentage Recovery of loans range
		No. of MFIs	Amount	No. of MFIs	Amount	
CBs (Public, Private and Foreign)	2008-09	522	3,718.93	1,762	4,977.89	70-100
	2009-10	645	8,038.61	1407	10,095.32	80-100
	% growth	**23.5**	**116.2**	**(20.1)**	**102.8**	
RRBs	2008-09	59	13.40	153	31.20	87-100
	2009-10	46	24.14	103	52.22	100
	% growth	**(22)**	**80.1**	**(32.7)**	**67.4**	
Coop. Banks	2008-09	0	0.00	0	0.00	NA
	2009-10	0	0.00	3	0.007	90
	% growth	**NA**	**NA**	**NA**	**NA**	**NA**
Total All Banks	**2008-09**	**581**	**3,732.33**	**1,915**	**5,009.09**	
	2009-10	**691**	**8062.74**	**1,513**	**10,147.54**	
	% growth	**18.9**	**116.5**	**(21.0)**	**102.6**	
SIDBI	2009-10	88	2665.75	146	3808.20	NA
Total of all Banks and SIDBI to MFIs	**2009-10**	**779**	**10728.49**	**1659**	**13955.74**	

can be gauged from the above numbers and if India is to stand among the comity of developed nations, there is no denying the fact that poverty alleviation & reduction of income inequalities has to be the top most priority. India's achievement of the MDG of halving the population of poor by 2015 as well as achieving a broad based economic growth also hinges on a successful poverty alleviation strategy. In this backdrop, the impressive gains made by SHG-Bank linkage programme in coverage of rural population with financial services offers a ray of hope.

The state accepted the challenge to move from the old paradigm of subsidized credit delivery to sustainable micro banking. By moving towards packaging of credit to meet the needs of the poor, the system had sorted out problems of arbitrage between the cost of credit available from the institutions that were sponsored by the state and the local players. Even the problem of improper identification of the "beneficiary" – leading to a heavy leakage was plugged. The question of continuing access to these services was therefore successfully addressed by embracing the methods of microfinance. Now after a conscious shift towards micro banking – they offer complete financial services of a bank to the poor and to people who transact in small amounts. It is claimed that this new paradigm of unsecured small scale financial service provision helps poor people take advantage of economic opportunities, expand their income, smoothen their consumption requirement, reduce vulnerability and also empowers them. Former World Bank President James Wolfensohn said "Microfinance fits squarely into the Bank's overall strategy. As you know, the Bank's mission is to reduce poverty and improve living standards by promoting sustainable growth and investment in people through loans, technical assistance, and policy guidance. Microfinance contributes directly to this objective. The emphasis on microfinance is reflected in microfinance being a key feature in Poverty Reduction Strategy Papers.

17

ROLE OF MFI IN SUSTAINABLE DEVELOPMENT OF INDIAN RURAL SECTOR

Piali Haldar & Anshu Kumar

Introduction

In India, financial inclusion has become a national and a government imperative in the last few years, and it has become a burning issue for discussion. Micro financial services have emerged as a powerful instrument for poverty alleviation in our economy. Microfinance institutions, also known as MFIs, are playing very important role in our society by offering financial services to underserved and impoverished communities. They provide both credits and deposits to the people who farm or fish or herd; operate small or micro enterprise where goods are produced, recycled, repaired, or traded; provide services; work for wages or commissions; gain income from renting out small amounts of land, vehicles, draft animals, or machinery and tools; and to other individuals and local groups in rural as well as urban areas.

The challenges are many in front of MFIs today, they are how to provide banking services and how to ensure the economic progress of financially excluded. The financial institutes have to develop a business model which will predominantly focus on serving the poor were there is lack of awareness and trust on the financial services. There is lot opportunity in front of the MFIs to unleash the untapped potential by improving the bankability and thereby ensuring the sustainable development of our economy.

This paper seeks to answer the question that is how to reach out to over 700 million citizens across six lakh villages, and meet the financial need of the rural poor and improve their self confidence and status in the society. An effort is made to suggest how to improve the economic condition of the rural poor for sustainable development of our economy.

Rural India A Glance

Rural India with a vast population spread in 630,000 villages with 12 percent world population attracts the attention of all and it has been realized by everybody that there is large potential market for financial products in rural India. Lots of changes are happening in rural India due to heavy government expenditure for rural development. The aspiration of the rural people are growing very fast, they are also putting their best efforts to be a part of mainstream economy. Seeing the opportunity many MFIs are jumping into rural market to meet their expectations without much prior planning.

And statistic reveals that the rural households contribute to 45 per cent of the total household income of the country, the saving income percentage in rural is 30 percent higher than urban. 48% of the households do not have access to the banking service. The income distribution is very skewed with some of this villages are reaping the rewards of Green Revolution and enjoying good standard of living, while others are still grappling with the basic issues of water, electricity, education, health etc.

According to NCEAR segmented the rural household on the basis income.

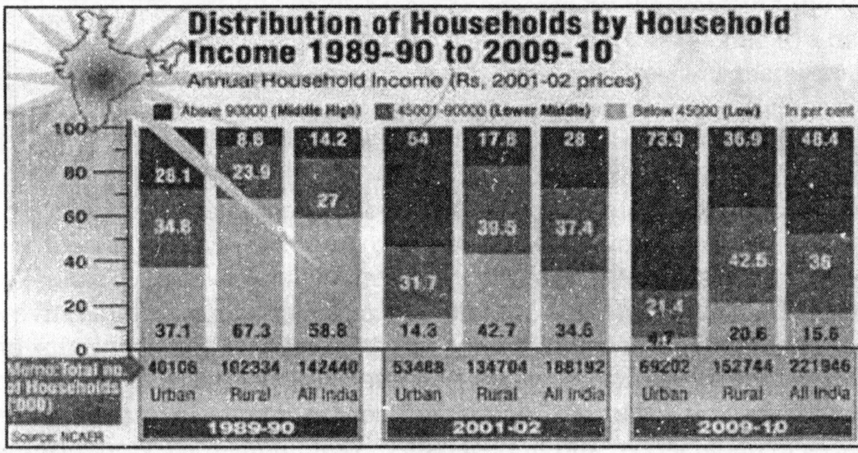

Figure 1

The statistics given in the table was published in NCAER's publication **Indian Market Demographics Report 2002, where** NCAER's projected distribution of income by household class from 1989-90 to 2009-10.The income bands have been collapsed into three, which we now call Low Income (L), Lower Middle (LM) and Middle High (MH). The lower income class which was 67.3 percent in 1989-90 reduced to 42.7 percent in 2001-02 and expected to reduce 20.6 by 2009-10. The banking system is able to meet only 20% of the credit needs of the rural poor.

There 6 lakh villages in India scattered in 28 states and 6 union territories and they are different from one another. Some of the villages have large population while some of them have very less. The villages can be segmented on the population size and on population density also. The no. of inhabited villages are 593,154 out of total number of villages is 638, 691 in India as per Census 2001.

Table 1

Population	*No of Villages*	*% of Total Villages*
Less than 200	92,541	15.6
200-500	127,054	21.4
501-1000	144,817	24.4
1001-2000	129,662	21.9
2001-5000	80,313	13.5
5001-10000 & above	18,758	3.2
Total no of villages	593,154*	100.0

All the state and union territories are not equally developed in India. Rural areas in some of the states are very well developed and the agricultural sector is also doing very well, in some place rural industrialization is happening at very fast pace, they are equipped with latest agricultural inputs while some of them are far behind. They are still following the traditional method of agriculture, and they are detached from the developing economy. They are confined to their village and their small society.

There are almost twice as many 'lower middle income' households in rural areas compare to urban areas.

Financial Scenario

The question one need to answer is that how to reach out to over 700 million citizens across six lakh villages, although there is growing awareness and agreement on the importance of financial inclusion, the same consensus doesn't seem to reflect around its 'definition' and the 'execution process to achieve' financial inclusion. Historically, the Reserve Bank of India (RBI) and the Government of India (GOI) had made efforts to increase banking penetration in the country, some of these measures include the *creation of State Bank of India in 1955; nationalization of commercial banks in 1969 and 1980; initiating the Lead Bank Scheme in 1970; establishing Regional Rural Banks (RRBs) in 1975; introducing a Self-Help Group (SHG)-Bank Linkage Programme in 1992 and formulating the Kisan Credit Card scheme in 2001.*

First time in November 2005, banks were *advised to make available a basic banking 'no-frills' account with low or nil minimum stipulated balances as well as charges to expand the outreach of such accounts to vast sections of the population* from low income group, both in urban and rural areas.

To reduce difficulties in opening bank accounts owing to procedural hassles, *know your customer (KYC) procedures for opening accounts has been simplified.* The Reserve Bank has directed banks to *make available all printed material used by retail customers in English, Hindi and the concerned regional language.* Bank nationalization in India marked a *paradigm shift* in the focus of banking as it was intended to *shift the focus from class banking to mass banking.* The rationale for creating Regional Rural Banks was also to take the banking services to poor people. The branches of commercial banks and the RRBs have increased from 8,321 in the year 1969 to 68,282 branches as at the end of March 2005. The average population per branch office has decreased from 64,000 to 16,000 during the same period.

The new Branch Authorization Policy of Reserve Bank *encourages banks to open branches in these under banked states and the under banked areas in other states.* The new policy also places a lot of emphasis on the efforts made by the Bank to achieve, inter alia, financial inclusion and other policy objectives. But the study of Distribution of Commercial Bank Branches-Region /State/Union Territory shows that, *there are certain under-banked states such as Bihar, Orissa, Rajasthan, Uttar Pradesh, Chhattisgarh, Jharkhand, West Bengal and a large number of North-Eastern states such as Assam, Manipur and Nagaland, where the average population per branch office continues to be quite high compared to the national average of 15,000 people per bank branch.*

The study also shows that even after the implementation of the new Branch Authorization Policy of Reserve Bank, out of a total of 811 new branches that were opened during July 2007-June 2008 only 3.82% branches were actually opened in the un-banked areas. During the same corresponding period in 2008-09, 677 new branches were authorized to operate and out of which 5.12% were opened in the un-banked areas.

Another benchmark employed to assess the degree of reach of financial services to the population of the country, *is the quantum of deposit accounts (current and savings) held as a ratio to the adult population.* In the Indian context, taking into account the state wise population (Estimated, March 2006), the ratio of demand deposit accounts (data available as on March 31, 2009) to the total adult population was only 69% as is evident in Coverage of Banking Services.

Within the country, there is a wide variation; For instance, the ratio for the states like Kerala, Tamilnadu, Delhi, and Punjab is over 100%, whereas Bihar is marked by a low coverage of 34%. In the North Eastern States like Nagaland and Manipur, the coverage is a meager 27% and 25%, respectively. The Northern Region, comprising the states of Haryana, Chandigarh and Delhi, has a high coverage ratio of 83%. Compared to the developed world, the coverage of our financial services is quite low. For instance, as per a recent survey commissioned by British Bankers' Association, 92% to 94% of the population of UK has either current or savings bank account.

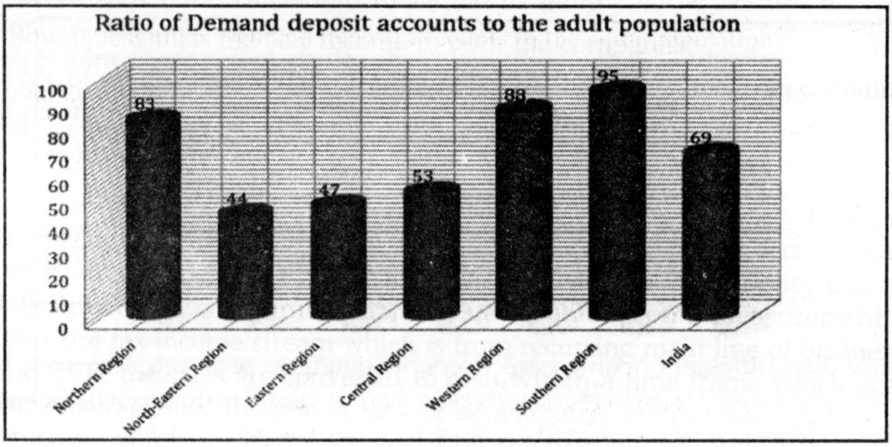

Figure 2

Indian banks, especially those in the public sector, have made substantial efforts to tap the country's rural population. But expanding through branches has been a costly endeavor. Out of 50 public sector and private sector banks, 26 appointed BCs, through which eight million no-frills accounts were opened till March 31, 2009. Using BCs is gaining popularity, with the RBI recently adding six more types of correspondents, including shop owners and public call center operators.

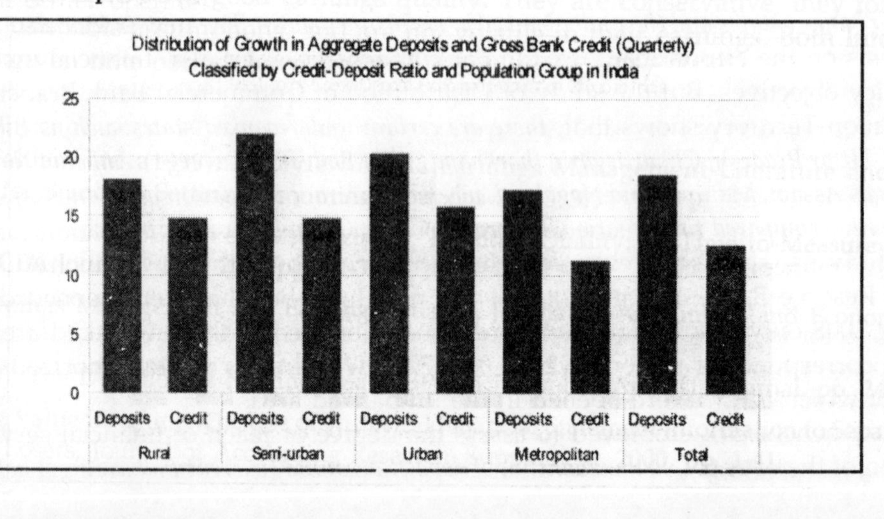

Population Group wise distribution of Deposits and Credits of Scheduled commercial banks shows that percentage share of deposits is lower in rural areas as compared to Urban and Semi urban areas and the share of credit is lower than that of deposits in all areas. This clearly brings out banks aspiration to earn good margins by investing funds into high potential areas, instead of strictly abiding by the RBI norm of priority sector lending to under developed and undeveloped areas.

The distribution of Commercial Bank branches in India- Bank Group and Population Wise clearly shows the dispersion of branches among rural, semi-urban, urban and metropolitan areas, by the various bank groups. It is evident that RRBs (77%) and Local Banks (43%) branches are in rural and semi-urban areas, they are followed by State Bank Group (65%); other nationalized banks (56%); whereas foreign banks seems to be only concentrating on urban and metropolitan areas (98%) and just have 2% branches in rural and semi urban areas. This reiterate the need to sensitize the private banks and the foreign banks to open branches in semi-urban and rural areas.

Micro Financial Institutions

Microfinance institutions, also known as MFIs, offer financial services to underserved and impoverished communities.Microfinance also refers to small scale financial services for both credits and deposits- that are provided to people who farm or fish or herd; operate small or micro enterprise where goods are produced, recycled, repaired, or traded; provide services; work for wages or commissions; gain income from renting out small amounts of land, vehicles, draft animals, or machinery and tools; and to other individuals and local groups in developing countries in both rural and urban areas'- Marguerite S. Robinson. Both public sector as well as private sector offers the micro finance services in India. They can be broadly categorized into two categories namely, formal institutions and informal institutions. The former category comprises of Apex Development Financial Institutions, Commercial Banks, Regional Rural Banks, and Cooperative Banks that provide micro finance services in addition to their general banking activities and are referred to as micro finance service providers. On the other hand, the informal institutions that undertake micro finance services as their main activity are generally referred to as Micro Finance Institutions (MFIs).

The former micro finance service providers include apex institutions like National Bank for Agriculture and Rural Development (NABARD), Small Industries Development Bank of India (SIDBI), and, Rashtriya Mahila Kosh (RMK), while at retail level Commercial Banks, Regional Rural Banks, and Cooperative banks provide micro finance services. Today, there are about 60,000 retail credit outlets of the formal banking sector in the rural areas comprising 12,000 branches of district level cooperative banks, over 14,000 branches of the Regional Rural Banks (RRBs) and over 30,000 rural and semi-urban branches of commercial banks besides almost 90,000 cooperatives credit societies at the village level. On an average, there is at least one retail credit outlet for about 5,000 rural people. This physical reaching out has provided savings, credit and other banking services to rural India.

The micro finance initiative in private sector can be traced to the initiative undertaken by Ms. Ela Bhat for providing banking services to the poor women employed in the unorganised sector in Ahmedabad City of Gujarat State. Shri Mahila SEWA (Self Employed Women's Association) Sahakari Bank was set up in 1974 by registering it as a Urban Cooperative Bank. Since then, the bank is providing banking services to the poor self-employed women working as hawkers, vendors, domestic servant etc. As on March 2003, the MFI had a membership of 30,000, 70 per cent of whom are from urban area. The deposit and loan portfolio stood at Rs.623.9 million ($ 13.86 million) and Rs.133.6 million ($2.97 million) respectively. Though the MFI is making profit, yet the SEWA bank model of MFI has not been replicated elsewhere in the country.

With the current phase of expansion of the SHG – Bank linkage programme and other MF initiatives in the country, the informal micro finance sector in India is now beginning to evolve. The MFIs in India can be broadly sub-divided into three broad categories of organizational forms as given in Table 3. While there is no published data on private MFIs operating in the country, the number of MFIs is estimated to be around 800. However, not more than 10 MFIs are reported to have an outreach of 100,000 micro finance clients. An overwhelming majority of MFIs are operating on a smaller scale with clients ranging between 500 to 1500 persons per MFIs. The geographical distribution of MFIs is very much lopsided with concentration in the southern India where the rural branch network of formal banks is excellent. It is estimated that the share of MFIs in the total micro credit portfolio of formal & informal institutions is about 8 per cent.

Table 3
Legal Forms of MFIs in India

Types of MFIs	*Estimated Number**	*Legal Acts under which Registered1.*
Not for Profit MFIs a.) NGO – MFIs b.) Non-profit Companies	 400 to 500 10	Societies Registration Act, 1860 or similar Provincial ActsIndian Trust Act, 1882 Section 25 of the Companies Act, 19562.
Mutual Benefit MFIs a.) Mutually Aided Cooperative Societies (MACS) and similarly set up	200 to 250	Mutually Aided Cooperative Societies Act enacted by State Government3.
For Profit MFIs institutions a.) Non-Banking Financial Companies (NBFCs)	6	Indian Companies Act, 1956Reserve Bank of India Act, 1934
Total	700 - 800	

According to Forbes magazine, seven microfinance institutes in India are in the list of the world's top 50 microfinance institutions.

Bandhan, as well as two other Indian MFIs—Microcredit Foundation of India (ranked 13th) and Saadhana Microfinance Society (15th) – have been placed above Bangladesh-based Grameen Bank (which along with its founder Mohammed Yunus, was awarded the Nobel Prize). Besides Bandhan, the Microcredit Foundation of India and Saadhana Microfinance Society, other Indian entries include Grameen Koota (19th), Sharada's Women's Association for Weaker Section (23rd), SKS Microfinance Private Ltd (44th) and Asmitha Microfinance Ltd (29th). A major problem still remains today is developing a business model that will led to sustainable development of rural India.

Sustainable Development

Microfinance institutions are doing great job in increasing awareness and importance of access to financial services for social upliftment as well as sustainable development for rural poor living in backward areas. All over the world microfinance policies have helped in achieving sustainable development of rural sector. Sustainable development has been defined in many ways, but the most frequently quoted definition is from *Our Common Future*, also known as the Brundtland Report.

"Sustainable development is development that meets the needs of the present without compromising the ability of future generations to meet their own needs. It contains within it two key concepts:

- *the concept of **needs**, in particular the essential needs of the world's poor, to which overriding priority should be given; and*
- *the idea of **limitations** imposed by the state of technology and social organization on the environment's ability to meet present and future needs."*

All definitions of sustainable development require that we see the world as a system—a system that connects space; and a system that connects time.

There is a need for an all round effort to develop the fledgling Microfinance Industry for tackling the problem of poverty and sustainability. The Government of

India directed the RBI to issue suitable instructions to the banks to bring in "inclusive growth". Accordingly, the Reserve Bank of India advised all banks to provide facilities, such as insurance, money transfer (remittances), social security, etc under the umbrella of "Financial Inclusion". RBI has issued Know Your Customer (KYC) norms for identification of an individual /corporate opening an account. It resulted in banks liberalized the norms to open "no-frills" accounts under which minimum balance amount was reduced/not insisted upon for savings accounts. It has also relaxed allowing accounts to be opened with "self declaration' of address and introduction by an account-holder of the bank. For financial inclusion hassle-free credit up to 25000/- is also granted to individual beneficiaries of rural households depending upon the economic activity they undertake under the newly introduced "General Purpose Credit Card (GCC)" scheme. Opening no-frills account is not an end itself but to meet the genuine financial needs of rural family.

For sustainable development the financial institution have to cater the financial needs of a rural family, and they are:

- Working capital for their existing activities.
- Investment for additional income generation.

Meeting consumption needs such as expenses towards marriage, health, house repair, child's education etc.The financial needs are different between poor and non poor, educated and non educated and between farm and non farm sector.

Most of the financial needs of the rural India are met by friends and relatives, since there is lack of financial service in rural India due to physical and social infrastructure, lack of understanding and knowledge, lack of technology, lack of support, lack of confidence.

For the Indian growth story to become sustainable, encompassing financial inclusion is a must. It is also important that each of the stakeholders in the growth process understand the immense value of inclusive growth. For the private sector too there are immense opportunities to reach at the "bottom" of the pyramid. This is the segment of the economy that is serviced primarily by informal channels of financial intermediation. The private sector should be able to discover where these opportunities lie. They should also be able to integrate these opportunities with their business strategy and business model for future growth.

Financial Inclusion and Sustainable Economic Development

Financial inclusion is an essential pre-condition to build uniform economic development, both spatially and temporarily, and ushering in greater economic and social equity. There are several government and non-government programs aimed at reducing poverty and bringing greater equity in the country. Financial inclusion can transform them into productive and self-sustainable projects. The micro-credit programme launched through numerous Non-Government Organizations has found fancy with the banking industry and can prove to be an excellent tool to bring in greater equity through financial inclusion.

No-frills account when promoted extensively plough backs the returns from these projects into bank coffers, thus encouraging the savings habit and ensuring that banks act as a repository of savings and sources of credit. This will make banking enter into the daily routine of a common man. Besides nurturing the habit of saving among the masses, it will remove the apprehensions and fear from their mind towards the financial products and services. This will encourage un/under-banked consumers to enter into or make better use of the financial mainstream. It will also persuade people to take credit for setting up new ventures. In a way provision of easy credit will encourage the first generation entrepreneurs to initiate new venture; aggravate the capital formation in the society; create new employment opportunities and thus will help in escalating the economic development of the country.

Model for Financial Inclusion

The topic of financial inclusion is at the center stage of policy agenda. Both the Reserve Bank of India (RBI) and the ministry of finance have taken it up as a priority, setting aside other things such as consolidation in the industry. The bet seems to be on the business correspondent (BC) model, which envisages non-bank outlets (such as kirana stores) supporting banking transactions for customers who do not have access to a bank branch. While the direction is right, we need to think and act more boldly to make any significant impact on the problem in a short time.

The model discussed below will be instrumental in bring hundred percent financial inclusion in our country:

Stage I: Create Awareness & Financial Literacy

Intensive awareness, education and promotion drive to create an in-depth impact on the masses.

- Government should promote introduction of basic banking – relevance, services, merits as a topic in secondary and higher secondary classes in all education institutions.
- Government sponsored publicity campaigns through all medias – radio, television, newspapers, e-choupal, village panchayat, movies, local stage shows etc.
- Banks should design and organize aggressive education cum promotion campaigns in unbanked parts of urban, semi – urban and rural areas to enhance financial literacy and awareness, as well as to remove the doubts and apprehensions that the masses have towards the banking sector.

Stage II: Basic Banking

The banks need to adopt a considerate approach towards this new clientele, to remove their qualms and disbeliefs. It is necessary that the basic banking should be comprehensive in scope and have attractive USPs that can lure people at large :

- All banks should allow no frill accounts i.e. savings accounts which can be opened with a nominal amount of Rs.5/- or even with zero balance .They should allow 6-7 withdrawals in the accounting period and should not restrict the number of deposits.

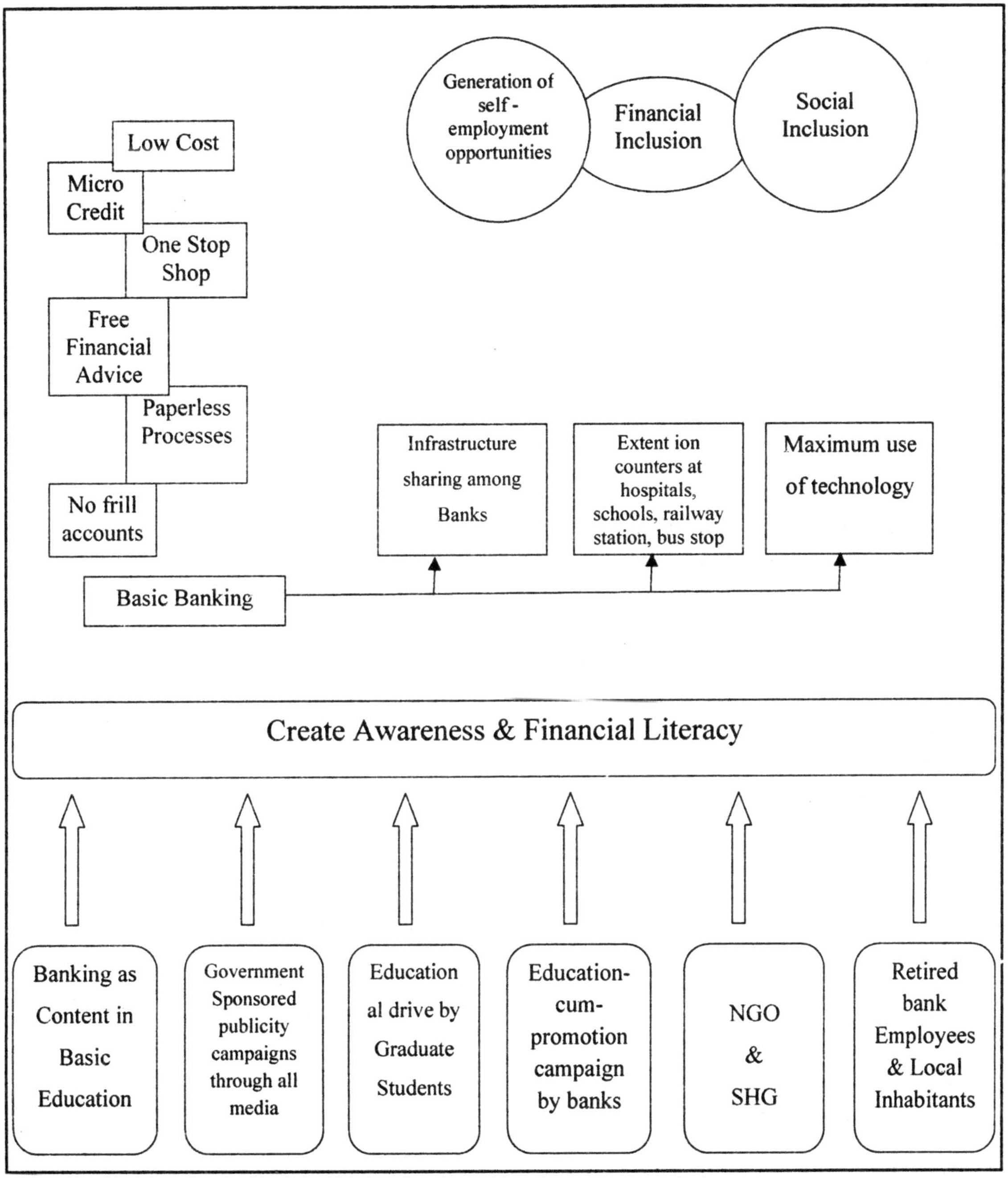

Figure 3

- RBI along with banks should toil hard to reduce the amount of paper work in relation to the opening of an account as well as in getting small credits . This would reduce the complexity and also speed up the processing at banks.
- Banks should make sure that local people are positioned in the front offices, so that the general public does not have to endure with language problem and does not have to suffer perceived / actual racial discrimination.

- It is all the more necessary for the banks that besides offering the conventional products and services they should set up teams who can understand the needs and requirements of the common man and design innovative products and services having greater suitability and desirability. Also banks should work as one stop store and offer diversified products in banking and insurance.
- Despite the risk, financing of first time entrepreneurs is a must for financial inclusion and growth. Banks should arrange and provide technical advice for these entrepreneurs. They will have to tone up their risk assessment and risk management capacities, and provide for these facilities.
- Banks should give free financial counsel to low-income households and small entrepreneurs.
- The pricing of the product should be also done keeping in mind the pockets of the potential clientele. The cost burden should proportionately be shifted to high potential sectors, who can afford a little upswing in their banking cost.

Stage III: Innovative Strategies

Basic banking itself needs to be supported by innovative strategies, in order to improve the reach and reduce the operating cost of the banks.

- Infrastructure sharing amongst banks and other organizations will help in lowering the operating cost and thus the cost benefit can be transferred to customers.
- Bank should open small extension counters at organization providing public utility services such as local schools, primary health care centers, village mandies, farmers' associations, cold storages and warehouses, railway stations , bus stops etc.
- This should simultaneously be supplemented by mobile banks. Wherever it is not economical to set up a branch, credit camps / loan 'melas' must be organized on weekly basis , to disburse small loans on easy terms .
- Greater use of technology should be made by the banks to improve their reach, speed of processing, as well as to cut down the operating cost.

Last but not the least the Government of India should initiate a 'civil rights law' prohibiting discrimination by banks against low and moderate income neighborhoods. This will create a pressure on banks to play an important role in bringing financial inclusion in the country.

This model will result in: improved financial literacy; make banking enter into the daily routine of the masses, broaden the deposit base, wider disbursement of credits, larger number of transactions. Jointly it will lead to formalized and systematic banking, faster economic growth, new employment opportunities in the society and financial as well as social inclusion.

Challenges

There are lots of challenges to unleash this opportunity at bottom of the pyramid. The challenge is to make the system efficient so that the financial services can reach out to every individual.

Lack of access to banking service by the poor led to lots of leakage at different level. For example if government can make the payment of wages for National Rural Employment

Guarantee Act (NREGA) to the beneficiaries through the "Electric Benefit Transfer (EBT) method it can minimize the transaction leakages.

Lack of physical and social infrastructure led to poor banking service led to poor saving into formal financial system. Financial institution need better physical and social infrastructure improve saving habits of the poor and this may led to better investment, this may increase low cost deposits, that will offer banks an opportunity to reduce their dependence on bulk deposits and help them to better manage both liquidity risks and assets-liability mismatches.

There is **lack of understanding and knowledge** of financial services available for the poor from different financial institutes. The spread of financial literacy programme is need of the day among the rural poor especially for inclusive growth.

There is **lack of technology** in rural areas, there is lot of scope of improvement in increasing wireless and broadband connectivity to support the rural banking service. EBT can be used to connect the system of various banks for increasing the efficiency of the banking system.

There is **lack of support** from the financial institutions, they have to improve upon its delivery mechanism, they have to develop innovative products especially for the poor and launch these products for agriculture and micro, small and medium enterprises sectors. Many times they do not have age and income proof documents for opening bank account, these issues need to be handled.

There is **lack of confidence** in financial institutions due to unfriendly and unemphathetic attitude of the banks to the customers. Non-transparency, burdensome terms and conditions attached to the financial products many a times create a barrier.

Conclusion

With nearly two-third of the population still living in the rural areas, and large part of this population is out reach of basic facilities, and having very less opportunities in front of them. Financial inclusion is must for ongoing economic expansion which is waiting at our door steps. This is essential not only for strengthening the inclusive character of the growth process, but also to address the demographic issues associated with unplanned development which is not addressing the problem of inequality and regional imbalance. Thus it is important to take every such step that will allow our economy to develop in all areas that will ensure the overall sustainable growth, so that our economy should be able to support specially the vulnerable sections of our population to improve their access to basic amenities and opportunities for livelihood.

References

Baljeet Singh, The Microfinance Promise in Financial Inclusion: Evidence from Pacific Region, School of Economics, University of the South Pacific.

Dr. A.K. Chakravarti, e-Financial Inclusion, Towards Accelerating Inclusive Society Goals Using ICT.

Dr. K.C. Chakrabarty (2006), Financial Inclusion: Concept, Issues and Roadmap.

Dr. Reena Agarwal, 100% Finnacial Inclusion: A Challenging Task Ahead, Conference on Global Competition & Competitiveness of Indian Corporate, IIMK.

John D. Conroy (2006), Financial Inclusion as an Organizing Principle for Poverty Alleviation: The Need for a Systematic Approach to Eliminate Financial 'exclusion'.

Inclusive Growth: The Role of Financial Education by Shyamala Gopinath, Deputy Governor, RBI.

No-frills Bank Accounts: Financial Inclusion is Good Economics by C.J. Punnathara, Business Line Thursday, June 8, 2006.

S.S. Sangwan, Financial Inclusion and Self Help Groups.

Taking Banking Services to the Common Man – Financial Inclusion by V. Leeladhar.

Appendix

Appendix Table 1
Distribution of Commercial Bank Branches in India – Bank Group and Population Group-wise

Bank/Population Group-wise Distribution of Commercial Bank Branches in India (As on 30.06.2009)

		Number of Branches				
		As on June 30, 2009 @				
Bank Group	*No. of Banks #*	*Rural*	*Semi-urban*	*Urban*	*Metropolitan*	*Total*
State Bank of India and Associates	7	5609	4907	3094	2650	16260
		-34.5	-30.2	-19	-16.3	-100
Nationalised Banks	19	13363	8646	8842	8244	39095
		-34.2	-22.1	-22.6	-21.1	-100
Other Public Sector Banks	1	56	112	196	202	566
		-9.9	-19.8	-34.6	-35.7	-100
Old Private Sector Bank	15	846	1564	1354	937	4701
		-18	-33.3	-28.8	-19.9	-100
New Private Sector Banks	7	275	1116	1389	1484	4264
		-6.4	-26.2	-32.6	-34.8	-100
Foreign Banks in India	32	4	4	53	234	295
		-1.4	-1.4	-18	-79.3	-100
Regional Rural Banks	86	11632	2750	671	91	15144
		-76.8	-18.2	-4.4	-0.6	-100
Non-Scheduled Commercial Banks (Local Area Banks)	4	11	20	13	-	44
		-25	-45.5	-29.5	(-)	-100
Total	171	31796	19119	15612	13842	80369
		-39.6	-23.8	-19.4	-17.2	-100

Note :
: As on June 30, 2009.
@ : Population group wise classification of branches is based on 2001 Census.
1. Number of branches data excludes administrative offices.
2. Data for June 2009 are provisional.
3. Figures in parentheses are percentage to the total in each group.

Source: Reserve Bank of India.

Appendix Table 2
State wise Deposits and Credits of Scheduled Commercial Banks in India (March 2009)

State wise Deposits and Credits of Scheduled Commercial Banks in India (March 2009)

		No. of Accounts in '000			
Region/State/UT's	*No. of Offices*	*Saving Accounts*	*Credit Accounts*	*Total No. of Accounts*	*Population*
Northern Region	14069	110429	11198	121627	146,169,000
Haryana	2192	17302	1634	18936	23,314,000
Himachal Pradesh	957	5459	557	6016	6,455,000
Jammu and Kashmir	984	7107	587	7694	10,941,000
Punjab	3324	26033	2093	28126	26,059,000
Rajasthan	4033	27504	3474	30978	62,276,000

Contd.

State wise Deposits and Credits of Scheduled Commercial Banks in India (March 2009)

Region/State/UT's	No. of Offices	Saving Accounts	Credit Accounts	Total No. of Accounts	Population
		No. of Accounts in '000			
Chandigarh	307	2248	190	2438	1,103,000
Delhi	2272	24774	2664	27438	16,021,000
North-Eastern Region	2181	15920	2001	17921	41,084,000
Arunachal Pradesh	77	521	57	578	1,169,000
Assam	1421	11488	1301	12789	28,665,000
Manipur	81	493	74	567	2,308,000
Meghalaya	205	916	115	1031	2,470,000
Mizoram	94	324	60	384	946,000
Nagaland	85	481	91	572	2,119,000
Tripura	218	1697	303	2000	3,407,000
Eastern Region	13670	104078	12192	116270	245,149,000
Bihar	3904	27038	3796	30834	90,752,000
Jharkhand	1747	12648	1327	13975	29,299,000
Orissa	2733	17215	3077	20292	38,887,000
Sikkim	71	288	36	324	576,000
West Bengal	5178	46625	3932	50557	85,216,000
Andaman and Nicobar Islands	37	264	25	289	419,000
Central Region	16244	134999	14178	149177	281,485,000
Chhattisgarh	1243	8112	948	9060	22,594,000
Madhya Pradesh	4052	26002	3508	29510	66,390,000
Uttar Pradesh	9844	93923	9002	102925	183,282,000
Uttarakhand	1105	6962	720	7682	9,219,000
Western Region	12664	110396	31287	141683	161,757,000
Goa	420	3319	185	3504	1,492,000
Gujarat	4435	37257	3225	40482	54,979,000
Maharashtra	7767	69366	27867	97233	104,804,000
Dadra and Nagar Haveli	24	226	5	231	266,000
Daman and Diu	18	227	4	231	216,000
Southern Region	22974	186480	39200	225680	236,540,000
Andhra Pradesh	6635	60211	12014	72225	80,712,000
Karnataka	5950	43884	8469	52353	56,258,000
Kerala	4170	28956	5703	34659	33,265,000
Tamil Nadu	6080	52200	12804	65004	65,135,000
Lakshadweep	11	43	5	48	72,000
Puducherry	128	1187	206	1393	1,098,000
India	81802	662302	110056	772358	1,112,184,000

Appendix Table 3

State and Population Group-wise Distribution of Offices Opened by Commercial Banks - 2008 and 2009

	Number of Offices										
		Opened during April 1, 2008 to March 31, 2009					As on March 31, 2009				
	As on March 31, 2008	Rural	Semi-Urban	Urban	Metro-politan	Total	Rural	Semi-Urban	Urban	Metro-politan	Total
State / Union Territory	(1)	(2)	(3)	(4)	(5)	(6)	(7)	(8)	(9)	(10)	(11)
Andaman & Nicobar	37	-	-	-	-	-	17	20	-	-	37
Andhra Pradesh	6351	72	73	129	75	349	2388	1537	1696	1077	6698
Arunachal Pradesh	74	-	3	-	-	3	50	27	-	-	77
Assam	1381	13	17	20	-	50	788	334	307	-	1429
Bihar	3792	17	46	35	16	114	2356	846	433	281	3916
Chandigarh	297	1	-	15	-	16	24	1	287	-	312

Contd.

	Number of Offices										
		Opened during April 1, 2008 to March 31, 2009					As on March 31, 2009				
	As on March 31, 2008	Rural	Semi-Urban	Urban	Metro-politan	Total	Rural	Semi-Urban	Urban	Metro-politan	Total
State / Union Territory	(1)	(2)	(3)	(4)	(5)	(6)	(7)	(8)	(9)	(10)	(11)
Chhattisgarh	1183	11	22	38	-	71	654	254	346	-	1254
Dadra & Nagar Haveli	21	1	2	-	-	3	5	19	-	-	24
Daman & Diu	18	-	-	-	-	-	-	18	-	-	18
Delhi	2149	3	5	-	159	167	56	36	-	2219	2311
Goa	409	2	13	-	-	15	159	265	-	-	424
Gujarat	4289	37	53	29	75	194	1486	989	649	1357	4481
Haryana	2064	20	53	57	8	138	691	468	924	118	2201
Himachal Pradesh	910	26	14	11	-	51	729	160	72	-	961
Jammu & Kashmir	978	11	7	11	-	29	547	192	268	-	1007
Jharkhand	1668	14	35	33	-	82	974	366	410	-	1750
Karnataka	5732	36	71	63	90	260	2166	1208	1343	1274	5991
Kerala	4053	3	81	51	-	135	332	2712	1142	-	4186
Lakshadweep	10	1	-	-	-	1	8	3	-	-	11
Madhya Pradesh	3878	22	83	71	35	211	1756	977	787	569	4089
Maharashtra	7465	41	74	112	191	418	2143	1415	1171	3147	7876
Manipur	76	2	1	2	-	5	35	21	25	-	81
Meghalaya	194	1	6	4	-	11	124	30	51	-	205
Mizoram	92	1	-	2	-	3	55	14	26	-	95
Nagaland	83	-	3	-	-	3	35	51	-	-	86
Orissa	2633	31	52	42	-	125	1654	514	588	-	2756
Punducherry	112	6	4	6	-	16	28	33	67	-	128
Punjab	3207	30	65	28	28	151	1123	965	743	526	3357
Rajasthan	3903	17	53	48	26	144	1756	993	861	431	4041
Sikkim	71	-	-	-	-	-	46	25	-	-	71
Tamil Nadu	5772	49	156	88	70	363	1709	1839	1445	1140	6133
Tripura	208	4	6	1	-	11	110	58	51	-	219
Uttar Pradesh	9446	89	132	140	90	451	4806	1776	1731	1568	9881
Uttarakhand	1056	19	15	16	-	50	570	290	246	-	1106
West Bengal	5054	26	41	45	33	145	2319	626	945	1306	5196
Total	78666	606	1186	1097	896	3785	31699	19082	16614	15013	82408

Notes:

1. Population group classification is based on 2001 census.
2. Data on number of offices is inclusive of administrative offices.
3. Data for 2009 are provisional.

Source: Master Office File (latest updated version) on commercial banks, Department of Statistics and Information Management, RBI.

PART THREE

Human Resource Management in Sustainability of Development

18

MANAGING CHANGE IN HR

Nimmi Agarwal, Agnibesh Samanta & Rohit Parashar

Introduction

In merger two separate companies form a new company;while an acquisition takes place when one company takes over controlling interest of another company. In merger both companies' stocks are surrendered and new company stock is issued in its place. In case of acquisition, the acquiring company retains its identity, while the acquired company ceases to exist. Mergers & acquisitions (M&A) are increasingly being used by firms to become stronger and maintain their position in the complex and global business economy.

There is a need for firms to systematically address a variety of human resource issues and activities in their merger and acquisition because the human resource systems vary across organizations owing to the differencespoorly managed HR issues in mergers and acquisitions have been the major reason for these failures.M&A activity presents a different set of challenge for the HRmanagers in both acquiring and acquired firm's .HR manager face this challenge as the economy improves. HR managers also play a strategic role at each stage ofM&A process and Preparing for the change can be a major HR issue. According to the corporate reports M&A activity is heating up, with the cash-rich players eager to buy the talent and products they need to compete effectively as the economy rebounds (itknowledgeexchange).

Mergers and Acquisitions

Types

- *Horizontal Merger*: - In the horizontal merger, two companies of the same market & same product line is merged together & form a new company.

  Example- Bank of Mathura with ICICI bank.

- *Vertical Merger*: - When a company combines itself with a distributor or retailer, this type of merger is called the vertical merger.

  Example- Pixar Disney merger

- *Conglomerate Merger*: - when two unrelated business firms merged together to form a new company, this type of merger is called the conglomerate merger.

  Example-Walt-Disney & American broadcasting company
- *Market-extension Merger*: - In market-extension merger, the two companies of the different markets selling the same products are merged together.

  Example- Acquisition of Eagle Bancshares Inc. by the RBC Centura.
- *Product-extension Merger*: - Product extension merger takes place between two companies selling different products into same market place are merged together. The products of these companies are related to each-other.

Reasons

- Reasons behind any merger and acquisition and one of those reasons are to get the talented employees in the organization through merging.
- Sometime the purpose of the merger is to acquire another company's assets, in terms of a particular product or brand.
- Survival in the emerging economy.
- To promotes growth.
- To become more powerful in this emerging economy.

Challenges

- In the stage of M&A, focused on the customer throughout the process.
- Reduce the cultural differences because it is the main reason of mergers fail.
- Keeping the key talent is a major challenge.
- In the process of integrating the workforce.
- Integrationof people, processes, technology and policies.

The Human Side of M&A Activity

Mergers and acquisitions are hypothesized that the combined company will have the greater value than the two separate companies. Mergers and acquisitions represent the extreme in change for a business as well as human side. Due to these kinds of activities human resource systems face the challenges in the organizational culture, sectorial differences and national cultural differences. More often, interpersonal conflict arises because corporate staff and division managers have differing perspectives on what their company wants from a merger. It is found that many boards and senior management teams only pay lip service to the idea of giving priority to the human side of the merger. Cultural differences which is a big issue in M&A because clash of cultures set the stage for a spectacular corporate collapse. People issues occur at every stages of M&A activity. In the integration stage, people issues include:

- Combining work culture
- Proper Communications
- Keeping the talent

Three Stage Model of Mergers and Acquisitions

Mergers and acquisitions create a difficult work environment for employees (due to different policies, procedures, and culture), with job redundancy and futures in question. The HR issues to be addressed in three stages of the M&A process. Hence, every stage of the M&A process demonstrates a new challenges as well as new opportunities to create value by managing people effectively. The three stages shown are (1) pre-combination; (2) combination and integration of the companies; and (3) solidification and advancement of the new entity

Stage 1: Pre-combination

In this stage HR pay an important role to identify the key people and to take immediate steps to keep them engaged with the company. An important aspect of this stage is to understand the similarities and differences between the two companies at the beginning, so as to compatibility could be determined at the initial stage, and relevant decision regarding merger and acquisition could be taken. It is essential to bring conflict out to the surface and deal with it.A 2006 white paper from the Economist Intelligence Unit revealed that 67 percent of survey respondents pointed to cultural integration as both the most important people issue and the most critical success factor in an M&A deal (Bundy& Hukins). In this stage HR also have to deal with designations and work processes. HR managers play a greater role to integrate compensation strategies and practices are a key component of successful mergers and acquisitions. HR also selects an outplacement service to support the individuals affected. A critical issues faced by HR include the integration manager to supervise the various integration teams and selection of the individual who will run the new company.

A handful of industry-changing newsmakers drove the market last year, but M&As among mid-size companies also saw increased activity in 2003, according to FactSetMergerstat LLC, a global mergers and acquisitions research firm in Santa Monica, Calif (HR Magazine, May, 2004).

Stage 2: Combination and Integration

The important aspect of this stage is to designing and implementing teams. According to Gary Forsee, chairman and CEO of Sprint Nextel Corporation, from the time the merger was announced employees expect straight talk, whether the news is good or bad (HR Magazine, March, 2007).Layoff plays a critical role in this stage because it not only affects those who lose their job but also affect the staff members who must take on additional work tasks as a result. During this stage HR managers could have worked with sales to quickly develop a focused training program that would have leveraged the combined company's strongest relationships instead of alienating its key customers.

According to a 2003 survey of 132 senior executives worldwide by professional services firm Towers Perrin of Stamford, the most common responsibility given to HR during M&As is to provide ad hoc advice to senior managers, rather than carrying out a structured and formal role (HR Magazine, May, 2004).

Hence the primary responsibilities of HR managers during this phase would be to developing the strategies for retaining people examining compensation & benefit programs and also creating & implementing a plan for establishing the communication with the newly merged organization. To adapt the target company's cultural characteristics is central to HR due diligence.

Human resources staff should establish a good agreement with both the upper management and other staff members from both companies. Another HR issue in a merger is the assimilation of new employees.

Satish Pradhan,chief,Group Human Resources, says acquisitions have evolved from the initial stage of looking at financial strategy, to looking at employees and answering the question, what will we look like and do we have the right mix of people (epaper.times ofindia).

Stage 3: Solidification and Advancement of the New Entity

The HR Issues in this stage is -

- Management and trade unions needs to be dealt with utmost care.
- Compensation structure and performance appraisal systems.
- Designations for the employees.
- Assessing the new HRM policies and practices.
- Solidifying staffing.
- Establish leadership.
- Readjusting and fine-tuning.

Role of the HR Department in M&A Activity

- Reviewing the target company's compensation policies to compare organizational philosophy and cultural fit.
- Train managers on the nature of change.
- Due diligence.
- Implement strategies for employee communications & keep an eye on it.
- Design and guide the integration effort.
- Manage the program to retain key talent.
- HR also has to manage outplacement & de-selection process.
- Manage the labor relations
- HR can act as a facilitator, and also as a coach to individual executives.
- Educating financial and operating executives about possible risks and costs.
- Stopped recruitment at few months before the M&A plan.
- Picturing the job descriptions at the target company.
- Bringing the new organization into the corporate structure.
- Possible activities: Human audit, human costs, people quality, personnel policies, employee relations and the organizational structure.
- Discovering and embracing new roles for the HR leader.
- Oversees progress of people-related cooperation and make secure workforce momentum is sustained.
- HR managers help to the development of and the accomplishment of the organization-wide business plan and objectives.

Conclusion

In today's global business world ,the reality of M&A transactions is that they are always complex and made more difficult by the fact that each party has unique behavioral patterns that define its culture and the success of M&As entirely depends on the people drive the business. With the increase in the mergers and acquisitions, an excess of opportunity lies before HR function to get properly involved in the activity. That's why it is necessary to involve HR Professionals in Mergers and Acquisitions discussions as it has an impact on key people issues and it helps achieve the success of M&A.

"A One of the best things you can do as a manager is stand in front of staff and have a discussion. Our technology really helped, but these 'coffee talks' led to open discourse because the employees want to look at the company leaders in the eye." ***—Vice-president, HR Hewlett-Packard, Hugo Bague on successful merger with Compaq***

References

Bundy, B., & Hukins, E. (2009). The Impact of Culture on M&A. London: Mercer Limited.

HR Magazine, May, 2004 by Susan J. Wells.

HR Magazine, March, 2007.

http://itknowledgeexchange.techtarget.com

http://www.globalhrnews.com

http://lite.epaper.timesofindia.com

Leo Lingham -Management Consulting/Questions Answered

Towers Watson: HR Consulting (magazine)

19

MANAGING CHANGE IN ORGANIZATIONS

G Vani

Introduction

Change is an inevitable aspect of life. It is the essence of any entity that has life or whose existence finds validity in the presence of life. Even time would lose its significance in the absence of change. As change manifests itself in a variety of ways, it does not hold the same connotation across people, situations, and contexts. Times change, people change, things change, situations change, and so do organizations.

Organizational change may be defined as the adoption of a new idea or a behavior by an organization (Daft 1995). It is a way of altering an existing organization to increase organizational effectiveness for achieving its objectives. Successful organizational change must continually focus on making organizations responsive to major developments like changing customer preferences, regulatory norms, economic shocks and technological innovations. Only those organizations that are able to undertake suitable change programs, can sustain and survive in a changing and demanding economic order in their bid to remain ahead of others in the race.

Organizational change programs require a great deal of planning before implementation. People's reluctance to change their style of working or to learn a new method of performing tasks makes them oppose change. It thus becomes imperative for managers to undertake comprehensive change-related programs in organizations to counter the resistance of employees.

Organizational change implies a change in the employees' manner of working and behavior. The change may sometimes increase the workload of employees drastically and put undue pressure on them, leading to stress. Under severe stress, performance of employees declines and this in turn affects performance of the organization.

Forces of Change

Change in general, indicates any act of making something different. Given the rate at which competition is increasing in business, organizations have learnt that change is necessary not only to compete, but to survive in the business.

Internal Forces: any change in organization's internal factors may also necessitate change.

- **Change in the top Management:** change in the top management and consequent change in the ideas to run the organization also leads to change in the system, structure and processes. Each manager brings his own ideas and way of working into the organization. The formal or informal relationships may change because of changes in top management.
- **Change in the Size of the Organization:** Change in the organization's size leads to change in the internal structure and complexity of the operations in the organization.
- **Performance Gaps:** when a gap between set target and actual results is identified, organizations face the forces to change and reduce the gap.
- **Employee Needs and Values:** with changing needs and values of the employees, organizations change their policies. For example, attractive financial incentives, challenging assignments, vertical growth opportunities etc.
- **Deficiency in Existing Organization:** sometimes, changes are necessary because of deficiency in the present organization. It may be in the form of unmanageable span of management, large number of managerial levels, lack of co-ordination between various departments, obstacles in communication, multiplicity of committees, lack of uniformity in policy decisions and so on.

External Forces: the present-day environment is dynamic and will continue to be dynamic. Change is social, political, economic, technological, and legal environment force organizations to change themselves.

- **Technology:** advancements in technology are reshaping jobs and industries. Technological developments are taking place at such a fast pace today they yesterday's technology becomes obsolete by tomorrow. Organizations that fail to keep up with the pace will lose their customers to competitors.

For example the telecommunications and entertainment industries are converging to form the multimedia industry. Moreover, many companies in the IT industry are now offering media services.

- **Business Scenario:** due to rapid changes in the business scenario with increasing competition and global economy, the needs and demands are also changing among the customers, suppliers and other stakeholders. There are two types of forces which may affect the competitive position of an organization-other organizations supplying the same products and, buyers who are buying the product. Any change in these forces may require suitable changes in the organization.
- **Environmental and National Factors:** environmental factors such as economic, political and demographic and legal factors play a vital role in devising organizational policies and strategy.

For example: organizations may have to change their employment policies in accordance with the government policy, demand of the non-government organizations and changing economic conditions of a country.

- **Social Changes:** social changes reflect in terms of people's aspirations, their needs, and their way of working. It has taken place because of several forces like level of education, urbanization, feeling of autonomy, and international impact due to new information sources.

Resistance to Change

Resistance to change goes hand-in-hand with change activities from individuals or from the culture and structural elements of the organization. There is no standard from in which resistance can be observed in the organization.

Individual Source of Resistance: individuals may resist change because of the following reasons:

- **Habit:** human being tends to develop habits. Instead of considering all the possible alternatives for each decision, he depends on habits for most of his responses. Changing one's habits is a painful task.

For example, an employee maybe habituated to busy life style in the city. It is very natural for him to resist, if he is transferred to a branch located in some rural area.

- **Security:** people are generally concerned about their security and resist any change that threatens their safety and security.

  For example, when a company introduces new sophisticated machinery or equipment that are likely to replace manual labor, its employees will feel insecure about their jobs an resist the company's automation efforts.

- **Economic Factors:** employees would resist change if it is likely to decrease their income or sources of earnings.

For example, if an organization undertakes restructuring and job redesigning, workers may resist it out of fear that it will decrease their productivity and affect their remuneration.

- **Fear of the Unknown:** people associated change with uncertainty. They fear the unknown and the insecurity resulting from it. They are anxious about their ability to adapt to the requirements of a new system.

For example, when computers replaced manual systems, many people developed a negative attitude towards computers for the fear of not being able to acquire the necessary compute skills.

- **Selective Information Processing:** individuals from their own perceptions about people and the world around them and like to stick to these perceptions and do not like to receive any information that contradicts their perceptions.

  For example, employees may listen to their colleagues who tell them about the negative consequences of automation but ignore what managers say about the benefits of computerization. Employees perceive that automation is a threat to their jobs and therefore accept only the information that supports their perception.

- **Social Factors:** people also resist change when they anticipate that the change might affect their status in the society adversely. When jobs are redesigned, they develop a sense of insecurity regarding their position in the organization and consequently resist the effort.

Organizational Resistance: organizational resistance can be seen in public sector undertakings in India. The structural inertia in the bureaucratic organizations also hinders change.

- **Structural Inertia:** organizations always attempt to maintain a steady and balanced state that is conductive to employees. They have inbuilt mechanisms to achieve that state of equilibrium. When change program is initiated in the organization, the structural inertia created y these inbuilt mechanisms offer strong resistance.

For example, if a good number of employees and managers leave the company foı various reasons, the work load on the remaining employees and managers will increase.

- **Limited Focus of Change:** an organization consists of many sub-systems that are interrelated and interdependent. Change in one system will affect other systems as well therefore, one cannot introduce change in a subsystem without considering its impact on the rest of the system.
- **Threat to Expertise:** the expertise of specialized group may be threatened by changes in organizational patterns.

For example, a general manager may prefer to make crucial decisions himself rather than delegating them to his subordinates due to the fear that decentralizing the process of decision-making would threaten is expertise.

- **Economic Factors:** people feel attached to the organization for satisfying their needs and economic needs-physiological, job security etc. employees perceive that they will be affected by the change in the terms of their needs satisfaction in the following ways like sill obsolescence, fear of economic loss, reduced opportunities for incentives etc.

John P Kotter's 'Eight Steps to Successful Change'

American John P Kotter (b 1947) is a Harvard Business School professor and leading thinker and author on organizational change management. Kotter's highly regarded books 'Leading Change' (1995) and the follow-up 'The Heart Of Change' (2002) describe a helpful model for understanding and managing change. Each stage acknowledges a key principle identified by Kotter relating to people's response and approach to change, in which people see, feel and then change.

Kotter's eight step change model can be summarised as:

- **Increase Urgency** - inspire people to move, make objectives real and relevant.
- **Build the Guiding Team** - get the right people in place with the right emotional commitment, and the right mix of skills and levels.
- **Get the Vision Right** - get the team to establish a simple vision and strategy, focus on emotional and creative aspects necessary to drive service and efficiency.
- **Communicate for Buy-in** - Involve as many people as possible, communicate the essentials, simply, and to appeal and respond to people's needs. De-clutter communications - make technology work for you rather than against.
- **Empower Action** - Remove obstacles, enable constructive feedback and lots of support from leaders - reward and recognise progress and achievements.
- **Create Short-term Wins** - Set aims that are easy to achieve - in bite-size chunks. Manageable numbers of initiatives. Finish current stages before starting new ones.
- **Don't Let Up** - Foster and encourage determination and persistence - ongoing change - encourage ongoing progress reporting - highlight achieved and future milestones.
- **Make Change Stick** - Reinforce the value of successful change via recruitment, promotion, and new change leaders. Weave change into culture.

Benefits and Significance of Change Management

Benefits and Significance

The subject matter holds a tremendous importance for both individual and organization. Let us discuss some of the benefits from organization perspective.

Understanding Environment (Society, Government, Customers): It is important for organization to understand, assess and gauge the dynamics in its external environment in order to envisage and establish an appropriate relationship with various actors like government, customers and society. Therefore managers by knowing the subject of change management can better be prepared to understand whatever is going on in the environment.

Objectives, Strategy Formulation & Implementation (to develop competitive advantage): Second is consequent upon knowing the impact of change at extraneous level on its own internal dynamics, and the foremost is objective setting and seeking competitive advantage.

- Employees (trained, high performing work practices, reliable organisation) The employees are the recipient of change plan. One such perpetual concern of senior managers is to make organization highly reliable, therefore employees ought to be trained and high performing one in today's hyper competitive world.
- Technology Issues

Technology is considered the engine of growth in today's world. Perhaps the greatest challenge for contemporary organizations is the acquisition and integration of technology in its strategy, structure and process. As such the concern of top managers is how to avoid organization being obsolete and how to cope and absorb the impact of changing information and communication technologies which have decisively influencing production and consumption behavior.

Globalization: The management of international economic and political forces what is today known as internationalization and globalization is yet another important factor influencing decision making of organization. No organization or nation can stay independent and indifferent to whatever is happening at international (political) level. For instance the impact of September 11 events have been tremendous on the economies and organizations of developing countries like Pakistan. Similarly supra – national institutions are becoming more assertive over nation states not only in political terms but also on social issues like child labor and gender issues. So government and states are considered somewhat less sovereign in imposing their will over their subjects (individual and organizations) against the ever increasing and complex interdependencies amongst states. For example the compulsions and legal provisions of international treaties like WTO and ISO certification regimes have decisively influenced the organizations and economies of the developing world. Hence imperative for managers, CEOs and entrepreneurs from smaller or larger organizations alike, of different sectors of economy, is to understand the complexities of globalization and its impact on organization' business.

The Relationship of Management with Change-Management: The relationship can be understood along the following lines. First, we have to consider that change management is a subject with cross-cutting theme, applicable across various traditional functional areas like management, marketing, production, finance and comprehensively with more recent strategic management concepts. For instance, this is related with marketing where the concern might be new product or market development, or can be related with production like the introduction or acquisition of new technology or skills. Viz. the finance – budgetary allocations, revisions and cost-cutting strategies, and for HR the concern is behavioral modification, formation and accumulation of technical and managerial knowledge, skills and values.

Strategic Management Domain: Within the strategic domain we have two concerns: One is Strategy formulation, that is formulating mission, vision and objectives after going through environmental assessment (a key feature of strategic management), and second pertains to strategy implementation means organization structure, culture and politics. While the whole focus of the popular framework of strategic management is the development and sustenance of competitive advantage of a firm or organization, at multiple levels of strategy making – functional, business, corporate and societal levels.

Enhanced Collaboration and Communication: Encouraging dialogue and circulating the information people need to know leads to a more cooperative, and more productive, environment.

Higher Retention Rate for Employees: A carefully thought-out approach to change reduces stress and turmoil and encourages people to stay loyal to your organization.

Better Customer Service: An effective organization with good morale and knowledgeable employees can deliver the benefit most changes are designed to provide - better and more cost effective service to clients.

Conclusion

Organizational change management is the perspective of business leadership from the top looking down into the organization. The focus is around broad change management practices and skills that will help the organization understand, accept and support the needed business change. The emphasis is on communications, training and the overall culture or value system of the organization. Individual change management is the management of change from the perspective of the employees. They are the ones who ultimately must implement the change. The focus for individual change management is around the tools and techniques to help employees through the transition. Managers and supervisors must provide the coaching required helping individuals understand their role and the decisions they make in the change process. Overall, change management is about helping people through change. It is the process, tools and techniques for proactively managing the people side of change in order to achieve the desired business results.

Examples of Effective Change Management in India

Change Management at HP Consultancy Operation in UK

On May 2002, two leading players in the global computer industry- Hewlett-Packard Company (HP) and Compaq Computer Corporation (Compaq) completed the merger which they had announced in September 2001. Care was taken to avoid many difficulties that usually crop up after mergers or acquisitions, like poor communication. To overcome communication problems, one-to one briefings were conducted, and information via e-mail and websites, etc., were sent to inform the employees about the merger, plans for the new company, and the role each of them would have to play after the merger.

Following the merger, the leadership team of the HP consultancy operation in the UK, which had about 800 employees, felt that there, was some sort of uneasiness in the organization. They decided to conduct some research on the factors that were causing the erosion of employee motivation and sought the help of workforce performance consultant Javier Bajer. Bajer joined HP as a consultant for three weeks and conducted a secret research operation about employee satisfaction in the organization. He collected feedback through informal discussions with about 150 employees at various levels of the organizational hierarchy.

When Bajer presented his findings to the leadership, it was surprised to learn that serious issues had surfaced in the organization which had severely damaged staff morale and motivation. There were problems relating to staff development, access of employees to organizational resources, lack of clarity about competitors, etc. the leadership on its part also tried to find out the causes for the breakdown in employee motivation after the merger. It found that even though it had worked hard prior to the merger, it had not indicated that it was in favor of it. Another finding was that there was only one-way communication with employees and that their problems were not properly attended to.

To reinstate motivation among the employees, the management started an all-inclusive 'people plan'. One aspect of this was an 'action event'-in which the employees were allowed to actively participate in solving business problems rather than being told what to do. A two-day long decision making session was conducted for 50 employees, who represented all the employees. Six months after the action event, an evaluation was done which showed that the event had been a success and that the level of motivation and commitment of the employees in the organization had improved.

Agilent Technologies-Transparency in Operations

Agilent Technologies, (Agilent) a spin-off of Hewlett-Packard, was headed by CEO Ned Barnholt from 1999 to 2005. Barnholt built Agilent into the world's leading developer and manufacturer of test, measurement, and moitoring devices. Under Barnholt's leadership, Agilent introduced many new products each year, and made technology innovation the basis of its enduring strategy. In 2001, Agilent faced a severe crisis on account of the economic slump of that year and the September 11 attack in the USA. Even though sales were low, the management headed by Barnholt tried various measures like a ten percent salary cut for all to avoid layoffs. When these measures proved futile, the company decided to reduce its workforce consisting of about 47,000 employees by one-fourth.

Management wanted to ensure that the downscaling operations were as transparent a possible. They maintained regular contact with the employees through the intranet, meetings, e-mail etc. these contacts, which were held both in groups and on an individual basis, were aimed at making the employees fully aware of what was happening.

Bharat Heavy Electricals Ltd.

The organizational set up of the heavy electrical industry working under two separate companies i.e., Heavy Electricals India Ltd. and Bharat Heavy Electricals Ltd. come up for review in 1971 in the wake of a grave power crisis. A committee was set up by the government to look into the working of these two enterprises. One of the recommendations made by the committee was that HEIL controlling the Bhopal unit should be merged with BHEL to ensure optimum utilization of available resources. Although different plants followed different standards and practices of decision was taken to merge the two companies and integrate the operations of different operating divisions. Though HEIL and BHEL were big employing 20,000 and 25,000 people respectively, it was strongly felt that, unless the different heavy electrical units worked in an integrated manner, the objective of providing better service to the customer could not be achieved. There was full awareness of the problems to be faced particularly in the human aspect associated with such integration. Individual interest were bound to come to conflict with overall organizational interests. Two steps were taken (Krishnamurty, 1977).

- The first step was to explain to all employees the benefits of integration. A series of meetings were held with various groups of employees at all levels. The rationale of reorganization was explained to them and their ideas were sought. An attempt was made to create an atmosphere in which all employees irrespective of their status and functional back-ground, could freely discuss and contribute their suggestions. This gave the employees a sense of involvement and belongingness to the organization. During the second year after the merger a few eminent management consultants from the UK visited BHEL's divisions. They were pleasantly surprised to find hardly any visible signs of merger with all divisions working as one organization.
- Another thing essential for bringing about a successful merger was the development of a bias towards optimism. Change can be effective only if a climate exists in which people are optimistic, feel a psychological freedom in their innovative attempts, and perceive an opportunity for their own growth and development in the process. They were given an opportunity to contribute in the planning and organization of their jobs. A system of responsibility-oriented functioning based on centralized policy formulation and decentralized execution and administration was adapted. In day-to-day functioning the executives were given full freedom to take their decisions as long as they were in line with the annual approved budgeted commitments and were within the policy guidelines.

References

Radha R. Sharma, Change Management, Concepts and Applications, the McGraw-Hill Companies, pg. 1.

Management Process and Organization Behavior, Sikkim Manipal University, B1127.

"Preparing for Organizational Change o Employee Self Management- The Managerial Transition.". Organizational Dynamics, 10 August 2003, *http://search.epnet.com.*

"Organization Development and Social Change." The Banyan Tree: A Textbook for Holistic Health Practitioners. *http://www.healthlibrary.com/reading/banyan2/8intro.htm*

Mirza S. Saiyadain, Human Resources Management, Third Edition, Tata McGraw Hill, pg.191.

Adapted from Cotam, Chris and Javier Bajer.: How HP Employees Changed the Business –in 36 Hours." SCM Volume8, Issue 1 December/January 2004.

Adapted from Tapscott, Don "They'll find out Anyway." *<http://www.intelligent enterprise.com/030630/ 611change1_1jhtml>june30,2003.*

20

CROSS CULTURAL ISSUES AND MANAGING DIVERSITY

K. Sanjeeva Rao

Introduction

The workforce of the 21st century is increasingly diverse and multicultural. The trend of globalization is providing opportunities for Indian firms to reach foreign markets. The business model of many upcoming industries like the information technology sector is dependent heavily on the foreign markets. This increases the need of professionals working in foreign cultural settings. The merger and acquisition activity especially the cross-border acquisitions have reached much higher levels. The trend of acquisitions is not only restricted to the new sectors like Information Technology, Telecom and Business Process Outsourcing, but core sector companies like Manufacturing (For Example: Bharat Forge acquiring Carl Dan Peddinghaus in Germany) and Mining (For Example: Sterlite group acquiring mines in Australia) have observed spurt in such activities too. The Pharmaceutical companies have widened their reach in world market with examples like Ranbaxy and DRL having presence in many countries. The globalization dreams present a new challenge for the Indian firms; the challenge to develop competent managers who would be able to work in new environments efficiently and will act as a bridge between the parent company and its subsidiaries. The globalization will also bring new employees to the Indian firms, the ones with different origin, language and national culture adding complexities to the culture of Indian organizations. The firms thus need to develop systems and processes not only to train managers for expatriate assignments but also to handle cultural diversity. This task can be achieved by well designed cross-cultural training programs which will help employees in coping up with the stress and cultural shock while dealing with a new culture. The need for cross-cultural training will be for both: Indian expatriates and employees dealing with expatriates of other origins. The cross-cultural training will also be required for the Indian companies getting into Business Process Outsourcing as the clients belong to culturally different environments. Working effectively in cross-cultural context is becoming vital competence for aspiring managers (Harris and Kumra, 2000).

Effective cross-cultural communication is necessary to build and maintain business relationships. To support their organizations, HR professionals can develop HRM practices and policies that promote cross-cultural training and reward managers for their part in educating employees on effective cross-cultural communication. HR must be knowledgeable about cross-cultural factors-on both the domestic and global fronts-in human resource management. By promoting education in cross-cultural competencies throughout the organization, HR can better serve the company to successfully achieve its mission and goals.

Why Cross Cultural Awareness?

"...the single greatest barrier to business success is the one erected by culture." Edward T. Hall and Mildred Reed Hall

Working, meeting, dealing, entertaining, negotiating and corresponding with colleagues or clients from different cultures can be a minefield.

Understanding and appreciating intercultural differences ultimately promotes clearer communication, breaks down barriers, builds trust, strengthens relationships, opens horizons and yields tangible results in terms of business success.

The Nature and Impact of National Cultural Differences

It is useful to identify clear framework for analyzing and understanding national cultural differences. Such frameworks have been developed by researchers and consultants such as Hofstede and Trompenaars. While the respective merits and drawbacks of different frameworks are widely discussed, I feel that use of one framework is helpful to illustrate the major issues which need to be considered. For this purpose I have selected Hofstede's basic model.

In his original work Hofstede identified four key dimensions which impact on natural cultural differences. These are:

- **Individualism/Collectivism**: This dimensions reflect the extent to which individuals value self-determination as opposed to their behavior being determined by the collective will of a group or organization.
- **Power-distance:** At the core of this dimension lies the question of involvement in decision making. In low power-distance cultures, employees seek involvement and have a desire for a participative management style. At the other end of this scale, employees tend to work and behave in a particular way because they accept that they will be directed to do so by the hierarchy or the organization.
- **Uncertainty Avoidance:** This dimension is concerned with employees' tolerance of ambiguity or uncertainty in theri working environment. In cultures which have a high uncertainty avoidance, employees will look for clearly defined, formal rules and conventions governing their behaviour.
- **Masculinity/Femininity:** This is possibly the most difficult dimension to use in an organization context. In practice, the difficulty is more to do with terminology and linguistics, in Hofstede's work the dimension related to values. In highly "masculine cultures" dominant values relate to assertiveness and material acquisition. In highly "feminine cultures" values focus on relationship among people, concern for others and quality of life.

General Cross Cultural Awareness Training, and Culture/Country Specific Training

The term "cross cultural training" refers to a variety of different training courses. Each in essence aims to develop awareness between people where a common cultural framework does not exist Cross cultural awareness training deals with the manifestations of culture in the workplace and has many applications. Its main purpose is to evaluate and constructively tackle the challenges cross cultural differences can bring to the workplace. A few examples of the courses we cover can illustrate the different applications of cross cultural awareness training:

- **Cross Cultural Team Building** Training will aim to raise team members' awareness of each other culturally in order to foster mutual trust, respect and understanding. The result of which will be clearer lines of communication.
- **Cross Cultural Management** Training aims to equip management staff with the knowledge and skills to effectively supervise a multi-cultural staff. Cross cultural awareness training results in a more convivial and understanding work environment.
- **Cross Cultural Negotiation** Training assists negotiators involved with foreign clients or customers with whom they are discussing possible terms and conditions.
- **Cultural Diversity Training** offers HR staff support in helping them understand their responsibilities to ethnic minority staff and/or look at ways of nurturing harmonious inter-personal relationships at work.
- **Culture Specific Training** is generally aimed at individuals or teams that regularly visit a foreign country or who frequently interact with overseas clients or colleagues. Such training usually focuses on areas such as values, morals, ethics, business practices, etiquette, protocol or negotiation styles with reference to one country. This better equips participants with the key skills that will help in building successful business relationships.

Example: Relocating to Another Country

If you are relocating to a country with a higher group orientation, make sure that you are aware of the need for colleagues to consult a larger group before making decisions; therefore, early stages of decision-making may take more time than you expect, although implementation may be generally more rapid than you expect.

If you are relocating to a country with a higher individual orientation, be aware that individuals whose role or position enables them to speak on behalf of the larger group without directly consulting them will often make decisions quickly. You can also expect that you will need to take more individual responsibility for your job performance than you may be used to.

The following six best-practice strategies for assuring that offshore teams will develop the required cross-cultural competency in American business culture:

Tip #1. Get Executives to Value Cross-cultural Training

Build commitment from the highest level possible in the company that training offshore teams in American business culture is a valued (and funded) strategy in support of productivity, and assign clear ownership and accountability for the execution of this strategy.

Tip #2. Make the Training a Team Effort

Get involvement of specialized high-level outside expertise, the business units involved in the offshore relationship, and internal training and HR functions in developing the best possible model for delivering the training.

Tip #3. Bring in Outside Experts

For best results, use training content and delivery by specialists with direct experience and in-depth knowledge of both American and Indian culture, as well as expertise in the field of cross-cultural communication.

Tip # 4. Train on Both Shores

In the case of American companies, provide coordinated training of the offshore Indian teams in American business culture and training of the onshore American teams in Indian business culture.

Tip #5. Integrate Training into New Employee Orientation

For both American companies with operations in India and Indian providers of outsourcing services, integrate training in American business culture as part of the regular induction processes for new employees. This applies not only to those who may be going to the United States, but all those who will be working with American counterparts, whether face-to-face or virtually.

Tip #6. Reinforce the Training with Mentoring

Engage onshore and offshore business unit heads and project leaders in reinforcing the content of the training. This involves ongoing mentoring of the offshore teams in the elements of American business culture that need to be practiced for success in working with Americans.

The 10 Benefits of Cross Cultural Training

Cross cultural differences can and do impede upon communication and interpersonal relationships. In the business world this occurs daily, where people from different cultures interact and are expected to perform and make decisions. Cross cultural training aims to develop awareness between people where a common cultural framework does not exist in order to promote clear lines of communication and better relationships.

Cross cultural training has many benefits to be gained by both participants and businesses. For participants in cross cultural training, the 10 main benefits are that it helps:

- **People Learn About Themselves:** Through cross cultural training, people are exposed to facts and information about their own cultures, preconceptions, mentalities and worldviews that they may otherwise not have contemplated. Cross cultural training helps people learn more about themselves through learning about others.
- **Encourage Confidence:** Cross cultural training promotes self-confidence in individuals and teams through empowering them with a sense of control over previously difficult challenges in the workplace.
- **Break Down Barriers:** All of us have certain barriers such as preconceptions, prejudices and stereotypes that obstruct our understanding of other people. Cross cultural training demystifies other cultures through presenting them under an objective light. Through learning about other cultures, barriers are slowly chipped away thus allowing for more open relationships and dialogue.
- **Build Trust:** When people's barriers are lowered, mutual understanding ensues, which results in greater trust. Once trust is established altruistic tendencies naturally manifest allowing for greater co-operation and a more productive workplace.

- **Motivate:** One of the outcomes of cross cultural training is that people begin to see their roles within the workplace more clearly. Through self-analysis people begin to recognise areas in which they need to improve and become motivated to develop and progress.
- **Open Horizons:** Cross cultural training addresses problems in the workplace at a very different angle to traditional methods. Its innovative, alternative and motivating way of analysing and resolving problems helps people to adopt a similarly creative strategy when approaching challenges in their work or personal lives.
- **Develop Interpersonal Skills:** Through cross cultural training participants develop great 'people skills' that can be applied in all walks of life. By learning about the influence of culture, i.e. the hidden factors upon people's behaviours, those who undertake cross cultural training begin to deal with people with a sensitivity and understanding that may have previously been lacking.
- **Develop Listening Skills:** Listening is an integral element of effective and productive communication. Cross cultural training helps people to understand how to listen, what to listen for and how to interpret what they hear within a much broader framework of understanding. By becoming good listeners, people naturally become good communicators.
- **People Use Common Ground:** In the workplace people have a tendency to focus on differences. When cross cultural communication problems arise the natural inclination is to withdraw to opposing sides and to highlight the negative aspects of the other. Cross cultural training assists in developing a sense of mutual understanding between people by highlighting common ground. Once spaces of mutual understanding are established, people begin to use them to overcome culturally challenging situations.
- **Career Development:** Cross cultural training enhances people's skills and therefore future employment opportunities. Having cross cultural awareness gives people a competitive edge over others especially when applying for positions in international companies with a large multi-cultural staff base.

The above benefits are but a few of the many ways in which cross cultural training positively affects businesses through staff training and development.

Effectiveness of having Diversity in Workforce

Why should companies concern themselves with diversity? Many managers answered this question with the assertion that discrimination is wrong, both legally and morally. But today managers are voicing a second notion as well. A more diverse workforce, they say, will increase organizational effectiveness. It will lift morale, bring greater access to new segments of the marketplace, and enhance productivity. In short, they claim, diversity will be good for business. Research stated that the Canadian companies leading the way in the area of diversity management have discovered that by embracing the elements of ethnic and cultural diversity in their workforce they have enhanced their ability to understand and tap new markets, both within Canada and abroad. Research generated from a variety of fields predicts that important benefits will accrue from demographic heterogeneity in organizations by increasing the variance in perspectives and approaches to work that members of different identity groups can bring(e.g., Thomas and Ely, 1996).

Importance of Managing Diversity

As the companies of today are getting more and more diverse, the need of managing the diverse workfare is increasing. All Countries specially USA and Canada are having more diverse workforce every day. So it is becoming important for the companies manage the diversity to get better results out of employees. Research stated that Forward-thinking Canadian organizations have recognized that competing successfully in the new global marketplace requires more than the latest technology, most efficient production processes, or most innovative products. Canadian organizations' competitive strength is increasingly contingent on human resources. Competing to win in the global economy will require an ability to attract, retain, motivate and develop high- potential employees of both genders from a variety of cultural and ethnic backgrounds. The challenge facing today's corporate leaders is to foster an organizational culture that values differences and maximizes the potential of all employees. In other words, leaders must learn to manage diversity.

The Role of Language

Today, communicating in the global marketplace requires new perspectives and new communication skills. In fact, the appropriate use of language in cross-cultural settings often depends on the situation. Thus, when developing HRM policies, practices and initiatives, it is important to consider the role of language in cross-cultural environments. For example, to roll out new initiatives worldwide, it may be necessary (and often required by law) to translate HRM policies and programs into other languages.

Example: Colgate-Palmolive Company is an example of an organization that has effectively communicated key HRM programs to its global workforce. Keeping in mind the different languages spoken in the firm, two critical HRM core value initiatives, Valuing Colgate People and Managing with Respect were translated into 10 languages. Valuing Colgate People includes a section on the company's business ethics, code of conduct and business practice guidelines. These initiatives set the stage for the organization's strategy to become a best place to work.

Understanding Body Language

When working with people from different cultures and/or countries, organizational leaders must know how to "read" body language, a key communication factor in high-context cultures. Misunderstanding body language can lead to inaccurate expectations. With many Western companies now doing business with India, a good example of a common cross-cultural difference is one of the head gestures by Indians. As cross-cultural trainer and management consultant Craig Storti explains, the Indian head gesture for "yes" appears similar to how Westerners shake their head to indicate "no." When seeing this gesture, Westerners may think that the Indian has disagreed, when that is not necessarily so. Taking time to understand communication through body language can make the difference in a positive or negative outcome. These various points are representative of the many scenarios that require flexibility and knowledge about language and cross-cultural communication.

Cultural Perceptions of Organizational Justice

There are three broad categories of organizational justice: 1) procedural justice (fairness of methods used); 2) interactional justice (the quality of treatment); and 3) distributive justice (perception of process and fairness of the outcome).

In a culturally diverse workforce, perceptions of justice may vary due to cultural values. A recent study examined cultural factors that influence how employees form overall justice perceptions in the United States, China, Korea and Japan. The study examined employee reactions in industry sectors such as finance, education, service, information technology and manufacturing. According to the study, the effect of perception of fairness on turnover is greater for Americans than for Chinese or Koreans. Americans are more likely to leave their organization as a result of perceived organizational injustice than are Japanese, Chinese or Korean employees.

Cross-Cultural Decision-Making

Whether in a domestic or global workplace, HR needs to be cognizant of cross-cultural decision-making and the corresponding influence on HRM. By being aware of cultural differences in the decision-making process (e.g., the reasons for making decisions, the various ways that decisions are made in different cultures, the party responsible for making those decisions—individuals, groups, various levels within the organization—and the ways decisions are implemented), HR can better gauge culturally appropriate decisions and work with managers of other cultures in the decision-making process.

Cross-Cultural Performance Feedback

Lack of cross-cultural sensitivity in the performance appraisal process can result in negative impact on communication, employee morale, teamwork and turnover. To get better performance results in culturally diverse employee populations, companies may need to re-examine and redefine their performance standards to ensure cultural bias does not influence the performance appraisal process. In a collectivist or high-context culture, such as India and Japan, where in-group harmony and interpersonal relationships are highly valued, it is recommended to give feedback in a manner that is subtle, indirect and non-confrontational. Researchers suggest that for certain feedback processes, such as 360-degree feedback, which involves explicit feedback, employees be trained to understand and utilize such feedback, particularly if it does not match their cultural orientation of communication. Presented by authors Milliman, Taylor and Czaplewski, the following mini-case study illustrates a critical incident in which cultural differences in the performance feedback process contributed to an unexpected response.

Example: Mini-Case Study: Cross-Cultural Performance Feedback

Fred, a team leader in software engineering at a U.S.-based multinational enterprise, leads a virtual work group. His team is working on a new product and is under pressure to meet quality standards and get the product to the marketplace. Some of his team members are located in Malaysia. Since the team was provided with technology for global communications, such as electronic group software and teleconferencing, the company did not provide cross-cultural training. Fred writes an e-mail to his counterpart team leader, Hisham, in Malaysia to inform him that the testing process must end and the next phase of the project must now go forward. Hisham does not respond to Fred's e-mail for many days, and the Malaysian team continues to do testing on the product. For the final stage of the project, Fred flies to Malaysia. Two weeks after the U.S. deadline has passed, the project is successfully completed.

Within the company's goal to operate as a global company, one of the new practices is 360-degree feedback. In his supervisory role, Fred gathers the required feedback and then meets with Hisham. Fred informs Hisham that while he performed well on the project, there were issues upon which he could improve. Fred documents the feedback in an e-mail to Hisham, with a copy to Hisham's supervisor in Malaysia. From Fred's viewpoint, he has completed the performance appraisal in accordance with the company standards, feeling that he has been both fair and transparent. Back in the United States the following week, Fred is quite surprised to learn that Hisham, immediately following the performance appraisal meeting, applied for a transfer to another team. Fred recalls that Hisham was quiet during the performance appraisal. He thinks that the transfer is for the best, particularly if Hisham cannot deal with constructive criticism. After all, Fred knows that the success of the project is what is most important.

In this mini-case study, different cultural dimensions are involved: 1) Malaysia is a high-context culture where communication requires awareness of facial expressions, tone of voice and eye contact, and 2) the United States is a low-context culture where people depend more on words than on external expressions for meaning. Differences in collectivism-individualism also explain the miscommunication between Fred and Hisham. Collectivism emphasizes creating harmony and loyalty between people. Yet, due to Fred's direct and assertive approach in the performance appraisal, Hisham experienced individual criticism and consequently suffered a loss of "face" for his team. On his end, Fred acted within the values of his individualistic culture and emphasized individual responsibility, not group responsibility, in Hisham's performance appraisal. Clearly, Fred is unawareof the cultural context in which he spoke to Hisham. Had Fred received cross-cultural training regarding the Malaysian workplace and appropriately communicated his feedback, Hirsham may not have requested the transfer.

Developing Global Mindset

From a cross-cultural viewpoint, Paul Evans, Vladimir Pucik and Jean-Louis Barsoux, experts in global HR management, point out that it is "global mindset"—a state of mind—that differentiates global managers. Global mindset is the ability to work effectively across organizational, functional and cross-cultural boundaries. The strongest mechanism to develop global mindset is the international assignment. HR can foster development of global mindset by ensuring that talented employees worldwide—no matter their passport country—have equal access to opportunities. Focused learning programs can also promote global mindset.

Example: Multinational corporations such as Unilever, Johnson & Johnson and General Electric have effectively used in-house experiential action-learning programs for a broad cross-section of high-potential employees to speed up the development of global mindset.

Career Perspectives Across Cultures

Recent studies look at career beliefs, social networking and the influence of political, social and economic changes on career concepts in nations around the world. One study explores career-life success and family social support among successful women in Argentina, Canada and Mexico. In all three countries, women now consider broader measures of career success than have been traditionally viewed, such as learning and contributing to society. In Canada and Mexico, many women now see receiving recognition in the workplace as evidence of career success. A study in Russia notes that new career beliefs and behaviors are emerging, in great part due to multinational corporations entering Russia and introducing Western ideas about career development (e.g., mentoring and coaching, management education and training, professional development).

Culture Shock

Failure to identify cultural issues and take action can lead to a culture shock. In order of priority, the most often found symptoms of culture shock are[3]:

- feeling isolated
- anxiety and worry
- reduction in job performance
- high nervous energy
- helplessness.

Not coping with culture shock symptoms when they appear can lead to a very negative situation.

References

Bodley, J.H. (1999), Cultural Anthropology: Tribes, States, and the Global System (3rd edition). United Kingdom: Mayfield Publishing Company.

Society for Human Resource Management. (n.d). Glossary of Human Resources terms. Retrieved May 14, 2008, from *www.shrm.org*

Society for Human Resource Management (2007), The 2007-2008 Workplace Trends List. Alexandria, VA: Author.

Society for Human Resource Management (2008), Workplace Forecast. Alexandria, VA: Author.

Gelfand, M.J., Erez, M., & Aycan, Z. (2007), Cross-cultural Organizational Behavior. Annual Review of Psychology, 58, 479-514.

Carter, L. (2005), Best Practices in Leading the Global Workforce: How the Best Global companies Ensure Success throughout their Workforce. Burlington, MA: Linkage.

Storti, C. (2007), Speaking of India: Bridging the Communication Gap when Working with Indians. Boston: Intercultural Press.

(25) Kim, T-Y, & Leung, K. (2007), Forming and Reacting to Overall Fairness: A cross-cultural Perspective. Organizational Behavior and Human Decision Processes, 104, 83-95.

Moran, R.T., Harris, P.R., & Stripp, W.G. (1993), Developing the Global Organization: Strategies for Human Resource Professionals. London: Gulf Publishing Company.

Aycan, Z. (2005), The Interplay between Cultural and Institutional/Structural Contingencies in Human Resource Management Practices. The International Journal of Human Resource Management, July, 16(7), 1083-1119.

Milliman, J., Taylor, S., & Czaplewski, A.J. (2002), Cross-cultural Performance Feedback in Multinational Enterprises: Opportunity for Organizational Learning. HR. Human Resource Planning, 25(3), 29-44.

Evans, P., Pucik, V., & Barsoux, J-L. (2002), The Global Challenge: Frameworks for International Human Resource Management. New York: McGraw-Hill Irwin.

Inkson, K., Khapova, S.N., & Parker, P. (2007), Careers in Cross-cultural Perspective. Career Development International, 12(1), 5+.

Lirio, P., Lituchy, T.R., Ines Monserrat, S., Olivas-Lujan, M.R., Duffy, J.A., Fox, S., et al. (2007), Exploring Career-life Success and Family Social Support of Successful Women in Canada, Argentina and Mexico. Career Development International, 12(1), 28-50.

Khapova, S.N. (2007), Dynamics of Western Career Attributes in the Russian Context. Career Development International, 12(1), 68+.

21

LEADERSHIP DEVELOPMENT IN THE CONTEXT OF SUSTAINABLE GROWTH

Dhananjay Singh

Introduction

The borderless economy presents before us one wonderful gift- 'Uncertainty'. The globalised world provides economic growth and abundant opportunities to be seized by individuals and corporations. The question is- How professionals assess and proactively respond to ever changing scenarios. And in the fast changing world, Leadership plays a very pivotal role. Is the science of Leadership based on foundation of Plato's Republic, Army functioning, McGregor's Theory of X and Y onwards lack the art of real life management of today's world, The question is: Is the ever fast changing world and its implications too complex to handle with today's knowledge and expertise.

Arieu, A. has defined Leadership as "a person capable of inspiring and associate others with a dream." This definition pulls two or more persons of a group towards a common goal.

In pursuit of common goals, the organizations come across the challenges of managing teams and there day to day operations. The day to day operations are end result of team work and cohesiveness of various teams to delver results. The teams provides assets to the organization to move on and shift orbits in the globalised world.

Employees & Teams are being rated on a grid where potential is on one axis and performance is on the other. This gives an opportunity to employees to understand 'where they are' and 'what they should do'.

The Leader looks up to the talent pool for organizational growth and sustainability. The teams look up to the Leader. This mutual working and hand holding is taking organization to places !

However, in the history of humanity, it has been observed that when individuals and organizations focus only on short term and individual goals- we face leadership crisis. With leadership crises comes the challenge of sustainable growth. The best intentions and policies fail to ride the rare sustainable wave due to self-centeredness.

In order to avoid 'leadership void', the organizations build Leadership Pipeline. The Leadership pipeline is encouraged at all levels and this serves as one critical way to sustain growth in the globalized environment.

Objectives

- To identify atleast one Talent Management Intervention of Aditya Birla Group
- To identify pre-requisite for leadership role in Aditya Birla Group
- To identify atleast two behavioral competency being tracked and measured in Aditya Birla Group
- Understanding how Talent Management will enhance business performance

Methodology

Secondary Research - books and web papers.

Talent Management

Talent management gained prominence in the decade of 1990's. HR professionals used the term to focus on the management of human resources which included a pool of talent. Mr David Watkins popularized the term Talent Management in 1998.

Talent Management refers to the skills of attracting good (talented) employees in the organization. This also includes developing and retaining employees to meet today's and tomorrows organization needs.

Talent Management helped organizations to understand that building talent pool and managing them to achieve organizational goals is a common responsibility. Unlike earlier unsaid believe that it is only HR Function.

In the last 20 years, the organizations has evolved multiple Talent Management strategies. These strategies differ from industry to industry and company to company. Specialized Talent Management strategies are developed to attract and retain employees at all levels. Large organizations invest a lot of time and money on Talent Management as this becomes the Competitive edge and strategic advantage.

Talent Management at Aditya Birla Group

The Aditya Birla Group is –

- World's largest aluminum rolling company
- world leader in viscose staple fiber
- one of the leading cement producers in India and eighth-largest globally
- fourth-largest producer of carbon black in the world
- fourth-largest producer of insulators black in the world
- fifth-largest producer of acrylic fiber in the world

The growing businesses of ABG requires Talent. The talent required must have multiple capabilities. ABG prefers to make products rather than 'buy and trade'. This puts more pressure on the Group to manage Talent and make businesses sustainable.

All employees, across the Senior, Middle, and Junior Management, have talent and potential that can be harnessed. The Group invests differentially in different talents.

ABG has a Common Talent Management Framework. At ABG, the steps involved in Talent Management are as under-

- Awareness about concepts and principles of Talent Management- The group provides detailed concepts and principles of Talent Management to the employees. The idea is to provide clarity on the expectations of the oragnisation and career Road map to the individuals.

- Talent dialogue with HR and Business Head – The employee and the HR Head/ Busienss Head sit together and discuses potential, performance and possibilities available to the employees.
- Providing Development Support to individuals- Through Career Stages Module, IDP booklet & Workshops the Group supports the career Development to individuals.
- Individual Development Plans(IDPs) –IDPs focus on a developmental action plan for 3-5 years. IDPs provide step-by step developmental objectives and career goals. The document defines the responsibility of employee and the supervisor in selecting learning activities in achieving these objectives and goals.
- Development Assessment Centers (DACs) - DAC assess people for their potential. The Assessment is done on multiple relevant competencies for current, as well as next two career stages. DAC is done for all managers identified as talent pool across all managerial levels.
- Institutionalization of Talent Management Process – In order to make a continuous process, ABG believes in Institutionalizing the Talent Management Process. The feedback system has been designed to provide the critical inputs so that with changing times the organization may not only adjust proactively but also lead change.

Pre-requisite for Leadership Role

"We have good corporals and good sergeants and some good lieutenants and captains, and those are far more important than good generals" — Gen William T. Sherman

Traditionally organizations have been looking up to leaders for direction. In the current time the Leader-follower equations have changed. It is rightly said, 'Leadership is action not position'. The fact that each manager, in a globalised world, plays both the roles of leader and follower.

In India, Professional Management is taking over traditional ways of managing business. The mindset is changing fast. The results are showing up for the empowerment. India Inc is growing.

Pre-requisite for Leadership Role in Aditya Birla Group

Aditya Birla Group has grown 15 times in last 15 years!

This speaks about the Talent Management and Leadership in ABG. The Pre-requisite for Leadership Role at Aditya Birla group is willingness to go beyond the comfort zones of one's city and immediate surroundings and requirements will signal to the organization, willingness to invest in one's own future. Hence, being mobile in ABG count's. At ABG, Career management is not a one way street where the organization strives to meet individuals aspirations, whereas individuals are unwilling to accept even temporary dislocation and disruption at a time when organization needs them. Naturally the organization would be levitating more towards those who stand by the organization at such moments of truth.

Behavioral Competencies

Competency provides ability to individuals to contribute to their job, in-turn to organization and its goals. The Competency is the ability of an individual to perform a job in satisfactory manner. Mr Richard Boyatzis coined the term Behavioral Competencies. The competency is an action by individuals and teams in a given situation or context.

This report focuses only of the Endeavour of ABG in developing Behavioral competencies.

As a part of Behavioral Competencies, ABG focuses on following-

- Business Acumen
- Vision and Strategy
- Promotes Team Work
- Develop Self and Others
- Customer Focus
- Innovates & Improves
- Gets Results
- Influencing
- Communication

Developing the Leadership Pipeline – Action Learning

Prof Reginald Revans is the founder of action learning. In 1940, Action Learning evolved in UK. In Action Learning, the Teams are encouraged to meet together in small groups. They share their experiences and follow it up with question and answer session. The Question and Answer sessions are based of the inputs received during such meeting. Keeping diverse functioning of ABG, a lot of conscious work has been done in Action Learning.

At ABG, the participants are encouraged to study their own actions and experience with an objective to improve performance. Action Learning has helped ABG employees to learn-by-doing and teaches through examples.

The learning happens in conjunction with others, in small groups. ABG has developed a Leadership Pipeline by taking following initiatives in Action Learning-

- by involving Top Management
- Ideas Unlimited Session with Chairman
- Project/Task forces: Unit/Business/inter-business/group level
- Line to staff switch
- Cross Functional rotation
- Job enlargement/enrichment
- "Pratibimb' – Online 360 Feedback Process

Senior Leaders Programme

In order to build the Leadership Pipeline, ABG has built various Senior Leaders Programmes. In a typical Senior Level Programme, following critical steps are involved-

- High potential managers selected from talent pool
- The High Potential Managers work on a project of strategic significance
- ABG provides supporting infrastructure to help the individual learn
- At conclusion of project, team members presents it's recommendations
- The presentation is made to Business Head & Chairman

India's first Multinational, Aditya Birla Group has tremendously benefited by such programmes. They have helped the Group to manage their businesses globally.

Understanding how Talent Management will enhance Business Performance

Armstrong and Baron focused on Performance and Performance Management. They defined performance management as 'a process. The Performance of the employees which includes Talent Pool, contributes to the effective management. ABG has implemented the Talent Management policies to make their products and services globally. By Individuals and teams contributions ABG has delivered high levels of organizational performance. ABG has ensured, by understanding 'what is to be achieved', the roadmap to develop people. ABG goes on to stress that it is 'a strategy which relates to every activity of the organization. ABG promotes a culture where actions are-

- **Strategic** – Employees are encouraged to think about broader issues and longer-term impact,
- **Integrated** – employees link their actions to all aspects of the business, personnel and environment.

In order to make Group globally Competitive, Aditya Birla Group has focused on following areas–

- Job Design
- Recruitment, Selection and assessment
- Performance Management
- Learning and Development
- Talent movement
- Rewards

Limitations and Suggestions for Future Research

Two limitations of the study merit attention and consideration in future research.

First, only secondary data has been used. In future, Primary Research will help to check whether 'what looks' is consistent with 'what people feel' on the ground. Second, research should include more than one organization so that in future comparative study between the two or more organizations can be done.

Conclusion

Aditya Birla Group believes in Attracting, developing and retaining people with the aptitude and abilities to meet current and future organizational needs.

In the process of Talent management and Leadership Development, ABG builds standardized, systematic and seamless approach in managing talent which helps in developing leaders for their diverse businesses & makes them sustainable.

Aditya Birla Group believes, I quote- "Meritocratic organizations are built on the strong foundation of values and not on the quicksands of opportunism. For us, our values-integrity, commitment, passion, seamlessness and speed, reflect the soul of the organization." - Mr Kumar Mangalam Birla, Chairman, Aditya Birla Group. Unquote- for sure ABG believes in Leadership Development to build Sustainable Growth.

References

http://www.adityabirla.com

http://en.wikipedia.org/wiki/Leadership

http://en.wikipedia.org/wiki/Talent_management

http://govleaders.org/dynamic_followership.htm

http://en.wikipedia.org/wiki/Action_learning

Global Strategic Management, Ms Neeta Baporikar, Himalaya Publishing House, 2008.

The Talent Management Handbook, Lance A Berger & Dorothy R. Berger, Tata McGraw-Hill Publishing Company Limited, 2004

Presentation made by Mr Anil Sinha, Aditya Birla Group on 21 August, 2010 at AIMA 9th National HRM Summit.

22

MENTAL HEALTH PROMOTION AT WORKPLACE: A KEY FOR ORGANIZATION GROWTH AND DEVELOPMENT

Dolly Lavania

Central Aim of the Research

The aim is to identify impact of mental health on employee's as well as organization's performance and to provide guidance on developing and implementing mental health strategies at the workplace for overall productivity. It is intended as a resource to help employers protect and improve the mental health of their workforce.

Objectives

- To examine the impact of mental health problems in the workplace.
- To examine the importance of work for persons with mental health problems.
- To find out the importance of mental health at workplace, its relevance to organization performance/productivity.
- To consider the role of the workplace in promoting good mental health practices for employees.

Research Methodology

Descriptive research with convenience sampling through non-probability method had been undertaken for conducting the study.

Target Source

The data and other relevant information had been collected by employers and occupational health professionals.

Implementation

Productive employment is important in achieving a decent living standard, social and economic development, and personal fulfillment. Mental health problems in the workplace carry a heavy toll for the individual and his or her family, for the workplace, and for society as a whole.

It outlines the types of mental health problems that may be encountered in the workplace, together with their consequences and costs, and proposes systematic strategies to prevent and reduce their impact on the person concerned and on the workplace.

Introduction

Mental Health: The World Health Organization defines positive men-tal health as "a state of well-being in which every indi-vidual realizes his or her own potential, can cope with the normal stresses of life, can work productively and fruitfully, and is able to make a contribution to her or his community".

Mental Illness: mental illness is a recognized, medically diagnosable illness that results in the significant impairment of an individual's cognitive, affective or relational abilities. Mental disorders result from biological, developmental and/or psychosocial factors and can be managed using approaches comparable to those applied to physical disease (i.e., prevention, diagnosis, treatment and rehabilitation)

Although the terms are often used parallel, mental health and mental illness is not the same thing. A fundamental difference between mental health and mental illness is that everyone has some level of mental health all of the time, just like physical health, whereas it is possible to be without mental illness. While poor mental health, also referred to as languishing, is at the other end. On the horizontal axis, having a serious mental illness is at one end of the continuum, while having no symptoms of a mental illness is at the other end. Ultimately, this means that someone can be mentally healthy with a mental illness and that someone can have poor mental health without a mental illness

The three most significant determinants of mental health are:

- Social inclusion;
- Freedom from discrimination and violence;
- Access to economic resources.

Myths about Mental illness and the Workplace

The following are major myths and facts regarding the impact of mental illness on the workplace

Mental Illness is the same as Mental Retardation: These are two distinct disorders. A diagnosis of mental retardation is chiefly characterized by limitation in intellectual functioning as well as difficulties with certain daily living skills. In contrast, among persons with psychiatric disabilities, intellectual functioning varies as it does across the general population.

Recovery from Mental Illness is not Possible: Long-term studies have shown that the majority of people with mental illnesses show genuine improvement over time and lead stable, productive lives. As medications were discovered helped to alleviate the symptoms of mental illness.

People with Psychiatric Disabilities cannot Tolerate Stress on the Job: People with a variety of medical conditions, such as cardiovascular disease, multiple sclerosis, and psychiatric disorders, may find their symptoms exacerbated by high levels of stress. In essence, all jobs are stressful to some extent.

Mentally Ill and Mentally Restored Individuals are Unpredictable, Violent, and Dangerous: A scholarly review of the research literature by Cornell University indicates that none of the data give any support to the sensationalized caricature of the mentally disordered served up in the media.

Common Mental Health Problems

Stress: when a person feels they don't have the resources to cope with the demands placed upon them. Symptoms may be emotional e.g. irritability, tearfulness and physical i.e. aches and pains, high blood pressure etc. The person may find it difficult to make decisions or perform tasks and may be unable to attend work.

Depression: Depression is a mood disorder that is typically characterized by a lowered mood and loss of interest or pleasure in usually enjoyable activities. While occasionally lowered mood is normal, depression is distinguished by its severity, persistence, duration and the presence of particular symptoms, such as sleep disturbances. Motivation can be affected and people may experience thoughts of life not being worth living, which in extreme cases can lead to suicidal behavior.

Anxiety: While some anxiety is normal, and moderate levels can even improve a person's performance, people with anxiety disorders have specific and recurring fears that they recognize as irrational, unrealistic and debilitating. Severe anxiety can impair a person's ability to understand new information, plan activities or undertake complex tasks.

Burnout: It is characterized by feelings of intense fatigue, a sense of isolation and loss of control, as well as a feeling of accomplishing nothing at work. It is often accompanied by insomnia, headaches, gastrointestinal symptoms, a variety of muscular and joint pains, and lapses in memory.

Other Mental Health Problems

Psychotic Conditions/Schizophrenia: In contrast to depression and anxiety, which are common in the general and the working population, psychosis is very uncommon. Psychosis is a term used when a person appears to lose touch with reality. People may hear, see or believe things that aren't real to others (e.g. hearing voices, thinking that others are 'out to get them'). If the illness becomes chronic (long-term) the person may withdraw from the outside world and neglect themselves.

Bipolar Disorder/manic Depressive Illness: Both terms are used to describe this condition, where a person may 'swing' between episodes of extreme low mood and depressive symptoms to being 'high' or elated. During a manic episode a person may have high energy levels, grand or unrealistic ideas and become reckless (e.g. taking risks, overspending). People may go through the mood cycles at different rates and times.

Self Harm and Suicide: People may hurt themselves deliberately in order to deal with problem emotions. Methods can include self-neglect, cutting, burning or overdosing. Suicidal behavior may occur when a person feels they have no other options. It may be a cry for help, a mistake or a deliberate act.

Personality Disorders: The Royal College of Psychiatrists states that there are many types of personality disorder and that they can be difficult to diagnose accurately. This depends on the type of disorder they have, how it manifests itself and how this affects their lives. Many people with mental health problems will have conditions that fluctuate, and it may be that they can go for long periods without having any particular difficulties.

A Few Facts about Employment and Mental Health Problems

- The World Health Organization estimates that by 2020 depression will become the second most important cause of disability in the world after heart diseases.

- According to a 2005 report from mental health charity Mind, nearly three in every 10 employees will have a mental health problem in any one year. the great majority of which will be depressive and anxiety disorders.
- According to the Royal College of Psychiatrists, at some point in their life, around one in five women and one in 10 men will suffer from depression. At any given time, one in every 20 adults is experiencing a serious 'major' depression.
- According to statistics from the September to December 2006 Labor Force Survey: Only 25.8 per cent of people with depression, bad nerves or anxiety who are of working age are actually in work. Only 13.5 per cent of people with mental illness, phobias, panic or other nervous disorders that are of working age are actually in work. People with mental health problems have the lowest employment rate of all disabled people of working age, at only 21 per cent.
- According to a Unum Provident survey published in March 2007, the sectors that registered the highest level of mental health related illness were public administration, education and health, while the lowest level was found in construction. Ten million working days were lost due to stress, depression and anxiety in 2005/06.
- The National Institute of Mental Health estimates that more than 3 million adults aged 18-69 have a serious mental illness. Estimates of unemployment among this group are 70-90%, a rate higher than for any other group of people with disabilities.
- In a CBI survey of over 800 companies, 98% of respondents said they thought that the mental health of employees should be a company concern.

Factors Associated with the Development of Mental Health Problems in the Workplace

Mental health can be badly affected by both external as well as internal factors.

External Factors

Globalization: Globalization affects individuals, families and the society generally. It has the potential to promote development and increase the wealth of the community by improving the national economy. Changes in the workplace that increase the income of employees, facilitate access to education and training, and improve working conditions will have a positive effect on the mental health of employees. However, globalization may also have a negative impact on employment and working conditions. The growth of large multinational companies has been accompanied by greater decentralization, outsourcing and flexible work environments, with wide variations in the conditions of work and in exposure to occupational hazards.

Urbanization and Migration: The need to find work has also resulted in many workers moving to other countries with a stronger employment sector or better working conditions. The International Labour Organization estimates that there are about 120 million workers living outside their country of origin, representing 3% of the global labour force. While migration can have a positive effect on the mental well-being of an employee, it can also cause stress through an increased risk of exposure to poverty and exploitation, difficulties in integrating into a new community, and the loss of family and other social support networks.

Information Technology: Information and communication technology can allow work to be performed in different physical locations. Workers may therefore be located geographically distant from the traditional workplace. Such developments create new challenges for employees. While some may enjoy the freedom associated with working at home, for many the isolation and loss of social support associated with working alone causes stress and increases the risk of developing a mental health problem.

Internal Factors

Stress and Work-life Balance Issues: Stress is a necessary part of everyday life. Indeed, some degree of stress or pressure is considered healthy. Underemployment can lead to boredom, apathy and a loss of energy and motivation. But conversely, excessive stress can lead to fatigue, impaired judgment and decision making, exhaustion and the onset of serious health problems – both mental and physical. Physically, stress is implicated in the development of coronary heart disease, certain types of cancer, and a host of other ailments including stomach ulcers, skin rashes, migraine, asthma, and increased susceptibility to infections.

***Discrimination*:** The way people living with mental illness are treated, intentionally or unintentionally, due to stigma. People with mental illness are often treated with disrespect, experiencing such behaviors as exclusion, bullying, aggression, ridicule and devaluation. Such discrimination can result in limits and barriers to many of life's opportunities.

Stigma: Stigma is not just a matter of using the wrong word or action. Stigma is about disrespect. It is a personal attitude and belief that negatively labels a group of people. Stigma creates fear and consequently results in discrimination which discourages individuals and their families from getting the help they need. One study found that 30 percent of people who experience mental illness have experienced stigma in the workplace.

Social Exclusion: People with disabilities, particularly psychiatric disabilities, face numerous barriers in obtaining equal opportunities – environmental, access, legal, institutional and attitudinal barriers which cause social exclusion. For people with mental illness, social exclusion is often the hardest barrier to overcome and is usually associated with feelings of shame, fear and rejection. It is clear that mental illness imposes a heavy burden in terms of human suffering, stigmatization of the mentally ill and their families and economic costs. Unfortunately, the burden is likely to grow over time as a result of ageing of the global population and stresses resulting from social problems and unrest, including violence, conflict and natural disasters.

Consequences of Mental Health Problems in the Workplace

The consequences of mental health problems in the workplace can be summarized as follows:

Absenteeism

- Increase in overall sickness absence particularly frequent short periods of absence
- Poor health (depression, stress, burnout)
- Physical conditions (high blood pressure, heart disease, ulcers, sleeping disorders, skin rashes, headache, neck- and backache, low resistance to infections).

Work Performance

- Reduction in productivity and output
- Increase in error rates
- Increased amount of accidents
- Poor decision-making
- Deterioration in planning and control of work

Staff Attitude and Behavior

- Loss of motivation and commitment
- Burnout
- Poor timekeeping,
- Labor turnover (particularly expensive for companies at top levels of management).

Relationships at Work

- Tension and conflicts between colleagues; poor relationships with clients
- Increase in disciplinary problems.

Impact of Mental Health Problems

The workplace can contribute positively to a person's mental health, may exacerbate an existing problem, or may contribute to the development of a mental health problem. The failure to prevent, recognize and treat mental health problems in the workplace has an impact on employers, employees and their families, and the community generally.

Employers

Mental health problems have an impact on employers and businesses directly through increased absenteeism, reduced production, increased costs, and reduced profits. They also affect employers indirectly through factors such as reduced morale of staff, increased absenteeism and many others. In many developed countries, 35–45% of absenteeism from work is due to mental health problems.

Increased costs Indirect costs may be a result of:

- Poor performance at work.
- Staff illness and shortages that can threaten the quality of service or product supplied.
- Reduced morale among staff.
- High staff turnover (costs of recruitment, induction and training).
- Early retirement.
- Management time to deal with issues associated with mental health problems.
- Providing temporary cover for colleagues.
- Complaints and possibly litigation associated with mental health problems.
- Cost to governments of health care and rehabilitation.

Employees and their Families

For individuals, mental health problems can lead to a reduced quality of life, as well as having significant economic and social effects. Absence from work is likely to affect the person's income. In combination with the costs of health care, this may cause significant financial hardship for employees with mental health problems. Many workers, particularly those in low-paid employment or small workplaces, do not have insurance that covers the cost of ill-health or absence from work. These employees are often not able to access the health services they need to treat their mental health problem, and may not be able to afford the time off work required for recovery. In addition, individuals with mental health problems often experience stigma and discrimination (World Health Organization, 2001).

The financial and personal burden of having a mental health problem can create a negative cycle that, without effective treatment, may lead to a worsening of the mental health problem. Families also experience the impact of mental health problems. They may have economic difficulties related to the reduced income and increased health care costs, the stress of coping with altered behavior, disruption to the household routine, and restricted social activities.

The Community

The cost of mental health problems to the overall community includes the cost of treatment, particularly when this includes hospitalization. The most important component of the cost of treating depression is hospitalization other costs to the community include those related to the loss of productivity, loss of lives, consequences of untreated illnesses (for example, increased numbers of people in prison), social exclusion and human rights abuses. Mental health problems in the workplace adversely affect the national economy.

Assessment of Costs relating Mental Illness

		Data	
Costs	*Category*	*Quantitative*	*Qualitative*
Linked to absenteeism	Days lost	Benefits paid to the absent employee. Professional health insurance contributions Overtime for colleagues.	Management and human resources' time
	Replacement of absent employee	Job advert fees and temporary staff agency fees Extra salary costs for insecure jobs	Recruitment, training and apprenticeship time Extra work for colleagues during the transitory period Slowing of pace/decline in results
Linked to Presenters	Drop in productivity	Penalties linked to extended deadlines	More errors Reduced quality Drop in innovation Loss of ability to win a market/satisfy clients
	Risks linked to a decline in collective and interpersonal relationships (harassment, conflicts with management, etc.) Stress-related industrial accidents	Legal fees: lawsuits and grievances Increase in costs of resulting absenteeism. Increase in work insurance premiums. Rise of benefits for work stoppages.	Management's time spent on adaptations within the team Tarnished image for clients/group Reduced attractiveness of company Management and human resources time

Why is Mental Health Important for a Successful Business?

There are many reasons why employers should make mental health promotion in the workplace a priority. The mental health of employees is an im-portant health determinant.

In today's global econo-my it is an important driver for successful business. More and more companies realize that the commit-ment of employees is crucial for the success of the organization.

In recent decades the increasingly global nature of our economies, and the advances in workplace technology, mean that the nature of work is chang-ing rapidly. This affects the content, organization and intensity of people's work, which increasingly requires more skills and competences in terms of innovation, communication and social intelligence. These rapid changes in the nature of work can be rewarding for employees, however, they can mean that employees may experience more pressure and demands upon their cognitive, social and psycho-logical skills. Mental health is crucial: both for the formation of these skills and their effective use in the workplace.

The workplace can provide a healthy culture and en-vironment that is psychologically supportive to the workforce. It is a challenge to employers as well as to employees to make the workplace a healthy workplace.

Workplace Health Promotion – Affecting Mental Health in Workplace

Mental health promoting actions and strategies are oriented to empowerment, choice and participation. They strengthen protective factors, lessen risk factors and build on the social determinants of health. A healthy workplace can help a person to cope with change and difficult circumstances, which is particularly im-portant in challenging economic conditions and is the key to the achievement of the objectives on growth and jobs including:

Productivity and Performance: Mental health promotion can also boost productivity and performance. A good working environment can help to increase morale, teamwork and communi-cation. Staff turnover is lower and so are the asso-ciated costs of recruitment and training. A healthy workplace can help people to cope with change and difficult circumstances, which is particularly im-portant in challenging economic conditions.

Reputation: By developing mental health promotion pro-grammes and policies, one can enhance the public reputation of the organization. This can improve the business reputation amongst potential future recruits, and it may increase chances of gain-ing public contracts. It can also improve the repu-tation amongst the wider public and customers as an organization that demonstrates corporate social responsibility. Good organizational reputation will be associated with a healthy and stimulating work-place where personal development is part of the organization learning culture.

No Health without Mental Health: There is good evidence to show that poor mental health and stress can lead to an increase in a range of physical illnesses. These include coronary heart disease, stroke and diabetes. This can happen di-rectly by mental distress affecting physiological vulnerability, but also indirectly by increasing the dependence upon negative lifestyle factors such as smoking and alcohol consumption. These are ma-jor social and workplace issues but also mean that there is a compelling business case to act now.

Creating a Healthy Workplace: Any employer who wishes to create a healthy work environment for their staff will need to develop policies and procedures to ensure that their approach is systematic and thorough, and its results would be tangible.

A Workplace Mental Health Policy

"A mental health policy for the workplace helps to define the vision for improving the mental health of the workforce and to establish a model for action A mental health policy for the workplace can be developed separately, or as part of a broader health and safety policy. Putting the policy in place involves the following steps:

Step I. Analyzing the mental health issues.

Step II. Developing the policy.

Step III. Developing strategies to implement the policy.

Step IV. Implementing and evaluating the policy.

Step I. Analyzing the Mental Health Issues

A coordinating body, such as a steering committee or working group, should be established to guide the assessment of the workforce, facilitate consultation with the various stakeholders and coordinate the development of the workplace mental health policy. This body should ensure that all key stakeholders are involved in developing the policy. All available relevant information should be assembled. Such information might include: human resources data (e.g. absenteeism records or number of resignations); occupational health and safety data (e.g. accidents or risk assessments), financial data (e.g. the cost of replacing employees who are on long-term disability leave) and health data (e.g. common health problems among the workforce).

Step II. Developing the Policy

A workplace mental health policy usually comprises a vision statement, a statement of the values and principles on which the policy will be based, and a set of objectives. These components need not be dealt with sequentially; often they are developed simultaneously. The vision statement presents a general image of the future of mental health in the workplace. It should set high expectations as to what can be achieved, while at the same time being realistic.

Workplaces have their own values and culture, which should be reflected in a policy. The values and principles underlying the workplace mental health policy should strike a balance between the various interests of the different stakeholders. Objectives should respond to the identified issues and aim to improve the mental health of the workforce. They should be specific and achievable within a specified timeframe of the policy.

Step III. Developing Strategies to Implement the Policy

The first task is to review the options for strategies, which can be divided into five main categories:

- Increasing employee awareness of mental health issues.
- Supporting employees at risk.
- Providing treatment for employees with a mental health problem.
- Changing the organization of work.
- Reintegrating employees with a mental health problem into the workplace.

Finally, the plan to implement the policy has to be formulated. The plan should outline the objectives, specific strategies to be used, targets to be achieved and activities to be carried out. The timeframe, responsible people, outputs and potential obstacles should be clearly identified.

Step IV. Implementing and Evaluating the Policy

The main actions in implementing and evaluating a mental health policy in the workplace include:

- Generating support and collaboration.
- Coordinating implementation.
- Training.
- Establishing a demonstration project.
- Evaluating the outcomes.

The implementation process needs to be carefully coordinated and monitored. The plan should be reviewed and updated as necessary. A process for implementation should be established. An individual, a department or a committee might be given responsibility for the implementation of the plan. Regular reporting to the employer, employees, and funders of the policy should be part of the implementation plan. It is important to ensure that the people who will be leading the implementation process are properly trained to understand the issues associated with mental health in the workplace.

Findings

- Discriminatory practices and assumptions which can make people feel stigmatized.
- A loss of confidence as a result both of mental health problems but also enforced absence from work as a result of inflexible working practices
- The present moment there are too few supported employment schemes and insufficient information about the best models of practice although a variety of projects and policies in mental health agencies have a wealth of good ideas.
- Many work environments do not promote mental well-being.
- Employers are afraid that focusing on mental health problems will have unforeseeable consequences stigma.
- Employers do not want to employ people with mental health.
- Some employers and employees may feel that employees with mental health problems are weak, unreliable, potentially dangerous and less productive than other employees.
- Concern that mental health policy will reduce profits.
- Belief that the workplace is too small for a mental health policy.
- Resistance from stakeholders' insufficient resources.

Possible Solutions/Suggestions

- The need to clarify what is meant by 'mental health problems' and to move away from solely psychiatric classifications. Given the heterogeneity in psychiatric diagnostic categories (ie that two people with the same diagnosis can have very different problems) there is a need for epidemiological research to look in more detail at the kinds of problems people experience.
- The importance of placing mental health problems in a social and economic context rather than seeing them as problems lying within the individual.
- There is an urgent need to provide stable long-term funding to independent groups of service users .There is also a need for properly funded and independent advocacy.

- There is a need for mental health services to be focused less on simply 'maintaining' people but to design services that support people to recover from their difficulties.
- Mental health services need to offer more real choices about the kind of treatments available to service users, not just drug treatment or the government do differently to enable more people with mental health problems to work.
- Provision of incentives to employers to recruit and retain people with mental health problems
- Conducting a confidential survey of those organizations to see how many people would identify themselves as having a mental health problem.
- Government to appoint such a person would do a great deal to counter myths and stereotypes nothing.
- Provide information to employers on mental health and productivity.
- Encourage employer organizations to become involved in mental health.
- Encourage employer organizations to provide assistance to small workplaces.
- Encourage links between small workplaces and primary health care services.
- Provide information to stakeholders.
- Use influential people in the workplace to champion mental health.
- Provide relevant information on the impact of mental health issues in the workplace.
- Provide evidence of effective mental health interventions
- Show how other businesses have successfully implemented mental health programmes.
- Invite a speaker who has had experience of a mental illness to speak with staff to educate the workforce.
- Make sure that employers know about their legal responsibilities.
- Use experiences from other businesses to illustrate positive impact of employing people with mental health problems.
- Make sure that the activities reflect employees' concerns.

Conclusion

The feeling of being valuable - 'I am a valuable person' - is essential to mental health and is a cornerstone of self-discipline." —M. Scott Peck

Satisfying work remains one of the most sought-after goals of the adult population of most countries. Employers, employees and unions are starting to realize that, for this population, mental health problems are the single most important cause of disability responsible for a global burden of disease larger than that due to infections, AIDS, cancer and physical accidents. The impact of mental health problems on absenteeism, productivity and job satisfaction is only starting to be realized.

Integral to these themes is the identification of good practices by employers as well as vocational rehabilitation agencies and professionals. There are many factors involved in addressing the importance of work for people with mental health problems, as well as identifying effective practices that encourage employment, re-employment and retention. Social support systems, mental health professionals and employers all have a significant role in helping individuals define options, make choices, learn to manage potentially disabling conditions, and avoid long-term hospitalization. The ultimate goal is for individuals to obtain and/or return to gainful, worthwhile activity, such as meaningful work.

References

Barber Brendan (2005), *Representing and Supporting Members with Mental Health Problems*. London: Trade Union Congress.

Bird L. (2009), *The Fundamental Facts: All the Latest Facts and Figures on Mental Illness*. London: The Mental Health Foundation.

Cooper C. Cartwright S. (1996), *Mental Health and Stress in the Workplace: A Guide for Employers*. London: HMSO.

Doherty N. Tyson S.(1998), *Mental Well-being in the Workplace. A Resource Pack for Management Training and Development*. Norwich: HMSO.

Floyd M. Povall M, Watson G. (1994), *Mental Health at Work: Disability and Rehabilitation*. Series 5. London: Jessica Kingsley.

Grove Bob, Seymour Linda (2005), *Workplace Interventions for People with Common Menta Health Problems Evidence Review and Recommendations*. London: British Occupational Health Research Foundation.

Gray Penny (1999), *Mental Health at Work Place: Tackling the Effects of Stress*. Mental Health Foundation.

Gaston Harnois, Phyllis Gabriel (2000), *Mental Health at Workplace; Impact, Issues and Practices*. Geneva: World Health Organization.

Harvey Steve, Courcy Francois (2006), *Organizational Interventions and Mental Health in the Workplace*. London: Institut de recherche Robert Sauvé en santé et en sécurité du travail.

Lee Knifton, Verona Watson, Heleen den Besten (2009), *A Guide to Promoting Mental Health in the Workplace*. Europe: BKK Bundesverband/ENWHP Secretariat.

Grayling. VAR Spotcheck (1998), Mental *Health Awards Commissioned Report*. VA Research Ltd.

Payne Janice B, Trevor E. Fenton (2005), *Accommodating Mental Illness in the Workplace: Principles and Practices*. London.

Mental Health Policies and Programes in the Workplace (2005), World Health Organization.

Appendices

Note: All the following figures are in percentage.

Table 1
The Main Barriers to Employment for Adults with Mental Health Problems

Discriminatory practices	43
Loss of confidence	20
Lack of support	37

Table 2
Adults in Work Lose their Jobs following the Onset or Relapse of Mental Health Problems

Often just hearing that someone has a psychiatric diagnosis.	42
After a prolonged period off sick.	34
The person does not feel confident.	24

Table 3
Most Important Problems like to see the Social Exclusion Project Address in Relation to Mental Health and Social Exclusion

Increasing the funding of the benefits and raising the earning allowance.	24
The need to overcome discrimination in employment.	39
More supportive work environments and creative thinking about the kinds of support people need in order to be able to work.	37

Table 4
Organization Support to Employees with Mental Health Problems

Adjustment of workload.	8
Provision of challenging tasks and working conditions promoting learning.	16
Promoting a healthy lifestyle.	16
Improving the work/life balance.	18
Stimulating social support.	14
Offering individual counseling for employees with mental health problems.	11
Back-to-work program.	17

Table 5
Management Shows Its Commitment to the Health Policy

Endorsement of the policy.	26
Inclusion on the agenda at management meetings.	16
Signaling commitment.	58

Table 6
Services which Support People with Mental Health Problems

Involve service users more in planning and providing support.	27
Need for genuinely independent groups.	22
The independent sectorneeds to be more involved.	31
Offer more real choices about the kind of treatments available to service users.	20

Table 7
The Best Way to Help Adults with Mental Health Problems find and Keep Work

Provision of training to employers which should also include 'shop-floor' staff.	28
Need for adequate support for people at work including dedicated supported employment.	24
Offered a graduated return to work so that they can rebuild their confidence over time.	19
Set minimum quotas on large organizations for recruitment and retention of people with mental health problems.	29

23

WOMEN SUCCESS IN PUBLIC RELATIONS THROUGH EMOTIONAL INTELLIGENCE

Anshu Bhati & Jyoti Sharma

Worldwide working women are increasing in number and are becoming the integral part of the workforce ranging from blue-collar to white-collar jobs. It's no revolutionary fact in India too. Future trends also look bright as far as women are concerned. Women have surely made their mark in the PR business over the last 20 years, to the extent that there is now a major shortage of men coming into the profession, and that's official. According to latest membership figures released by the Institute of Public Relations (IPR), women now outnumber men by 60:40 - a massive swing since 1987, when figures highlighted the opposite at 20:80.

Women have entered Public Relations at a much faster rate than men over the last two decades (Andsager, 2005 et al), the most dramatic change has been the transformation of Public Relations from a male-dominated field to one in which women now constitute about 70 percent of practitioners, Hutton (2005) opined that the percentage of women in the field has been increasing methodically for the past two or three decades. If current trends stabilize, the percentage of women will eventually be about 80%—at all levels of experience—as older men retire from the PR work force. The fact to be noted is, the people in Public Relations profession is characterized with abilities and qualities as listening and communication, tolerance for frustration, style, enthusiasm, drive, stability, handling people, problem solver, intellectual curiosity, empathy and generating confidence. People with high Emotional Intelligence can be of help in Public Relations to serve the public effectively and efficiently, believing that the required characteristics for PR will be available in them. Women in PR have found a discipline where they can work and show self-confidence, assertiveness, a risk-taking attitude, and an accountability necessary for business success. Major appeal of PR to women was because it blended creativity and business.

Public Relations as defined by the newsletter *Public Relations News*, Public Relations is the management function, which evaluates public attitudes, identifies the policies and procedures of an individual or an organization with the public interest and plans and executes a program of action to earn public understanding and acceptance. Public Relations is about reputation management of organization as defined by Black (2003) "PR is about reputation–the result of what you do, what you say and what others say about you." PR practice is the discipline which looks after reputation – with the aim of earning understanding and support and influencing opinion and behavior.

Stating one of the important examples, Priyanka Seth, senior account manager, Corporate Voice, Weber Shandwick, opines, "PR, more than a profession is an art, women definitely make better PR professionals but it would be unfair to men if we call it solely a chick's art. Having said that, I do believe women are more tactful when it comes to the balancing act- be it calmness, creativity and assertiveness that make them communicate better and get their point across. All of us have had problems handling a difficult client and women are blessed with the virtue of patience with which they are able to draw a distinct line between assertion and aggression which helps them go a long way in the profession." This is the inherent quality of women to intelligently use emotions in the most critical situations. She has the balancing power of managing the crisis in most subtle manner maintaining optimum output.

Public Relations (PR) is the buzzword today in the management circles. It refers to the deliberate effort of an organization to build and maintain relations with the publics. It can be utilized effectively to communicate with internal and external publics of an organization. PR helps an organization and its publics (employees, consumers, stakeholders, media, government and society etc.) adapt mutually to each other. PR profession believes in truth more than the image created. The basic PR philosophy of doing first and than saying is looked forward by professional organizations for long-term image building and relationships. In today's competitive scenario, profit and non-profit organizations are practicing PR to leave a positive impression on publics' mind.

Endowed with natural communication skills, it is observed that women colleagues at Perfect Relations are quick to grasp the core issues of a situation and deliver quality work. Another area of strength is flexibility that goes a long way in surviving pressures that the job demands. Women multitask better, men grind much finer – that's the only distinction I can see between the sexes. Public relation professionals interact with all kinds of people in their different spheres of life, either at work or in their personal lives, and are undoubtedly really good listeners. No matter what kind of situation they're in, they always seem to know just what to say – and how to say it – so that other's are not offended or upset. Grunig et al., (2000) argue that public relations are an industry founded on feminist values, such as honesty, justice, and sensitivity, which will enhance the symmetrical communication patterns of public relations. They're caring and considerate, and even if they don't find a solution to our problem, they usually leave feeling more hopeful and optimistic. All theses qualities reflect their ability to use emotions intelligently. As women are generally found to have these qualities inbuilt, they are more successful in Public Relations profession.

PR Professionals are masters at managing their emotions. Feminist scholars such as Rakow (1989) suggest that women's emergence in public relations is an opportunity for more responsible and effective practice. Feminist scholars such as Rakow (1989) reject these concerns and suggest that women's emergence in public relations is an opportunity for more responsible and effective practice. They don't get angry in stressful situations. Instead, they have the ability to look at a problem differently and calmly find a solution. They're excellent decision makers, and they know when to trust their intuition. Regardless of their strengths, however, they're usually willing to look at themselves honestly. They take criticism well, and they know when to use it to improve their performance. People like this have a high degree of emotional intelligence, or EI. They know themselves very well, and they're also able to sense the emotional needs of others.

Emotional intelligence is a combination of competencies. These skills contribute to a person's ability to manage and monitor his or her own emotions, to correctly gauge the emotional state of others and to influence opinions. Goleman describes a model of five dimensions. Each area has its own set of behavioral attributes as follows.

- Self-awareness is the ability to recognize a feeling as it happens, to accurately perform self-assessments and have self-confidence. It is the keystone of emotional intelligence (Goleman, 1995). Female PR professionals confidently regulate the emotions of self and variety of publics to perform their roles and reach to optimal and appropriate results.
- Self-management or self-regulation is the ability to keep disruptive emotions and impulses in check (self-control), maintain standards of honesty and integrity (trustworthiness), take responsibility for one's performance (conscientiousness), handle change (adaptability), and be comfortable with novel ideas and approaches (innovation). Capability of self-management helps female PR professionals to manage the crisis communication management by thought generations in positive direction and obtaining positive results.
- Motivation is the emotional tendency guiding or facilitating the attainment of goals. It consists of achievement drive (meeting a standard of excellence), commitment (alignment of goals with the group or organization), initiative (acting on opportunities), and optimism (persistence reaching goals despite set backs). PR professionals use emotional intelligence to make effective decisions through self-awareness, communication and influence, and commitment and integrity. Female PR professionals who do not develop their emotional intelligence have difficulty in building good relationships with peers, subordinates, superiors and clients.

  Empathy is the understanding of others by being aware of their needs, perspectives, feelings, and concerns, sensing the developmental needs of others. Public relation executives provide an insight into socialising with clients and journalists as part of the job. 'We need people who can juggle tasks, keep calm and influence people - and women are good at that,' says Jo Marino, Head of Waterstones' in-house PR team. Here, the suggestion that clients and "contacts" are considered to be more equal within a relationship allows emotional labour to have a positive outcome for the individual that happens as a result of empathetic attitude for others, where they are able to understand others point of view and think on equal or similar lines and women are considered best at this. One of the major reasons for this count for the rearing environment that females get in their childhood where they learn to live many roles all together and handle them perfectly.

  Social skills are fundamental to emotional intelligence. They include the ability to induce desirable responses in others by using effective diplomacy to persuade (influence); listen openly and send convincing messages (communicate); inspire and guide groups and individuals (leadership); nurture instrumental relationships (building bonds); work with others toward a shared goal (collaboration, cooperation); and create group synergy in pursuing collective goals. Emotion and emotion management skills tacitly accompany the many activities performed by a public relations executive in delivering a personal service to journalists and clients– for example, negotiating and "selling-in" stories, pitching for accounts, crisis handling, as well as the day-to-day interactions with colleagues and "suppliers" (e.g. photographers), that are part of the job.

When people are asked what traits and qualities they admire in female Public relation leaders, the typical responses are that they are caring, engaging, authentic, positive thinkers, creative, patient, empathetic, charismatic and thoughtful. These qualities are not taught in college textbooks or graduate school courses. They are learned and developed by people who have come to understand the value of Emotional Intelligence.

In our competitive business world, Emotional Intelligence, or EQ, is more important than your IQ. Your ability to connect with people on a genuine human level and build rapport with them is essential if you want to climb the ladder of success, and stay at the top.

The realization by corporate organizations took their own time to recognize the concept of EI. Perhaps, the finding that successful managers who score highly on measures of emotional intelligence also tend to have high IQ scores and therefore emotional intelligence is not contradictory to traditional intelligence helped in its actual acceptance by the organizations. Still it advocates that higher IQ with low emotional concern and adaptability becomes the sole reason for intra personal and interpersonal conflicts in an organization. Today's organizations, particularly corporate are known to use IQ as a criterion for recruitment and emotional intelligence for promotions.

Emotional Intelligence is what can be said as "street smarts." EQ is a huge factor in communication and conflict resolution, both at work and home. Individuals with high levels of EQ have compassion, empathy, congeniality, patience, assertiveness and self-awareness. Again, the good news is that EQ can be learned.

The present study aims at understanding the role of Emotional Intelligence in women success in the various facets of Public Relations profession and how it can assist women Public Relations professionals in understanding importance of emotions in various situations. Women in PR have found a discipline where they can work and show self-confidence, assertiveness, a risk taking, and an accountability necessary for business.

It can be stated that our society places a greater communication burden-opportunity on women, teaching them to listen and thus begin to understand communication's most basic aspects. Indeed, many educators would agree that not only are most students women, but also the best students are women. They communicate, observe, listen and write better. And thus has the capability of understanding and expressing emotions with appropriate message in public relation.

Public Relations practitioners use emotions in communications. Emotions work negatively and positively in varied situations. In the Public Relations, there are constant interactions, which are occurring among the people. While some of these interactions are positive others are negative. The key aspect is that, Public Relations professionals must understand these interactions over time. When we use Emotional Intelligence, we are attuned to our emotions and can use them to channel others and our behavior for the optimum outcome. Public Relations is deliberate, planned and sustained effort to establish and maintain mutual relationship between organization and public. The aim of using emotions in Public Relations is not to avoid emotions, but to use them to guide others and ourselves to be more productive in a holistic manner.

Public opinions are called as product of Public Relations. PR professionals look forward to create favorable public opinion. An individuals opinion can be affected by multiple factors; events, media, others opinion, past experiences etc. Emotions therefore can be important stimuli in influencing public opinion. Public Relations practitioners devote considerable time and effort assessing and perhaps modifying the image that people, products or organizations make upon a variety of publics (DuBrin, 1969). PR professionals need to be emotionally balanced and have intellectual curiosity to read publics mind and alter it in the favor of organization and its products.

Women not only express their views differently from men, but they perceive what they see in a different way. Here they use their empathetic trait for perception and expression.

From physiological perspective, men's brain has about six and half times the amount of grey matter related to general intelligence than women. Conversely, women have nearly 10 times the amount of grey matter related to intelligence than men. Gray matter is the information processing centers. This physiological make up gives women more emotional intelligence, which is a kind of a skill that is required in profession of Public Relations and makes women successful.

Top management makes policies, strategies, plans and frameworks to successfully achieve the objectives of the organizations. It can be said that all these tools should be in the favor of the consumers and other stakeholders so that altering of opinion can really take place and therefore it is being opined that Public Relations Officer should reports to top management. S/he can contribute to policy formation in favor of various publics based on opinion surveys. They evaluate motives, thinking, and reasons, behind any acts of stakeholders in these surveys. Efforts are also being made to understand the underlying emotions behind any behavior amongst any group of public, this is why/how knowledge of emotions is must.

Corporations worldwide have become more and more concerned about the stakeholders in recent past. Diverse range of activities is undertaken by corporate under the umbrella of Corporate Social Responsibility (CSR). CSR is no more a buzzword rather every corporate in recent past has started dedicating decent amount on CSR activities. A concerning issues still remains with CSR, "public's faith"; corporate should handle publics feelings and emotions very carefully when it comes to CSR. CSR initiatives can be constructively handled and well managed by PR professionals in most appropriate manner. Public Relations is influencing behavior to achieve objectives through the effective management of relationships and communications as defined by British Institute of Public Relations, thus handling people is embedded in the profession. Women are considered best at this as they find themselves comfortable in working with diverse workforce and handle them appropriately. Gillian Rankin, a business psychologist at ML Consulting points out in PR Week, opined that, Women are better suited to PR because they naturally have better communication skills. He said further that 'Women are recognised at being better at relationship building, which is crucial for dealing both with clients and the media...Also they have empathy with people and more interested in interactive dialogue - listening as well as speaking.' interactive dialogue- listening as well as speaking.'

Public Relations professional's work depends a lot on client brief, "Better the brief, great will be the product". Conversion of client brief into the PR product requires listening and communication skills in the people. At the same time, Client expectations are sometimes far away from the realities creating problems and frustrations. Public Relations profession involves strict and intense deadlines. Media generally demands stories in short time. Specially, in times of crisis, things go ha-voc, pulses increases, media questions, community becomes demanding, and everybody amongst the stakeholders asks questions to the PRO, increasing the panic. The first step towards solution at such times is to use emotions in integrated manner by regulating them in positive direction, because panic results into frustration. Stability of words, actions, and thoughts is key at this point of time. PR professionals need to have tolerance to deal with and overcome from such situations.

Conclusion

Public Relation Professionals involve emotions to work with diverse publics in different situations. Researchers have developed a feminist perspective of public relations (Grunig, Toth, & Hon, 2000; Hon, 1995). This research primarily focuses on how women and feminist values can benefit the industry, positing that feminist values are intrinsic to the public relations profession. The fact can be concluded by stating that emotional intelligence is one of the vital components of women professionals in Public Relation executive for making their profession effective and successful. High Emotional Intelligence can facilitate them in Public Relations to serve the public effectively and efficiently.

References

Black C. (2003), *The PR Practitioner's: A Handbook,* New Delhi: Crest Publishing House.

Daniel Goleman (1995), *Emotional Intelligence: Why It Can Matter More Than IQ.* Bantam Books.

DuBrin, J. Andrew (1969), *A Management Psychologist Looks at the Public Relations Man,* The Public Relations Quarterly, Winter, 7-12.

Grunig, L.A., Toth, E.L., & Hon, L.C. (2000), Feminist Values in Public Relations. *Journal of Public Relations Research,* 12(1), 49–68.

Hon, L.C. (1995), Toward a Feminist Theory of Public Relations. *Journal of Public Relations Research, 7,* 27–88.

Hutton Games J. (2005), "The Myth of Salary Discrimination in Public Relations", *Public Relation Review,* 31, 73-83.

Rakow, L.F. (1989), From the Feminization of Public Relations to the Promise of Feminism. In E. L. Toth & C. G. Cline (Eds.), *Beyond the velvet ghetto* (pp. 287–298). San Francisco: IABC Foundation.

http://icbirmingham.icnetwork.co.uk/0150business/womeninbusiness/tm_headline=why-women-dominate-pr-profession%26method=full%26objectid=14780965%26siteid=50002-name_page.html

http://sme.franchiseindia.com/articles/Managing-a-Business/HR/New-Age-Power-Girls-318/

24

OCCUPATIONAL STRESS AND MID-CAREER CRISIS FOR INDIAN CORPORATE WOMEN IN THE SERVICE SECTOR

Manidipa Chatterjee

The Indian Corporate Women – An Introduction

In recent years there has been a complete resurgence of female employees in India, especially in the service sectors. Educated and skillful Indian women today occupy a large part of the progress wheel in the service sector. Their success is not limited in the IT enabled services alone but, also in the area of banking, insurance, tourism, marketing of financial products, retail, academics, hospitality, health-care, education and research etc. It is not uncommon to find women in command of commercial aircrafts.

The traditional concept of familial norms is slowly modifying itself to a nuclear family structure, there by scarcity of manpower remain as a persistent problem. Again patriarchy prevail in the Indian society from the time immemorial with the need to attend the official norms being considered to be much more important in case of father or men of the family. Though Indian women are today empowered with knowledge and education, but still they are deemed to be the primary caregivers of the family.

In the last 40 odd years India had witnessed women as Prime Minister and President. Many more women personalities had came in the forefront with remarkable achievements in their respective fields. The country also saw increasing incidents of violence and discrimination against women in the same period. Inspite of the progress in education and social status, contradictions are still prevailing in our society and Indian women executives are often placed in the midst of such events. Today women are amongst the most educated, liberated, articulated and free, and yet on the other hand they are the most oppressed. Media of all types are reflecting the progressive face of a woman.

Although women occupy significantly top management slots in various organizations, ranging from high-tech, manufacturing to consumer services, still they continued to be under represented in many areas in our society. Can such dichotomy about women's acceptability and status, co-exist? In answering this question one need to ponder about the real causes for her misery and her dilemma in choosing the actual role from the multiple expectations that arose from this dyadic entangle of work-family imbalance. With enhancement of socio-economic status, women are more prone to occupational mobility and accessibility but at the same time they are more susceptible to various role-conflict entangling themselves in a vicious cycle of stress.

Literature Review

Selye (1936) viewed stress as *the non-specifically induced changes within a biological system.* His concept of General Adaptation Syndrome (GAS), provides an automatic defense mechanism to help people cope with the external environmental demands. Mukhopadhyay (1989) compared a group of working mother with their non-working counterparts, in Kolkata, with respect to stress level measured in terms of their anxiety score and the result showed that anxiety and health score of the two groups of women are similar. Campbell and Boyd (2000) studied that women engaged in health care are more prone to occupational stress and violence. Swanson (2000) stated that occupational stress is a growing problem in US workplaces and may be a problem of particular magnitude for working women, in part because of gender specific job stressors (gender discrimination & difficulties combining work and family). Loutfi (2001) also investigated some of the dramatic changes in women's status notwithstanding the glaring inequalities that remain. These changes not only initiated a wide range of debate on the appropriate roles of men and women, but also gave deep reflection on the basic human values, including the place of work in life as a whole drawing together the ideas of different economists, lawyer, and statisticians. Martino (2003) vividly depicted relationship between work-stress and work place violence in the health sector. Bahl (2005) found out the reasons and consequences of workplace bullies, which are behind all forms of harassments, discrimination, abuse, conflict and violence. Bianchi et al. (2005) elucidated that demographic, sociological, technological and economic change occurring in the United States in the latter half of the 20th Century, dramatically altered family life, nature of work and the conditions of employment. Gopal (2005) analyzed the main factors that culminates stress among women with the introduction of MNC culture and also depicted the techniques of stress prevention. Michailidis and Georgiou (2005) conducted a study on occupational stress of the employees in the banking sector and the degree to which employees bring work related problems to home. Srivastava (2005) conducted a study in a public sector organization using the organizational role stress scale. He depicted that role stagnation; role erosion and total role stress are less at senior management level as compared to junior and middle management level. Buchanan and Boswell (2006) investigated the interrelations among role-integration-segmentation, role identification, reactions to interruptions and work-life conflict. In this study results from the field survey of the university staff revealed that how individuals integrate their work and life domains and the consequences of such integration on work-life conflict. Gunavathy and Suganya (2007) depicted the work-life imbalance among married women employees of BPOs. Messersmith (2007) published the same type of case oriented article on managing work-life conflict among information and technology workers. Abdullah et al. (2008) explained the occupational stress and its impact on the social and familial difficulties as well as job-satisfaction level of the workingwomen in the socio-economic perspective of Bangladesh. Budhiraja and Jyoti (2008) gave a vivid description of the challenges faced by women professional in this 21st. century. Kidwai et al. (2008) analyzed the impact of working status on the lives of the workingwomen at a teaching hospital in Karachi, Pakistan. Das and Dutta (2008) studied the causes, consequences and management of occupational stress among the employees of different service sector units in and around Kolkata. Ghosh and Das (2009) pointed out the impact and root causes of the emergence of stress at work place and provides the strategies to be adopted by companies to cope up with stress. Vidyavati (2009) examined the demographic and socio-economic profiles of women workers working in the ITES hub of Bangalore and identified the opportunities and challenges that they have to face everyday and how they are coping with stress.

Major Themes of the Article

This article is mainly reflecting the following themes:

- What are the major causes and symptoms of occupational stress for working women which generally demoralize them and make them difficult to concentrate in their day- to- day activities at office resulting in mental agony and strain?
- How far women are getting social support and the type of career impediments they have to face due to such inhibitions?
- How far Indian industries specially in the service sector are slowly realizing women as the assets of the company and the type of measures they are taking in order to retain them for the long- term benefit of the organization?

Causes and Symptoms of Stress on Working Women

Hans Salye (1936) defined stress as ***"An adoptive response to the external situation that results in physical, psychological and behavioural deviation for organizational participants".*** Individual and gender differences however result for a wide range of reactions to stressful situations. Today's technologically advanced busy urban culture is full of hassles, deadlines, frustrations and demands creating enormous day to day stress for an individual. Stress is not always bad. In small doses, it can help one to perform under pressure and motivate a person to do the best. But when one is constantly running in emergency mode, his mind and body pay the price. Various studies have shown that women are about twice as likely as men to suffer from depression and stress (Marano, 2003). This two-to-one difference persists across racial, ethnic, and economic divides.

Stress level of working women may be more than their non-working counterpart because she has to juggle with multiple roles in both professional and personal life. The various causes of stress can be due to (i) **Social and cultural causes** (ii) **Psychological causes** (iii) **Physical or biological causes**

Among the **social and cultural causes,** women's multiple roles as mother, wife and working professional make her more vulnerable to role strain leading to subsequent stress and depression. Depression is more common in women receiving less support in housework and child-care activities. Single working mothers are particularly at risk. Above all, women's relative lack of power and status in our society might lead to feelings of helplessness. This sense of helplessness places her at greater risk for depression. These feelings may be provoked by discrimination in the workplace leading to underemployment of women in many employable sectors in our economy. Gender discrimination at work place may generate the problem of *Glass ceiling* where a woman's career progression is restricted or *Glass wall* where in higher positions women are not allowed to take part in strategic decision making.

In finding the **Psychological causes** of stress many studies have shown that rate of depression is lower for the married compared to the single and divorced working women, which proves that marriage can be one of the factors of life satisfaction for many women. Again, the benefits disappear entirely for women whose marital satisfaction is low due to the lack of intimacy with spouse and marital strife. Unsuccessful marriage is another cause of depression for them. Women executives often suffer from psychological guilt complex as they are made to believe and realize that they are not able to focus on their families or rather neglect their families and children at the cost of their personal freedom. Sometimes in many traditional households their financial contribution in enhancing social security of their family remains ignored. Sometimes, family support and the role played by their husbands is also a cause for concern in the Indian social set-up although the problem varies from one situation to another. Many researches had elucidated that only a mere 30% of the corporate women (ref: D.Mukherjee, HRM Review, Jan 2009) in India are of the opinion that their husbands are supportive in sharing their responsibilities in the home front. Often many husbands want to co-operate with their working wives, but their eagerness to help are more often dampened and ridiculed by other family members.

Among the various **biological causes** of depression premenstrual problems or hormonal fluctuations during the menstrual cycle can cause the familiar symptoms of premenstrual syndrome (PMS), such as bloating, irritability, fatigue, and emotional reactivity. For many women, PMS is mild. But research shows that for some working women, symptoms are severe enough to disrupt their lives particularly when their work involve lot of stress and strain for long duration. Hormonal changes that occur during pregnancy can contribute to depression, particularly in women already at high risk. Many new mothers experience the *baby blues*. This is a normal reaction that tends to subside within a few weeks. However, some women experience severe, lasting depression even after long days of childbirth. This condition is known as Postpartum Depression. Postpartum Depression sometimes is influenced partly, by hormonal fluctuations. But in many cases it can be acute for working mothers just after the childbirth because she is in a dilemma of how to juggle her new role as a caregiver for her new born as well as tackling her old work place responsibilities.

Family demands and family attitudes were found to influence the frequency of absenteeism of women at workplace when they are unable to arrange for proper childcare arrangements. Thus there is a strong relationship between social support and mental stress and trauma in women. It relates to a woman's help-seeking attitude, social networks, kinship network and support network. Consistently women are more susceptible to increasing rate of psychosomatic diseases and psychological disorders in the present day world. Some of the major life decisions and life-events like an employed woman's attitude about marriage; pregnancy (whether she is ready for this new role or not) may also influence her level of perceived stress.

Various Symptoms of Stress on Women

From the above discussion it can be inferred that stress is not *one size fits all*, particularly when it comes to the genders. The symptoms of stress in women are the same as those for major depression.

Psychological symptoms of stress in women include feelings of guilt, hopelessness and worthlessness, suicidal thoughts or sleep disturbance (sleeping more or sleeping less), difficulty in concentrating, lack of energy and fatigue. Women are more likely to ruminate when they are depressed. This includes crying to relieve emotional tension, trying to figure out why she is depressed, and sharing with her friends about her depression. Men, on the other hand, tend to distract themselves when they are depressed. Thus the behavioural symptoms of stress are quite different for men and women. In many cases women are more likely than men to develop depression under lower levels of stress. Furthermore, the female physiological response to stress is quiet different from men because women produce more stress hormones than men. Some of the most common **behavioural symptoms** of stress are feeling tense or depressed leading to poor memory, concentration, addiction to increased alcohol consumption or smoking, anger/hostility or certain emotional outburst, mood swings, difficulty in making decisions as well as less interest in conjugal life in case of married women. **Biological or physical symptoms** of stress may be in the form of appetite and weight changes, menstrual problems, infertility, hormonal disbalance, gout, arthritics, headache & migraine, asthma, shortness of breathe, diabetes, insomnia, high blood pressure & hypertension, irritability, fatigue etc.

Causes of Occupational Stress of Women Executives in Service Sector and their career impediments:

Women from lower middle class are joining the workforce mainly for economic reasons and women from upper middle class are mainly joining the corporate sector for their career advancement. Majority of the working women are continuing their career even after marriage. But still in India, women had to work hard to proof themselves as half good as men. Occupational stressors are those variables at work place, which generate lot of stress and strain and for working women occupational stressors can be categorized into two groups. One group of stressors is in the **context to the work**. These are the psycho-social problems that a woman is facing at her work place, which is some how having major to minor disruptions in the work performance. The other groups of stressors are attached with the **content of the work** or the work itself. Thus the different types of occupational stressors are as follows:

Types of Occupational Stressors for Women

Category	*Context to Work*
1. Organizational Culture & function	Poor communication, low level of support from male collogues due to gender stereotypes, Male dominated Corporate network, lack of support from management for personal development.
2. Role of organization	Many new women employees suffer from Role ambiguity due to lack of information & support as well as role conflict due multiple responsibilities in the professional and personal fields.
3. Career development	Due to invisible glass ceiling, Career stagnation & uncertainty, under promotion or role stagnation leads to de-motivation among women
4. Decision latitude/ Control	Low participation of women in decision making, low representation of women in the company's board room leads to lesser control over work
5. Work place abuses, bullying and sexual harassments.	Social or physical isolation, poor relationships with superiors and co-workers, interpersonal conflict, feeling of insecurity
6. Work-home interface	Conflicting demands of work and home, low support at home from spouse and other family members, dual career problems

Contd.

Category	Context to Work Content of work
7. Type of Work, environment and heavy work load	Problems relating to scheduling of shifts, issues of health, intense management pressures, abusive calls specially in ITES and call centers. Constant monitoring of staff by technology and team leaders. Majority of ITES jobs are monotonous & repetitive leading to burn out syndrome.
10. Work schedule & night shift	Shift working, inflexible work schedules, unpredictable hours, long or unsocial hours specially in ITES and health sector leading to distortion in the body's natural rhythm and ill health.

Women have to make constant career choices and compromises and all the time they have to face with various hurdles in their career path. Let us highlight some of them:

- Still many women are lacking upgraded knowledge and skill and mostly after marriage they take a back seat for furthering their cognitive knowledge and skills because of family responsibilities, restrictions and prejudices.
- Uneven distribution of family responsibilities and work pressure at office mostly make them exhausted at the end of the day because men in most Indian families are still not ready to share the family responsibilities with his spouse.
- For many working women family is their topmost priority leading to work family conflict.
- Many women don't prefer to travel extensively and prefer jobs which are mostly in-house or soft categories or in lower positions where the challenges and risk are less. Those jobs are mostly average to low paid.
- Women are having fewer acceptances as a boss or due to persistence stereotypical roles as a care giver and in most cases men emotionally feel challenged while taking orders from female managers.
- Woman's career is influenced more by other people (mostly parents and spouse) opinion in Indian families rather than her own abilities to take a career of her choice.
- Lack of career counseling, inadequate interventions to remove stress disorders, inadequate support from family members and spouses make today's women more prone to take irrational decisions or in most cases quitting job at the peak of their career.

Views of Indian Corporate Sector regarding Women Executives

The women of the 90's have emerged as a qualitatively different breed. Apart from manufacturing lot of service industries emerged during this phase. The service industries offer more flexible work ethos where individual can be a part of the work regardless of their geographical location and work schedules. This trend had been reinforced by the widespread availability of enabling technologies such as user- friendly computer, hardware, software and virtual libraries. Women in future will have the opportunity to create virtual working environments at home, availability of flexible working hours and therefore can better deal with social and home responsibilities. Companies like Genpact, Wipro, TCS, Infosys, ICICI give higher preferences to women employees and some of them are also undertaking gender audit to assess effectiveness of women employees from entry to board level jobs. Although women did occupy top management slots in various organizations in service sector but inspite of that they continued to be underrepresented in many cases compared to men. According to the industry statistics, the number of employed women grew by almost 200 million over the last decade and reached to 1.2 billion in 2007 compared to 1.8 billion men in India. The decision to appoint Ms.Chanda Kochhar as the CEO of ICICI Bank to succeed K.V.Kamath, Ranjana Kumar of Indian Bank are the indicators showing the growing popularities of women managers in Indian Industries. But Indian companies seem to be trying hard for getting more women executives in their boardroom.

Companies world over are paying adequate attention for hiring competent women . Various research findings showed that women have more patience and more stress resistance capabilities then men, collaborative in their approach and have better social skill and commitment. But Indian companies seems to be trying hard for getting more women on board and some head hunters or consultancies are getting higher commissions for recruiting women. Companies today are also giving certain incentives for efficient women employees and to retain them for long term. But companies' also expect the women executives to be more agile and to accept more responsibilities moving beyond the comfort zone. The general trend in India is that still many women are forced to make a choice between having a family and having a career. Today more women friendly companies want their women executives to be a part of the "boys club" will become adept to a more masculine style of functioning. They will be ready to face more tough assignments, assertive as a leader just like men keeping aside their prejudices. But at the same time companies should also be accommodative in providing pro-women policies like maternity leave, flexible working hour, transferring them in the same city or place where their spouse are working.

Recently WLL Mentoring Programme of creating "Women Business Leaders 2011"- is a leadership learning experience for senior women executives conducted by Tata Management Training center on May 2011 last year conducted a survey over 700 senior executives, to find out why women executives need mentoring? Some of the key findings from the study are as follows:

- Gender- stereotypes in the work place and the gender –bias at top management.
- Male dominated corporate networks.
- Lack of support from senior management for diversity and inclusivity in the work place
- Invisible glass ceiling that leads to demotivation among women executives
- Aspiration- deficit among women due to socio-economic conditioning
- "Sting of rejection" in the past
- Motherhood pressure and feeling of guilt for children
- Understand the women's advantage and differential leadership styles that can be leveraged
- Build skills to navigate the labyrinth and corporate dynamics
- Share how other women are responding to these pressures and learn from their experiences.
- There is strength in numbers and high energy in bonding, where there is a gender minority

There are five main themes of the WLL programme as follows:

Program Themes of WLL

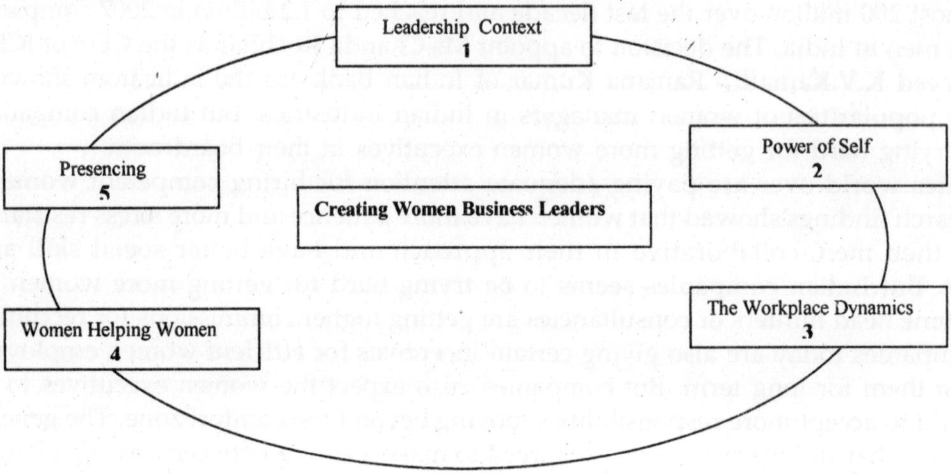

Theme 1

The Leadership Context: During this session, aspects related to personal, gender and cultural dimensions of women's leadership will be covered both in terms of "what" and also "how" women can exercise Contextual leadership and be masters of their context.

Theme 2

The Alchemy: Activating the Power of Self: "Alchemy neither composes nor mixes: it increases and activates that which already exists in latest state"- this session provide an opportunity to learn specific techniques and practices that create leadership excellence.

Theme 3

The Dynamics of women at workplace: The session will focus on building abilities in three areas:

- Self-Resilience
- Leading and Managing Change
- Global leadership and Mindset

Theme 4

Women Developing Women: Networking, Mentoring and Coaching will form the three pillars of this session. Women working together can create a powerful energy for achievement of each other's potential. The challenge is to examine and explore the nature of their engagement with each other and give a definite commitment towards activating the their latent energy for successful leadership.

Theme 5

In this final session the focus will be on evolving the future with actions in the present. The specific focus will be on consolidating and expressing the leadership challenges, Developing learning Partnerships and concretize ways in which women's leadership will find its voice, expression and Engagement.

Thus company initiatives for conducting this kind of training session for women executive proves that women are given utmost priorities in today's industrial organization and development for their highest future possibilities are indeed taken care of.

Stress Coping Mechanism for Women Executives in their Daily Life

Women find it harder to say "no" to other's requests and would often feel guilty if they could not satisfy everyone. Thus they often spend less time nurturing their own emotional and physical needs, as that might be perceived as "selfish" by social norms in many cases. At the individual level they should give priority for nurturing their own physical and emotional needs. This can be done by investing more time in developing their emotional health through the practice of resilience. To remain focused, flexible and positive in both bad and good times practicing regular stretching exercise, yoga, reading or writing in magazines, listening to music, engaging in spiritual reflection are some of the techniques of relaxation which are very necessary. Creating small opportunities and occasion for celebrating with friends and family members and spending quality time with loved ones can rejuvenate and strengthen the relationships with spouse and children. To reduce occupational stress maintaining friendly relationships at all level in the work place with peers, superiors and co-workers are very essential. Besides informal meetings with co-workers in lunch or coffee break, arranging for get together, picnic can reduce boredom and stress at work place. Many studies revealed that women in a highly stressful job are also suffering from various problems like infertility; premature menopause and many of them are unable to conceive due to higher level of stress hormones. For them, apart from general medication certain special treatment like talk therapy, individual psychotherapy and taking help from professional counselor, support group therapy, Biofeedback, relaxation training, changing some of the life style factors, reducing addictions are some of the ways of maintaining better health and energy and reducing the causes of stress. Reducing unrealistic goals and expectations can help to sort out her problems and to find out her own definition of success in life.

Conclusion

Since today's organization have realized the importance of women in the work place. For instance, numerous organization are providing EAP (Employer Assistance Programs) where a workforce can take counseling services from psychotherapist or professional psychologists. In the same way assistance cell for women employees are essential. Besides flexitime and crèche facilities for children of the working mother at the organization premises should be given due consideration in service sectors. Crèche facilities previously were only provided to women worker in factory but this system should be included in service sector where many women have to stay for long hours and night shift specially in ITES, health and banking sectors. So employers role will focus on giving women executives as much control over their jobs as possible and should provide proper training and development programme specially for talented women executives. Initiatives like inclusion of pro-women policies into their HR policy of the organization and creating workplace as a better, stress-free and exhilarating experience for women are the few steps forward towards the empowerment of women workforce in India.

References

Abdullah, R., Jahan, S. and Saha, S. (2008), Occupational Stress, Social and Family Difficulties and Job Contentment of Working Women: Bangladesh Perspective, *Journal of Business and Economics*, Vol.3, No.1, January, pp.139-143.

Bahl, T. (2005), The Workplace Bullies, *www.blonnet.com*

Bianchi, S.M., Casper, L.M., and King, R.M. (2005), *Work, Family, Health and Well-Being*, Lawrence Erlbaum Associates, London.

Budhiraja, J. and Jyoti, A. (2008), Work Place Challenges for Women in 21st. Century, HRM Review, The Icfai University Press, September.

Buchanan, J.B.O. and Boswell, W.R. (2006), Blurring Boundaries: Correlates of Integration and Segmentation between Work and Non-work, *Journal of Vocational Behaviour*, Vol.68, Issue 3, June, pp. 432-445.

Campbell, J.C and Boyd, D. (2000), Violence Against Women: Synthesis of Research for Health Care Professional, *A Research Report submitted to the U.S. Department of Justice by NIJ (National Institute of Justice)*, December.

http://www.ncjrs.gov/pdffiles1/nij/grants/199761.pdf

Das, J.K. and Datta, S. (2008), Management of Occupational Stress in the Service Sector: An Empirical Study, *Indian Accountancy Review*, Vol.12, No.2, pp.33-52.

Ghosh, K.B and Das, S. (2009), Stress at Work Place- A Mounting Concern, *HRM Review, Icfai University Press* , February Issue.

Gopal, V.V. (2005), Women and Workplace Stress, *Work Place Stress: Concepts and Cases, The ICFAI University Press*, PP.72-78.

Gunavathy,.J.S. and Suganya, N.P. (2007), Work Life Inbalances Among Married Women Employees of BPOs- A Study, *IJTD JOURN AL XXXVII:1, January-March*, pp.156-168.

Kidwai, W., Waheed, S., Ayub, S and Azam, S.I. (2008), Impact of Working Status on their Lives- A Survey of Working Women at a Teaching Hospital in Karachi, Pakistan, *Pakistan Journal of Medical Science Quartely*, Vol.24, No.4, *http://pjms.com pk/issues/julsep08/pdf/impact.pdf*

Loutfi, M.F. (2001), Women, Gender and Work, *International Labour Office.*

Marano, H.E. (2003), *More Women Suffer Depression*, published in Psychology Today, July Issue.

http://www.psychologytoday.com/articles/200307/more-women-suffer-depression

Martino, V.D. (2003), Relationship between Work Stress and Work Place Violence in the Health Sector, *working paper series published by the Steering Committee of the ILO/ICN/WHO/PSI*, Geneva

http://www.who.int/violence_injury_prevention/violence/interpersonal/Wvstresspaper.pdf

Messersmith, J. (2007), Managing Work-Life Conflict Among Information Technology Worker, *Human Resource Management, Fall 2007*,Vol 46,No.3, Published online in Wiley InterScience (*www.interscience.wiley.com*)

Michailidis, M. and Georgiou, Y. (2005), Employee Occupational Stress in Banking Work, *A Journal of Prevention, Assessment and Rehabilitation*, IOS Press, Vol.24, No.2, pp.123-137.

Mukhopadhyay, S. (1989), Working Status and Stress of Middle Class Women of Calcutta, *Journal of Biological Sciences*, 21; Cambridge University Press, pp.109-114.

Selye, H. (1936), The Nature of Stress, online edition from "The Best of Basal facts" edited and published by *ICNR (International Center for Nutritional Research, Inc., 1981).*

Srivastava, A.K. (2005), Role Stress Across Management Levels in an Organization, *The ICFAI Journal of Organizational Behaviour, The ICFAI University Press*, Vol. IV, No.4, October, pp.53-63.

Swanson, N.G. (2000), Working Women and Stress, *JAMWA*, Vol 55, No.2, Spring Issue.

Vidyavathi, K. (2009), Women Workers in the ITES Hub of Bangalore, *HRM Review, Icfai University Press*, February Issue.

http://www.willforumindia.com/downloads/wll-creating-women-Business-Leaders-2011.pdf

25

QUALITY OF WORK LIFE AS HR PRACTICE: THE MEDIATING LINK OF COMMITMENT

Jyoti Sharma

Introduction

Organizational Culture Analysis can determine the relative effectiveness of the organizational innovations to optimize organizational performance. It can also determine the relationship of workforce psychological characteristics (attitudes, behavioral preferences), and work environment attributes such as structure and culture and change processes with respect to performance outcomes. Results will enable the organization to identify and implement effective culture-based innovations that improve workforce performance.

Quality of work life is prescriptive concept; it attempts to design work environment so as to maximize concern for human welfare. It is goal, as well process. The goal is of creation of more involving, satisfying and effective jobs and environment for people at all levels of the organization. As a process quality of work life involves efforts to realize this goal through active participation. To improve the quality of life for employees during their time at work. This includes creating a healthier and more employee friendly environment as well as making improvements to the methods used by employees as part of their work. This is also a corporate social responsibility of the employer, as this can improve on the employees loyalty to the company.

The commitment level of the employee can be judged at different levels i.e. at job level, functional discipline and at organizational goal. However, it has been observed that organizational goals help in contributing to employee's committed and effective efforts towards the functional discipline of the organization in which individual's organizational commitment is placed above his or her self-commitment. Indeed the goals and the objectives of the organization should be clear to the employees that provide them ample opportunity to tax them their potentials. If any individual faces checks and unnecessary control it affects the working capability, hurting the emotional aspect of the person and affecting commitment level. Mathieu and Zajac (1990) and Benkhoff (1997) defined organizational commitment as the psychological attachment of workers to their organizations. Commitment to organization has also been found to relate positively to a variety of desirable work outcomes including employee job satisfaction, motivation and performance, and negatively correlated to absenteeism and turnover.

Literature Review

A high QWL environment is one in which people are essential members of an organization that challenges the human spirit, promotes personal growth and development, and achieves results. It is characterized by employee participation in the decision-making process and problem solving, excellent communication channels, good teamwork and collaboration, employees engaged in meaningful and challenging work, and employment security (Karasek and Theorell, 1990). A survey of 17,000 nurses in Canada revealed that 32.9 percent were dissatisfied with their present jobs, 36.0 percent reported a high risk of burnout, and 29.4 percent of nurses, under 30 years of age, were planning to leave their present job in the next year (Toronto Star, 2001). In studies on QWL, results indicated that staff become committed to an organization's mission, if the organization has in place programs which maximize employee development, promote a healthy work climate, and provide the tools and resources necessary to enhance staff performance (Donner et al., 1995).

Staff commitment particularly organizational commitment has emerged as a promising area of research within the study of industrial/organizational psychology. To a large extent, interest in the study of commitment has replaced an earlier emphasis on job satisfaction (Schneider, 1985). The latter construct was perceived as a logical correlate of job performance as workers became more satisfied with their work (Schwab and Cummings, 1970). Although there has been some ambiguity surrounding the broad construct of work commitment (Salancik, 1977), there appears to be some theoretical consensus and convergence of empirical findings about organizational commitment (Tett and Meyer, 1989, Morrow, 1983, Mowday et al, 1979). Organizational commitment has been used to refer to three aspects of staff attitudes (Mowday et al 1979) the extent to which an employee demonstrates a strong desire to remain a member of the organization; the degree of willingness to exert high levels of effort for the organization and belief in and acceptance of the major values and goals of the organization.

While these definitions stress the attitudinal components of commitment suggesting a bond between the individual and the organization, behavioural aspects of commitment have also been identified. Salancik (1977) has argued that commitment must be manifested not only in attitudes but also in actions. Bateman and Organ (1983) refer to these behaviours as employee citizenship behaviours. In particular, they point to indicators of performance, which go beyond the normal requirements of the job, such as helping co-workers with job-related problems, tolerating temporary impositions without complaint and cooperating in the times of crisis. With regard to organizational commitment, Tett and Meyer (1989) have reviewed a large number of studies that focused on the relationship between staff commitment and a number of organizational outcomes. They discovered strong relationships between staff commitment and both job satisfaction and job turnover. Mowday et al (1979) also found a relationship between organizational commitment and rates of absenteeism. Hence, the available research suggests that employees who exhibit organizational commitment are happier at their work; spend less time away from their jobs and are less likely to leave the organization.

Method

The Study - It is an exploratory study focused at understanding the relationship of quality of work life with employee's commitment amongst the executives.

Sample- The study was carried out on 200 executives working in manufacturing and service industry, who were selected on random basis. The respondents belonged to the senior and middle level. The extraneous variables of age, sex, education and other variables were controlled by randomization and elimination.

Tools For Data Analysis –Simple correlation was used for examining the relationship between variables under study.

Results

	O.Com	*CO*	*IO*
QWL	0.7010 **	0.7721 **	0.3633 **

** Significant at 0.01level

QWL- Quality of work life, O.Com- Organizational Commitment, CO- Concern for organization and IO- Identification with the organization

- The correlation between the variables has been found to be 0.7010 which is significant at 0.01 level. It shows that with positive level of quality of work life, organizational commitment also increases which positively impacts commitment of the employee.
- The correlation between the variables has been found to be 0.7721 which is significant at 0.01 level. It shows that with positive level of quality of work life, the dimension of organizational commitment i.e. concern for organization increases which positively impacts commitment of the employee.
- The correlation between the variables has been found to be 0.3633 which is significant at 0.01 level. It shows that with positive level of quality of work life, the dimension of organizational commitment i.e. identification of organization life also increases which positively impacts commitment of the employee.

Discussion

A high QWL environment is one in which people are essential members of an organization that challenges the human spirit, promotes personal growth and development, and achieves results. It is characterized by employee participation in the decision-making process and problem solving, excellent communication channels, good teamwork and collaboration, employees engaged in meaningful and challenging work, and employment security (Karasek and Theorell, 1990). The quality of work life is cooperative rather than authoritarian; evolutionary and open and rather static and rigid; informal rather rule bound; impersonal rather than mechanistic; mutual respect and trust rather than hatred against each other. Work-life balance is about people having a measure of control over when, where and how they work. It is achieved when an individual's right to a fulfilled life inside and outside paid work is accepted and respected as the norm, to the mutual benefit of the individual, business and society.

Organizational commitment has been defined and measured in several ways signifying a bond between the individual and the organization (Mathieu and Zajac, 1990). Morris and Sherman (1981) proposed an exchange approach in which commitment is the result of investments in the organization or a psychological approach in which commitment is depicted as a positive high-involvement orientation towards the organization. Mowday et al, 1979 and Mowday et al, 1982 suggested that organizational commitment is an internalization of the values and goals of the organization, a willingness to work hard on behalf of the organization and a strong desire to remain with the organization. This type of psychological commitment has been named as affective commitment (McGee and Ford, 1987; Gregersen and Black, 1992; and Mayer and Schoorman, 1992) whereas in the institutional commitment, individual works with a feeling of belongingness, sense of pride and sense of group achievements, with a spirit of dedication and determination in putting efforts to accomplish goals of organization.

The results of the research indicate the positive relation of quality of work life on organizational commitment and its dimensions namely i- concern for organization and ii- identification with the organization. The various studies referred to in the survey show that where innovations are motivated primarily by an improvement in quality of work life, such improvement can lead to improved performance with committed efforts. Despite the evidence that firms can reap considerable performance advantages through attempts at increasing the quality of working life through greater job enlargement, job enrichment, competence development and delegated participation, there is also considerable evidence that some firms are actually using such approaches in deference to short-run pressure for immediate results on the 'bottom-line' of the profit and loss account and rapid increases in stock market valuation.

The positive correlated value of quality of work life and organizational commitment is 0.7010 **, which is significant at .01 level. Assumptions are that participation measures affect all employees identically, regardless of gender, race, age and contractual status, can amplify social disadvantage. It is stated that a combination of participation and welfare measures appears to enhance organisational performance and the quality of working life. Policy support should focus on union recognition and activity within a human rights framework, since this can positively influence employees' behaviour towards organisational goals. Organizational commitment has been used to refer three aspects of staff attitudes that indicates the extent to which the employee demonstrate a strong desire to remain the member of the organization, the degree of willingness to exert high level of efforts for organization and belief and acceptance of the major goals and values of the organization. Behavior of "employee as citizen" is an indicator of performance which goes beyond the requirement of the job, such as helping co-workers with job related problems, tolerating temporary impositions without complaining and cooperating at the time of crisis. In a study conducted by Daud (2010), the level and relationship between quality of work life with organizational commitment amongst academic staff was determined in one of the leading public universities in Malaysia. A survey instrument was used to measure the perception of academic staff concerning their level of quality of work life and its relationship to organizational commitment. Based upon the study, the levels of QWL were found to be favorable and Organizational Commitment among staff was moderate.

Quality of work life ensures the committed efforts of the employees. The degree of influence accorded to employees is also important. Low levels of participation with little employee autonomy have been identified as a reason for disappointing results. Where introducing participation has raised employees' expectations, but there is little real improvement in employee influence, workers may express resentment and dissatisfaction. Where participation is only from the top down, workers may feel that they are being lectured and not listened. Even where participation is from the bottom up, workers may feel that management is using their ideas, with no return seen by employees.

The positive correlated value of quality of work life and concern for organizations is 0.7721 ** which is also found significant at .01 level. This evidence contends that when employees and organization has the feeling of belongingness for each other then concern for organization rises high which is considered in relation to quality of work life. Some studies, which have examined the business consequences of implementing family-friendly employment policies, have found benefits in doing so. Others have tried to determine whether employees have a say over work-life issues, and how instrumental it might be in establishing family-friendly employment policies. Employees appear to have a voice of some kind in larger organisations. Family-friendly policies appear to be more widespread and deeply embedded in enterprises, which recognise unions, though this association does not imply that unions have a more effective voice. Consultation – even with and among line managers– also appears to be rather restricted, with the possible exception of health services, where there is an organisational cultural tradition of consultation.

Humanistic values may contribute positively to firm performance and thereby enhance competitive advantage. New initiatives at the workplace developed in such a spirit would also develop the skills and thereby employability of individuals at a time of structural upheaval and enduring unemployment. The concept of increasing the participation of workers in decisions affecting their work lives is appearing more often on the labor-management agenda. The reasons for management interest include the need for increasing productivity and quality; increasing the quality of work life for the new worker, who is more educated, with a good work ethic but alienated and unmotivated under current management practice; and meeting foreign competition. Problems may arise for firms involved in forms of participation such as quality circles and quality of work life programs, when management aims of a streamlined work force and control of worker innovations clash with the workers' expectations of work place democracy inherent in such programs.

The positive correlated value of quality of work life and identification with the organizations is 0.3633 ** which is again found significant at .01 level. Individuals with high level of social support are less likely to experience the negative effects of emotional dissonance on organizational commitment. This happens when employees identify themselves with organization and quality of work life becomes the cause for it. They are emotionally satisfied and hence their committed efforts are reflected in their performance. Reichers (1986) and Welsch and LaVan (1981) discussed the discrepancy theory that provides the theoretical basis for a linkage between emotional dissonance, job satisfaction, organizational commitment and intention to turnover. According to it every employee has a threshold comparison level that represents the quality of expected outcomes from his or her employment. Emotional conflict is more closely identified with the job and is more proximate in the work environment than distant influences such as the organization. Feelings of job dissatisfaction are followed by alienation from the organization in the form of reduced organizational commitment (Mathieu and Hamel, 1989).

Employees dually committed to their organizations and careers reported the highest empowerment, willingness to engage in service recovery and work satisfaction. They were more aware of the supervisory use of legitimate, reward, expert and referent powers. According to Mueller et al (1994), many modern management techniques involve attempts to indirectly control employees by fostering organizational commitment. Managers try to reinforce employee loyalty as organizationally committed individuals are reported to be better performers, (Jauch et al, 1978). They are more aligned with enterprise goals, and are thought to be less likely than their uncommitted counterparts to seek employment elsewhere (Mowday et al, 1979). The concept of job involvement has received considerable attention in occupational psychology. Job involvement is defined as the degree to which one identifies with one's present job (Kanungo 1982; Lawler and Hall, 1970). Attention has also been paid to how job involvement is related to mental well being leading to commitment. Well-being is a many-faceted and value-laden concept (Campbell, 1976; Jahoda, 1958), but its primary indicator is its affective level and quality, in terms of positive affect e.g., feelings of happiness, satisfaction, high self-esteem and feelings of distress e.g., anxiety, depression, sense of hopelessness; Warr (1987). Some of the studies testing the relationship between job involvement and well-being have shown that involvement is related to a high level of well-being confirming commitment (Wiener et al, 1987; Castro, 1986). Involvement is also caused by the congruence between a person's needs and the characteristics of the job that is, by how well the job fulfills the individual's needs leads to commitment . Of these different reasons for job involvement, need fulfillment most closely relates to a known basis for well-being too.

Conclusion

When quality of work life is taken as HR practice in any organization it mediates as a link to the commitment of employees towards organization. Employees' association with management values and goals is increased by quality of work life in the organization, and they are more motivated and committed to achieving corporate goals. By catering for employees' social needs, through improved job security and satisfaction and quality of working life, higher performance is achieved. Alternatively, satisfying social needs can be treated as an end in itself. The research concludes that the quality of working life results in committed employees efforts.

References

Bateman, T., and Organ, D. (1983), Job Satisfaction and the Good Soldier: The Relationship between Affect and Employee "citizenship". Academy of Management Journal, 26 , 587-595.

Benkhoff, B. (1997), Ignoring Commitment is Costly: New Approaches establish the Missing Link between Commitment and Performance. Human Relations, 50, 701-726.

Campbell, A. (1976), Subjective Measures of Well-being. American Psychologist, 31, 117-124.

Castro, N. L. (1986), Working-class Women: The Relationship of Job Characteristics and Job Involvement to Psychological Well-being in Employed Mothers. Dissertation Abstracts International, 47, 3978.

Daud, N.(2010), Education and Management Technology (ICEMT), 2010 International Conference.Manage., Univ. Teknol. MARA Shah Alam, Shah Alam, Malaysia. Print ISBN: 978-1-4244-8616-8. Digital Object Identifier: 10.1109/ICEMT.2010.5657657 +Daud, N.

Gregersen, H.B. and J.S. Black (1992), "Antecedents to Commitment to a Parent Company and a Foreign Operation." Academy of Management Journal 35: 65-90.

Jahoda, M. (1958), Current Concepts on Mental Health. New York: Basic Books.

Jauch, L.R, Glueck, W.F., and Osborn, R.N. (1978), "Organizational Loyalty, Professional.

Karasek, R., Theorell, T. (1990), *Health, Work, Stress, Productivity, and the Reconstruction of Work Life*, Basic Books, New York, NY .

Kanungo, R.N. (1982), Work Alienation: An Integrative Approach. New York: Praeger.

Lawler, E., and Hall, D. (1970), Relationships of Job Characteristics to Job Involvement, Satisfaction, and Intrinsic Motivation. Journal of Applied Psychology, 54, 305-312.

Mayer R.C. and F.D. Schoorman (1992), Predicting Participation and Production Outcomes through a Two Dimensional Model of Organizational Commitment, Academy of management Journal 35, 671-684.

McGee, G.W. and R.C. Ford (or more?) Dimensions of Organizational Commitment : Reexamination of the Affective and Continuance Commitment Scales, Journal of Applied Psychology. 72:638-642.

Morris, J.H. and J.D. Sherman (1981), "Generalizability of an Organizational Commitment Model." Academy of Management Journal 24: 512-526.

Mathieu, J.E., and Hamel, K. (1989), A Causal Model of the Antecedents of Organizational Commitment Among Professionals and Nonprofessionals. Journal of Vocational Behavior, 34. 299-317.

Mathieu, John E. - Zajac, Dennis M. (1990), A Review and Meta-Analysis of the Antecedents, Correlates,and Cosequences of Organizational Commitment. Psychological Bulletin, Vol. 108, No. 2, 171-194.

Morrow, P. (1983), Concept Redundancy in Organizational Research: The Case of Work Commitment and Academic Research Productivity,". Academy of Management Review, 8, 486-500.

Mowday, R.T., Porter, L.W., and Steers, R.M. (1982), Employee-organization Linkages: The Psychology of Commitment, Absenteeism, and Turnover. San Diego, CA: Academic Press.

Mowday, R., Steers, R., and Porter, L. (1979), The Measurement of Organizational commitment. Journal of Vocational Behavior, 14, 224-247.

Mueller, C.W, Boyer, E. M.,. Price, J. L and Iverson, R D. (1994), "Employee Attachment and Noncoercive Conditions of Work: The Case of Dental Hygienists," Work and Occupations 21(2), 179-212.

Reichers, A.E. (1986), Conflict and Organizational Commitments. Journal of Applied Psychology, 71, 508-514.

Salancik, G. (1977), Commitment and the Control of Organizational Behavior and belief. In B.M. Staw and G. Salancik (Eds.), New Directions in Organizational Behavior (pp. 1-30). Chicago: St. Clair Press.

Schneider, B. (1985), Organizational Behavior. Annual Review of Psychology, 36, 573-611.

Schwab, D., and Cummings, L. (1970), Theories of Performance and Satisfaction: A Review. Industrial Relations, 9, 408-430.

Tett, R., and Meyer, J. (1989), Organizational Commitment, Job Satisfaction, Turnover Intention, and Turnover: A Meta-analytic Review. Unpublished Manuscript, University of Western Ontario, London, Canada.

Warr, P.B. (1987), Job Characteristics and Mental Health. In P.B. Warr (Ed.), Psychology at Work. London: Penguin.

Welsch, H.P., and LaVan, H. (1981), Inter-relationships between Organizational Commitment and Job Characteristics, Job Satisfaction, Professional Behavior, and Organizational Climate. Human Relations, 34, 1079-1089.

Wiener, Y., Muczyk, J.P., and Gable, M. (1987), Relationship between Work Commitments and Experience of Personal Well-being. Psychological Reports, 60, 459-466.

26

A STUDY ON TALENT MANAGEMENT SYSTEM AS AN EFFECTIVE TOOL FOR ORGANIZATION EFFECTIVENESS

Vijit Chaturvedi & Poonam Batra

Introduction

Talent consists of those individuals who can make a difference to organisational performance, either through their immediate contribution or in the longer-term by demonstrating the highest levels of potential.

Talent management is the systematic attraction, identification, development, engagement/ retention and deployment of those individuals who are of particular value to an organisation, either in view of their 'high potential' for the future or because they are fulfilling business/operation-critical roles.

This definition underlines the importance of recognizing that it is not enough to just attract individuals with high potential. Developing, managing and retaining those individuals as part of a planned strategy for talent is equally important, as is adopting systems to measure the return on this investment. More organisations are also now broadening their definitions, looking at the 'talents' of all their staff and working on ways to develop their strengths.

Need of Managing Talent in Workplace

Talent management is an organizational approach for leading people by building culture, engagement, capability, and capacity through integrated talent acquisition, development, and deployment processes that are aligned to business goals. The common components of talent management include acquisition of employee's career planning assessment succession planning, organization development, performance management team and individual development.

Specifically, effective talent management must be relentlessly focused on organizations' desired business outcomes. This differs from past views of talent management in that traditional approaches to talent selection and development focused on worthy, but HR-centric goals such as building a leadership bench, training and developing managers, or selecting the right people for the right job at the right time. Often these practices were functionally siloed, regionally fragmented and stood apart from other business practices and financial metrics.

To ensure perceived (and real) relevance for contemporary talent management practices, the shared lexicon in many organizations needs to shift dramatically. Everyone engaged in developing and implementing talent strategies must start by thinking as a Board, a CEO, or an owner of the organization. Walking in their shoes quickly reveals that their priorities, which can include such strategic priorities as driving revenue growth, penetrating new markets, horizontal integration, and driving cost efficiencies, have a decidedly different, business-oriented ring.

Talent management has never been more of an immediate concern than it is right now. But in the rush to fill a perceived talent management void, organizations must be careful not to rush into implementing initiatives or programs that are more about taking action than about implementing a well-crafted solution.

Careful planning, culminating in a sound talent strategy that is tightly connected to the organization's overall business strategies and business needs, is required for talent management to become ingrained in an organization's culture and practices. Only when this happens is it possible for talent management to be both effective and sustainable.

(http://www.ddiworld.com/pdf/ddi_employeeengagement_mg.pdf)

Organisations find greater value in formulating their own meaning of what talent is than accepting universal or prescribed definitions and there are considerable differences in how talent is defined across different industries and sectors. That said, it is helpful to start with a broad definition and, from our research, we have developed a working definition for both 'talent' and 'talent management'.

Review on Significant Role of Talent Management in Different Companies –An Indicator for Organization Effectiveness

St Luke's Communications, a leading performer in the UK advertising industry, has a reputation for attracting, retaining and motivating creative talent. Unlike its peers, the agency is very unconventional – in being completely co-owned as a co-operative and in continually challenging the status quo. It has the lowest talent turnover rates of any comparable company.

US electronic payment and Internet commerce provider, **First Data Corporation,** has built its successful global business over the last few years on systems and operational excellence. But, given a newer solutions focus within and fundamental change in financial services markets, it has been rethinking its talent management strategy and programmes. These shifts are as much the remit of organizational development executives as those in HR.

Agilent Technologies, a spin-off of **Hewlett-Packard (HP)**, is a world leader in talent management practices. This is partly based on HP's track record of over 30 years, but more recently, based on the work of its 15-person new HR global talent team and extended global talent network. Talent management is positioned strategically in the organization and directly integrates business and diversity strategies.

Founded in 1899, forest products group, **Carter Holt Harvey (CHH)**,is a leading employer in New Zealand with over 11,000 people in 33 separate businesses across the southern hemisphere. Such has been the group-wide impact of its HR function on people and performance improvement programmes over three years, that it was spun-off from the group in spring 2001 as a stand-alone business called Mariner7. CHH talent management directions/interventions are now provided by the outsourced former department, in addition to the development of a range of on-line tools.

Staffing and employment solutions organization, **Manpower plc**, has established a reputation over four decades for best employment practice in the UK and currently employs two groups of people – 1500 operations staff and, in the course of 12 months, around 200,000 contract workers, all of whom are on its payroll. But, despite its reputation, the company is rethinking talent management practices to sustain its market leadership.

The diversified manufacturing company, **International Paper**, has built a reputation over 100 years in North America and globally as a growth business and stable employer. It now has a global penetration in more than 50 countries. Since 1997, however, the corporation has been systematically rethinking its interpretation of talent management, which is leading to wide-ranging innovations in its positioning, talent practices and a in more compelling value proposition based on employee engagement.

SAB Ltd is the South Africa Beer Division of **South African Breweries plc**, South Africa's leading brewer. It enjoys a 98 per cent market share from 16 brands, in addition to strong business growth and a reputation for equitable employment and people practices. Despite continued success and some innovative talent management practices, SAB faces talent challenges driven by socio-political, economic and internal circumstances.

Over two decades or so, semiconductor industry leader **ST Microelectronics** has become used to the pace of change and the breakthroughs that characteristically reinvent the sector, or introduce 'un-thought-of' applications for its chips and integrated circuits. Despite complexity, the company has flourished and is in the world's top industry players. However, business/economic conditions are causing a rethinking of the position of talent management, its strategies and practices.

Features of a Talent Management Strategy

Key features of a talent management strategy include the following elements.

Alignment to Corporate Strategy

Ensuring that the talent strategy is closely aligned with the corporate strategy must be a priority. In developing a talent strategy, both internal and external factors should be taken into account. Strategic analysis from the business perspective should feed into an HR forecast which can help shape an organisation's tailored approach to talent management.

Inclusive versus Exclusive Approaches

Some organisations adopt an inclusive approach to talent management creating a 'whole workforce' approach to engagement and talent development, while others develop a more exclusive focus segmenting talent according to need.

Regardless of which approach organisations adopt, fairness and consistency must be applied in all talent management processes. Diversity considerations must also be built-into talent management processes to ensure that organisations are able to draw from the widest pools of talent possible.

Involving the Right People

Careful consideration needs to be paid to involving the right stakeholders in the talent management strategy. Clearly, HR specialists have an important role to play in providing support and guidance in the design and development of approaches to talent management that will fit the needs of the organisation.

Focusing on the Talent Management Loop

It is also important to focus attention on the four areas of the talent management loop, that is: attracting, developing, managing and evaluating talent.

Attracting Talent: The ability to attract external talent depends upon how potential applicants view the organisation, the industry or sector it operates in and whether they share the values of that organisation. The creation of an attractive employer brand is an important factor in attracting external talent. Where needed, lower financial rewards can be countered with alternative benefits and employer values such as social responsibility.

Developing Talent: Talent development should be linked to other learning and development initiatives. Appropriate learning and development interventions are required at relevant stages in a career path for talented individuals to achieve their maximum potential. Developing talent needs informal as well as formal learning interventions. These interventions will include conventional development activities but there is also the opportunity to use creative alternatives such as talent coaching and mobility.

Managing Talent: Active steps, plans and activities are needed to retain and engage talent required for the future health of the organisation. Investment in management, leadership and other development activities will positively impact on talent retention. Organisations should develop a performance culture where individuals take responsibility for the continuous improvement of business processes and their own skill development.

Tracking and Evaluating Talent Management: Evaluation of talent management is difficult but necessary to ensure that the investment is meeting organisational needs. Evaluation requires both quantitative and qualitative data which is valid, reliable and robust.

Role of Talent Management Process Development in Effective Talent Identification and Management

Talent management is a dynamic process that has to be continuously reviewed to ensure that organisational requirements are still being met in the light of changing business priorities. Ultimately, organisational success is the most effective evaluation of talent management

There are four steps that companies can take to quickly assess their talent management process and begin improving their talent management competency-

Step 1 – Identify Key Roles.- Analyze the key steps in each part of the talent life cycle (identification and attraction, hiring and inculcation, motivation and development, appraisal and reward, building and sustaining relationships) and map the key players and their roles and responsibilities to each stage.

Step 2 – Take an Inventory of Your Talent Management Skills- Identify the critical skills needed to play the key roles in the talent life cycle effectively. To what extent does your company employ people who possess them?

Step 3 – Measure the Right Thing- . Assess the measures you use to evaluate the performance of your talent management process at each life cycle stage such as offer-to-hire ratios, average tenures of new hires, performance ranking, skill fit to job requirements, etc.

Step 4 – Set Up a Process-Wide Feedback Loop. Everyone managing talent needs to understand the big picture and to connect their role and responsibilities to the overall objectives of the process. How is data captured in each stage of the life cycle reported and communicated? How are knowledge and experiences shared across the process? Where are the information gaps and missed communications?

Essential Elements in Effective Management of Talent Process

In such a competitive scenario, talent management has become the key strategy to identify and filling the skill gap in a company by recruiting the high-worth individuals from the industry. It is a never-ending process that starts from targeting people.. in order to make the talent cycle more effective following elements should be importantly focused to make it more effective-

Understanding the Requirement: It is the preparatory stage and plays a crucial role in success of the whole process. The main objective is to determine the requirement of talent. The main activities of this stage are developing job description and job specifications.

- **Sourcing the Talent:** This is the second stage of talent management process that involves targeting the best talent of the industry. Searching for people according to the requirement is the main activity.
- **Attracting the Talent:** it is important to attract the talented people to work with you as the whole process revolves around this only. After all the main aim of talent management process is to hire the best people from the industry.
- **Recruiting the Talent:** The actual process of hiring starts from here. This is the stage when people are invited to join the organization.
- **Selecting the Talent:** This involves meeting with different people having same or different qualifications and skill sets as mentioned in job description. Candidates who qualify this round are invited to join the organization.
- **Training and Development:** After recruiting the best people, they are trained and developed to get the desired output.
- **Retention:** Certainly, it is the sole purpose of talent management process. Hiring them does not serve the purpose completely. Retention depends on various factors such as pay package, job specification, challenges involved in a job, designation, personal development of an employee, recognition, culture and the fit between job and talent.
- **Promotion:** No one can work in an organization at the same designation with same job responsibilities. Job enrichment plays an important role.
- **Competency Mapping:** Assessing employees' skills, development, ability and competency is the next step. If required, also focus on behavior, attitude, knowledge and future possibilities of improvement. It gives you a brief idea if the person is fir for promoting further.
- **Career Planning:** If the individual can handle the work pressure and extra responsibilities well, the management needs to plan his or her career so that he or she feels rewarded. It is good to recognize their efforts to retain them for a longer period of time.
- **Succession Planning:** Succession planning is all about who will replace whom in near future. The employee who has given his best to the organization and has been serving it for a very long time definitely deserves to hold the top position. Management needs to plan about when and how succession will take place.
- **Exit:** The process ends when an individual gets retired or is no more a part of the organization.

Generally Adopted Strategies for Effective Talent Management

There are several ways to begin talent management work. Because the work is holistic, there isn't a linear path toward becoming a talent-centric organisation. Pick a starting place that works for you – one that captures the attention, and will fit well with the active participation, of the CEO.

Again, talent management is like change management: one may have to go after the low hanging fruit in order to gain acceptance and understanding.

Identify Critical Jobs. Talent management is about capturing/developing both the potential and performance of everyone. But it is not likely that HR will have the resources or the time to develop initiatives that address the needs of the entire workforce. Therefore, the best place to begin is by focusing on the jobs that have the biggest impact on the organisation. Just the exercise of identifying those jobs – and they are jobs not individuals – will provide great benefit. Once those jobs are identified, the next step is to look at retention/ recruitment needs for them.

Develop a Competency Framework. People who join organisations bring more than just their training or functional knowledge. They also bring skills and abilities, some of which relate to the specific job they may do, others that relate to their interpersonal qualities. Being successful – being talented – requires all these factors, in various degrees and combinations depending upon the level and nature of the position. Competencies define the skills, knowledge and abilities that are required for success. They contain specific behaviors that are expected, along with specific skills, and they relate closely to leadership models and company values. Developing a competency framework is an important first step to take in understanding what is required of talent – and for providing language that can be used consistently in recruitment and development.

Creating Tools/Process for Talent Conversations. According to many organisations, talent management is all about conversations. In fact, several companies have said that the act of having conversations about talent is just as important as the outcome of those conversations. Conversations provide honest feedback between managers and employees, setting the stage for development and improvement. HR has a big opportunity early on in its talent management work, and throughout the process, to provide tools, tips, processes and training for managers and employees alike, to make the talent conversations effective.

Determine Workforce Vulnerabilities. Workforce planning is the newest and still the least integrated of all the categories of talent management initiatives. Yet it is the one that commonsense tells us should be one of the starting points. With today's ageing/retiring baby boomers, outsourcing and off shoring of work, and many different styles of working, understanding the makeup of the workforce has never been more important.

Enhance the Performance Management Process. The fastest way to start integrating your disparate talent-related initiatives is to concentrate first on the initiative that touches more of the others: performance management. Performance management is the most integrative because it involves the greatest number of people in the organisation. Everyone has a manager, everyone has goals and everyone should have discussions about how they are performing. The rigor of your performance management process needs to be examined right when you start talent management thinking. One of your first efforts should be to make performance management a process, if not a part of the way people work, rather than just an annual event.

Motorola's performance management process contains just that sort of rigor. After five years, their process has evolved to include a series of behavioral-based assessments that are then calibrated so that talent is ranked relatively. The ranking forms the basis of decisions around professional development and leadership opportunities.

Structure Ways for the CEO to be Visibly Involved. Virtually all companies that excel in talent management do so with the visible, active participation – not just support – of their CEOs. Such involvement takes the form of sharing the values of talent with all employees; organizing town hall meetings to discuss or probe for employee feedback gathered; designing, as well as teaching, leadership development or high potential programs

Developing a Human Centric Organization - human-capital-centric organizations do things differently. They align all the systems and processes that identify, attract, and support talent. The characteristics of such organizations are-

- Business strategy is determined with talent considerations that drive human capital management practices
- Every aspect of the organization is obsessed with talent and talent management
- Performance management is one of the organization's most important activities
- The organization gives the same amount of attention and rigor to measures of talent costs, performance, and condition as it does to measures of equipment, materials, buildings, supplies, and financial assets the corporate board has the information and expertise to understand and advise on talent issues

Practices Promoting Effective Talent Management Growth in Organization

Drive talent management from the top of the organization to ensure that it will have support from senior managers and not fall into silos. Ensure that talent management efforts support key organizational strategies.

- Align all components of talent management to support optimal performance
- Manage talent with a long-range perspective but the ability to respond to changes
- Manage talent actively and strategically in good times or bad. A downturn in business performance is not an automatic signal to eliminate critical talent or cut back on training and development.
- Nurture talent-oriented corporate cultures Use talent management metrics
- Cultivate the skills needed to manage talent effectively on talent-related initiatives. They recognize that talent is the core of their business and want to be fully attuned to the needs of talent. Early on, determine an appropriate mix of ways for your CEO to visibly participate in the talent work
- Alignment with business strategy and goals
- CEO active involvement
- Talent mindset – the belief that talent is critical to the organisation now and in the future; that it can be developed; and that it differentiates culture and breeds competitive advantage
- Shared accountability – between HR/OD and the line; between 'talent' and the organisation

Outcome of Effective Talent Management

Therefore, talent management benefits those individuals deemed exceptional by providing them with tools, and processes to learn, grow, and remain 100 per cent engaged. Individuals get frequent and honest feedback on both their performance and their potential. They get a range of opportunities to progress – some that come from learning on the job or developmental assignments, others that come from structured courses or programs. Through facilitated discussions, individual managerial interaction and participation in programs for high potentials (that very often include personal contact with the CEO and top management) they get more of a chance to be proactive in shaping their career with the organisation.

According to the 2005 Hewitt Associates Best Employers in Asia study, best employer's record over 60 per cent higher revenue growth, 30 per cent higher growth in revenue per employee as well as half the recruitment costs of others. The talent management interventions employed by these 'best' companies include structures so that employees can meet their goals and frequent meetings with managers to discuss the work. At the core is the focus on the manager-employee relationship and creating a culture that values employees.

In addition the impact that talent management has on the financial or bottom line it also provides a wide range of benefits for the culture. By creating an environment in which frequent and honest feedback is the norm it promotes culture change. It also minimizes risk.

Many organisations that start out in talent management do so because of their perceived need for leadership or succession planning. While there is nothing wrong with that as a reason to start, what is actually being done is HR risk management. Organisations that know what positions are critical to them (and those may not necessarily reside just in the executive suite) and the likelihood of their ability to keep those positions filled with outstanding individuals, should the incumbent leave the organisation, are being strategic. They are also mitigating risk.

Additionally, organisations working actively in talent management have a much better understanding of what sustains employee engagement. They are working at defining their difference between good and great performance. Talent-centric organisations are crafting leadership values and behaviors, competency models and enriched performance management processes to ensure they achieve the competitive advantage that people can provide.

One such organisation is Pfizer. Since Pfizer's CEO Hank McKinnell has made talent one of his five business imperatives, the company has developed explicit values and expectations for leader behaviors. These are reinforced in the talent planning process and are used globally to align people to the strategy.

Lastly, one should care about talent management because it offers benefits or value to HR professionals directly .Particularly to those have wanted a seat at the strategic planning table or the confidence of senior leadership. All too often HR work has been seen as transactional or soft. But talent management is hardly transactional. It is holistic thinking, and is totally aligned to the achievement – in fact the creation –of business strategy.

Conclusion

Talent management provides value for HR because it places in a facilitative, business partner role, rather than in an administrative Facilitating talent reviews or talent discussions provides with an opportunity to show that one understand what the key business issues are and the human capital requirements for business success.

HR executives who are responsible for talent management should have frequent interaction with senior management, especially with the CEO. Since the CEO's involvement is required to make talent management successful, HR must coordinate and facilitate that involvement. Strategies should be developed to Attract, develop, and retains talent to ensure that people with the right skills and motivations to meet business needs are in the right place at the right time. Action planning activities should be fully integrated into an organization's performance management process.

Organisations working actively in talent management have a much better understanding of what sustains employee engagement. They are working at defining their difference between good and great performance. Talent-centric organisations are crafting leadership values and behaviors, competency models and enriched performance management processes to ensure they achieve the competitive advantage that people can provide.

References

Rudis, E. (2007), *CEO Challenge: Perspectives and Analysis 2007 edition.* (R-1418-08-RR). New York: The Conference Board.

Growing Global Executive Talent: High Priority, Limited Progress. (2008), Development Dimensions International (DDI) in Cooperation with The Economist Intelligence Unit. Pittsburgh, PA: Development Dimensions International.

Teng, A. (2007), *Making the business case for HR: Talent management aids business earnings.* HRO Today magazine, May.

Bassi, L. & McMurrer, D. (2006), *Human capital and organizational performance: Next generation metrics as a catalyst for change.* McBassi & Company white paper available online at *www.mcbassi.com,* April.

Integrated Talent Management Part 1: Understanding the Opportunities for Success (2008), IBM Institute for Business Value. Available online at *www.ibm.com,* July.

Kaplan, R. & Norton, P. (2000), *The Strategy-focused Organization.* Boston: Harvard Business School Press. See also: Blair, M. (1995), *Ownership and Control: Rethinking Corporate Governance for the Twenty-first Century (Chapter 6).* Washington, D.C.: Brookings Institution.

Lucier, C., Schuyt, R., & Tse, E. (2005, Summer), *CEO Succession 2004: The World's Most Prominent Temp Workers.* Strategy + Business, (39), 28-43.

Karlsson, O., Neilson, G., & Webster, J. (2008, Summer), *CEO Succession 2007: The Performance Paradox.* Strategy + Business, (51).

Integrated Talent Management Part 1: Understanding the Opportunities for Success. (2008 July).

Saba, J. & Martin, K. (2008), *Succession Management: Addressing the Leadership Development Challenge.* Aberdeen Group Research Report available online at *www.aberdeen.com,* October.

Howard, A. & Wellins, R. (2008), *Global Leadership Forecast 2008/2009.* Pittsburgh, PA: Development Dimensions International. Handfield-Jones, H., Michaels, E., & Axelrod, B. (2001, November/December). *Talent Management: A Critical Part of Every Leader's Job.* Ivey Business Journal, 66 (2), 53-58.

27

PRINCIPLES FOR SELECTION OF TEACHING AND TRAINING METHODS

K. Palani

Introduction

Education and training for management like any other educational process fulfils its role only by creating situations which are favourable to learning. That is why "all schemes for management education and executive development exploit or depend on the basic principles of human learning:" The teacher's knowledge, managerial and teaching experience and personality are all factors of primary importance and are intentionally mentioned at the beginning. To put it bluntly: the teacher has to have a clear and significant message to pass, and his personality has to be acceptable to the students or trainees so that effective communication links can be established quickly and easily. If these conditions are fulfilled a well chosen and properly used method is likely to ease and stimulate learning.

Objectives of Teaching & Training

- As a rule training needs and objectives of educational and training programmes in management are defined in terms of changes to be effected in knowledge, attitudes and skills which should afterwards lead to improved managerial action.
- Various training situations will be concerned with various types and levels of knowledge, attitudes and skills.
- A preliminary analysis of needs will help to identify what objectives a particular programme ought to have.
- Methods will then be selected with regard to their ability to impart new knowledge influence attitudes and develop practical skills.
- To teach employees the new techniques and ways of performing job or operations
- To prepare employees for higher level task and build up a second level of competent managers
- To improve the basic knowledge and skills to new entrants and enable them to perform their jobs well
- To equip the employees to meet the changing requirements of the job and the organization

Teaching Methods

Teachers are advised on teaching methods by their directors of studies, by senior colleagues in special "teaching methods" courses, through manual's, etc. But eventually each teacher has to assume personal responsibility for choosing the best methods for his particular teaching assignment. He ought to be able, therefore, to make a rational appraisal of his abilities and to try to employ methods likely to enhance, not reduce the impact he hopes to make. Role paying for example is an exercise requiring some knowledge of psychology, a lot of experience with various types of human problems in management and the ability to react quickly in discussions. That is why a teacher who does not possess these qualities, but has an analytical 'mind and experience in solving business problems, might give preference to the case study method.

Training the Trainers

In training trainers one should encourage teachers to use a greater variety of methods, but certainly not impose upon them which they would feel uneasy.

- The intellectual level and educational background of the participants;
- The participants, age and practical experience; and
- The social and cultural environment.

For example, in training programmes intended for supervisors, middle managers, small entrepreneurs who have had only a basic education and who have been away from school for a long time, lectures should be replaced by short talks using visual aids extensively concrete examples should be given and no high-level theories presented simplified case studies should be used instead of long and complex cases; simple programmed books should be recommended instead of the usual textbooks.

Practical Experience

In regard to the participants' practical experience, a distinction must be made between young people with little or no management experience, who first learn about management in a university or other type of school and participants with practical experience, either from managerial functions or from specialist work in various functional departments.

Much of the information is new to the students and it is difficult to link the teaching process with any previous experience. However, these students are open minded and often more receptive to new ideas than the later group. In training people with experience, only possible but absolutely essential to make an appeal to the participants experience by relating the teaching to it. However,. in this group some of the participants with practical experience may take the attitude of "knowing better in advance"; if so, the teacher's main problem may be how to change their air of self-complacency and make them aware of what they need to learn to do their jobs better. In such cases it is rarely sufficient for the teacher to talk about new methods and techniques of management. Practical assignments, case study discussions or simulation exercises are more likely to help the participants realize that they have gaps in knowledge and skills and that training may be the answer.

Managerial Experiences

Experienced managers have the capacity to learn directly from each other provided a favorable atmosphere is created and method are used which stimulate this learning,

Discussion groups, working parties, syndicates, consultancy assignments and practical projects carried out by groups of managers are well suited for this purpose.

The complexity of the problem is increased by social and cultural factors in the environment. It must be remembered that many of the participative teaching methods were developed in the United States- a country with its own particular social and cultural characteristics, High achievement motivation, little respect for formal authorities, priority given to action before contemplation -these and many other cultural factors may be absent in the country to which one or another teaching method is to be transferred.

Fortunately, educators are now aware of this problem and special studies are available on the question of transfer. A number of experts with considerable experience in developing countries have also confirmed that, in general any participative method may be used in any environment provided that it is instilled gradually with for knowledge of the environment, making the necessary modifications of the method and without hurting national pride.

B. Hawrylshym Model of Experences

In this connection B. Hawrylyshyn has developed a simple but interesting model based on the experience of the Centre d 'Etudes Industrielles in Geneva. In this model six participative methods are related to the general skills which a manager should possess whatever his special field of work or level may be in the hierarchy. Each method in the model can serve various purposes; however a method reaches its peak of effectiveness only in connection with a specific purpose. This can be well demonstrated with the case method pertinent data are given to the trainee in the description of the case. He has to diagnose and analyse the problem, consider alternative solutions, discuss those solutions and modify them after hearing his colleagues views. He does not have to make decisions or implement them; consequently he is not trained in the skill of decision-making and there is no reliable feedback on the correctness of his solutions.

The main lesson to be drawn from this model is that if training is intended to improve multiple skills (which is usually the case) a combination of teaching method must be used.

A similar type of analysis could be made to determine which methods are most likely to affect the managers' attitudes or impart a specific kind of knowledge.

Let us take the example of using specialist knowledge and experience in the preparation of management decision on complex business matters. It is of little use to lecture about the value of specialists to a manager who overestimates his own individual judgment and is not willing or perhaps able to use the specialist services which are available to him. Team work in syndicates, participation in business games or practical projects might make such a manager aware of his drawbacks so that he will begin to change his attitudes towards team work and the importance of specialists. His interest in new knowledge and skills will undoubtedly be awakened.

On his leadership style, communication abilities and behaviour in general, a manager may get more direct and stronger feedback from other participants in sensitivity training or as a member of a team working on a group project than in years of work 'in a managerial position.

Obviously, knowledge, skills and attitudes are inter-related and this must not be overlooked when setting the objectives of training and choosing teaching methods. Furthermore they are related to certain specific management functions or subject areas or, in many cases to multi-functional situations and inter-disciplinary problems.

Fuctiomal Area of Subjects

Various subject areas (finance, personnel/HR, operations research, general management etc.) have their own specific features. For example, operations research techniques are based on the extensive use of mathematics and statistics. It is usually taught through a combination of lectures (using. audio-video aids) and exercises during which the technique is practiced. This may be supported by reading assignments. In certain cases lectures may be replaced or supplemented with programmed books. However, the main thing from the management point of view is not to know the technique itself, but to know when and how it can be used. This ability can be developed through practical projects simulation exercise, business games, case studies, etc.

Attitude & Behavioural Aspect

The behavioral aspects of management, communication, leadership and motivation, training methods may be selected and combined in ways which give the participants numerous opportunities to analyze human behaviour and at the same time directly influence the attitudes and behaviour of the participants themselves. These programmes use case studies dealing with the "human side of the enterprises", business games emphasizing communication and relations between participants, role playing, sensitivity training and various other forms of group discussions, assignments and exercises.

It should be noted that it is often possible to choose from several methods, if we want to deal with a particular subject or problem. Thus the analysis of a balance sheet can be taught through the case study method, a combination of case study with role playing, a lecture, as a classroom exercise or by reading a text or a programmed book on the subject. This is possible because the principal methods are versatile enough to be made in teaching a number of different subjects. Lectures, discussion and case studies are being used in virtually all subject areas. However, in management education and training the principal problem is not how to deal with specific subject areas and functions, it is much more important to :

- Explain the relationship between various sides and' functions of the enterprises and show the highly complex character of the management process;
- Help the participants to avoid a one-sided and over simplified approach to multi-dimensional situations;
- promote general management skills, which essentially lie in an interdisciplinary approach to management, and to combine and co-ordinate the various functions of management.

Participative Methods

A sound use of participative methods can be of great help. A senior management seminar, for example, may start with a complex case study illustrating a business problem from multiple angles and arousing the participant's interest in specific subject areas, methods and techniques which, if properly integrated, will help them to take the right action in a complex situation. This may be followed in the second phase of the seminar by a more detailed study of these specific subject areas, methods and techniques. The final phase may be devoted to the integration of specialist knowledge and skills in general management through another complex case, business game or similar exercise or if possible through working on a practical project which requires this inter disciplinary approach.

Time & Material Factor

The choice of teaching methods are not independent of time, financial resources and other factors.

(a) **Preparation time** (which affects the cost of the teaching material as well varies for the different teaching material as well) varies for the different teaching methods. As a rule complex case studies and business games require long and costly preparation which includes testing with teachers or experimental groups, and making necessary revisions.

(b) **The length of the course** predetermines the kinds of methods which can be used. The longer the course the better are the chances that the teacher will be able to use business games, complex cases and practical projects. This is not to imply that participative methods should be eliminated from short appreciation or survey courses, however, only methods which are not time consuming and are liable to quickly pass the message can be used in these courses.

(c) **The time of day** is more important than many course designers would imagine. For example, in the post-lunch period (1400-1600) it is more desirable to have enjoyable and. attractive sessions which require active involvement.

The teaching facilities may. be a limiting fact6r in some institutes, or in courses given outside the institute e.g. ,in small towns. Factors such as the number of rooms available for group discussions or syndicates or the altered in advance.

Effective Learning and Teaching Methods

Principles of learning are not put into effect through the teaching method alone. Motivation to learn for example, depends on a number of other variables, such as the challenge of the participants' present or future job, his own "achievement motivation quotient" or the stimulation provided by the environment. However, the methods used in teaching and training can influence motivation to learn and therefore should be examined and applied with this in mind.

Motivation

The motivation to learn is enhanced if the presentation of the material is interesting, emphasises applicability and shows benefits to be drawn from application. To some extent this can be obtained through any methods are directly concerned with applying theoretical knowledge to real life situations. The diverse ways in which they can be combined and sequenced can add to the enjoyment of learning arid minimize participant fatigue.

Active Involvement

The principle of active involvement is perhaps the main "raison d etre" of participative teaching methods. As a rule, the deeper the involvement, the higher the motivation the more the participants retain and the better they are equipped to apply it. It should not be overlooked however that the method itself although considered as highly participative, does not assure that each person will be fully involved. Involvement also depends on organization of case study preparation, leadership style and other factors. The participant may also be passive if he considers the material to be of poor quality or the performance of the teacher to be below his own professional level.

Individual Approach

On-the-job training is a method which can be based on the training needs of one individual with full regard to his present and future job. It has. however, many limitations and that is why group training programmes should also involve work outside the enterprise. They must take into account the fact that individuals have different capabilities and learn at different places, have personal styles of study and application and should be subject to individual control of performance. The over-all course design and methods of teaching have to provide, therefore, not only work in groups and teams, but also the opportunity for individual reading, thinking exercising and application of knowledge use of teaching aids for individual learning like magnetic tapes, video-tapes, teaching machines, computer terminals accessible to individuals; the breaking down of group assignments and projects into assignment for each individuals;

Some methods are better suited than others for introducing new topics and ideas, for correctly sequencing them or for explaining the structure of a vast and complex area. That is why in certain situations the teacher cannot be without lectures and reading assignments feedback on one's competence and behaviour (as seen by the other course participants by the trainer and by the trainee himself); feedback on what was actually learned, and one's ability to effectively apply it.

Feed back

Direct feedback on the soundness of decisions is an integral part of business games, whereas in case discussions the only feedback on the individual's analytical abilities is the opinion of other participants and of the discussion leader. Strong feedback on behaviour rural patterns is provided by participation in role playing business games and sensitivity training (group dynamics). Practical exercises, consultancy assignments and application projects provide feedback on the practical usefulness of learning.

Conclusion

Thus, The principles requires that education and training help the individual to transfer what he has learned to live situations. Some teaching methods like lectures, study of literature or discussions do not play much attention to this transfer. On the other hand, in many participative methods the element of transfer is strong. For this reason the methods of simulation and practical application projects are considered by some teachers as the most effective ones. Examining teaching methods from the viewpoint of principles of learning shows the necessity to properly sequences and combine various teaching methods in order to secure the greatest impact on learning. It also explains why there is a growing interest in certain methods; those with high motivational feedback and transfer capabilities. This, of course, does not eliminate other methods which are needed for different purposes. Neither should it lead to an overestimation of a single method which in fact, may fulfill its role only in combination with other methods (business games) or serve only very special purposes (sensitive training).

References

Buckley, R and Caple, J. The Theory and Practice of Training, Kogan Page Ltd. London.

Craig, L.R. (1987), Training and Development - Hand Book: A Guide to HRD, McGraw Hill, New York.

Dugan, L. (1985), Training and Development, Addison – Wesley, New York.

ILO (1983), An Introductory Course in Teaching and Training Methods for Management Development- Sterling Publishers, New Delhi.

Mumford, A. (1986), Handbook of Management Development. Gower & Sons, London.

Training and Development Journal, ASTD, Sept. 1982, Feb-Aug. 1988.

Schein, H.E. and Bennis, G.W. (1965), Personnel 2nd Organizational Change through Group Methods, John Wiley & Sons, New York.

Beenet R. (Ed.) (1988), Improving Trainer Effectiveness. Gower Publishing Co. Aldershot.

Chaudhary, D.P. (1986), Training Methodology and Management. Sterling Pub., New Delhi.

Cooper, C.L. (1982), Theory of Management Learning John Wiley & Sons, New York.

Knowles, M. (1975), Self Directed Learning: A Guide to Learners and Teachers. Cambridge, New York.

Rushby, N.J. (1981), Selected Readings in Computer Based Learning. Kogan Page, -London.

Stuart, R. and Holmes, L. (1982), Successful Trainer Styles Journal of European Industrial Training, 6(4), 17-23.

Soydell T.H. (1990), A Guide to the Identification of Training Needs. 2nd edn. SACIE, London.

E Rrdinand (1988), 'Management Training Needs Analysis (TNA). 'Industrial and Commercial Training. Vol. 20, No. S, September/October. pp. 27-31.

Goldstein I.L. (1986), Training in Organisations: Needs Assessment, Development and Evaluation. 2n. Brooks/Cole Publishing Company. California.

Herbert Grand Doverspike D. (1990), 'Performance Appraisal in the Training Needs "Analysis Process: A Review Arid Critique.' Public Personnel Management. Vo1. 19.

Jackson T. (1989), Evaluation: Relating Training to Business Performance, Kogan Page, London. No. 3, fall. pp. 253-70.

Newby A.C and Bramely P. (1984), 'The Evaluation of Training Part II: The Organisational Context.' Journal of European Industrial Training, Vol. 8, No. 7. '

AN M Slom (1994), 'Coming in Frort the Cold: A New Role for Trainers.' Personnel Management. Vol 26, No. 1, January, pp. 24-7.

Olivas L. (1983), 'Designing and Conducting a Training Needs Analysis; Putting the Horse Vefore" The Cart.' Journal of Management Development. Vol. 2, No. 4.

28

ATTAINING GLOBAL SUSTAINABLE COMPETITIVE AVANTAGE IN THE 21ST CENTURY THROUGH HR FUNCTIONS USING WEB 2.0 TECHNOLOGIES

Tanushree Gulati

Introduction

The explosion of the social web is allowing us to connect with others in a previously impossible way, and the ability it's giving us to share information and ideas is actually reforming our learning process and the way we think: we are fast approaching a period of 'Business Enlightenment'. JR Johnson in the post "Social Media can Change the World through Common Ground" points out that as we are awakening to the power of this interaction on the web, the most progressive companies and individuals are the ones actively creating new business models around this information, hybrids that combine existing frameworks with new social models through the enhanced process of network and communication made possible by the advanced Web 2.0 technologies. This technology necessarily concentrates on the common applications/services such as blogs, video sharing, social networking and podcasting—a more socially connected Web in which people can contribute as much as they can consume. [8]

New modes of communication like Internet calling services of Skype or Yahoo! Voice turn a computer, a webcam and a headset into a video phone. Blogs, while not new, have grown in usage over the last few years and are now a common way for many people to communicate their ideas to a broad audience and, in most cases, to hear back from that audience. [12]

Advent of Web 2.0 Technology

The advent of Web 2.0 technology, popularly termed to indicate advanced Internet technology, has facilitated interactive information sharing, communication process, and collaboration on the World Wide Web. A Web 2.0 site allows its users to interact with other users or to change website content, in contrast to non-interactive websites where users are limited to the passive viewing of information that is provided to them. The virtual communities of Online Social Network Service users make it possible for individuals to potentially cross geographical and political boundaries in order to communicate in mutual interests or goals. Focusing on the talent pool of net users, social networks these days are working wonders as a conduit between cyberspace and human collective intelligence. [3]

Characteristics of Web 2.0

Some of the basic characteristics exhibited by a web 2.0 website are:

- "Network as platform" — delivering (and allowing users to use) applications entirely through a browser.
- Users owning the data on the site and exercising control over that data.

  An architecture of participation and democracy that encourages users to add value to the application as they use it. This stands in sharp contrast to hierarchical access control in applications, in which systems categorize users into roles with varying levels of functionality. [1]
- A rich, interactive, user-friendly interface based on Ajax or similar frameworks.
- Some social networking aspects.
- A public good. "Public goods" characteristically have jointness of supply and are no excludable

The elements of Web 2.0 are demonstrated in Figure 1 given below.

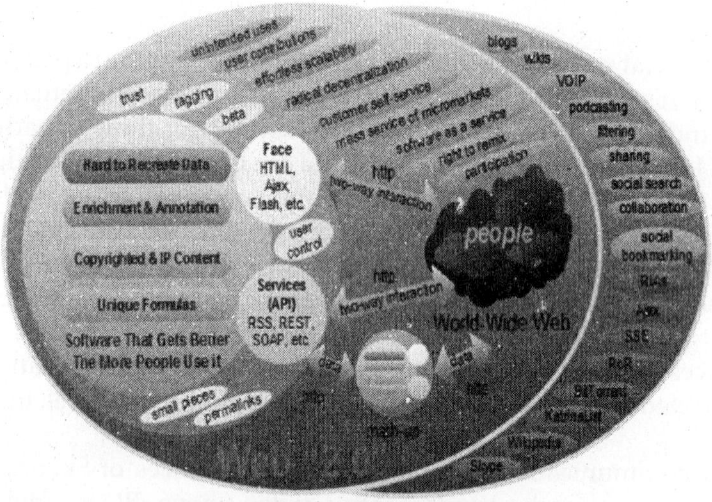

Source: http://web2.wsj2.com

Figure 1: Elements of the Web's Next Generation

Popular Examples of Web 2.0 Based Websites

Some of the popular Web 2.0 based Social Networking Sites are Orkut, World Flickr, You Tube, Blogs, Google AD sense, Wikipedia, LinkedIn, Myspace, Skype, Twitter, Yahoo Voice, Second Life, Technorati, Facebook to name a few. [4]

Online Social Networking Service (SNS) based on Web 2.0 Technologies

The evolution of web communities and hosted services such as social network services ("SNS") is a relatively recent phenomenon. SNS can broadly be defined as online communication platforms which enable individuals to join or create networks of like-minded users. SNS share certain characteristics:

- Users are invited to provide personal data for the purpose of generating a description of themselves or 'profile'.
- SNS also provide tools which allow users to post their own material (user-generated content such as a photograph or a diary entry, music or video clip or links to other sites5);
- 'Social networking' is enabled using tools which provide a list of contacts for each user, and with which users can interact. [2]

The Various activities revolving around the Process of Social Networking is demonstrated n Figure 2.

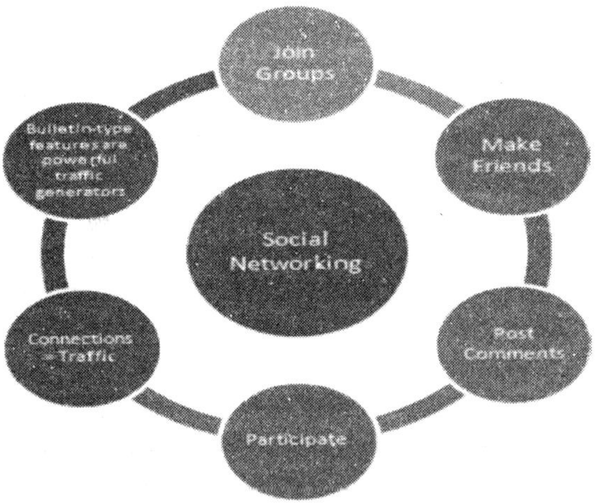

Figure 2: Various Activities Revolving Around the Process of Social Networking

The Implications of Social Networking Sites for HR in 21st Century

The recent growth of Social Networking websites such as Facebook, MySpace, LinkedIn to name a few, has significant ramifications for employers. Approximately 27% of employers report that they either check job candidate profiles on Social Networking Sites like Facebook, LinkedIn and MySpace, or conduct Google searches for online information. According to the Telegraph, Facebook now has 4.5 million regular users, making it one of the most popular sites in the UK.

The increased use of such sites means that employers need to have clear policies on Internet use. Policies should set out what staff are and are not allowed to access during their working hours. A ban on personal use of the Internet at work, or on accessing certain sites, is potential solutions. The latter has been adopted recently by organisations such as Transport for London, Lloyds TSB, the Metropolitan Police and Credit Suisse. Such a ban can, however, lead to a lowering in staff morale and create backlashes from employees as was recently discovered by the law firm Allen and Overy when it suspended employee access to Facebook. The staff complained and asserted that they were using the site to network with clients. Access was reinstated. With increasing amounts of employee time now being spent at work, particularly in certain industries (such as legal and financial services), an outright ban may seem a draconian step. Arguably, employees should be trusted to act responsibly and that companies could draw up guidelines allowing a **'lunchtime only' policy** for use of the sites.

Breach of Confidentiality

Careless use of the sites could also be in breach of the employees' duty of confidentiality, particularly where users of such sites, whether inadvertently or not, disclose their employer's confidential information and trade secrets to third parties.

The profile page of a subscriber to a Social Networking Site can be accessed by anyone else who is a member of the same network, subject to the security and privacy settings applied by the user. This means, for example, that an individual from an HR Department registered on Facebook could join the any global network and view profiles of other members of that network. This could be used by employers as a tool to find out more details about potential applicants. Existing employees could also be scrutinized.

Employers should, however, be extremely cautious of doing this as it could not only be regarded as misuse of personal data in breach of the Data Protection Act 1998 but could also lead to claims of discrimination if employers start basing *recruitment decisions* on the social habits of employees.

It is also worth bearing in mind that the terms of use of Facebook specifically prohibit the use of the site for "commercial" reasons; the action described above would surely constitute "commercial" use. It would therefore be against the terms of use of such networks for employers to create profiles for recruitment purposes and they could be removed by Social Networking Site owners.

Social Networking Sites provide convenient sources for information beyond what is stated in a job candidate's resume. Since this information resides in the public domain, it is freely available to potential employers. However, employers should be aware that these postings may include information that cannot be legally asked of the job candidate, such as:

- Race
- Religion
- Disability
- Family/marital status

Therefore, employers must be careful to ensure that all interviewing and hiring decisions are based on job-related criteria. Employers should also be aware that not all information posted on social networking sites is current or accurate. Moreover, users of these sites sometimes "pretext," or pretend to be someone else. Thus, some of the information may not have been placed on the site by the prospective applicant.

Adoption and Integration of New HR and Learning 2.0 Technologies

The third major change which is causing HR to change is the rapid adoption of new HR and Learning 2.0 ("social networking") technologies. It is now possible to upgrade an HRMS system which includes integrated functionality for goal alignment, performance management, succession planning, talent pooling, career management, and more. And in the area of enterprise learning, today's new learning management systems (LMS) now have social networking, collaboration, messaging, and content management embedded. [20]

Global Sustainable Cometitive Advantage

The success of developing economies around the world can be attributed to the global competitive advantages that they have been able to build over the years.

Many companies, specially the ones in micro and small sector do not even bother to use the Internet as a part of the hiring process. That's unfortunate, because there's a comfortable ground in which one can leverage the Internet to make the best informed hiring decisions. The Social Networking Sites and their network can be used to pool in candidates. One may ask the candidates for links to content online that demonstrate how they work, communicate, or think. It can be blogs, online profiles, articles or forum posts. Nowadays it has become indispensable for corporate talent hunt until and unless one has a good Web site, Facebook page, or some other online presence to serve as a talent magnet.

Attaining Sustainablity in 21st Century Through HR Using Online Social Networks Based on Web 2.0 Technologies

HRM Today is one of the leading free resources for HR Professionals in the world. A combination of a powerful Social Network where thousands of business professionals interested in human resources, human capital management and talent management strategy can exchange ideas and a central location for some of the best HR blogs on the Internet. HRM today is designed to elevate the profession of human resources to a more strategic and business-centric level of sophistication.

Social Networks can make the difference between personal success and obscurity. Appropriate use of Facebook, LinkedIn, Technorati and other sites can help build a brand.

It is an adage in business that "it's not *what* you know, it's *who* you know." Getting to know others who share interests, can provide resources, assist in making contacts, and help find new avenues for business development, is critical for building a reputation. A few hours of work pays dividends by developing, utilizing and expanding a Social Network to increase the value of a personal brand.

Online Social Networks connect millions of people by their interests, both professional and personal. Although there are many networking sites, and new ventures are popping up all the time, it would take too much effort to maintain a strong presence on all of them. Maintaining personal brand by focusing efforts on doing a quality job with a handful of established and respected social networking sites is today's trend in HR. [19]

Networking Site where professionals post a profile can be very simple or an entire on-line resume. Users can link to personal blogs and join groups of people interested in specific topics and business segments. A person or keyword search will likely turn up past and present colleagues to invite to become part of a personal network.

Facebook is a huge site with over 200 million users. A Facebook profile can be used for business or publicity. Since Facebook is so popular, it is now common for hiring managers, potential business partners, or anyone trying to find out about someone, to look for a Facebook account for that person. [18]

Currently, limited case law exists concerning Social Networking in the employment setting. Employers should establish policies that define their expectations regarding blogs, Tweets and other types of employee Social Networking as it relates to their place of employment. Such policies should prohibit the following types of activity:

- Harassment of co-workers or customers
- Interference or disruption of work caused by social networking
- Exposure of trade secrets or other proprietary information
- Disparaging or negative comments about the company or its employees

– Potential problems can be alleviated by training employees in the proper and improper uses of social networking at work or relating to their employment.[17]

For integration of HR and Web 2.0 Technology, specially SNS, there are numerous LMS (Learning Management System) like the Enterprise Social Software 2009 which offers information, insight, and objective analysis of social software: conversation (blogs, microblogs, forums, and discussion groups); connections (user profiles, groups and domains, social networking; collaboration (wikis, work spaces, project and process management, innovation); and content (content sharing, management, development, and search and discover). The software system also covers reporting and analytics. Corporate HR may find selection criteria lists, specific to corporate needs and priorities.

Towards "Business Enlightenment"

The immense scope of interaction through the Web 2.0 technologies has brought in a global sense of a shift of modern business techniques from the traditional. JR Johnson in the post "Social Media can Change the World through Common Ground" points out that as we are awakening to the power of this interaction on the web, the most progressive companies and individuals are the ones actively creating new business models around this information, hybrids that combine existing frameworks with new social models. [5]

Wim Rampen has also noticed a trend, as expressed in "Connecting the Dots", referencing Graham Hill's recent post, "A Manifesto for Social Business", and Mitch Lieberman's post "Social Just is...", both acknowledging the power of customer networks, looked at through the lens of Social Business. Hill laid out fifteen trends shaping the future of business, which clearly outline the fundamental shift underway. Hill would almost go as far to say that we are fast approaching a period of 'Business Enlightenment', based not so much on the linear thinking that drove the Enlightenment in the 18th Century, as on networked, emergent thinking which is driving so much new thinking in the 21st century.

Web 2.0 is the business revolution in the computer industry caused by the move to the internet as platform, and an attempt to understand the rules for success on that new platform. Chief among those rules is this: Build applications that harness network effects to get better the more people use them. (This is what he's elsewhere called 'harnessing collective intelligence.'). [13]

CONCLUSION

New technologies can be transformational, but to gain Global Sustainable Competitive Advantage today's HR has to make sure how they will force and enable the leverages of technologies like SNS for branding themselves. Online Social Network Sites are assuming the role of an effective futuristic tool to enhance corporate branding through the Advanced Web technologies. It is an invaluable tool for the corporate as well as individual professionals. There are also arguments supporting that success today is based on a person's ability to leverage power and influence within their *social networks,* to act as *"connectors"* between people and information, and in turn build social capital. [14] Online social networking sites are here to stay and HR departments need to be prepared with answers to employer and employee queries raised about their use. Education of staff, appropriate disciplinary action where necessary and definite policies for workplace access are key to ensuring that we all continue to work, "post", "tag" and "poke" happily.

However the recent surge of information flow through the internet has made it all the more necessary the need of a proper **knowledge management system**. With the changing times, branding HR through the ever-more advanced Web 3.0 technologies may assume paramount relevance for a successful business strategy to be formulated in this competitive world.

References

Eijkman, H. (2008), Web 2.0 as a Non-foundational Network-centric Learning Space. *Campus-Wide Information Systems*, Vol. 25, No. 2, pp. 93-104.

Niccolai, James (2008), Firms Tackle Social Networking. *Network World*, Southborough: Apr. 28, 2008. Vol. 25. Is. 16: p. 24.

Roberts, Bill (2008), Social Networking at the Office. *HR Magazine*, Alexandria: Mar. Vol. 53, Issue. 3: pp. 81-84.

Tredinnick Luke (2006), Web 2.0 and Business. *Business Information Review*, Sage Publications Vol. 23, No. 4, 228-230.

Vara, V. (2006), Office Co-opts Consumer Web Tools like 'wikis' and Social Networking. *The Wall Street Journal*, 12 September, pp. B1, B4.

Wyld, David C. (2008), Management 2.0: A Primer on Blogging for Executives. Management Research News Vol. 31 No. 6, pp. 448-483.

Gulati Tanushree, Dr. Singh S.K., Dr. Banerjee S., Dr. Gupta Sanjeev (2010), Social Networking – A Futuristic Tool to enhance Human Capital Management Functions. *Global Meltdown or Recession*, 11th International Seminar.

Anderson, P. (2007), What is Web 2.0? Ideas, Technologies, and Implications for Education. *JISC Tech Watch*, available at *www.jisc.ac.uk/media/documents/techwatch/tsw0701b.pdf*

Engestrom, J. (2005), Why Some Social Network Services Work and Others Don't – Or: The Case for Object-centered Sociality. Zengestrom.

Hinchcliffe, E. (2006), Review of the year's best Web 2.0 explanations. *http://web2. socialcomputingmagazine.com/review_of_the_ years_best_web_20_explanations.html.*

Microsoft, proof! Just six degrees of separation between us, *http://www.guardian.co.uk/technology/2008/ aug/03/internet.email.*

New Media Consortium (2007), Social Networking, the "third place," and the evolution of communication. 10 October. Retrieved 20 February 2008 from *www.nmc.org/evolution-communication.*

O'Reilly, Tim (2008), Web 2.0 Compact Definition: Trying Again.. O'Reilly Radar. *http:// radar.oreilly.com/archives/2006/12/web-20- compact-definition-tryi.html*

Venessa Miemis (2009) Is twitter a Complex Adaptive System? *http://www.memebox.com/futureblogger/ show/1908-is-twitter-a-complex-adaptive-system-*

[Accessed 21st Nov, 2010] available on world wide web: *http://www.communityintelligence.com/blogs/ public/archives/cat_definitions.html 9*

[Accessed 23rd Nov, 2010] available on world wide web: *http://en.wikipedia.org/wiki/Collective_ intelligence#Types_of_collective_intelligence.*

"Top 10 Best Practices in HR Management", 2010, White Paper, Business & Legal Reports, Inc., Margaret A. Carter-Ward, Editor in Chief.

Schawbel, Dan. *Me 2.0.* New York, NY: Kaplan Publishing, 2009.

Micek, Deborah and Warren Whitlock. *Twitter Revolution*, Las Vegas, NV: Xeno Press, 2008.

[Retreived on 21st February, 2011] available on world wide web: Restructuring HR: Where are we going, ***Posted on*** *October 26th, 2008.*

Annexure 1

Technologies Mentioned in the Text

Blogs (a sampling of popular blog services includes www.typepad.com, www.wordpress.com, www.blogger.com, and www.livejournal.com) are a form of online journal. A blog can have a single author or several. Most blogs allow readers to post comments in response to an article or post, but some do not.

Facebook (www.facebook.com) is a social networking site where users can set up a profile, create formal connections to people they know, communicate, and share preferences and interests. Facebook's fastest-growing demographic is users over 25.

Flickr (www.flickr.com) is an online photo site. Users upload photos; public photos may be viewed and commented on by others.

LinkedIn (www.linkedin.com) is a social networking site where users can set up a profile, create formal connections to people they know, communicate, and share preferences and interests.

MySpace (www.myspace.com) is a social networking site where users can set up a profile, create formal connections to people they know, communicate, and share preferences and interests.

Skype (www.skype.com) is an Internet calling service that enables two-party audio and video chat and multi-party audioconferencing. Skype can make computer-to-computer calls as well as computer-to-phone calls (land- or mobile phones).

Twitter (www.twitter.com) is a cross between instant messaging and blogging that allows a user to send a short (140-character) update. Users can also follow the updates of selected friends.

Yahoo! Voice (voice.yahoo.com) is an Internet calling service offered by Yahoo! Features include the ability to assign a phone number to your computer so that it can be called from land- and mobile lines; computer-to-computer calls from within Yahoo! Messenger; and computer-to-phone calls.

Second Life (www.secondlife.com) is a 3-D virtual environment created by Linden Lab. Residents create an avatar and may own land, build and create objects and clothing, and interact with each other in the setting of a user-created virtual world complete with its own economy.

YouTube (www.youtube.com) is an online video site owned by Google, Inc. Videos are uploaded by users and can be viewed free. Users can leave comments on video pages.

Google AD sense *(www.google.com)* allows users to earn money through posting Google ads on their websites.

Orkut Social-networking site (www.orkut.com) which allows the users to send messages and communicate with other members.

Wikipedia (*www.wikipedia.org*) is online encyclopedia wherein the users contribute by writing the articles, definitions, etc. It is completely edited and maintained by the users.

PART FOUR

Dynamics of Marketing & Sustainable Development

29

DISTRIBUTION STRATEGIES ADOPTED BY SMALL SCALE INDUSTRIES OF UTTARAKHAND

Gajendra Singh & Pratima Negi

Introduction

Prosperity of a Nation depends on the development of the nation's economy. Every nation has the responsibility to ensure economic development to improve the living standards of the people, eliminate poverty and backwardness. The process of economic development involves improvement in the Gross National Production (GNP) and depends upon the utilization of physical natural resources by the human resources to realize the productive potential of the nation. It requires increase in production and level of consumption. The Development of Business skills to enable the establishment and successful operation of Small Enterprises constitutes a major priority and pre-requisite for rapid economic growth in India.

A channel of distribution or distribution system for the product is the route taken by the title to goods they move from the producer to ultimate consumer or industrial user. In the words of Beckman "The course taken in the transfer of the title to the commodity constitutes its channel of distribution. It is the route taken by the title to a product in its passage from its first owner the agriculture producer or manufacturer, as the case may be, to the last owner, the ultimate consumer or the business user." The major participants in the distribution channel are producers, intermediaries and consumers. The producers produce the goods and services of the type needed by the consumers or industrial users. The intermediaries (wholesalers, retailers and facilitators) direct the products and services to consumers. The consumers are the ultimate link in the channel for whom goods are produced, and who purchased them.

The small scale industrial units play a crucial role in the progress of any developing country like India. They represent a stage in economic transition from traditional to modern technology, such a tendency is a witness in the growth of small-scale units. Small Scale Industries are mostly found in village and semi urban areas. If they are encouraged further, the smaller firms and the countryside can benefit from modern industrialism. The small-scale unit use less amount of scarce factor viz. capital. In India capital is a scarce commodity; in spite of this cause small units can be established with a small amount of capital, small scale industries are also adaptable to a large extent to the changing conditions and habits of the people. Uttarakhand being a newly formed state has a large number of small scale industries functioning in the rural and the literally interior areas of the state. These units produce the required material of the people near to them. So the products produced are woolens, carpets or the handicrafts which they can produce easily with the local raw material. Keeping all the conditions in mind the study help in examine and analyzing the small scale industries in respect of product they produce and the product strategies adopted by these industries in the state.

Review of Literature

The broad review of literature regarding the study is as follows: **Saxena B.C (1964)** studied the practices and problem of cotton marketing of small scale units in Punjab. He pointed out that nearly the small growers themselves to the regulator market for the final requirement brought 85% of the produce. **Bhanshali (1987)** examined the performance of small-scale industry. He pointed out that the marketing activity is one of the important criteria to measure the development of Entrepreneurship. He suggested that the entrepreneur should go in for adopting certain specific Marketing Strategies for the products of small scale industrial sector. **Apparao P.B and Reddy T. Subbi (1988)** examined the internal courses of marketing. They observed that the poor quality of the product, the high cost of production, operations in a sellers market, competition with large-scale producers – all these results in the marketing problems of small scale units. **Hooda R.P. (1991)** study focused on the marketing practices in small scale industry. He examined the marketing practices in terms of Product, Price, Place and Promotion. The study suggested having the marketing orientation in small-scale industry as the small scale units are not using any marketing activities. **Rao, D. Nageswara (2002)** examined to know in detail the problems faced by the Cotton growers in marketing their products. He observed that the cotton industries are not adopting marketing policies like storage, Advertising, Distribution channels. **Mag V., Xavier Joseph A. (2002)** examined the analysis the production and sales performance, marketing of Khadi and Village Industries product. He observed that the awareness on quality, pricing, customer satisfaction, and effective marketing management not considered by the same (KVI).

Objective of the Study

The Small Scale units are the backbone of the industrial structure in the state. These units are manufacturing a variety of goods ranging from tiny needles to sophisticated electronic goods. This study proposes information regarding the product of the small scale unit in the state of Uttarakhand. The study is done on the basis of several parameters out of which there are (a) to examine the reason of setting up the unit at a particular area, (b) to evaluate the various functions the salesman are required to perform, (c) to analyzes the distribution system of small scale enterprises, and (d) to examine whether the activities undertaken to maintain the relation with the dealers are sufficient or not.

Research Methodology

The study is based on both the primary as well as secondary data. The primary data will be collected on the basis of questionnaires administered to various Small scale Industries in the state of Uttaranchal. The information will be sought from the entrepreneur of Small Scale

Industry regarding reason of having unit at particular location, salesman functions, distribution system & strategies etc. The secondary data was collected from published and unpublished records and reports of the central Government and Government of Uttaranchal. The units will be selected by using the stratified random Sampling technique. The sample of study will be 150 units in State of Uttaranchal. The product groups are: Shawl/Sweater, Carpet & Handicraft. I shall select Dehradun, Pauri, Chamoli, Udam Singh Nagar, Almora and Pithoragarh on the basis concentration of Industries. The study will cover the period from 2005 to 2009. The data collected on the basis of questionnaire would be tested with the help of test of significance besides using various other statistical techniques like average, correlation, regression and trend analysis etc.

Analysis & Interpretation

In this study we had taken a sample of total 150 respondents, belonging to small scale industries. The Table-1 shows the demographic profile classification of 150 respondents. Demographic profile contains four main basis on which these respondents are further divided are main product of the enterprise, age of the entrepreneur, qualification and location of the unit. On the basis of main product of the enterprise 34 respondents manufacture shawls/

Table 1
Demographic Profile

Demographic Base	*Classification*				*Total*
Main product of the enterprise	Shawl/Sweater 34	Carpets 113	Handicrafts 03		150
Age of the entrepreneur	18-25 years 24	26-45 years 108	45 & above 18		150
Qualification	Primary 97	High School 29	Intermediate 18	Graduate 6	150
Location of the unit	Inside the town 52		Outside the town 98		150

sweater, 113 respondents manufacture carpets and the remaining 3 respondents manufacture handicrafts. Further on the basis of the age of the entrepreneurs, 24 respondents fall under the age category of 18-25 years, 108 respondents comes under the age category of 26-45

Table 2
Main Product of the Enterprise & Reason for Setting up the Unit in Present Location

			Reason for Setting Up the Unit in Present Location				
			Parental Land	*Nearness to Home Town*	*Transportation Facility*	*Labour Availability*	*Total*
Main product of the enterprise	shawl/sweater	Count	22	0	3	9	34
	carpets	Count	50	3	12	48	113
	handicrafts	Count	3	0	0	0	3
Total		Count	75	3	15	57	150

	Value	*df*
Pearson Chi-Square	8.017(a)	6
N of Valid Cases	150	

years and 18 respondents come under 45 & above age category. Among 150 respondents, on the basis of qualification 97 respondents have primary education, 29 respondents have high school education, 18 respondents have done intermediate and the remaining 6 respondents have done graduation. And lastly on the basis of location of the unit, 52 respondents have their unit located inside the town and 98 respondents have their unit located outside the town.

According to Table-2 there are total 150 respondents. Out of them 22 respondents who deal in shawl/sweater said that the parental land is the reason for setting up the unit in present location, no respondent who deal in shawl/sweater said that the nearness to home town is the reason for setting up the unit in present location, 3 respondents who deal in shawl/sweater said that the transportation facility is the reason for setting up the unit in present location and 9 respondents who deal in shawl/sweater said that the labour availability is the reason for setting up the unit in present location. 50 respondents who deal in carpets said that the parental land is the reason for setting up the unit in present location, 3 respondent who deal in carpets said that the nearness to home town is the reason for setting up the unit in present location, 12 respondents who deal in carpets said that the transportation facility is the reason for setting up the unit in present location and 48 respondents who deal in carpets said that the labour availability is the reason for setting up the unit in present location. 3 respondents who deal in handicrafts said that the parental land is the reason for setting up the unit in present location, no respondent who deal in handicrafts said that the nearness to home town is the reason for setting up the unit in present location, no respondent who deal in handicrafts said that the transportation facility is the reason for setting up the unit in present location and no respondent who deal in handicrafts said that the labour availability is the reason for setting up the unit in present location. Since calculated value of chi-square for degree of freedom 6 at 5% level of significance is 8.017 is less than tabulated value 12.592, therefore null hypothesis is accepted, i.e. Main product of the enterprise & reason for setting up the unit in present location are independent.

Table 3
Main Product & Functions the Salesman are Required to Perform

			Which of the following Functions the Salesman is Required to Perform?					
			Seeking Orders	*Providing Delivery*	*Collecting Payments*	*Introducing New Items to Dealers/ Customers*	*Gathering Market Information*	*Total*
Main product of the enterprise	shawl/sweater	Count	10	18	0	3	3	34
	carpets	Count	0	98	12	3	0	113
	handicrafts	Count	0	3	0	0	0	3
Total		Count	10	119	12	6	3	150

	Value	*df*
Pearson Chi-Square	54.816(a)	8
N of Valid Cases	150	

According to Table-3 there are total 150 respondents. Out of them 10 respondents who deal in shawl/sweater said that seeking orders is the function the salesman are required to perform, 18 respondents who deal in shawl/sweater said that providing delivery is the function the salesman are required to perform, no respondent who deal in shawl/sweater said that collecting payments is the function the salesman are required to perform, 3respondents who deal in shawl/sweater said that introducing new items to dealers/ customers is the function the salesman are required to perform and 3 respondents who deal in shawl/sweater said that gathering market information is the function the salesman are required to perform. No respondent who deal in carpets said that seeking orders is the function the salesman are required to perform, 98 respondents who deal in carpets said that providing delivery is the function the salesman are required to perform, 12 respondents who deal in carpets said that collecting payments is the function the salesman are required to perform, 3 respondents who deal in carpets said that introducing new items to dealers/ customers is the function the salesman are required to perform and no respondent who deal in carpets said that gathering market information is the function the salesman are required to perform. No respondent who deal in handicrafts said that seeking orders is the function the salesman are required to perform, 3 respondents who deal in handicrafts said that providing delivery is the function the salesman are required to perform, no respondent who deal in handicrafts said that collecting payments is the function the salesman are required to perform, no respondent who deal in handicrafts said that introducing new items to dealers/customers is the function the salesman are required to perform and no respondent who deal in handicrafts said that gathering market information is the function the salesman are required to perform. Since calculated value of chi-square for degree of freedom 8 at 5% level of significance is 54.816 is more than tabulated value 15.51, therefore null hypothesis is rejected, i.e. Main product of the enterprise & functions the salesman are required to perform are independent.

Table 4
Main Product & Distribution System

			Which Distribution System do you follow?		
			Selling through Every Possible Outlet	*Selling through Out Dealer in One City Area*	*Total*
Main product of the enterprise	shawl/sweater	Count	28	6	34
	carpets	Count	89	24	113
	handicrafts	Count	3	0	3
Total		Count	120	30	150

	Value	*df*
Pearson Chi-Square	.976(a)	2
N of Valid Cases	150	

According to Table-4 there are total 150 respondents. Out of them 28 respondents who deal in shawl/sweater said that they follow selling through every possible outlet distribution system and 6 respondents who deal in shawl/sweater said that they follow selling through out dealer in one city area distribution system. 89 respondents who deal in carpets said that they follow selling through every possible outlet distribution system and 24 respondents who deal in carpets said that they follow selling through out dealer in one city area distribution system. 3 respondents who deal in handicrafts said that they follow selling through every possible outlet distribution system and no respondent who deal in handicrafts said that they follow selling through out dealer in one city area distribution system. Since calculated value of chi-square for degree of freedom 2 at 5% level of significance is .976 is less than tabulated value 5.991, therefore null hypothesis is accepted, i.e. Main product of the enterprise & distribution system is independent.

Table 5
Main Product & Activities Undertaken to Maintain the Relation with Dealers

			To what extent the following activities are undertaken in order to maintain has the relation with dealers?			
			Free Gift	*Special Deals*	*Easy Credit Terms*	*Total*
Main product of the enterprise	shawl/sweater	Count	0	24	10	34
	carpets	Count	33	71	9	113
	handicrafts	Count	0	3	0	3
Total	Count		33	98	19	150

	Value	*df*
Pearson Chi-Square	21.488(a)	4
N of Valid Cases	150	

According to Table-5 there are total 150 respondents. Out of them no respondent who deal in shawl/sweater said that the free gift activities are undertaken in order to maintain the relation with dealers, 24 respondents who deal in shawl/sweater said that the special deals activities are undertaken in order to maintain the relation with dealers and 10 respondents who deal in shawl/sweater said that the easy credit terms activities are undertaken in order to maintain the relation with dealers. 33 respondents who deal in carpets said that the free gift activities are undertaken in order to maintain the relation with dealers, 71 respondents who deal in carpets said that the special deals activities are undertaken in order to maintain the relation with dealers and 9 respondents who deal in

Table 6
Age of the Entrepreneur & Reason for Setting Up the Unit in Present Location

			Reason for Setting up the Unit in Present Location				
			Parental Land	*Nearness to Home Town*	*Transportation Facility*	*Labour Availability*	*Total*
Age of the entrepreneur	18-25 years	Count	9	0	0	15	24
	26-45 years	Count	57	0	15	36	108
	46 & above	Count	9	3	0	6	18
Total		Count	75	3	15	57	150

	Value	*df*
Pearson Chi-Square	33.263(a)	6
N of Valid Cases	150	

carpets said that the easy credit terms activities are undertaken in order to maintain the relation with dealers. No respondent who deal in handicrafts said that the free gift activities are undertaken in order to maintain the relation with dealers, 3 respondents who deal in handicrafts said that the special deals activities are undertaken in order to maintain the relation with dealers and no respondent who deal in handicrafts said that the easy credit terms activities are undertaken in order to maintain the relation with dealers. Since calculated value of chi-square for degree of freedom 4 at 5% level of significance is 21.488 is more than tabulated value 9.488, therefore null hypothesis is rejected, i.e. Main product of the enterprise & activities undertaken to maintain the relation with dealers are dependent.

According to Table-6 there are total 150 respondents. Out of them 9 respondents who aged between 18-25 said that the parental land is the reason for setting up the unit in present location, no respondent who aged between 18-25said that the nearness to home town is the reason for setting up the unit in present location, no respondent who aged between 18-25 said that the transportation facility is the reason for setting up the unit in present location and 15 respondents who aged between 18-25 said that the labour availability is the reason for setting up the unit in present location. 57 respondents who aged between 26-45 said that the parental land is the reason for setting up the unit in present location, no respondent who aged between 26-45 said that the nearness to home town is the reason for setting up the unit in present location, 15 respondents who aged between 26-45 said that the transportation facility is the reason for setting up the unit in present location and 36 respondents who aged between 26-45said that the labour availability is the reason for setting up the unit in present location. 9 respondents whose age is 46 & above said that the parental land is the reason for setting up the unit in present location, 3 respondents whose age is 46 & above said that the nearness to home town is the reason for setting up the unit in present location, no respondent whose age is 46 & above said that the transportation facility is the reason for setting up the unit in present location and 6 respondents whose age is 46 & above said that the labour availability is the reason for setting up the unit in present location. Since calculated value of chi-square for degree of freedom 6 at 5% level of significance is 33.263 is more than tabulated value 12.592, therefore null hypothesis is rejected, i.e. Age of the entrepreneur & reason for setting up the unit in present location are dependent.

Table 7
Age of the Entrepreneur & Functions the Salesman are Required to Perform

			Which of the following functions the salesman is required to perform?					
			Seeking Orders	*Providing Delivery*	*Collecting Payments*	*Introducing New Items to Dealers/ Customers*	*Gathering Market Information*	*Total*
Age of the entrepreneur	18-25 years	Count	0	18	6	0	0	24
	26-45 years	Count	10	83	6	6	3	108
	46 & above	Count	0	18	0	0	0	18
Total		Count	10	119	12	6	3	150

	Value	*df*
Pearson Chi-Square	19.415(a)	8
N of Valid Cases	150	

According to Table-7 there are total 150 respondents. Out of them no respondent who aged between 18-25 said that seeking orders is the function the salesman are required to perform, 18 respondents who aged between 18-25 said that providing delivery is the function the salesman are required to perform, 6 respondents who aged between 18-25 said that collecting payments is the function the salesman are required to perform, no respondent who aged between 18-25 said that introducing new items to dealers/customers is the function the salesman are required to perform and no respondent who aged between 18-25 said that gathering market information is the function the salesman are required to perform. 10 respondents who aged between 26-45 said that seeking orders is the function the salesman are required to perform, 83 respondents who aged between 26-45 said that providing delivery is the function the salesman are required to perform, 6 respondents who aged between 26-45 said that collecting payments is the function the salesman are required to perform, 6 respondents who aged between 26-45 said that introducing new items to dealers/customers is the function the salesman are required to perform and 3 respondents who aged between 26-45 said that gathering market information is the function the salesman are required to perform. No respondent whose age is 46 & above said that seeking orders is the function the salesman are required to perform, 18 respondents whose age is 46 & above said that providing delivery is the function the salesman are required to perform, no respondent whose age is 46 & above said that collecting payments is the function the salesman are required to perform, no respondent whose age is 46 & above said that introducing new items to dealers/customers is the function the salesman are required to perform and no respondent whose age is 46 & above said that gathering market information is the function the salesman are required to perform. Since calculated value of chi-square for degree of freedom 8 at 5% level of significance is 19.415 is more than tabulated value 15.507, therefore null hypothesis is rejected, i.e. Age of the entrepreneur & functions the salesman are required to perform are independent.

Table 8
Age of the Entrepreneur & Distribution System

			Which distribution system do you follow?		
			Selling through Every Possible Outlet	*Selling through Out Dealer in One City Area*	*Total*
Age of the entrepreneur	18-25 years	Count	12	12	24
	26-45 years	Count	90	18	108
	46 & above	Count	18	0	18
Total		Count	120	30	150

	Value	*df*
Pearson Chi-Square	18.750(a)	2
N of Valid Cases	150	

According to Table-8 there are total 150 respondents. Out of them 12 respondents who age between 18-25 said that they follow selling through every possible outlet distribution system and 12 respondents who age between 18-25 said that they follow selling through out dealer in one city area distribution system. 90 respondents whose age is 26-45 said that they follow selling through every possible outlet distribution system and 18 respondents whose age is 26-45 said that they follow selling through out dealer in one city area distribution system. 18 respondents whose age is 46 & above said that they follow selling through every possible outlet distribution system and no respondent whose age is 46 & above said that they follow selling through out dealer in one city area distribution system. Since calculated value of chi-square for degree of freedom 2 at 5% level of significance is 18.750 is more than tabulated value 5.991, therefore null hypothesis is rejected, i.e. Age of the entrepreneur & distribution system are dependent.

Table 9
Age of the Entrepreneur & Activities Undertaken to Maintain the Relation with Dealers

			To what extent the following activities are undertaken in order to maintain has the relation with dealers?			
			Free Gift	*Special Deals*	*Easy Credit Terms*	*Total*
Age of the entrepreneur	18-25 years	Count	6	18	0	24
	26-45 years	Count	18	71	19	108
	46 & above	Count	9	9	0	18
Total		Count	33	98	19	150

	Value	*df*
Pearson Chi-Square	16.292(a)	4
N of Valid Cases	150	

According to Table-9 there are total 150 respondents. Out of them 6 respondents whose age is 18-25 said that the free gift activities are undertaken in order to maintain the relation with dealers, 18 respondents whose age is 18-25 said that the special deals activities are undertaken in order to maintain the relation with dealers and no respondent whose age is 18-25 said that the easy credit terms activities are undertaken in order to maintain the relation with dealers. 18 respondents whose age is 26-45 said that the free gift activities are undertaken in order to maintain the relation with dealers, 71 respondents whose age is 26-45 said that the special deals activities are undertaken in order to maintain the relation with dealers and 19 respondents whose age is 26-45 said that the easy credit terms activities are undertaken in order to maintain the relation with dealers. 9 respondents whose age is 46 & above said that the free gift activities are undertaken in order to maintain the relation with dealers, 9 respondents whose age is 46 & above said that the special deals activities are undertaken in order to maintain the relation with dealers and no respondent whose age is 46 & above said that the easy credit terms activities are undertaken in order to maintain the relation with dealers. Since calculated value of chi-square for degree of freedom 4 at 5% level of significance is 16.292 is more than tabulated value 9.488, therefore null hypothesis is rejected, i.e. Age of the entrepreneur & activities undertaken to maintain the relation with dealer are independent.

Table 10
Qualification & Reason for Setting up the Unit in Present Location

			Reason for Setting up the Unit in Present Location				
			Parental Land	*Nearness to Home Town*	*Transportation Facility*	*Labour Availability*	*Total*
Qualification. academic	Primary	Count	49	0	12	36	97
	High School	Count	14	0	0	15	29
	Intermediate	Count	6	3	3	6	18
	Graduate	Count	6	0	0	0	6
Total		Count	75	3	15	57	150

	Value	*df*
Pearson Chi-Square	34.708(a)	9
N of Valid Cases	150	

According to Table-10 there are total 150 respondents. Out of them 49 respondents have primary education said that the parental land is the reason for setting up the unit in present location, no respondent have primary education said that the nearness to home town is the reason for setting up the unit in present location, 12 respondents have primary education said that the transportation facility is the reason for setting up the unit in present location and 36 respondents have primary education said that the labour availability is the reason for setting up the unit in present location. 14 respondents have high school education said that the parental land is the reason for setting up the unit in present location, no respondent have high school education said that the nearness to home town is the reason for setting up the unit in present location, no respondent have high school education said that the transportation facility is the reason for setting up the unit in present location and 15 respondents have high school education said that the labour availability is the reason for setting up the unit in present location. 6 respondents have intermediate education said that the parental land is the reason for setting up the unit in present location, 3 respondents have intermediate education said that the nearness to home town is the reason for setting up the unit in present location, 3 respondents have intermediate education said that the transportation facility is the reason for setting up the unit in present location and 6 respondents have intermediate education that the labour availability is the reason for setting up the unit in present location. 6 respondents who have done graduation said that the parental land is the reason for setting up the unit in present location, no respondent who have done graduation said that the nearness to home town is the reason for setting up the unit in present location, no respondent who have done graduation said that the transportation facility is the reason for setting up the unit in present location and no respondent who have done graduation said that the labour availability is the reason for setting up the unit in present location. Since calculated value of chi-square for degree of freedom 9 at 5% level of significance is 34.708 is more than tabulated value 16.919, therefore null hypothesis is rejected, i.e. Qualification & reason for setting up the unit in present location are dependent.

According to Table-11 there are total 150 respondents. Out of them 10 respondents who have primary education said that seeking orders is the function the salesman are required to perform, 81 respondents who have primary education said that providing delivery is the function the salesman are required to perform, 6 respondents who have primary education

Table 11
Qualification & Functions the Salesman are Required to Perform

			Which of the Following Functions the Salesman is Required to Perform?					
			Seeking Orders	*Providing Delivery*	*Collecting Payments*	*Introducing New Items to Dealers/ Customers*	*Gathering Market Information*	*Total*
Qualification	Primary	Count	10	81	6	0	0	97
	High School	Count	0	17	3	6	3	29
	Intermediate	Count	0	18	0	0	0	18
	Graduate	Count	0	3	3	0	0	6
Total		Count	10	119	12	6	3	150

	Value	*df*
Pearson Chi-Square	61.685(a)	12
N of Valid Cases	150	

said that collecting payments is the function the salesman are required to perform, no respondent who have primary education said that introducing new items to dealers/ customers is the function the salesman are required to perform and no respondent who have primary education said that gathering market information is the function the salesman are required to perform. No respondent who have high school education said that seeking orders is the function the salesman are required to perform, 17 respondents who have high school education said that providing delivery is the function the salesman are required to perform, 3 respondents who have high school education said that collecting payments is the function the salesman are required to perform, 6 respondents who have high school education said that introducing new items to dealers/customers is the function the salesman are required to perform and 3 respondents who have high school education said that gathering market information is the function the salesman are required to perform. No respondent who have intermediate education said that seeking orders is the function the salesman are required to perform, 18 respondents who have intermediate education said that providing delivery is the function the salesman are required to perform, no respondent who have intermediate education said that collecting payments is the function the salesman are required to perform, no respondent who have intermediate education said that introducing new items to dealers/ customers is the function the salesman are required to perform and no respondent who have intermediate education said that gathering market information is the function the salesman are required to perform. No respondent who have done graduation said that seeking orders is the function the salesman are required to perform, 3 respondents who have done graduation said that providing delivery is the function the salesman are required to perform, 3 respondents who have done graduation said that collecting payments is the function the salesman are required to perform, no respondent who have done graduation said that introducing new items to dealers/customers is the function the salesman are required to perform and no respondent who have done graduation said that gathering market information is the function the salesman are required to perform. Since calculated value of chi-square for degree of freedom 12 at 5% level of significance is 61.685 is more than tabulated value 21.026, therefore null hypothesis is rejected, i.e. Qualification & functions the salesman are required to perform are dependent.

Table 12
Qualification & Distribution System

			Which Distribution System do you Follow?		
			Selling through Every Possible Outlet	*Selling through Out Dealer in One City Area*	*Total*
Qualification	Primary	Count	76	21	97
	High School	Count	23	6	29
	Intermediate	Count	18	0	18
	Graduate	Count	3	3	6
Total		Count	120	30	150

	Value	*df*
Pearson Chi-Square	8.049(a)	3
N of Valid Cases	150	

According to Table-12 there are total 150 respondents. Out of them 76 respondents who have primary education said that they follow selling through every possible outlet distribution system and 21 respondents who have primary education said that they follow selling through out dealer in one city area distribution system. 23 respondents who have high school education said that they follow selling through every possible outlet distribution system and 6 respondents who have high school education said that they follow selling through out dealer in one city area distribution system. 18 respondents who have intermediate education said that they follow selling through every possible outlet distribution system and no respondent who have intermediate education said that they follow selling through out dealer in one city area distribution system. 3 respondents who have done graduation said that they follow selling through every possible outlet distribution system and 3 respondents who have done graduation said that they follow selling through out dealer in one city area distribution system. Since calculated value of chi-square for degree of freedom 3 at 5% level of significance is 8.049 is more than tabulated value 7.815, therefore null hypothesis is rejected, i.e. Qualification & distribution system do you follow are independent.

Table 13
Qualification & Activities Undertaken to Maintain the Relation with Dealers

			To what Extent the Following Activities are Undertaken in order to Maintain has the Relation with Dealers?			
			Free Gift	*Special Deals*	*Easy Credit Terms*	*Total*
Qualification	Primary	Count	18	63	16	97
	High School	Count	3	26	0	29
	Intermediate	Count	9	6	3	18
	Graduate	Count	3	3	0	6
Total		Count	33	98	19	150

	Value	*df*
Pearson Chi-Square	22.314(a)	6
N of Valid Cases	150	

According to Table-13 there are total 150 respondents. Out of them 18 respondents who have primary education said that the free gift activities are undertaken in order to maintain the relation with dealers, 63 respondents who have primary education said that the special deals activities are undertaken in order to maintain the relation with dealers and 16 respondents who have primary education said that the easy credit terms activities are undertaken in order to maintain the relation with dealers. 3 respondents who have high school education said that the free gift activities are undertaken in order to maintain the relation with dealers, 26 respondents who have high school education said that the special deals activities are undertaken in order to maintain the relation with dealers and no respondent who have high school education said that the easy credit terms activities are undertaken in order to maintain the relation with dealers. 9 respondents who have intermediate education said that the free gift activities are undertaken in order to maintain the relation with dealers, 6 respondents who have intermediate education said that the special deals activities are undertaken in order to maintain the relation with dealers and 3 respondents who have intermediate education said that the easy credit terms activities are undertaken in order to maintain the relation with dealers. 3 respondents who have done graduation said that the free gift activities are undertaken in order to maintain the relation with dealers, 3 respondents who have done graduation said that the special deals activities are undertaken in order to maintain the relation with dealers and no respondent who have done graduation said that the easy credit terms activities are undertaken in order to maintain the relation with dealers. Since calculated value of chi-square for degree of freedom 6 at 5% level of significance is 22.314 is more than tabulated value 12.592, therefore null hypothesis is rejected, i.e. Qualification & activities undertaken to maintain the relation with dealers are dependent.

Table 14
Location of the Unit & Reason for Setting up the Unit in Present Location

			Reason for Setting up the Unit in Present Location				
			Parental Land	*Nearness to Home Town*	*Transportation Facility*	*Labour Availability*	*Total*
location of the unit	inside the town	Count	34	0	3	15	52
	outside the town	Count	41	3	12	42	98
Total		Count	75	3	15	57	150

	Value	*df*
Pearson Chi-Square	8.539(a)	3
N of Valid Cases	150	

According to Table-14 there are total 150 respondents. Out of them 34 respondents whose unit location is inside the town said that the parental land is the reason for setting up the unit in present location, no respondent whose unit location is inside the town said that the nearness to home town is the reason for setting up the unit in present location, 3 respondents whose unit location is inside the town said that the transportation facility is the reason for setting up the unit in present location and 15 respondents whose unit location is inside the town said that the labour availability is the reason for setting up the unit in present location. 41 respondents whose unit location is outside the town said that the parental land is the reason for setting up the unit in present location, 3 respondents whose unit location is outside the town said that the nearness to home town is the reason for setting up the unit in present location, 12 respondents whose unit location is outside the town said that the transportation facility is the reason for setting up the unit in present location and 42 respondents whose unit location is outside the town said that the labour availability is the reason for setting up the unit in present location. Since calculated value of chi-square for degree of freedom 3 at 5% level of significance is 8.539 is more than tabulated value 7.815, therefore null hypothesis is rejected, i.e. Location of the unit & reason for setting up the unit in present location are dependent.

Table 15
Location of the Unit & Functions the Salesman are Required to Perform

			Which of the Following Functions the Salesman is Required to Perform?					
			Seeking Orders	*Providing Delivery*	*Collecting Payments*	*Introducing New Items to Dealers/ Customers*	*Gathering Market Information*	*Total*
location of the unit	inside the town	Count	10	33	3	6	0	52
	outside the town	Count	0	86	9	0	3	98
Total		Count	10	119	12	6	3	150

	Value	*df*
Pearson Chi-Square	34.768(a)	4
N of Valid Cases	150	

According to Table-15 there are total 150 respondents. Out of them 10 respondents whose unit location is inside the town said that seeking orders is the function the salesman are required to perform, 33 respondents whose unit location is inside the town said that providing delivery is the function the salesman are required to perform, 3 respondents whose unit location is inside the town said that collecting payments is the function the salesman are required to perform, 6 respondents whose unit location is inside the town said that introducing new items to dealers/customers is the function the salesman are required to perform and no respondent whose unit location is inside the town said that gathering market information is the function the salesman are required to perform. No respondent whose unit location is outside the town said that seeking orders is the function the salesman are required to perform, 86 respondents whose unit location is outside the town said that providing delivery is the function the salesman are required to perform, 9 respondents whose unit location is outside the town said that collecting payments is the function the salesman are required to perform, no respondent whose unit location is outside the town said that introducing new items to dealers/customers is the function the salesman are required to perform and 3 respondents whose unit location is outside the town said that gathering market information is the function the salesman are required to perform. Since calculated value of chi-square for degree of freedom 4 at 5% level of significance is 34.768 is more than tabulated value 9.488, therefore null hypothesis is rejected, i.e. Location of the unit & functions the salesman are required to perform are dependent.

Table 16
Location of the Unit & Distribution System

			Which Distribution System do you Follow?		
			Selling through Every Possible Outlet	*Selling through Out Dealer in One City Area*	*Total*
location of the unit	inside the town	Count	43	9	52
	outside the town	Count	77	21	98
Total		Count	120	30	150

	Value	*df*
Pearson Chi-Square	.361(b)	1
N of Valid Cases	150	

According to Table-16 there are total 150 respondents. Out of them 43 respondents whose unit location is inside the town said that they follow selling through every possible outlet distribution system and 9 respondents whose unit location is inside the town said that they follow selling through out dealer in one city area distribution system. 77 respondents whose unit location is outside the town said that they follow selling through every possible outlet distribution system and 21 respondents whose unit location is outside the town said that they follow selling through out dealer in one city area distribution system. Since calculated value of chi-square for degree of freedom 1 at 5% level of significance is .361 is less than tabulated value 3.841, therefore null hypothesis is accepted, i.e. Location of the unit & distribution system do you follow are independent.

Table 17
Location of the Unit & Activities Undertaken to Maintain Relation with Dealers

			To What Extent the Following Activities are Undertaken in order to Maintain has the Relation with Dealers?			
			Free Gift	*Special Deals*	*Easy Credit Terms*	*Total*
location of the unit	inside the town	Count	15	24	13	52
	outside the town	Count	18	74	6	98
Total		Count	33	98	19	150

	Value	*df*
Pearson Chi-Square	15.735(a)	2
N of Valid Cases	150	

According to Table-17 there are total 150 respondents. Out of them 15 respondents whose unit location is inside the town said that the free gift activities are undertaken in order to maintain the relation with dealers, 24 respondents whose unit location is inside the town said that the special deals activities are undertaken in order to maintain the relation with dealers and 13 respondents whose unit location is inside the town said that the easy credit terms activities are undertaken in order to maintain the relation with dealers. 18

respondents whose unit location is outside the town said that the free gift activities are undertaken in order to maintain the relation with dealers, 74 respondents whose unit location is outside the town said that the special deals activities are undertaken in order to maintain the relation with dealers and 6 respondents whose unit location is outside the town said that the easy credit terms activities are undertaken in order to maintain the relation with dealers. Since calculated value of chi-square for degree of freedom 2 at 5% level of significance is 15.735 is more than tabulated value 5.991, therefore null hypothesis is rejected, i.e. Location of the unit & activities undertaken to maintain relation with dealers are dependent.

Conclusions & Suggestions

Small industry sector has performed exceedingly well and enabled our country to achieve a wide measure of industrial growth and diversification. By its less capital intensive and high labour absorption nature, SSI sector has made significant contributions to employment generation and also to rural industrialization. This sector is ideally suited to build on the strengths of our traditional skills and knowledge, by infusion of technologies, capital and innovative marketing practices. This is the opportune time to set up projects in the small-scale sector. It may be said that the outlook is positive, indeed promising, given some safeguards.

Distribution decisions have a broad impact on the marketing program used by a firm because middlemen can provide a wide variety of marketing functions. Middlemen perform a number of important functions in the distribution of products. The specialized efforts of distribution channel members generate place utility, possession or ownership utility, time utility for the consumers. Channel intermediaries have many roles. One is to perform the distribution at a lower cost per unit then the manufacturer could, and to balance the production efficiencies of the supplier with the purchasing needs of the supplier with the purchasing need of the consumers. Another role is to break down the large volumes produced into the small quantities bought. Intermediaries like dealers can minimize the number of transactions involved in the selling process. In some markets, dealers may assist in cash management & lead the marketing and promotional efforts too.

On the basis of the above given analysis and interpretation of the data, following conclusions can be drawn out. The analyses of tables are done on the basis of certain demographical basis. These demographical bases are main product of the enterprise, age of the entrepreneur, qualification and the location of the unit. Moreover it can be concluded from the above given analysis of tables that distribution system adopted by the small scale units in the state is one of the important tool and technique of effective marketing. There are around 75 respondents are agree that the parent land is the reason for setting up the unit at present location, 3 respondents are agree that the nearness to home is the reason for setting up the unit at present location, 15 respondents are agree that the transportation facility is the reason for setting up the unit at present location and 57 respondents are agree that the labour availability is the reason for setting up the unit at present location on the basis of main product of the enterprise, present age of the entrepreneur, academic qualification, family occupation and the location of the unit.

In the today's dynamic & highly competitive environment, salesman plays an important part. Salesman is the connecting link between sellers and buyers at every step, i.e., from the collection of raw materials to the finished goods/products. 10 respondents are agree that seeking orders is the function that salesman are required to perform, 119 respondents are agree that providing delivery is the function that salesman are required to perform, 12 respondents are agree that collecting payment is the function that salesman are required to perform, 6 respondents are agree that introducing new items and products to dealers and customers is the function that salesman are required to perform and 3 respondents are agree that collecting or gathering market information is the function that salesman are required to perform.

The concept of the distribution system becomes very simple to understand in terms of the route which manufacturers opt, to make their product available to his customers/ consumers at right time, place and price. The distribution system can be a direct or indirect. On the basis of main product of the enterprise, age of the entrepreneur, qualification and the location of the unit the 120 respondents sell their product through every possible outlet where as the remaining 30 respondents sell their product through dealers in one city area. A channel of distribution or distribution system for the product is the route taken by the title to goods they move from the producer to ultimate consumer or industrial user.

Companies try to forge a long term relationship with distributors (dealers). They often use positive motivators, such as higher margins, special deals, premiums, display allowances, and sales contests. 33 respondents are agree that they use free gifts are the activities undertaken to maintain the relationships with their dealers, 98 respondents are agree that they use special deals are the activities undertaken to maintain the relationships with their dealers and 19 respondents are agree that they use easy credit terms are the activities undertaken to maintain the relationships with their dealers.

On the basis of the above analysis of data and conclusion it becomes very clear that the condition of the small scale industries in the state of Uttarakhand with respect to distribution is critical. Government makes various schemes for promotion and distribution of them, but the actual help in form of policies and financial cannot make them to survive or aren't reach them. Generally Small firms typically starts and follow local operation selling in a limited market, using existing intermediaries. This channel of distribution is also got effected by the various reason due to which a particular unit is located at a certain area.

Salesman creates new wants and preferences. It involves establishing a cordial and binding relationship between the company and its customers and is based on annual trust. Some important functions of salesman are: seeking orders, providing delivery, collecting payments, introducing new items to dealers/customers and gathering market information etc. A company needs to view its intermediaries in the same way it views its end users. It needs to determine intermediaries' needs and construct a channel positioning such that its channel offering is tailored to provide superior value to these intermediaries. Most producers see gaining intermediaries' cooperation as a huge challenge.

Proper marketing facilities and the related policies should be framed by the government which actually works out in the market. Support by various governmental or non-governmental organizations being required by the entrepreneurs so that their product can grow and survive long in the market. The entrepreneurs of the state prefer to rely on the conventional distribution methods. The choice of middlemen too is totally based of convenience, those who are ready to sell are selected as distributors, therefore, the middlemen dictate terms. The units are not competent or resourceful enough to opt direct distribution option. The goods are generally distributed locally or to certain extent, regionally. Very few think of venture at the national level and the international reach is just a distant dream.

References

Ahmad and Nisar (1987), "Problems and Management of Small Scale and Cottage Industry", Deep & Deep Publications, Delhi.

Mag, V. and Xavier, J. (2002), "Production and Marketing of KVI Products in Virudhunagur District" *Indian Journal of Marketing*, Vol.XXX11, No. 12, pp. 23-26.

Merani, S.T. (1965), "Reflections on Development of Small Scale Industries", *Productivity Management Journal*, Vol.6, No.1, Spring.

Mohan, K.K. (1971), "Small Industry Enterprise Handbook", *Productivity Service International*, Bombay.

Narula, B.S. (1966), "Development of Small Industries: Some Suggestions", *The Economic Times*, Vol. 6.

Oliver, Rober W. (1966), "The Role of Small Scale Manufacturing in Economic Development", Washington D.C.

Rao, D. Nageswara (2002), "A Study of Marketing of Cotton in Coastal Andhra Pradesh", *Indian Journal of Marketing*, Vol. XXXII, No. 12, pp. 13-15.

Saraogi, A.R. (1984), "Industrial Growth in India–Turning Obstacles into Opportunities", *Indian Management*.

Schumpeter, J.A. (1934), "The Theory of Economic Development", Cambridge, M.A: Harvard University Press.

Sharma, A.P. (1988), "Marketing Problems of Small Scale Industries in Marketing in India– Cases and Readings by S. Neelamegham (Eds.)", Vikas Publishers, New Delhi.

Sharma, G.D. (1984), "How to Start Your Own Small Scale Industry", Vision Books, New Delhi.

Shashi Bala (1984), "Management of Small Scale Industries", Deep & Deep Publications, Delhi.

Singh Balajit (1961), "The Economics of Small Scale Industries, A Case Study of Small Scale Establishments of Moradabad", Asia, Bombay.

Singh R. and Agnihotri, A.K. (1989), "Marketing of Machine Tools in Small Sector, Small Enterprise Development", *Management and Extension Journal*, Vol. 16, No. 4.

Singh, P.I (1992), "Marketing Strategy to Tap Rural Market", *Journal of Rural Development*, Vol.11, No.2, pp.175-185.

Tambi, J.M.L (1988), "Marketing Strategy for Small Scale Industries in Marketing in India Cases and Readings by S. Neelamegham (Eds.)", Vikash, New Delhi.

30

SUSTAINABILITY MEASURES FOR EFFICIENT MARKETS AND GOOD GOVERNANCE: AN IMPACT STUDY ON THE EXTENSION OF TRADING HOURS IN INDIA

Deepak. R

Introduction

A gargantuan leap was taken by Securities and Exchange Board of India (SEBI) on October 2009 when it decided to extend the trading hours on major exchanges of India mainly National Stock Exchange (NSE) and Bombay Stock Exchange (BSE). This step would help in integrating the local markets with the global markets leading to efficient delivery of information flow, thus leading the efficient markets.

This decision was received with lot of skepticism by the trading and investing community throughout the country. It was stated that the Banks' Real-Time Gross Settlement (RTGS) system, a funds transfer mechanism where transfer of money takes place from one bank to another bank on a real time and on gross basis was not in place which would disrupt the functioning of exchanges by not allowing the traders/brokers to make margin payment during the extended time periods. There also existed concerns of undesirable speculation and day-trading by the speculators and trading community.

But the main reason existed from the belief that National Stock Exchange (NSE) was losing its commerce to Singapore stock exchange which had recently launched a derivative product on NSE's Nifty index called SGX Nifty. NSE had a belief that Nifty's volumes were reallocated to Singapore stock exchange which opened two and half hours earlier to Indian markets. Foreign institutional investors and hedge funds found it better to invest in Singapore stock exchange due to this lead-lag with respect to trading timings. Singapore stock exchange first half trade ends at 12.30 pm which corresponded to Indian markets commencing at 9.55 am. By extension of the trading hours to 9.00 am from the previous time of 9.55 am, the market would be able to assimilate information quickly, leading the efficient markets and regaining its lost volumes to other markets.

SEBI on October 2009 issued a circular under section 11 of SEBI act, allowing the exchanges to extend the trading hours from 9 am to 5 pm. In order to understand the sentiments of market participants on this issue, BSE and Association of Exchange Members of India (ANMI) conducted surveys among the brokers and trading members. The results clearly showed that more than half of the respondents were opposed to this circular and wanted to retain the old market timings. Inspite of all this opposition, on January 4th, 2010, the trading hours of both BSE and NSE were extended. The market sentiments played a major role on the historic day of implementation. BSE reached its 22 month high closing at 17,559 whereas NSE volumes decline to its lowest of '37,897crores which was earlier seen in March 2009.

Research Problem

The extension of trading hours by the act of SEBI certainly was received with lot of pessimism among the investing community. The major aim of extension was mainly to integrate the Indian markets with the global markets, thus leading to efficient markets in the long run. Since, there were concerns that NSE was losing business to Singapore Stock Exchange in the derivative and spot markets. It was thus felt a necessity to understand the after effects of the implementation of SEBI act of extension of trading hours on the prices and volumes of NIFTY index market in India.

Objectives of Study

- To understand the reaction of Nifty spot market prices and volumes around the date of implementation of SEBI act on extension of trading hours.
- To examine the equality of means and variances for the price and volume returns before and after the extension of market timings.

Hypotheses

Two hypotheses were tested for Nifty index spot price returns & volume returns. The tests are one sided & hence single tail tests.

Alternative Hypothesis 1: All the price returns after the change in the trading hours (Jan 4, 2010 to July 24, 2010) are significantly greater than price returns before the change in the trading hours (Jan 4, 2009 to July 24, 2009). Symbolically

$$Ho: \mu_1 = \mu_2$$

$$H1: \mu_1 > \mu_2$$

Alternative Hypothesis 2: All the volume returns after the change in the trading hours (Jan 4, 2010 to July 24, 2010) are significantly greater than volume returns before the change in the trading hours (Jan 4, 2009 to July 24, 2009). Symbolically

$$Ho: \beta 1 = \beta 2$$

$$H1: \beta 1 > \beta 2$$

Literature Review

Extension of trading hours is not a new phenomenon. There are several instances across the world when the futures or options markets opened or closed prior to or later than cash markets. In USA, the DJIA futures from Chicago Board of Trade (CBOT) and S&P500 futures from Chicago Mercantile Exchange opened earlier than NYSE.

In European countries, namely Germany, Italy and Switzerland we notice extension of trading hours. In South Africa, futures markets open 30 minutes earlier to cash markets.

In Asia-Pacific region, especially in Australia and Malaysia, the futures markets open earlier than the cash markets. In certain countries namely Austria and France, the cash markets trading starts early when compared to the futures markets.

After the extension of trading hours in either the cash markets/futures markets, the primary question to be addressed was whether it lead to change in volatility. Few studies related to the impact of extension of trading hours on the information flow between cash and futures markets (Chang, Jain and Locke (1995), Ho and Lee (1998), Fong and Frino (2001)) concluded that there existed new trading patterns after the extension.

The research would thus be focused on the volatility of the stock markets before and after the extension of the trading hours in India and whether investors can gain abnormal returns during such a regulatory change.

Data and Sources

For the study, the data obtained was secondary in nature. The NSE Nifty spot index prices and volumes from period January 1st 2009 to July 30th 2010 was retrieved from official website of NSE. The date of implementation of extension of market timings has been considered as January 4th 2010.

Methodology

In order to understand the behaviour of the markets towards the extension of the trading hours, three methods were followed:

Event Study Methodology (Brown and Warner, 1985) was adopted which enables to compute Cumulative Abnormal Returns (CAR) of the respective index price and volumes surrounding the implementation day. The main aim is to find whether the extension led to significant change in the price and volumes of nifty index. January 4th 2010 was considered the event day on which extension of market timings was brought into effect. 60 days surrounding the event day (30 days before and 30 days after the event) has been considered as event window. 212 days prior to the last day of the event window (i.e. -280 to -31 days from the event day) has been considered the estimation window.

The index price and volume returns for Nifty were calculated as shown below:

$$r_t = (\ln p_t - \ln p_{t-1}) * 100$$

Where Rt is the price return in period t, Pt refers to daily closing price of the index at time t and Pt-1 refers to daily closing price of the index at time t-1.

$$vr_t = (\ln v_t - \ln v_{t-1}) * 100$$

Where vr_t is the volume return in period t, v_t refers to daily volumes of the index at time t and v_{t-1} refers to daily volumes of the index at time t-1.

For Nifty index, Nifty 500 which is a broad market index was taken as a proxy for market index The estimation window price returns and volume returns were regressed against Nifty 500 to determine the 'constant' and the 'regression coefficient' to calculate the expected returns during the 'event window'.

$$\overline{r}_{it} = \alpha_i + \beta_i \overline{r}_{mt} + \xi_{it} \text{ and } v\overline{r}_{it} = \alpha_i + \beta_i v\overline{r}_{mt} + \xi_{it}$$

where

$\overline{r}_{it}$ = expected return of Nifty price returns on day t

$\overline{vr}_{it}$ = expected return of Nifty volume returns on day t.

$\overline{r}_{mt}$ = price return of the market index on day t i.e. Nifty 500.

$\overline{vr}_{mt}$ = volume return of the market index on day t.

β_i = systematic risk component

α_i = Intercept term

ξ_{it} = white noise error term on day t with zero mean and constant variance.

The α_i and β_i were estimated from day -211 to -31 day from the event day (day '0' is defined as the event day on which the market timings were extended) to calculate abnormal returns from day -30 to day +30 around the event day. The difference between the actual return and expected return during the event window is considered as the abnormal return.

The abnormal price return is calculated as follows:

$$AR_{it} = r_{it} - (\alpha_i + \beta_i \overline{r}_{mt})$$

The abnormal volume return is calculated as follows:

$$AVR_{it} = vr_{it} - (\alpha_i + \beta_i \overline{vr}_{mt})$$

where AR_{it} = abnormal return on price return and AVR_{it} = abnormal return of volume returns. Cumulative abnormal returns are the sums of daily average of abnormal returns over the event time. The cumulative abnormal price returns for period t = a until t = b is defined as follows:

$$AR_{ab} = \sum_{i=a}^{b} AR_t$$

and the cumulative abnormal volume returns for period t=a until t=b is defined as follows:

$$AVR_{ab} = \sum_{i=a}^{b} AVR_t$$

assuming independence across days, the t statistic for cumulative abnormal returns for a period of T days from day 'a' to day 'b' was calculated by

$$CAR_t = \frac{CAR_t}{\sqrt{\text{variance of } AR_t x T}}$$

T-TEST for testing difference between sample means: Here under the null hypothesis of no difference in the returns before and after the event day, the t-test was conducted at 0.05 level of significance.

The standard error of the difference between the two means since population standard deviation is unknown was calculated as follows:

$$\hat{\sigma}_{\bar{x}_{after}-\bar{x}_{before}} = \sqrt{\frac{\hat{\sigma}^2_{after}}{n_{after}}} + \sqrt{\frac{\hat{\sigma}^2_{before}}{n_{before}}}$$

To estimate the common variance or an unbiased estimator of population variance, the weighted average of sample variances were considered with weights being equal to degrees of freedom used.

Thus pooled estimate of population variance was estimated as shown below:

$$s_p^2 = \frac{(n_{after}-1)s^2_{after} + (n_{before}-1)s^2_{before}}{n_{before}+n_{after}-2}$$

Thus degree of freedom would be equal to number of sample before and after the event minus two. Because we are doing upper tailed test at 0.05 level of significance, the critical value of t is 1.671.

Thus standardized't' statistic is calculated as shown below:

$$t = \frac{(\bar{x}_{after}-\bar{x}_{before})-(\mu_{after}-\mu_{before})H_0}{\hat{\sigma}_{\bar{x}_{after}-\bar{x}_{before}}}$$

If the standardized difference between the two samples means lies within the acceptance region, we would accept the null hypothesis of no difference between the means of returns before and after the event day. Finally F-test was done for testing the difference between sample variances before and after the event day.

Analysis and Findings

At the outset, from Figure 1, we can observe that the nifty has recovered immensely from a low of 2700 levels during 2009 to around 5500 levels presently. Markets have gained confidence of the investors in bringing nifty from the lows to new highs in a very short span of time.

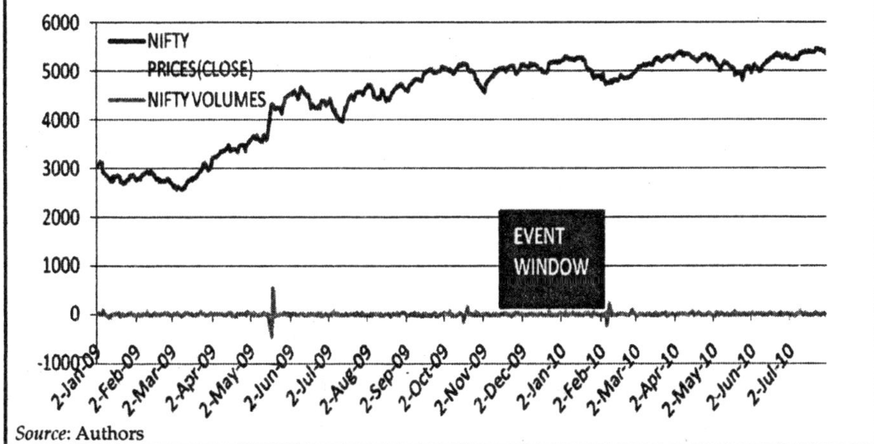

Source: Authors

Figure 1: Nifty Price and Volumes for Period January 1, 2009 to August 9th 2010

The market players' opposition (or market sentiments) to the change in the timings of the markets during the event window period can be clearly observed in terms of reduced prices after the implementation.

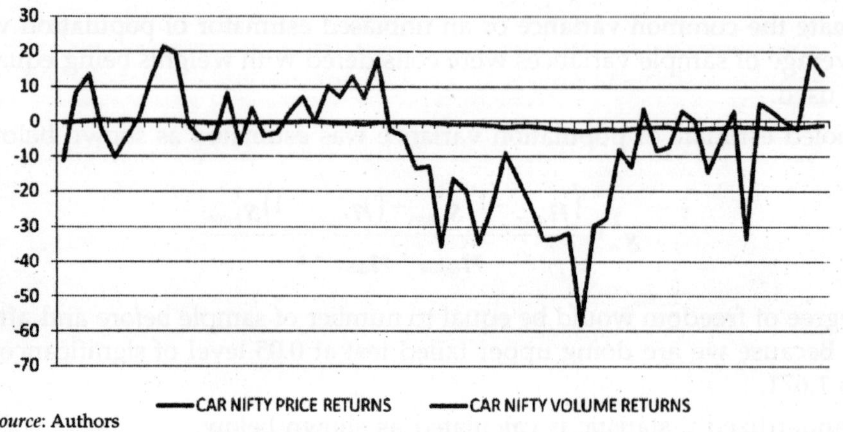

Source: Authors

Figure 2: Cumulative Abnormal Returns for the Event Window of Nifty Price and Volume Returns

As seen in Figure 2, thirty trading days prior to the announcement of the extension in trading hours till the actual date of announcement of the bonus issue the cumulative abnormal price and volume returns remained positive with correction after the announcement of the extension of trading hours. The cumulative abnormal returns were found to be negative for atleast two weeks from the event day, which confirms the negative market sentiments towards extension of trading hours. The descriptive statistics in the Table 1 and Table 2, clearly point to the fact that there were pointable differences before and after the event day. The average price returns declined from around 9 to negative 24 percentage after the extension of trading hours. But the volumes after the event day showed tremendous improvements.

But was there a statistically significant change in the prices and volumes before and after January 4th 2010 was of interest in the study.

The findings from the three methodologies followed are as follows:

Event Study Methodology

Though SEBI had issued the circular on extension of trading hours in 2009, the market was found to be pessimistic about the change. From table 3 we can observe that, for the five days preceding the extension, the abnormal price returns were 0.53%, 0.07%,-0.018%,-0.23% and 0.108% respectively and five days after the extension were -0.24%,-.04%,-0.05%,-0.16% and -0.51% respectively. On the event day, the cumulative abnormal price return was found to be -0.29%.

Similarly for the change in volumes, the abnormal returns five days prior to event day were -5.87%,10.89%,-20.19%,-1.56 and -9.43% respectively and five days after the event day were -22.66%,19.24%,-3.60%,-14.89% and 11.50% respectively.

The Cumulative Abnormal price returns after the event day were found to be statistically equivalent to zero, thus specifying that though market expected the announcement; it adjusted the prices of the 30 shares accordingly with a negative bias/sentiments. The Cumulative

Abnormal volume returns after the event day were found to be statistically equivalent to zero thus supporting the proposition that the NSE is semi-strong form efficient. The information flow from the extension of timings was found to gradually amplify negatively in the share prices and positively in the volume returns.

Table 1

Descriptive Statistics of Nifty Price Returns during the Event Window

NIFTY PRICE RETURNS IN EVENT WINDOW(BEFORE)		*NIFTY PRICE RETURNS IN EVENT WINDOW(AFTER)*	
Mean	0.090164933	Mean	-0.248894233
Standard Error	0.202692948	Standard Error	0.21710705
Median	0.009225707	Median	-0.004712226
Mode	#N/A	Mode	#N/A
Standard Deviation	1.110194998	Standard Deviation	1.189144285
Sample Variance	1.232532934	Sample Variance	1.414064132
Kurtosis	0.771033931	Kurtosis	0.524614541
Skewness	0.600847515	Skewness	-0.663997135
Range	5.163372707	Range	5.224598936
Minimum	-2.02900066	Minimum	-3.139898953
Maximum	3.134372047	Maximum	2.084699983
Sum	2.704947978	Sum	-7.466826999
Count	30	Count	30

Source: Authors

Table 2

Descriptive Statistics of Nifty Volume Returns during the Event Window

NIFTY VOL RETURNS IN EVENT WINDOW(BEFORE)		*NIFTY VOL RETURNS IN EVENT WINDOW(AFTER)*	
Mean	-0.383612586	Mean	0.161057226
Standard Error	3.299657218	Standard Error	11.58462744
Median	-2.028274179	Median	-0.994674283
Mode	#N/A	Mode	#N/A
Standard Deviation	18.0729669	Standard Deviation	63.45161772
Sample Variance	326.6321327	Sample Variance	4026.107791
Kurtosis	0.453437743	Kurtosis	10.6301389
Skewness	0.393922578	Skewness	-0.169270608
Range	82.24270409	Range	453.8742039
Minimum	-40.01972563	Minimum	-230.9132291
Maximum	42.22297846	Maximum	222.9609747
Sum	-11.50837758	Sum	4.831716782
Count	30	Count	30

Source: Authors

The t-test for Equality of Mean Returns around the Event Day

The t-test for the equality of means at 95% level of confidence for the abnormal returns during 30 days prior and 30 days after the extension of the trading hours, the t value being 1.671 suggests that the null hypothesis is accepted. As seen in the Table 4, this leads us to the conclusion that there is no statistically significant difference in the mean of the abnormal returns prior to and after the announcement of the bonus issue. This is consistent with the findings of the Cumulative Abnormal Average returns.

The F-test for Equality of Variances around the Event Day

The F-test for equality of variances around the event day suggests non-acceptance of the null hypothesis that there is significant difference in the distribution pattern of the variances between before and after the extension of the trading hours.

Table 3
t-values of CAAR Around the Event Date for NSE Nifty Price and Volume Returns

LAG	ABNORMAL NIFTY PRICE RETURNS	CUMULATIVE ABNORMAL NIFTY PRICE RETURNS	t CAR	LAG	ABNORMAL NIFTY PRICE RETURNS	CUMULATIVE ABNORMAL NIFTY PRICE RETURNS	t CAR	LAG	ABNORMAL NIFTY VOLUME RETURNS	CUMULATIVE ABNORMAL NIFTY VOLUME RETURNS	t CAVR	LAG	ABNORMAL NIFTY VOLUME RETURNS	CUMULATIVE ABNORMAL NIFTY VOLUME RETURNS	t CAVR
-30	-0.213004268	-0.213004268	-0.57408	1	-0.24533735	-0.838977887	-2.26117								
-29	0.132030574	-0.080973694	-0.21824	2	-0.0443462	-0.88332409	-2.38069	-29	-11.166107	-11.16610701	-0.59092	1	-22.663656	-35.5763663	-1.57029
-28	0.335014675	0.254040982	0.68468	3	-0.05371766	-0.937041752	-2.52546	-28	19.0417763	7.875669287	0.415867	2	19.24501369	-16.33135261	-0.73657
-27	0.210199349	0.46424033	1.2512	4	-0.16289398	-1.099935728	-2.96449	-27	5.4983277	13.37399698	0.712174	3	-3.60198194	-19.93333455	-0.90398
-26	-0.169452948	0.294787382	0.79449	5	-0.51734852	-1.617284251	-4.35882	-26	-15.933612	-2.559614691	-0.13532	4	-14.8960578	-34.82989238	-1.55358
-25	0.240570021	0.535357404	1.44287	6	0.259826612	-1.35745764	-3.65855	-25	-7.5720849	-10.13164964	-0.53776	5	11.5077581	-23.32163428	-1.04163
-24	-0.397490327	0.137867077	0.37157	7	-0.07883302	-1.436290658	-3.87101	-24	5.50873937	-4.622910262	-0.24394	6	14.29704058	-9.0245937	-0.39826
-23	0.091447769	0.229814846	0.61804	8	-0.28989256	-1.726183214	-4.65231	-23	5.67939156	1.056481301	0.055313	7	-7.72303195	-16.74762565	-0.73408
-22	-0.084461348	0.144853497	0.3904	9	-0.5237406	-2.249923811	-6.06387	-22	11.0017277	12.05820897	0.626376	8	-7.31421455	-24.06184021	-1.03893
-21	0.021356136	0.166209634	0.44796	10	-0.26548521	-2.515409016	-6.77989	-21	9.18506262	21.24327159	1.099685	9	-9.6334695	-33.69530971	-1.43182
-20	-0.128452138	0.037757495	0.10176	11	-0.19214738	-2.707556399	-7.29726	-20	-1.7912939	19.45197766	1.001652	10	0.207425022	-33.48788468	-1.40567
-19	-0.366526431	-0.328768936	-0.88608	12	0.329425281	-2.378131118	-6.40941	-19	-20.728416	-1.276438561	-0.06509	11	1.534796086	-31.9530886	-1.30985
-18	-0.202585583	-0.531354519	-1.43208	13	0.191214171	-2.186916947	-5.89406	-18	-3.6457705	-4.922209098	-0.25427	12	-26.2373837	-58.1904723	-2.32421
-17	0.179408134	-0.351951386	-0.94856	14	-0.3241938	-2.511110744	-6.76781	-17	0.15342417	-4.768784923	-0.24403	13	28.45031387	-29.74015843	-1.24987
-16	0.260256556	-0.091694829	-0.24713	15	0.262942655	-2.248168089	-6.05914	-16	12.8521364	8.083351452	0.409816	14	1.975516184	-27.7649966	-1.21257
-15	-0.261182584	-0.352877414	-0.95106	16	0.709302767	-1.538865321	-4.14747	-15	-14.57041	-6.487058489	-0.32783	15	19.32782568	-8.437170919	-0.35748
-14	-0.001313276	-0.354190689	-0.9546	17	0.025295633	-1.513569688	-4.07929	-14	10.191566	3.704507523	0.187469	16	-4.74891866	-13.18608957	-0.56038
-13	0.077395347	-0.276795342	-0.746	18	-0.12637498	-1.639944664	-4.41989	-13	-7.9833997	-4.278892196	-0.21531	17	16.63400994	3.44792037	0.142246
-12	0.096296449	-0.180498893	-0.48647	19	-0.60946804	-2.2494127	-6.06249	-12	0.90792791	-3.37096429	-0.16836	18	-12.0124224	-8.56450206	-0.35072
-11	0.053946598	-0.126552295	-0.34108	20	0.064801715	-2.184610986	-5.88784	-11	5.70059573	2.329631437	0.114989	19	1.156329658	-7.408172402	-0.29825
-10	0.112703784	-0.013848511	-0.03732	21	0.272097975	-1.912513011	-5.1545	-10	4.59211708	6.92174852	0.338128	20	10.33551543	2.927343031	0.112841
-9	-0.271779692	-0.285628202	-0.76981	22	0.082556499	-1.829956512	-4.932	-9	-7.2088886	-0.287140113	-0.01387	21	-2.76757673	0.159766306	0.005987
-8	-0.126793809	-0.412422011	-1.11154	23	0.363253696	-1.466702816	-3.95298	-8	10.2044235	9.917283432	0.474568	22	-14.585642	-14.42587568	-0.50964
-7	-0.145396419	-0.55781843	-1.5034	24	-0.2645784	-1.731281219	-4.66605	-7	-3.0259455	6.891337921	0.327437	23	7.923457766	-6.502417915	-0.22555
-6	-0.206633862	-0.764452292	-2.06031	25	0.092654856	-1.638626364	-4.41634	-6	5.69699055	12.58832847	0.590552	24	9.29161382	2.789195905	0.090862
-5	0.539131832	-0.225320461	-0.60727	26	-0.22659785	-1.865224214	-5.02705	-5	-5.8711941	6.71713436	0.311413	25	-36.2969031	-33.50770721	-1.0188
-4	0.070643038	-0.154677422	-0.41688	27	-0.08305468	-1.948278896	-5.25089	-4	10.8932268	17.61036113	0.806735	26	38.45032498	4.942617776	0.196769
-3	-0.018295773	-0.172973195	-0.46619	28	0.371708824	-1.576570072	-4.24909	-3	-20.197766	-2.587405045	-0.11766	27	-2.08291207	2.859705702	0.190429
-2	-0.236632202	-0.409605397	-1.10395	29	0.218357235	-1.358212837	-3.66058	-2	-1.5648483	-4.152253358	-0.1909	28	-3.31639889	-0.45668819	-0.02687
-1	0.108340727	-0.301264669	-0.81195	30	0.174680114	-1.183532723	-3.18979	-1	-9.434438	-13.58669131	-0.61528	29	-1.80562533	-2.262313521	-0.11512
0	-0.292375864	-0.593640533	-1.59995					0	0.67398101	-12.9127103	-0.57937	30	20.55305254	18.29073902	0.718034

Source: Author

Table 4
t- test of Means in NSE Nifty Price and Volume Returns

TEST OF DIFFERENCE FOR EQUALITY IN THE MEAN PRICE RETURNS AROUND THE EVENT DAY		TEST OF DIFFERENCE FOR EQUALITY IN THE MEAN VOLUME RETURNS AROUND THE EVENT DAY	
S SQUARE P	1.370559	S SQUARE P	2254.097461
SQUARE ROOT OF S SQUARE P	1.170709	SQUARE ROOT OF S SQUARE P	47.47733628
S.E OF DIFFERENCE	0.307443	S.E OF DIFFERENCE	12.46815934
STANDARDIZED 'T' STATISTIC	1.102835	STANDARDIZED 'T' STATISTIC	-0.043684861
CRITICAL T	1.671	CRITICAL T	1.671

Source: Author

Table 5
F-test of Variances in NSE Nifty Price and Volume Returns

F-Test Two-Sample for Variances(NIFTY PRICE RETURNS)				F-Test Two-Sample for Variances(NIFTY VOLUME RETURNS)		
	BEFORE	*AFTER*			*BEFORE*	*AFTER*
Mean	0.090164933	-0.24889		Mean	-0.383612586	0.161057
Variance	1.232532934	1.414064		Variance	326.6321327	4026.108
Observations	30	30		Observations	30	30
df	29	29		df	29	29
F	0.871624495			F	0.081128512	
P(F<=f) one-tail	0.356946074			P(F<=f) one-tail	7.27439E-10	
F Critical one-tail	0.537399965			F Critical one-tail	0.537399965	

Source: Author

Conclusion

Extension of the trading hour on national stock exchange though was received with lot of pessimism from the investing community, statistically the mean returns around the event day were found to be the same. The market sentiment played a vital role in the negative returns for the first two weeks after the extension of the trading hour. The variances of the price and volume returns were found to be significantly different thus confirming better informational flow thus leading to efficient markets.

References

James L. Davis, Eugene F. Fama, and Kenneth R. French, "Characteristics, Covariances and Average Returns, 1929 to 1997, "Journal of Finance 55, No. 1, (2000), pp. 389-406.

Leo H.Chan, Kam C.Chan and Louis T.W.Cheng (2002), "The Effect of Extended Trading Hours on the Informational Flow Between Cash and Futures Market", May.

Mohanty.P. (2001), "Efficiency of the Market for Small Stock, NSE Research Initiative, April.

Robert F.Whitelaw, "Time Variation and Covariations in the Expectation and Volatility of Stock Returns,"Journal of Finance 49(1994), pp.515-42.

Rajnish Mehra and Edward Prescott (1985), "The Equity Premium: A Puzzle," Journal of Monetary Economics, March.

Nai-Fu Chen, Richard Roll, and Stephen Ross (1986), "Economic Forces and the Stock Market, "Journal of Business, Vol 59.

Shrinivas. R. Patil (2010), "Extension of Trading Hour in Stock Market: An Insight", Portfolio Organizer, March, pp. 19-23.

Chan, Kalok (1992), A Further Analysis of the Lead-lag Relationship between the Cash Market and Stock Index Futures Market. Review of Financial Studies 5, 123-152.

Ho, Richard Y.K., and Raymond S.K. Lee (1998). Market Closure Effects on Return, Volatility, and Turnover Patterns in the Hong Kong Index Futures Market. Journal of International Financial Markets, Institutions and Money 8, 433-451.

Kawaller, I.G., P.D. Koch, and T.W. Koch (1993), Intraday Market Behavior and the Extend of Feedback between S&P 500 Futures Prices and the S&P 500 Index, Journal of Financial Research, 16, 107—121.

Webliography

Increase in Market Hours of Trading, Discussion paper, retrived from *www.sebi.gov.in/commreport/trading.pdf*

Tania Kishore Jaleel (2010), "Early Trading Hours Fail to Bring in Volumes", The Hindu Business line, April 19.

www.nseindia.com

www.bseindia.com

www.sgx.com

http://www.sgx.com/wps/portal/marketplace/mp-en/prices_indices_statistics/indices

31

DESIGNING AN INTERNATIONAL ADVERTISING STRATEGY

Amit Thukral

Objectives of the Study

- To find out the different advertising strategies used by the global marketers.
- To find out the reasons behind opting a particular advertising strategy.

Methodology

The method of research design is exploratory based on field/Laboratory research observation & analysis module.

Introduction

Advertising is a paid form of communication intended to persuade an audience (viewers, readers or listeners) to purchase or take some action upon products, ideas, or services. It includes the na-me of a product or service and how that product or service could benefit the consumer, to persuade a target market to purchase or to consume that particular brand. These messages are usually paid for by sponsors and viewed via various media. Advertising can also serve to communicate an idea to a large number of people in an attempt to convince them to take a certain action

Advertising in global scenario is viewed as an critical issue. As World can be divided into different regions, countries and different markets. Each geographical area possesses different cultural and social features which differentiates one market from another .Different subcultures exists in the different parts of the world. There are different social groups which are formed on the basis of income and their standard of living. Acceptability and the success of an advertisement campaign depend on its compatibility with these features. So it has to be designed while keeping these features in mind. It results to the adoption of differentiated strategy or an standardized strategy of advertising.

Literature Review

Factors Influencing Communication Decisions

It is a well known fact that the culture of a country influences the consumer's behavior.

Custom-ers are quite sensitive about the cultural aspect depicted in marketing communication. Advertising themes incorporating social acceptance, mutual dependence, respect for elders and tradition, harmony with nature, use of seasons, innovation and novelty, changing family role are often effective. Islamic countries impose certain restrictions on the presentation of women in TV commercials. The most stringent law regarding presentations of women is in Saudi Arabia where the TV commercials can show only a veiled woman or her back. Procter and gamble had to adopt an unusual strategy in Saudi Arabia .Since the focus had to be on the prospect s hairs, the ad showed the hair of a women from the back and another veiled woman from the front (Joshi, Rakesh Mohan, 2008).

Translation from one language to another is crucial in international communications. The literal translation may fail to convey the desired message across the countries due to cultural factors. Pepsi used the German translation of the slogan "come alive with Pepsi" in its ad campaign in west Germany. However the slogan was translated to German actually meant "come out of the grave with Pepsi" and failed to generate any market response from the customer (Joshi, Rakesh Mohan, et al. 2008).

The level of literacy plays an important tool in deciding what communicating tool message should be used in an international market. Market segment with lower level of adult literacy need to be addressed by way of more audio visual content rather than a written message. It should be ensured that the visuals convey the desired message rather than the text part of the communication (Joshi, Rakesh Mohan, et al. 2008)

Culture has been broadly divided as high context and the low context culture .Countries like Japan, China,, India and middle east generally have high context cultures where the contextual background of the communication is extremely significant. In high context cultures, the customers look keenly at the details of the sales executives and the company. Therefore advertising campaign in such cases should aim at establishing the firm's credibility and background. There should be clarity in presentation. Jargons and slangs should be avoided. One should speak slowly and without a strong accent, unlike western markets (Joshi, Rakesh Mohan, et al. 2008).

Ethnocentrism and the self-reference criterion. The *self-reference criterion* refers to the tendenc-y of individuals, often unconsciously, to use the standards of one's own culture to evaluate other. For example, Americans may perceive more traditional societies to be "backward" and "unmotivated" because they fail to adopt new technologies or social customs, seeking instead to preserve traditional values. In the 1960s, a supposedly well read American psychology professor referred to India's culture of "sick" because, despite severe food shortages, the Hindu religion did not allow the eating of cows. The psychologist expressed disgust that the cows were allowed to roam free in villages, although it turns out that they provided valuable functions by offering milk and fertilizing fields. *Ethnocentrism* is the tendency to view one's culture to be superior to others. The important thing here is to consider how these biases may come in the way in dealing with members of other cultures. It should be noted that there is a tendency of outsiders to a culture to overstate the similarity of members of that culture to each other. In the United States, we are well aw-are that there is a great deal of heterogeneity within culture; however, we often underestimate the diversity within other cultures. For example, in Latin America, there are great differences between people who live in coastal and mountainous areas; there are also great differences between social classes.*

Advertising Strategies Used by Global Marketers

Standardized Advertising Strategies

Standardizing a communication policy consists of operating a communication in all the foreign markets which is identical to the one in the domestic market, with the existing socio-cultural diff-erences. Furthermore, the company will use the same promotional arguments, the same positioni-ng, the same advertising messages, the same concepts, the same images, the same slogans. The global trademarks which use this strategy include Coca-Cola, Perrier and Benetton. When a standardized communication campaign is envisaged, this is generally considered as the media of television, and to lesser extent hoardings. However, in the case of hoardings, or a television advertisement, the text and the script have to be translated into the language of the country.**

Proponents of the standardization school assume that due to faster communication there is a con-vergence of markets and that consumers are becoming increasingly similar. The standardization school assumes that markets are driven "toward a converging commonality" by technology and increased communication (Levitt, 1983). Followers of this school assume that art, literature, taste-s, thoughts, religious beliefs, culture, living conditions, language, and, as a consequence, advertising is converging. Furthermore, they believe that even though people are different their basic physiological and psychological needs are the same. All promotional efforts must be adapted to so-me degree even if that only means a translation into the local language (Harvey, 1993). The decision to standardize or adapt advertising is based on the different views of the world. Those who prefer standardization are mainly concerned with reduction of advertising costs and consistent brand and image worldwide. Other benefits of standardization include sharing of experience and effective use of advertising budget. Other benefits of standardization include sharing of experience, effective use of advertising budget, etc. Cost reductions from standardization of advertising mainly originate from economies of scale and scope (Onkvisit and Shaw, 1990) highlight several advantages as a result of cost reduction. Standardized advertisement themes provide consistent brand images worldwide (Kirpilani, 1988).

Adaptation or Differentiated Advertising Strategies

Adapting a communication campaign consists of altering its different components to the characteristics of each country. The company designs a specific communication for each target market, t-he chosen stance for these markets can be different to the one used in the domestic market.***

The adaptation school holds the opposite view compared to the standardization school. The reason for adaptation of advertising is to create a differential advantage through local sensitivity and increased communications effectiveness (Hite and Fraser, 1990). Those who argue for adaptation generally points to difference among nations in terms of cultures, stages of economic development, political and legal system, customer values and lifestyles (Cavusgil ,1993). The purpose of adaptation is to gain differential advantage by adapting the advertisement to gain maximum effectiveness in terms of response and sales (Onkvisit and Shaw,et al. 1990). The advantage with a decentralized advertising function is that it allows responsiveness and adaptation to culture, infrastructure and competition. The visual and verbal parts of advertising are particularly sensitive to adaptation and use of local language, models and scenery increases the probability for the advertisement to be effective.

Other reasons for adaptation are accurate positioning arguments and price discrimination (Shoham, 1995).

Compromise School

Onkvisit and Shaw,et al. (1990) believe that the difference between standardization and adaptation is in degree rather than kind and that the difference between them should be seen as a continuum. This view is supported by Link (1988) who argues that companies can be placed on a globalization continuum. On the left side are companies with highly decentralized, multi-domestic operations and products. On the right side are the totally integrated and globally advertised brands and companies. In the middle are companies that increasingly standardize brands or products, but still adapt to local differences.

Reasons behind Opting a Particular Strategy

- Values that are strongly held with in the general market. The rate and direction of value changes occurring within the pertinent culture.
- Similarities and dissimilarities in demographic factors like literacy level, income, etc.
- Product variables – the degree of universality of the product. Product categories are usually divided into consumer durable, consumer non-durable and industrial goods. Boddewyn (1986) found that industrial goods had the highest level of standardization followed by consumer durables and consumer non-durables.
- One critical base for the deployment of standardization or adaptation of the marketing mix, including advertising, is the existence of global, or at least regional, market segments. Some authors argue that global segments do exist while others have a different view. One proponent of global markets is Levitt et al. (1983) who argues that markets are converging. Also Onkvisit and Shaw et al. (1990) suggest that there is an increasing homogeneity of markets that drives opportunities for standardization.
- Kirpalani et al. (1988) found that there is a significant relationship between the headquarter control and the extent of advertising standardization. They also found that the degree of headquarter control depends on the country-of-origin of the headquarter. Canadian and Japanese tend to exercise more control than do the US and Western Europe MNCs. Tai (1-997) found that there is a significant relationship between who makes the decision and the standardization of advertising decisions. Strategic decisions are more likely to be made jointly by headquarter and subsidiary while tactical decisions were most likely to be made by the subsidiary. The results from this survey indicate that corporations in the four Asian markets (China, Hong Kong, Singapore and Taiwan) do not adopt neither a fully standardized nor a differentiated approach to advertising. The reason for having a decentralized decision-making structure is to meet local consumer requirements. The overall conclusion is that organizational arrangements seem to have a substantial impact on the decision to standardize or adapt international advertising.
- Governmental variables – the restrictions on mass-communication.

Recommendations and Conclusion

Marketers have to analyze the cultural influences and the pace of acculturation in the foreign market, demographic factors, and the product category to design the appropriate advertising strategy. The most justifiable school-of-thought of international advertising is the compromise school that not only recognizes local differences but also some degree of advertising standardization is not only possible but also desirable. Marketers have analyze the differences and similarities in the business environment of the target country to design the appropriate advertising strategy.

References

Shoham, A. (1995), "Global Marketing Standardization", Journal of Global Marketing, Vol. 9, Nos. 1/2, pp. 91-117.

Tai, H.C. (1997), "Advertising in Asia: Localize or Regionalize?", International Journal of Advertising, Vol. 16, pp. 48-61.

Cavusgil, S.T., Zou, S. and Naidu, G.M. (1993), "Product and Promotion Adaptation in Export Ventures: An Empirical Investigation", Journal of International Business Studies, Third Quarter, pp. 479-506.

Boddewyn, J.J., Soehl, R. and Picard, J. (1986), "Standardization in International Marketing: Is Ted Levitt in fact Right?", Business Horizon, Vol. 29 No. 6, pp. 69-75.

Harvey, M.G. (1993), "Point of View: A Model to Determine Standardization of the Advertising Process in International Markets", Journal of Advertising Research, pp. 57-64.

Hite, R. and Fraser, C. (1990), "Configuration and Coordination of Global Advertising", Journal of Business Research, Vol. 21

Joshi, Rakesh Mohan (2008), International Marketing, Oxford University Press, pp. 498-99.

Kirpalani, V.H., Laroche, M. and Darmon, R.Y. (1988), "Role of Headquarter Control by Multinationals in International Advertising Decisions", International Journal of Advertising, Vol. 7, pp. 323-33..

Levitt, T. (1983), "The Globalization of Markets", Harvard Business Review, Vol. 61 No. 3, pp. 69-81. Proponents.

Onkvisit, S. and Shaw, J.J. (1990), "Global Advertising: Revolution or Myopia", Journal of International Consumer Marketing, Vol. 2 No. 3, pp. 97-112.

Websites

*http://www.consumerpsychologist.com/**

*http://www.eur-export.com/anglais/apptheo/marketing/comm/comstandadapa.htm***

*http://www.eur-export.com/anglais/apptheo/marketing/comm/comadapa.htm****

32

CHANGING GLOBAL MARKETING ENVIRONMENT

K.G. Chaubey, Shanti Ranjan Upadhyay & Jyoti Bajpai

Changing Global Marketing Environment

Bank of America (BofA) is one of the best-known brands in banking, so it's no surprise that when NationsBank acquired BofA it adopted that name. What is more surprising is how a small southern bank—North Carolina National Bank before it was renamed Nations Bank—grew so quickly that it was ultimately able to acquire BofA, Fleet Bank, and other giant competitors. In fact, the innovative marketing strategy planning that originally fueled growth at NationsBank continues to make the new Bank of America unique. BofA has offices in 31 countries and serves clients from 150 countries. It provides banking services for corporations, manages trusts for the wealthy, and offers investment services. But what differentiates BofA is that it has grown primarily by becoming a "local bank" that serves large numbers of final consumers and small businesses in communities across the land. Its banking centers are in 5,800 locations, and it has the largest network of ATMs—16,800 of them. It was also a pioneer in e-commerce and now, serving 14 million customers online, is the world's largest online banker. The bank's customers benefit from this strategy. For the first time, consumers can count on easy access to their hometown bank virtually anywhere they live, work, play, and travel. BofA is right there—in person, online, or via telephone or ATM.

Along with that convenience, BofA has raised the stakes for service quality in banking.

How did managers at NationsBank know which opportunities to pursue and turn into strategies? Part ot the explanation is that they evaluated not only customer needs and competitive rivals, but also trends in the external market environment. Even though the marketing environment is constantly changing, they spotted new trends and took advantage of them. Strength catapulted the bank ahead when the Internet opened the door to online services. Moreover, using online banking to expand the retail customer base fit with the marketing program the bank had been pursuing for years. Consider, for example, how changes in the competitive and legal environments have shaped the bank's strategies for acquiring new customers. Regulations once governed how banks could operate, interstate banking was restricted, and many states limited the **Changing Global Marketing Environment.**

Evaluating Opportunities in the Changing Marketing Environment

Number and location of branch offices. As regulations began to ease, banking became more competitive and more marketing-oriented. For example, in college towns the bank targeted students with special accounts to build relationships that would last when they moved to new locations after graduation. By the time interstate banking was allowed, the firm already had experience managing many branches—and the financial resources to acquire other banks and their customers. Initially they screened opportunities to focus on banks in Sun Belt states where population and income growth was rapid, regulations were more favorable, and consumers were less satisfied with available banks. NationsBank's customer base grew quickly—and it held on to new customers by improving the value they received from their banking relationship. Although NationsBank was very profitable and growing rapidly, it did not have the international reputation of banks like Citicorp that were based in big financial centers. That was a weakness during a period when economies were becoming more global. However, the merger with BofA helped to offset that weakness. Because the bank operated in many regions across the United States, managers were less provincial than managers of many other banks.

Quickly saw and responded to cultural shifts that were taking place. For example, BofA's banking centers in Texas and Florida served many Hispanic customers and the Atlanta bank had a large proportion of African American customers. As society became more multicultural, the bank recruited associates (employees) from diverse ethnic backgrounds and made BofA a welcoming place for them to work and bank. Now BofA is one of the best companies in America for minority workers. Similarly, it offers flexible hours and other progressive benefits to help ease the pressure on dual career families. Having a loyal group of associates has helped build a team culture where everyone tries to win in the market by providing excellent and efficient service. Catherine Bassinet, a global marketing executive, put it this way, "Our strong brand is a significant competitive advantage, and in building it everything matters. The substance of our people, culture, process, and presence uniquely sets us apart."

Learning Objectives

In the present scenario it's expected that a marketing manager must analyze customer needs and choose marketing strategy variables within the framework of the marketing environment and how it is changing.

When you finish this chapter, you should

- Know the variables that shape the environment of marketing strategy planning.
- Understand why company objectives are important in guiding marketing strategy planning.
- See how the resources of a firm affect the search for opportunities.
- Know how the different kinds of competitive situations affect strategy planning.
- Understand how the economic and technological environment can affect strategy planning.
- Know why you might be sent to prison if you ignore the political and legal environment.
- Understand the cultural and social environment and how key population trends affect strategy planning.

- Understand how to screen and evaluate marketing strategy opportunities.
- Understand the important new terms.

The Marketing Environment

The marketing strategy planning process requires narrowing down to the best opportunities and developing a strategy that gives the firm a competitive advantage and provides target customers superior customer value. This narrowing-down process should consider the important elements of the marketing environment and how they are shifting. A large number of forces shape the marketing environment. The direct market environment includes customers, the company, and competitors. The external market environment is broader and includes four major areas:

- Economic environment
- Technological environment
- Political Environment
- Legal environment
- Cultural and social environment

The marketing manager can't control the variables of the marketing environment. That's why it's useful to think of them as uncontrollable variables.

Objectives Should Set Firms' Course

A company must decide where it's going, or it may fall into the trap expressed so well by the quotation: "Having lost sight of our objective, we redoubled our efforts." Company objectives should shape the direction and operation of the whole business. It is difficult to set objectives that really guide the present and future development of a company. The marketing manager should be heard when the company is setting objectives. But setting whole-company objectives—within resource limits—is ultimately the responsibility of top management.

The following three objectives provide a useful starting point for setting a firm's objectives. They should be sought *together* because in the long run a failure in even one of the three areas can lead to total failure of the business. A business should-

- Engage in specific activities that will perform a socially and economically useful function.
- Develop an organization to carry on the business and implement its strategies.
- Earn enough profit to survive.

These objectives are important, but top executives often don't state their objectives clearly. If objectives aren't clear from the start, different managers may hold unspoken and conflicting objectives.

A good mission statement should focus on a few key goals rather than embracing everything. It should also supply guidelines when managers face difficult decisions. For example, three basic objectives provide guidelines a mission statement helps set the course **Work 1** Marketing Strategy Planning, Competitors, Company, and External Market Environment

Best opportunities to pursue* _ *Evaluating Opportunities

- Screening criteria

- Planning grids
- Planning for multiple products

Competitors

- Current
- Prospective

Company

- Objectives
- Resources

External Market Environment

- Economic
- Technological
- Political and legal
- Cultural and social

It is not a substitute for more specific objectives that provide guidance in screening possible opportunities. For example, top management might set objectives such as "earn 25 percent annual return on investment" and "introduce at least three innovative and successful products in the next two years." Of course, when there are a number of specific objectives stated by top management, it is critical that they be compatible. For example, the objective of introducing new products is reasonable. However, if the costs of developing and introducing the new products cannot be recouped within one year, the return on investment objective is impossible.

To avoid such problems, the marketing manager should at least be involved in setting company objectives. Company objectives guide managers as they search for and evaluate opportunities—and later plan marketing strategies. Particular *marketing* objectives should be set within the framework of larger company objectives. Although Work 2, firms need a hierarchy of objectives—moving from company objectives to marketing department objectives. For each marketing strategy, firms also need objectives for each of the four Ps—as well as more detailed objectives. For example, in the Promotion area, we need objectives for personal selling, mass selling, *and* sales promotion. **Toyota** provides an example. One of its company objectives is to achieve high customer satisfaction. So the R&D people design vehicles to meet specific reliability objectives. Similarly, the production people work to cut manufacturing defects. The marketing department is in turn, sets specific customer satisfaction objectives for each and every product. That leads to specific promotion objectives to ensure that the sales and advertising people don't promise more than the company can deliver. Dealers and customer service people, in turn, work to quickly fix a problem the first time it's reported.

Company's objectives and marketing objectives should be realistic and achievable. Overly ambitious objectives are useless if the firm lacks the resources to achieve them.

Company Resources May Limit Search for Opportunities

Every firm has some resources—hopefully some unique ones—that set it apart. Breakthrough opportunities—or at least some competitive advantage—come from making use of these strengths while avoiding direct competition with firms having similar strengths. To find its strengths, a firm must evaluate its functional areas (production, research and engineering, marketing, general management, and finance) as well as its present products and markets. The knowledge of people at the firm can also be a unique resource. By analyzing successes or failures in relation to the firm's resources, management can discover why the firm was successful—or why it failed—in the past. Some opportunities require large amounts of capital just to get started. Money may be required for R&D, production facilities, marketing research, or advertising before a firm makes its first sale. And even a really good opportunity may not be profitable for years. So lack of financial strength is often a barrier to entry into an otherwise attractive market. In many businesses, the cost of producing and selling each unit decreases as the quantity increases. Therefore, smaller firms can be at a great cost disadvantage if they try to win business from larger competitors.

Financial strength producing capability and flexibility Work 2 A Hierarchies of Objectives-Production objectives, Finance objectives, Company objectives, Marketing objectives, Human resource objectives, R&D objectives.

Campbell Soup Company has strengths that make it a very tough competitor in the consumer market. Knorr, doesn't have as large a consumer advertising budget or as much shelf space in supermarkets. However, in the restaurant market, chefs often want ingredients that are different from what consumers have at home—and that's strength for Knorr.

Some firms are finding that they have the greatest flexibility by not having any "in-house" manufacturing at all. Sara Lee, the company that markets brands like Hanes and L'eggs, is a good example. Sara Lee sold its manufacturing facilities for many of these textile-related markets. Sara Lee says it doesn't have a competitive advantage in manufacturing. Further, as its needs change in various markets around the world it will buy products from whatever suppliers are best able to meet its specifications. Our marketing strategy planning framework helps in analyzing current marketing resources. In the product area, for example, a familiar brand can be a big strength. Starbucks is famous for its coffee beverages. When Starbucks introduced its Coffee Ice Cream, many people quickly tried it because they knew what Starbucks flavor meant.

Finally, thorough understanding of a target market can give a company an edge. Many companies fail in new product-markets because they don't really understand the needs of the new customers or the new competitive environment.

Analysising Competitors & the Competitive Environment

The **competitive environment** affects the number and types of competitors the marketing manager must face and how they may behave. Although marketing managers usually can't control these factors, they can choose strategies that avoid head-on competition. And where competition is inevitable, they can plan for it. Understanding the differences among these market situations is helpful in analyzing the competitive environment, and our discussion assumes some familiarity with these concepts.

The best way for a marketing manager to avoid head-on competition is to find new or better ways to satisfy customers' needs and provide value. The search for a breakthrough opportunity—or some sort of competitive advantage—requires an understanding not only of customers but also of competitors. That's why marketing managers' turn to ***competitor analysis*** —an organized approach for evaluating the strengths and weaknesses of current or potential competitors' marketing strategies. The basic approach to competitor analysis is simple. You compare the strengths and weaknesses of your current target market and marketing mix with what competitors are currently doing or are likely to do in response to your strategy. The initial step in competitor analysis is to identify potential competitors. It's useful to start broadly and from the viewpoint of target customers. Companies may offer quite different products to meet the same needs, but they are competitors if customers see them as offering close substitutes. For example, disposable diapers, clothe diapers, and diaper rental services all compete in the same generic market concerned with baby care. Identifying a broad set of potential competitors helps marketing managers understand the different ways customers are currently meeting needs and sometimes points to new opportunities. For example, even parents who usually prefer the economy of cloth diapers may be interested in the convenience of disposables when they travel. Usually, however, marketing managers quickly narrow the focus of their analysis to the set of ***competitive rivals*** —firms that will be the closest competitors. Rivals offering similar products are usually easy to identify. However, with a really new and different product concept, the closest competitor may be a firm that is currently serving similar needs with a different type of product. Although such firms may not appear to be close competitors, they are likely to fight back—perhaps with a directly competitive product—if another firm starts to take away customers. A successful strategy attracts copycats who jump in for a share of the profit. Sometimes a creative imitator figures out a way to provide customers with superior value.

In a competitor analysis, you also consider ***competitive barriers*** —the conditions that may make it difficult, or even impossible, for a firm to compete in a market. Such barriers may limit your own plans or, alternatively, block competitors' responses to an innovative strategy. For example, Competitor analysis in the Japanese market for disposable diapers. P&G was about to replace its original Pampers, which were selling poorly, with a new version that offered improved fit and absorbency.

Grocery stores and drugstores are very small, frequent restocking by wholesalers is critical. So getting cooperation in the channel was a potential competitive barrier for P&G. To overcome this problem, P&G changed its packaging to take up less space and offered wholesalers and retailers' better markups.

A marketing manager should actively seek information about current or potential competitors. Although most firms try to keep the specifics of their plans secret, much public information may be available. Sources of competitor information include trade publications; alert sales reps, middlemen, and other industry experts. In business markets, customers may be quick to explain what competing suppliers are offering. The Internet is a powerful way to get information about competitors. A firm that puts all of its marketing information on a public website for customers also makes it readily available to competitors.

Competitor Analysis

P&G's Current Strengths, Planned Strategy and Weaknesses and Weaknesses Target Market(s), Product, Place, Promotion, Price, (Potential)-Competitive Barriers: Upscale, modern parents who can afford disposable diapers Improved fit and absorbency ; brand-name imagery weak in Japan ; Distribution through independent wholesalers to both food stores and drugstores , but handled by fewer retailers ; Heaviest spending on daytime TV, heavy sales promotion, including free samples ; Improve wholesaler and retailer margins; faster deliveries in channel; change package to require less shelf space Same as for P&G Brand familiarity but no longer the best performance Press retailers to increase in-store promotion; change advertising and/or improve product Same as for P&G, but also budget-conscious segment that includes cloth diaper users Two brands for different market segments—and more convenient package with handles Distribution through 80% of food stores in best locations but if P&G takes customers, cut price on premium brand.

A firm that faces very stiff competition may find that the competitive environment and the opportunities are much better in another country.

The Economic Environment

The **economic and technological environment** affects the way firms—and the whole economy—use resources. We will treat the economic and technological environments separately to emphasize that the technological environment provides a *base* for the economic environment. Technical skills and equipment affect the way companies convert an economy's resources into output. The economic environment, on the other hand, is affected by the way all of the parts of a macro-economic system interact. This then affects such things as national income, economic growth, and inflation. The economic environment may vary from one country to another, but economies around the world are linked. The economic environment can, and does, change quite rapidly. The effects can be far-reaching and require changes in marketing strategy. Even a well-planned marketing strategy may fail if a country or region goes through a rapid business decline. As consumers' incomes drop, they must shift their spending patterns. They may simply have to do without some products. In contrast to the cultural and social environment, economic conditions can move rapidly and require immediate strategy changes.

Technological Environment

Technology is the application of science to convert an economy's resources to output. Technology affects marketing in two basic ways: with new products and with new processes (ways of doing things). The **Internet** is a system for linking computers around the world. The idea of linking computers in a network is not new. Even so, the Internet expands the network concept to include any computer anywhere and the World Wide Web makes the exchange of information easy. As a result, this technology is radically changing just about every aspect of marketing. Consider the arena of promotion. The invention of TV changed marketing because it suddenly made it possible for a sponsor to broadcast a vivid message to millions of people at the same time. Now, the Internet makes it possible for that sponsor to select any of millions of messages and to simultaneously narrowcast any of them to millions of different individuals. It is just as easy for customers to request the information in the first place, or to respond electronically once they have it. Thus, the Internet's capability radically changes our ideas about how firms communicate with customers, and vice versa. Similarly, the Internet is creating totally different approaches to pricing. Airlines run online auctions of seats that might otherwise go unsold. To check out an online auction, go to www.ebay.com.

The global economy is connected Technology affects opportunities Technology transfer is rapid Internet technologies are reshaping marketing In hindsight, new approaches such as these seem obvious—given that the technology is available. But they are not obvious up front—unless you're really looking for them.

The Political Environment

The attitudes and reactions of people, social critics, and governments all affect the political environment. Consumers in the same country usually share a common political environment, but the political environment can also affect opportunities at a local or international level. Strong sentiments of ***nationalism*** —an emphasis on a country's interests before everything else—affect how macro-marketing systems work. They can affect how marketing managers' work as well. Nationalistic feelings can reduce sales—or even block all marketing activity—in some international markets. For many years, China has made it difficult for outside firms to do business there—in spite of the fact that Technology and ethical issues Nationalism can be limiting in international markets, Many competitors offer products for computer networks, so AT&T wants customers to focus on its special capabilities and network products that are superior because they go beyond just connecting computers.

The international competition fostered by the moves to unify Europe provided impetus for other cooperative trade agreements, including the ***North American Free Trade Agreement* (NAFTA),** which lays out a plan to reshape the rules of trade among the U.S., Canada, and Mexico. NAFTA basically enlarges the free-trade pact that had already knocked down most barriers to U.S.–Canada trade, and over a 15-year period it will eliminate most such barriers with Mexico. It also establishes a forum for resolving future trade disputes.

The changes that result from NAFTA may ultimately be as significant as those in Europe. Talks are under way to explore the concept of expanding NAFTA to create a free-trade zone for 34 countries across North, South, and Central America.

Consumerism is a social movement that seeks to increase the rights and powers of consumers. In the last 45 years, consumerism has spread to many different countries, but it was born in America. The basic goals of modern consumerism haven't changed much since 1962, when President Kennedy's "Consumer Bill of Rights" affirmed consumers' rights to safety, to be informed, to choose, and to be heard. U.S. consumerism was much more visible in the early days. Consumers staged frequent boycotts and protest marches and attracted much media attention.

The Legal Environment

Changes in the political environment often lead to changes in the legal environment and in the way existing laws are enforced. The legal environment sets the basic rules for how a business can operate in society. To illustrate the effects of the legal environment, we will discuss how it has evolved in the United States. However, laws often vary from one country to another. American economic and legislative thinking is based on the idea that competition

The law now bans the shipment of unsanitary and poisonous products and requires much testing of drugs. The Food and Drug Administration (FDA) attempts to control manufacturers of these products. It can seize products that violate its rules—including regulations on branding and labeling. Federal legislation— which affects interstate commerce—marketers must be aware of state and local laws. There are state and city laws regulating minimum prices and the setting of prices, regulations for starting up a business (licenses, examinations, and even tax payments), and in some communities, regulations prohibiting certain activities—such as telephone selling or selling on Sundays or during evenings. The old rule about buyer–seller relations— let the buyer beware —has changed to *let the seller beware.*

Cultural and Social Environment

The **cultural and social environment** affects how and why people live and behave as they do—which affects customer buying behavior and eventually the economic, political, and legal environment. Many variables make up the cultural and social environment. Some examples are the languages people speak, the type of education they have, their religious beliefs, what type of food they eat, the style of clothing and housing they have, and how they view work, marriage, and family. Demographic data and trends tell us a lot about a society and its culture. Understanding the demographic dimensions is also important to marketing strategy planning, so it's useful to look at some key demographic patterns. When summarizes data for representative countries from different regions around the world.

Conclusion

Businesses need innovative strategy planning to survive in our increasingly competitive markets. In this, we discussed the variables that shape the environment of marketing strategy planning and how they may affect opportunities. First we looked at how the firm's own resources and objectives may help guide or limit the search for opportunities. Then we went on to look at the need to understand competition and how to do a competitive analysis. Then we shifted our focus to the external market environments. They are important because changes in these environments present new opportunities, as well as problems, that a marketing manager must deal with in marketing strategy planning.

The economic environment—including chances of recession or inflation—also affects the choice of strategies. And the marketer must try to anticipate, understand, and deal with these changes—as well as unfamiliar market that a manager in a distant country might otherwise overlook. Further, a local citizen who knows the marketing environment may be able to identify an "obvious" problem ignored even in a careful analysis. Thus, it is very useful for the analysis to include input from locals—perhaps cooperative middlemen. The farther you go from familiar territory, the greater the risk of making big mistakes. But not all products, or marketing mixes, involve the same risk. Think of the risks as running along a "continuum of environmental sensitivity."

Some products are relatively insensitive to the economic and cultural environment they're placed in. These products may be accepted as is—or they may require just a little adaptation to make them suitable for local use. Most industrial products are near the insensitive end of this continuum. At the other end of the continuum, we find highly sensitive products that may be difficult or impossible to adapt to all international situations. Consumer products closely linked to other social or cultural variables are at this end. For example, some cultures view dieting as unhealthy; that explains why products like Diet Pepsi that are popular in the United States have done poorly there. This continuum helps explain why many of the early successes in international marketing were basic commodities such as gasoline, soap, transportation vehicles, mining equipment, and agricultural machinery. It also helps explain why some consumer products firms have been successful with basically the same promotion and products in different parts of the globe. Yet some managers don't understand the reason for these successes. They think they can develop a global marketing mix for just about *any* product. They fail to see that firms producing and/or selling products near the sensitive end of the continuum should carefully analyze how their products will be seen and used in new environments— and plan their strategies accordingly. If the risks of an international opportunity are still hard to judge, it may be wise to look first for opportunities that involve exporting. This gives managers a chance to build experience, know-how, and confidence over time. Then the firm will be in a better position to judge the prospects and risks of taking further steps. Risks vary with environmental sensitivity What if risks are still hard to judge? Industrial products Basic commodity-type consumer products Consumer products that are linked to cultural variables Insensitive.

33

GLOBAL BRANDING STRATEGY

S.K Tannan

Introduction

Though Globalization was a battle cry of the last decade of the 20th Century, however, this phenomenon is not unique or new to this period. In the 19th Century, colonialism was a major force of globalization and created a multitude of cross-border trade links. During this period, goods bearing a brand name were sent abroad in large quantities. However, many of the cross-border trade links bearing branded goods were limited to neighboring countries and to the countries' colonial empires; British brands found their way to India, French branded goods to Indo-china and Dutch brands to Netherlands' East Indies.

The next big spur for globalization came after the Second World War, when new consumer brands came to Europe and Asia. The third big push for branding came in the wake of the erosion and subsequent demise of communism. The fall of the Berlin Wall opened up previously inaccessible markets to foreign brands, not just only in Eastern and Central European markets, but also other markets such as Chile and South Africa, However, the biggest impetus came from the opening up of China, which is not only a massive market, but also a massive production location for U.S, Japanese and European Brands.

The anti-capitalist and anti-globalization movement argued that global brands essentially had too much power and were the cause of a variety of evils and injustices in world society. But such a movement is ignoring the importance of globalization and brands to the economic and social development of all nations. Brands have been successful because people want them; and every organization's need to protect its reputation and also its corporate value is the most efficient impetus for them to behave well.

The economic importance of brands on a national and international stage is undeniable. For an example, when the GDP of Thailand was around $115 billion in 2001, the combined value of the world's two most valuable brands (Coca-Cola and Micro-soft) was around $134 Billion. If a brand delivers what it promises, behaves in a responsible way, and continues to innovate and add value, people will continue to vote for it with their wallets, their respect and even their affection. However, if a brand takes its position as granted and becomes complacent, greedy and less scrupulous in its corporate practices, people will stop voting for it, with potentially disastrous effects for the brand and its owner.

The effect that the intensified globalization had had on brands has been spectacular. New brands are seemingly born global. Brand portfolios that have been built up through decades of acquisitions are rationalized to focus attention on a limited number of strategic brands. Long established brands have enhanced their dominant positions across the globe, threatening less market savvy local brands.

Some of the global brands managed to become local institutions by filling a local role in societies where they operate, while others dominate their category as global monoliths.

The supposed supremacy of global brands and the inadequacy of the local brands has become a debatable issue. It has been argued that consumers across the globe are becoming more a like, require the same mass-produced products at reasonable prices, and that brands should not bother to adapting to the local needs and cultural preferences.

However, the past decade has shown that the contention that the consumers are becoming more similar is incorrect. Far from homogenizing, markets have fragmented over the past decade, and people around the world have asserted their local identities. This has happened not despite, but because of globalization. As people interact more with the outside world, they become increasingly sophisticated in their attitudes and behaviors, not content to take foreign brands at face value.

Defining a Global Brand

A brand is a construct and not a living and breathing organism. Brands are created, stimulated and applied by people working in organizations seeking to create worthwhile experiences for their customers that will induce behavior beneficial to the organization. This calls for some careful preparation and planning.

Global brands are defined loosely as brands that are available across multiple geographies, without specifying any lower limit or any continental requirements. The revenue these brands generate also does not matter, nor does the manner in which they present themselves in each society.

The Strategic Planning Cycle

The strategic planning for a brand starts with an understanding of an organization's business strategy. Strategizing for business is not something that is exclusive to the business world. Not-for profit organizations also have a need for this type of activity, particularly those that are dependent on donations from the general public. The business strategy is aimed at achieving a particular consumer behavior. Only if consumers actually purchase, use goods, pay a higher price or donate more, the objectives of a business strategy will be met.

The objectives of a business strategy may include a larger market share, increased returns, higher margins, and increased shareholder's value. Brands are designed to persuade consumers to show the behavior that will make the objectives come true for the organization. Thus, the influence of business strategy on the brand strategy is direct and compelling.

It is the task of the brand management to translate the business strategy into the brand expression. However, the brand expression does contain the materials with which brand managers are able to shape their brands. The marketing mix in its turn aims to translate the brand expression into actual products or services, with a specific price, to be sold at specific outlets, to be promoted through specific communication activities and channels, and to be supported by specific service. The influence of the marketing policy is indirect, in that the correct translation of the brand into the marketing mix determines whether the consumers are provided with correct experience of the brand.

Having translated the business strategy into the brand expression, which in turn has guided the marketing activities, brand management has seemed to have done its job.

The Brand Environment

Many factors influence a brand than the business strategy and the subsequent efforts of the organization and its affiliates to bring about the brand. A brand operates in an environment consisting of, on the one hand, the elements of the strategic planning cycle and, on the other hand, organizational conventions, competitive forces, market structures, cultural factors, consumer motivation and media attention: the lenses and filters through which consumers perceive and experience the brand.

The brand environments consist of the brand itself-expression, perception and recognition-surrounded by internal and external factors that have an influence on the brand. Only by taking these factors into consideration can management understand the entire brand proposition, and how it is affected in different markets.

The problem facing brand managers is how to unravel all these elements and turn their insights into policies that will unlock the full potential of their brand in a particular market, and across multiple markets at the same time. This requires a common framework that can be used across markets in order to obtain equivalence of brand analysis. A framework ensures not only that global brand management talks the same brand language and follows the same procedures as local brand management, but also that it becomes clear which internal or external factors that are uniquely influencing to particular societies or segments of societies.

The Management of Global Brands

One of the key issues facing the management of brands today is how to deal with a brand as it stretches across multiple societies and geographies. . There is always a conflict between finding an optimum fit of the brand with local circumstances, and the desire to obtain brand consistency across markets. Frequently, the decisions are made on the basis of organizational constructs rather than on the basis of an understanding of the brand and the various internal and external influences on it. This leads to tensions between global and local brand management that can result in power struggles about the ownership of the brand.

Global and local brand management need to understand each other's viewpoints on the brand and the resulting need for adaptations, the possibilities for obtaining sustainable competitive advantage, and the opportunities for standardization. A compelling brand is a interest of all those affected by it.

It is of utmost importance that global and local brand management must have a common basis for their brand strategy and planning. The common basis needs to provide a shared language, definitions, interpretations, assessments and most importantly a clear understanding of the relationships between the factors that shaped a brand in its global and local context.

The past decade or so has seen the increasing popularity of brand standardization. Brand standardization can reap huge benefits in terms of economies of scale: centralized production, increased leverage among distribution partners, one advertising campaign across markets, the same brand extensions everywhere, reduction in brand management staff etc. for many brand managers, their brands can only be considered truly global if they are the same in every respect everywhere. In reality, only very few precious brands to claim this title.

At the same time, other voices emerged lambasting global brands for their detrimental effects on environment: on workers in developing countries, on local brands, on the mental well being of children, on public spaces and so on. Global brands are being portrayed as epitomes of degradation, exploitation and manipulation. Anti-globalization activists raised questions such as "Are global brands forces of destruction in the third world? Should local brands be protected in order to defend local culture?", and "How can local brands be stopped?

Developing countries need not be the victims of globalization. If they can learn to use the classic rich-nations tricks of branding and marketing, they can turn the forces of global markets to their advantage. Each brand has its own specific potential for standardization across and adaptation to culturally and structurally diverse markets. One of the right questions to ask is,

- "How can a brand best provide value to its shareholders, those directly affected by the brand, dispersed across countries, markets, societies and geographies?"
- Do consumers value the brand enough to buy and use it?
- Do employees value it enough to want to work for it?
- Do distributors value it enough to carry it?
- Do shareholders value it enough to invest in it?
- Do communities value it enough to welcome it in their midst?
- Who these stakeholders are and how they relate to each other may differ by brand and also by location where the brand is present.

Branding is a deeply humanistic discipline seeking to connect the various processes of an organization, in order to get people to rally around the purposes and principles of the brand and provide unique value to stakeholders. The unique characteristics of a brand can best be extended across societies by understanding that brand's sensitivity or vulnerability to particular factors: both internal and external to the brand's organization.

Although each brand is unique, it is possible to categorize brands in a manner that helps us to understand to which factors certain types of brands are most susceptible. This kind of understanding is useful not only to all those corporate managers eager to make a success of their brand around the globe, but also to those who are responsible for a local brand that is faced with better endowed global competitors. In fact, this type of knowledge is useful to everyone with a vested interest in particular brands, such as Governments, non-governmental organizations (NGO's), employees, distribution partners, suppliers, local communities and even anti-globalization activists.

The Global Brand Proposition Model

The model combines the strategic planning cycle with the brand environment into an analysis tool that can be applied both globally and locally. It allows global and local analysis to be linked together. The model consists of two parts: an internal analysis and external analysis.

The Internal Analysis

The internal analysis is essential for gaining an understanding of how the brand's global and local organizational constructs shape the brand expression or multiple brand expressions. Issues such as business strategy, corporate culture, organizational structures, the brand's significance to the organization and the relationship between global and local brand management teams all play a role in shaping brand expression elements. These individual elements, in their turn, should guide global and local marketing activities.

The way the brand defines its advantages over the competition, its legacy and principles, and its character have a specific influence on product and service development, channel choice, advertising, staff demeanor, delivery and supply chain management. More important is to know how well these processes connect up in order to provide consumers with the required brand experience. For example, to realize a specific brand expression may require a rethinking on the organizational structure by which the brand is managed.

The External Analysis

The external analysis focuses on how local conditions act as licenses through which the consumers or particular consumer segments observe the brand, and how these circumstances affect consumer's understanding of the brand itself, and in relation to other brands. Specific situational factors affect brand perception elements in a particular manner, thereby influencing brands that are considered as being especially adapt at individual elements. The resulting brand recognition relates the perception of the brand to those in the environment, both competitive brands and related brands, either brand within the same organization or others that provide enhancement of the brand.

The findings of the external analysis provide new input for the internal analysis. The analysis of the brand perception, in particular, provides a starting point for further strategic planning. As the brand perception holds the meaning and significance of the brand to the consumers, it is the main focus area that global and local brand management will want to influence.

As a result, the model functions as a constant and consistent feedback loop. Each step of the process will help refine or redefine global and local brand propositions.

Brief Resume of the Contributor: S.K Tannan: Professor, Institute of Productivity and Management, Ghaziabad. After serving the various Chambers of Commerce and Industry Associations for about 25 years, he is in the teaching profession for the last 5 years and has served the various institutes like Apeejay Institute of Marketing, New Delhi; National Institute of Sales, New Delhi and Western International University, New Delhi. He has to his credit about 40 articles published in reputed trade journals besides about 10 books on different areas of management written for National Institute of Sales, New Delhi. He has also contributed in designing the course structures and reading materials for various institutes. He has also conducted a training program on the export documentation and procedures for the electronic industry in India. He has attended number of international Conferences/ Seminars and presented the papers.

References

Global Brand Strategy: Unlocking Brand Potential Across Countries, Cultures and Markets by Sicco Van Gelder published by Kogan Page India, New Delhi, 2004.

Brands and Branding by Rita Clifton and John Simmons published by the Economist in Association with Profile Books Limited, 2006.

Global Strategic Management by Dr M. Mahmoudi Maymand published by Deep and Deep Publications Private Limited, 2005.

Immutable Laws of Internet Branding by Al Ries and Laura Ries published by Harper Business, 2000

INDEX

A

Action

- Learning, (UK), 190
- Research Project, 142

Addiction, Types, 81

- Computer Addiction, 82
- Cyber Relationship Addiction, 81
- Cyber Sexual Addicts, 81
- Information Overhead, 81
- Net Compulsion, 81

Aditya Birla Group, (ABG), 188, 189, 190, 191

- Common TM Framework, 188
- Leader in Viscose Staple Fibre, 188
- Leading Cement Producer, 188
- Producer of Arylic Fibre, 188
- Producer of Carbon Black, 188
- Producer of Insulator Black, 188
- Role of Leadership, 188
- Senior Leaders Program, 190
- World's Largest Aluminum Rolling Company, 188

Administration, 88

Advertising, 287, 288, 289

- Strategies, 289

Africa/East Asia's Growth, 3

African American Customers, 293

Agilent Technologies, 176, 232

Agricultural Commodities, 116, 117

AIDS, 203

Airports, 11

- Delhi, Kalkotta, Chennei, Mumbai, 11

All India Council of Technical Education (AICTE), 61, 62

American Business Culture, 180

Amma, (SHGs), 39

Andhra Pradesh, 144

Anganwadi, 39

Anti-Globalization Movement, 302

Arjun Sengupta Committee Report, 57

Army Functioning, 187

ASA (Activists for Social Alternative), 142

Asia's Total Agriculture Land, 11

Asian

- Countries, 4
- Development Bank (ADB), 35

Asia-Pacific Region, 279

ASSEFA (Association for Sarva Seva Farmers), 142

Asset Performance, 129-140

Attacks in USA, 176

Australia and Malaysia, 278

Azim Premji, 25

B

Bandhan, 152

Bangladesh and Pakistan, 11

Bank

- Nationalization in India, 149

Of America, 292, 293
Banks Nationalization, 129
Basic
Banking, 152
Infrastructure, 4
Behavioral Competencies, 189, 190
Best Practice Strategies for Cross Cultural Competency, 180
Bharat
Forge, 178
Heavy Electrical Ltd (BHEL), 177
Bhoomi Centre, 96
Bluebook, 76
Body Language, 183
Bombay Stock Exchange (BSE), 277, 278
Borderless Economy, 187
BOT, 15
Projects, 6
BPL Families, 45
Brand
Environment, 303
Managers, 303
Standardization, 303
Branded Goods, 301
Branding, 304
Brazil, 4
British
Bankers Association, 150
Brands, 301
Raj, 62
Bush Administration's Clear Skies Initiative, 108
Business
Planning, 52
Process Outsourcing (BPO), 178, 215
Related Skills, 47
School Campuses, 57-60
Strategy, 237

C

Canadian (s)
And Japanese, 290
Companies, 181
Organization, 183
Cancer, 203
Capital
Market Development, 138
Markets, 5
Micro Enterprise, 43
Carl Dan Peddinghens Germany, 178
Carpets, 263
Carter Hold Harvey (CHH), Talent Management Model, 232
Causes of Stress, 215
Biological Causes, 215
Psychological Causes, 215
Social and Cultural Causes, 215
CDF (Cooperative Development Forum), 142
Central European Markets, 301
Change Management, Benefits and Significance, 174
Chicago Board of Trade (CBOT), 278
Child Labour. 174
China, 4, 6, 115, 299, 301
Civil Aviation Infrastructure, 8
Combination and Integration, 167
Commercial
Banks, 129, 141, 142, 149, 151
Skill, 45
Commercialization of Education, 56
Commodity
Based Economy, 114
Futures, 116
Markets, 113
Markets in India, 113

Trading, 113

Communication (s), 179

Skills, 183, 208, 211

Technologies, 79

Compensation Structure, 168

Compromise Schools, 290, 291

Compulsive Internet, 81

Consumer

Bill of Rights, 299

Services, 213

Consumerism, 298

Consumers And Recyclers, 107

Containers Deposit Legislation, 107

Cooperative Banks, 142

Corporate

Employment, 55

Governance Practices, 105

Social Responsibility (CSR), 211

Country Council, 94

Credit

Market, 129

Schemes, 25

Union, 142

Crisis of Market, 121

Cross Border

Acquisitions, 178

Trade Links, 301

Cross Cultural

Communications, 178

Decision Making, 184

Differences, 181

Issues, 178-186

Performance, 184

Trainer, 183

Training, 179

Awareness, 180

Benefits, 181

Cultural and Social Environment, 299

Currency Market, 139

Custom Procedures, 4

D

Data Networking Services, (DNS), 79

Debt Market, 121

Decade of Commodities, 115

Decentralization, 5

Of Economic Power, 23

Decision Making, 52

Process, 225, 226

Dehra Dun—Pithoragarh, 261

Democracy Project, 94

Democratization of MBA Education to Privatization, 56

Depression, 216, 217

Of Internal Addicts, 83

Derivative, 134

And Global Market, 113

Explained, 113

Markets, 113-119

Performance in India, 113-119

Developed Economies, 130

Development of Financial Sector, 138

DIC (District Industrial Centres), 30

Direct

Foreign Investment (FDI), 4

Sequence Spread Spectrum Radiology, 79

Discussion Groups, 242

Distribution

Concept, 275

Methods, 275

Of Commercial Banks in India, 151

Strategies, 259-275

System, 259, 261, 264, 267, 270, 271

District
  Ernakulam, 36, 39, 40
  Jhalawar, 97
  Sitapur (MP), 96
Diversity Management, 182
Divorced Working Women, 216
Domestic
  And Global Market, 113
  Markets, 5
Dutch Brands, 301

E

e-Administration, 88
Earnings Quality Assistance, (EQA), 70-75
  Models, 71
  Performance of Infosys, 70
  Performance of TCS, 70
Ecological Security, 64
e-Commerce, 87
Economic
  Development, 4, 23, 24, 143, 153, 259
  Environment, 298
  Environmental and Social Problems, 64
  Exchange, 4
  Growth, 3-5, 52, 103, 129-140, 187
  Shocks, 170
  System, 24, 103
Economies, 200
Economists Intelligence Unit, 167
Economy, 3, 4, 120, 121, 138, 147, 259
  Rural, 141
Ecosystem, 103
  Services, 109
e-Democracy System, 88
Education, 171
  And Training, 196
  Training, 240
Educational
  And Training Program, 240
  Facilities, 29
  Process, 240
  System, 62
Effective Change Management in India, Examples, 175-176
e-Governance, 87-102
  Benefits, 100
  Categories of Application, 92
  Initiative in India, (EGI), 95
    Karntaka, 96
    Kerala, 96
    Madhya Pradesh, 96
    Rajasthan, 97
    Uttar Pradesh, 96
  Models, Explained, 89-90
  Projects (In States), 100
Electricity Generation, 3
Electronic
  Delivery of Service, 87
  Goods, 260
  Graft Management Cetnre (EGM), 93
Emerging Markets, 138
  Korea, 138
  Malaysia, 138
  Thailand, 138
Emotional Intelligence, 207-212
Empirical Research Partners, 70
Employees and Unions, 203
Employer Assistance Program (EAP), 221
Employment
  Generation, 24, 24, 43, 274
  Growth, 3
  Opportunities, 42, 141
  Policies, 228

Empowerment, Economic, Social and Cultural, 141

Energy, 11

- Hydro Projects, 11
- Non-Conventional, 11
- Renewable, 11
- Wind, 11

Entrepreneurial

- Activity, 52
- Class, 5
- Development Training Program (EDP), 23
- Traits, 22
  - Development, 22
  - Skills, 22

Entrepreneurs

- Personal Qualities, 53, 54
- Socio-Economic Profiles, 45
- Trained and Developed, 22

Entrepreneurship, 22-24

- Development, 42-56, 59
- Future, 55
- Growth in India, 24
- Impact of-, 45

Environmental

- Friendly Power, 4
- Impact, 108
- Resources, 68

e-Seva

- Andhra Pradesh, 98
- Centres in Andhra Pradesh, 93

Ethical Business Practices, 64

Ethno Centrism, 288

European

- Brands, 301
- Commission, 68
- Countries, 278

F

Fall of Berlin Wall, 301

FIIs (Foreign Institutional Investment), 120-128

Financial

- Inclusion, 147, 153, 154, 157
- Infrastructure, 35
- Institutions (FIs), 27, 30, 129
- Instruments, 113
  - Futures, 113
  - Options, 113
- Literacy, 152
- Market Development, 4
- Market, 138
- Reporting, 64
- Sector of Indian Economy, 129
- Services, 146, 147, 151, 156
- Services to Poor and Underprivileged, 141

Five Year Plan (11th), 6, 34

Food and Drug Administration, 299

Foreign Markets, 178

Formal Financial System, 141

Forward

- Market Commission (FMC), 114
- Trading, 115

Fossil Fuel, 107

FRIENDS Janeseva Kendras, 96

Fun Data Corporation, US, Electronic—Internet Provider, 232

Funds Transfer Mechanism, 277

Futures

- Contracts, 116
- Market Trades, 114
- Trade, 117

G

Gender

- Discrimination, 215

Issues, 174
General Adaptation Syndrome, (GAS), 214
Global
Branding Strategy, 301, 305
Brands Defined, 302
Business Economy, 165
Copper Demands, 114
Economy, 64, 171, 200, 298
Entrepreneurship Monitor, 51
Financial Reporting, 64
Leader Force, 196
Management, 303
Marketers, 289
Marketing Environment, 291-300
Marketplace, 183
Markets, 43
Oil Demands, 114
Reporting Initiative (GRI), 65, 67
Village, 64
Globalization, 8, 23, 87, 120, 174, 178, 190, 290, 301, 302
And Liberalization of Economy, 127
And Privatization, 129
Of Trade, 114
GPS
Mobile Application, 78
Receiver, 78
Working, 78
Gram Panchayat, 44
Grameen
Bank (Bangladesh), 35, 152
Model, 142
Green
Revolution, 148
Washing, 107
Examples, 107
Group
Insurance, 142
Training Program, 245
Gujarat State Financial Corporation, 25
Gyandoot, 96

H

Handicrafts, 263, 265
Heavy Electrical Industry, 176
Hindu Religion, 288
Hispanic Customers, 293
Hofstade's Model, 179
Human Resource (HR), 179, 184, 236, 239
Functions, 169, 180
Issues, 165, 166, 168
Management, 184, 185
Managers, 165, 167
Needs, 184
Policy, 221
Practice, 229
Professionals, 169, 188, 238
Risk Management, 238
Specialists, 233
Human Resource Management, (HRM), 184
Policies, 183
Policies and Practices, 168
Program, 183

I

ICDS (Integrated Child Development Services), 38
ICICI Bank, 124, 142
IIFC, UK, 15
IIM
Ahmedabad, 57, 59
Bangalore, 59
Impact on Economy, 120
Inclusive
Growth, 141

Maritime Infrastructure, 20
Income
Generation, 4
Tax Act, 1961, 6
India,
20th Largest Maritime Country, 8
Coastline, 8
India's
International Trade, 8
Market Capitalization, 138
Ports, 8
Indian
Business Schools, 56
Corporate Sector, 218
Corporate Women, 213-223
Derivative Market, 114
Economic Policy, 129
Economy, 114, 120, 129, 130, 144
Financial System, 139
FOREX Derivatives, 119
Industries, 215
Information Technology Managers, 70-75
Infrastructural Financial Companies, 15
Investors, 115
Management Education System, 57
Management Education, 56, 57, 61, 63
Markets, 121, 277
Micro Finance, 142
Population, 43
Railways, 6
Road Networkm, 6
Rural Sector, 147-161
Rural Women, 42
Society, 26
Stock Market, 120-128
Trust Act, 144
Women, 27, 28, 42, 213
Industrial
Business, 42
Development, 25
Growth, 274
Industrial
Investment Corporation, 25
Organizational Psychology, 225
Policy, 24, 25, 32
Structure, 260
Training Institutions, 29
Industrialization, 24, 51, 103, 129
Industries, 120, 178
Infections, 203
Information
And Technology Workers, 214
Process Centres, 211
Security System, 92
Technology, 88, 89, 178, 196
Action Plan, 90
And e-Governance, 90
And Manufacturing Hub, 11
e-Governance, 88
Enabled Services, (ITES), 213, 215, 221
Infrastructure, 90
Standard Association (ITSA), 93
System Planning, 91
Information, Communication and Technology, (ICT), 64, 87, 88, 92, 196
Infosys, 70
Infrastructure, 5, 6, 22
And Competition, 289
Development, 3-21
In India, 5
Facilities, 3, 5, 6
For Teachers, 61

Investment, 3
Port, 4
Ports, Shipping, 8
Power, 8
Projects, 5, 6
Rural, 5
Sector, 4
Services, 3, 6
Sharing, 156
Sub-Sectors, 6
Airports, 6
Irrigation, 6
Ports, 6
Railways, 6
Roads, 6
Telecommunication, 6
Telecommunication, 8
Infusion of Techniques, 274
Innovative Strategies, 156
Institutional Loans, 25
Insurance, 213
Instruments, 136
Integrated Rural Development Program, (IRDP), 35
Intermediate Education, 269, 271
Internal
Addicts, 81-86
Non-Addicts, 81-86
International
Labor Organization (ILO), 196
Markets, 299
Trade, 8, 64
Internet Technologies, 298
Islamic Countries, 288

J

Japan, China, India and Middle East, 288
Job Security, 229

K

Karnataka, 144
Kerala—Punjab, 150
Kisan Credit Cards (KCC) Scheme, 149
Kudumbashree, 36
Mission, 36, 39
KYC (Know Your Customer), 149, 153

L

Labour Management Agenda, 228
Leadership
Defined, 187
Development, 187-192
Pipeline, 187, 190
Role, 187, 189
Styles, 242
Legal Environment, 299
Liberalization, 23, 26
And Privatization, 129
License Raj, 129
Lincoln, Abraham, US Pres., 88
Local Brands, 302
LOKMITRA and JAN MITRA Pilot Projects, 97
Lokvani Kiosk Centre, 96

M

Macro-Marketing System, 299
MACS (Mutually Aided Cooperative Society Act), 142, 144
Malaysia, 184, 185
Management
And Trade Unions, 168
Education, 240
System, 92
Teachers, 61
Managerial
Education, 56-63
In India, 56-63

System, 60
Managing Diversity, 183
Manufacturing, 178
Market
Capitalism, 105
Economy, 138
Health At Workplace, 193-206
Health Key for Organizational Growth, 193-206
Health Promotion, 193-206
Players, 282
Research, 51, 52
Marketing
Communications, 288
Program, 274
Services, 275
Strategy Planning, 300
Markets, 289, 290, 296, 302, 303
And Governance, 277-286
Mental
Disorder, 194
Myths About, 194
Health (MH), 193
Problems, 193-199
Stress, Depression, Anxiety, Burnout, 195
Illness, 194
Retardation, 194
Mergers and Acquisitions (M&A), 165, 178
Activity, Role of HR Department in-0, 168
Human Side, 166
Models, 166
Transactions, 168
Types, 165
Micro
Credit, 35, 35, 42, 49, 144
Centered Enterprises in India, 42-50
Foundation of India, 152
Institutions (MCIs), 42
Enterprise (s), 34-37, 42, 44, 49, 93
Development, 43
Program, 43
In India, 43
Finance, 141-146
For Sustained Development, 34-40
Institutions (MFIs), 142-144, 151
Services, 147
Insurance, 141
Pension, 141
Remittance, 141
Sustainability, 108
Mid-Career Crisis, 213-223
Millennium Development Goals, (MDGs), 146
Mine Revolution in Commodity, 114
Mining, 178
Ministry of
Railways, 17
Road Transport, 17
Mixed Economy, 24
MMS (Multimedia Service), 77
MNC Culture, 214
Mobile Technology, 76-80
Global Positioning System (GPS), 76, 78
Laptop and Notebook Computers, 76, 77
Mobile Phones, 76
Palmtop Computers, 76, 77
Wireless Debit/Credit, 76, 78
Modern
Industries, 259
Management Techniques, 228
Mohammad Yunus, Founder of Grameen Bank of Bangladesh, 152
Monitoring Devices, 176
Motivation, 244

Motorola's Performance, 237

Multi-cultural Workforce, 178

Multi-national Corporations (MNCs), 23, 64, 130, 196

Multi-State Cooperative Societies Act, 144

Mutual Funds, 134

N

National

- Bank of Agriculture and Rural Development (NABARD), 151
- Cultural Differences, 179
- Economy, 196
- e-Governance Plan of Indian Govt, 98
- Institute of Mental Health, 196
- Maritime Development Program, 8, 20
- Policy Research Council, 90
- Service Scheme (NSS), 49
- Stock Exchange, (NSE), 277, 278, 279

Nationalization of Commercial Banks, 141

Netherlands East Indies, 301

Neuroticesin, 83

New

- Bank Authorization Policy (RBI), 149
- Technologies, 11, 28

Non-Farm Employment, 34

Non-Governmental Organizations, (NGOs), 29, 30, 44, 115, 142, 304

- Micro Finance Institutions, 144

North

- American Free Trade Agreements (NAFTA), 299
- Carolina National Bank, 292
- East States, 150

Nuclear Power Generation, 20

O

Occupational Stress, 213-223

- Of Women, 217

On-Line

- Gambling, 81
- Pornography, 81
- Relationship, 81
- Social Network Service, (SNS), 247
- Status Enquiry of Passport Application, 88
- Trading, 115

On-the-Job Training, 245

Open Trade Regime's Infrastructure Projects, 5

Operational Research Techniques, 243

Opportunities for Women, 31, 32

- In Rural Areas, 32

Option Market, 117

Organizational

- Change Management, 175
- Change Program, 170-177
- Culture, 166, 228
- Development, 231
- Justice, 183
- Performance, 224, 231
- Skills, 105

Other Mental Problems, 195

Outlet Distribution System, 263, 273

P

PACS (Primary Agricultural Credit Societies), 142

Pakistan, 11, 174

Panchayats, 36

Participatory Methods, 243, 244

Pension, 71

Performance

- Appraisal System, 168
- Improvement Program, 45
- Management, 231

Personal Digital Aids, 77, 78

Personality and Depression, 81-86

Pharmaceutical Companies, 178

Physical Accidents, 203
Planning, 5, 53, 170, 231, 235, 238
  Skills, 104
Plato's Republic, 187
Political Environment, 298
Port
  Infrastructure, 4
  Projects, 8
Ports/Shipping/Infrastructure, 8
Position of Women in Society, 42
Poverty
  Alleviation, 147
    Program, 43
  Eradication, 141
    Program, 36
  Reduction, 4
Power
  Generation, 8
  Infrastructure, 8
Primary State Level Development Banks, 142
Prime Minister's Employment Generation Program (PMEGP), 36
Principles of Leaning, 244
Priority Sector, 141, 151
Private
  Entrepreneurship, 130
  Participation, 5
Product Groups, 261
  Carpet and Handicrafts, 261, 262
  Shawl/Sweater, 262
Product Stewardship, 106, 107
Productivity and Performance, 200
Professional Organization, 208
Project
  Bhoom Centre, 96
  FRIENDS, 96
  Lokvani, 96
Psychiatric Disabilities, 194
Public Administration Operation, 87
Public Relations
  Business, 207
  Leaders, 210
  Philosophy, 208
  Practioners, 210
  Profession, 207
  Professionals, 208, 211, 212
Public-Private Partnership (PPP), 6, 15
  Projects, 15
Purdue University, 55

Q

Quality
  Business Education, 56
  Management Education, 56
  Of Earnings, 70
  Work Life (QWL), 224-229
    Environment, 225, 226

R

Radio Technology, 79
Rajiv Gandhi Udyami Mitra Yojna, 36
Ranbaxy, 178
Rashtriya Mahila Koshm (RMK), 151
Recession, 120, 127
Recruitment and Training, 200
Reforms in Indian Economy, 130
Regional
  Integration, 4
  Rural Banks (RRBs), 141, 142,,149, 152
  Socio-Economic Development, 4
Reservations, 115
Respondents
  Primary Education, 262, 268, 269, 270, 271
  School Education, 262, 268, 269, 270, 271

Retailers, 107

Risk Management, 114

  Mechanism, 114

Road Infrastructure, 4, 6

Role of

  Language, 183

  Talent Management, 231

Royal College of Psychiatrists, 196

RTGS System, 277

Ruchishree, 39

Rural

  Banking System, 141

  Banks, 141

  Economy, 141

  Enterprises, 38

  Entrepreneurship, 34-40

  India, 147

  Industrialization, 149, 274

  Infrastructure, 5

  Micro Entrepreneurship, 34

S

Saadhan Micro Financial Society, 152

Satyam Scam, 70

Scheduled Commercial Banks, 151

School Education, 45

Schooling in Capitalist America, 61

SEBI (Securities and Exchange Board of India), 120, 277, 282

Sector,

  Automobiles, 127

  Financial, 138

  Indian Rural, 147-161

  Information Technology, 124, 130, 178

  Infrastructure, 4

  Maritime, 8

  Micro Finance, 141, 152

  Pharmaceutical, 124, 130

  Telecom, 11, 20

Self Employed Women Association (SEWA), 151

  Banks, 152

Self-Help Groups (SHGs), 39, 44, 45, 48, 142, 144, 149

  Bank Linkage Model, 142, 144

  Bank Linkage Program, 146, 149, 151

Service

  Industries, 218

  Sector, 213-223

SGSY, 35

Sharda Women's Association of Weaker Section, 152

Singapore Stock Exchange, 277

Single Window Agencies, 30

Small

  Industries Development Bank of India (SIDBI), 151

  Industry Sector, 274

  Scale

    Industrial Units, 259

    Industries, 23, 260

    Industry of Uttarakhand, 259-275

    Industry Sector, 274

    Sector, 23

    Units, 260

Smart Phones, 77, 78

SMS (Short Message Service), 77

Social

  Changes, 171

  Empowerment, 49

  Entrepreneurship, 56, 57, 58

  Exclusion, 197, 199

  Infrastructure, 157

  Learning, 249

  Networking, 185

Problem, 58
Skills, 209
Support System, 203
Up-Lift, 152
Societies Registration Act, 144
Socio-
Cultural Differences, 289
Economic
Development, 22
Security, 64
South Korea, 82
Standardized
Advertising Strategies, 289
Communication Policy, 289
School, 289
State
Cooperative Societies Act, 144
Financial Corporation, 30
Status of Women, 42
Steps to
Develop Information System, 92
Successful Change, 173
Strategic Planning, 302
Stress, 197, 225
Coping Mechanism, 221
On Women, 216, 217
Psychological, Behavioral, and Biological, 216, 217
Sub-Prime Crisis, 121, 127
Subsidies, 11, 37, 38, 44
Supra-National Institutions, 174
Sustainability Management, (SM), 103-110
Global Warming, 103
Habitat Distribution, 103
Management Role-, 104
Over Population, 103
Pollution, 103
Species Extinction, 103
War, 103
World Profile, 103-111
Sustainability, 106
Economic Benefits, 106
Environmental Benefits, 106
Social Equity Benefits, 106
Sustainable
Development, 22-33, 56, 64, 141, 152
Role of Micro Finance Institutions in-, 147-161
Economic Development, 153
Sustained Growth (SG), 3, 21

T

Talent
Centric Organizations, 238, 239
Conversations, 236
Management, 188-191, 231
At Aditya Birla Group, 188
Defined, 188
Intervention, 188
Loop, 234
Practices, 232
Skills, 234
Strategy, 233
Strategy Features, 233
System (TMS), 231-239
Tamil Nadu, 144
Tata Management Training Centre, 219
TCS, 70
Teacher and Training (TT), Objectives, 240
Teaching
And Training Methods, 240-246
Mechanism, 245
Methods, 241, 242, 244, 245

Technological
- Advance (Advancement), 8
- Advancement, 87, 139
- Changes, 28
- Environment, 298
- Funds, 44
- Innovations, 170
- Transfer, 298

Technology, 4, 120
- For Global Communication, 184

Telecom, 178
- Market, 8

Telecommunication
- Industry in India, 8
- Infrastructure, 8

Theory of Savings, 132

Thermal Electricity Generation, 15

Thin Screen Technology, 77

Tier I Business Schools, 61

Tier II Business Schools, 61

Tourism, 213

Trade Rules and Regulations, 4

Trading
- Hours, 278, 279
- In Commodity Futures, 135

Traditional
- Industrialist, 25
- Methods of Agriculture, 149

Training
- And Counseling, 29
- And Trainer, 241
- Program 29, 30, 167, 241

Transparency, 64
- In Operations, 176

Triple Bottom Line Reporting (TBLR), 64-69

TV Commercials, 288

U

UGC-AICTE-DEC Joint Committee, 62

UK, 177
- Advertising Industry, 231

UN
- ESCAP, 3
- Industrial Development Organization (UNIDO), 27, 28
- Millennium Development Goals, 4

Under-Banked States, 149
- Bihar, 149
- Orissa, 149
- Rajasthan, 149
- Union Territories, 149

University
- Education, 62
- Grants Commission, 62

Up-gradation Program, 61

Urbanization, 171
- And Migration, 196

US, 6, 214, 242, 299
- And Canada, 183
- And Western European MNCs, 290
- Based Multinational Enterprises, 184
- Canada Trade, 299
- Consumerism, 299
- Dept of Defence, 78
- Economy, 127
- Recession, 121
- System, 56

US—Japan, 184

Uttarakhand, 260, 261

V

Violence and Discrimination against Women, 213

Vocational Training, 29

W

Weaker Sections, 42

WEB 2.0
- Advent of-, 247
- Based WEBSITES, 248
- Characteristics, 248
- Techniques, 247-253

White Collar Jobs, 207

WiFi, 76, 79

WLL Monitoring Program, 219, 220

Women
- Economic and Social Status, 42
- Entrepreneurs, 26-29, 30, 31, 42, 43
  - Guidance Cell, 30
  - How to Develop-, 29
  - In India, 27
  - Role of-, 26
- Entrepreneurship, 22-33, 47
- Executives, 221
- Micro Enterprises, 49
- Status, 43
- Success in Public Relations, 207-212
- Thrift Groups (WTGs), 142
- Training Program, 30

Women's
- Development Corporation, 30
- Occupation, 43
- Participation, 29
- Polytechnics, 29
- Technical Training, 29

Workforce, 178, 182, 183, 184,

Working Women, 207, 214

Workplace, 193-207, 217, 221, 224, 236
- Health Promotion, 200
- Mental Health Policy, 200, 201
- Planning, 236

World Economic Farms, 4

World Economy, 57, 127

World Health Organization, (WHO), 194, 195
- Defined Mental Health, 194

World War II, 301